Regulating Preventive Justice

Like medicine, law is replete with axioms of prevention. 'Prevention is better than cure' has a long pedigree in both fields. Seventeenth-century jurist Sir Edward Coke observed that 'preventing justice excelleth punishing justice'. A century later, Sir William Blackstone similarly stated that 'preventive justice is . . . preferable in all respects to punishing justice'. This book evaluates the feasibility and legitimacy of state attempts to regulate prevention. Although prevention may be desirable as a matter of policy, questions are inevitably raised as to its limits and legitimacy – specifically, how society reconciles the desirability of averting risks of future harm with respect for the rule of law, procedural fairness and human rights.

While these are not new questions for legal scholars, they have been brought into sharper relief in policy and academic circles in the wake of the September 11 terrorist attacks. Over the past 15 years, a body of legal scholarship has tracked the intensified preventive focus of anti-terrorism law and policy, observing how this focus has impacted negatively upon traditional legal frameworks. However, preventive law and policy in other contexts, such as environmental protection, mental health, immigration and corruption, has not received sustained focus. This book extends that body of scholarship, through use of case studies from these diverse regulatory settings, in order to examine and critique the principles, policies and paradoxes of preventive justice.

> Whereas earlier scholars looked upon preventive justice as a source and means of regulation, the powerfully argued contributions to this volume provide forceful reasons to consider whether we would do better to talk about regulating preventive justice.
>
> Professor Lucia Zedner, Oxford University

Tamara Tulich is a Lecturer at the Faculty of Law, University of Western Australia, Australia.

Rebecca Ananian-Welsh is a Lecturer at the TC Beirne School of Law, University of Queensland, Australia.

Simon Bronitt is a Professor at the TC Beirne School of Law, University of Queensland, Australia.

Sarah Murray is an Associate Professor at the Faculty of Law, University of Western Australia, Australia.

Regulating Preventive Justice

Principle, Policy and Paradox

Edited by
Tamara Tulich, Rebecca Ananian-Welsh, Simon Bronitt and Sarah Murray

Routledge
Taylor & Francis Group
LONDON AND NEW YORK

First published 2017 by Routledge

2 Park Square, Milton Park, Abingdon, Oxfordshire OX14 4RN
711 Third Avenue, New York, NY 10017

Routledge is an imprint of the Taylor & Francis Group, an informa business

First issued in paperback 2018

British Library Cataloguing in Publication Data
A catalogue record for this book is available from the British Library

Library of Congress Cataloging in Publication Data
Names: Tulich, Tamara, editor.
Title: Regulating preventive justice : principle, policy and paradox / Edited by Tamara Tulich, Rebecca Ananian-Welsh, Simon Bronitt and Sarah Murray.
Description: New York : Routledge, [2016] | Includes bibliographical references and index.
Identifiers: LCCN 2016035260 | ISBN 9781138658189 (hbk) | ISBN 9781315620978 (ebk)
Subjects: LCSH: Preventive law.
Classification: LCC K579.P74 R44 2016 | DDC 364.4--dc23
LC record available at https://lccn.loc.gov/2016035260

ISBN: 9781138658189 (hbk)
ISBN: 9780367025199 (pbk)

Typeset in Galliard
by Taylor & Francis Books

Contributors

Rebecca Ananian-Welsh is a Lecturer at the University of Queensland's TC Beirne School of Law. Rebecca's research focuses on courts and the separation of powers, particularly in the national security and organised crime contexts. She has spoken widely on these topics in Australia and overseas, has published in leading journals, and is co-editor (with Professor Jonathan Crowe) of *Judicial Independence in Australia: Contemporary Challenges, Future Directions* (2016, Federation Press). Before joining the TC Beirne School of Law, Rebecca was an academic member of the Laureate Fellowship Project 'Anti-Terror Laws and the Democratic Challenge' at the University of New South Wales. Rebecca has also held positions with the Federal Attorney-General's Department and with DLA Piper Sydney.

Peter Billings is an Associate Professor at the TC Beirne School of Law and a Fellow of the Centre for Public, International and Comparative Law. In 2014 he was a Senior Visiting Research Fellow at the School of Law, University of Warwick. His research interests are in particular areas of public law and public international law: particularly, administrative law, constitutional law, immigration and refugee law, social welfare law and the law relating to Indigenous Australians. Peter has published several book chapters in edited collections on administrative law and refugee law, reports, and peer-reviewed journal articles in Australia, United Kingdom, United States and international journals, including *University of New South Wales Law Journal, Melbourne University Law Review, Journal of Social Security Law, Public Law, Northern Ireland Legal Quarterly* and *International Journal on Minority and Group Rights.*

Simon Bronitt was appointed Professor of Law and Deputy Dean (Research) in the TC Beirne School of Law, commencing in June 2014. Previously, he served as the Director of the Australian Research Council Centre of Excellence in Policing and Security, hosted by Griffith University (2009–14). Before moving to Queensland in 2009 to take up this position, Simon was a member of the Australian National University College of Law (1991–2009). During that time he served as Sub Dean in 1997–8, and was promoted to Professor in 2005. During his time at the Australian National University (ANU), he held a number of research leadership roles, including Director of the National Europe

Centre, an EU-funded Centre, in the Research School of Humanities (2003–8) and Director of the Australian Centre for Military Law and Justice, ANU (2009). Drawing on comparative and interdisciplinary perspectives, he has published widely on criminal justice topics ranging across terrorism law and human rights, comparative criminal law, covert policing, family violence and mental health policing. His key publications include two textbooks, *Principles of Criminal Law* (3rd edition, Thomson Reuters, 2010) and *Law in Context* (4th edition, Federation Press, 2012).

Susan Donkin is a member of the Griffith Criminology Institute and a Lecturer at the School of Criminology and Criminal Justice at Griffith University. Her PhD examined pre-emptive anti-terrorism legislation across time and place, comparing how/whether measures such as control orders are used in different jurisdictions, and identifying how they compare to similar historical precedents, such as internment. A modified version of her thesis examining control orders in light of crime prevention theory and practice has been published as part of the Springer Brief Series in International and Comparative Criminology.

Teneille Elliott is a doctoral candidate at the National Security College, ANU. Her doctoral research is assessing the effectiveness and appropriateness of Australia's legislative response to counter the security threat of foreign fighters. Teneille teaches at ANU on transnational security issues in the Asia-Pacific region, and Australia's national security laws. Prior to joining ANU, Teneille worked as a lawyer within Australia's national security community. Most recently, she was the Adviser to the former Independent National Security Legislation Monitor, Bret Walker SC, from 2011 to 2014. Teneille advised the Monitor on the operation, effectiveness and implications of Australia's counter-terrorism and national security legislation.

Keiran Hardy is a Lecturer in the School of Criminology and Criminal Justice at Griffith University. He previously worked as a Research Fellow in the Gilbert + Tobin Centre of Public Law at the University of New South Wales on the ARC Laureate Fellowship 'Anti-Terror Laws and the Democratic Challenge'. He earlier completed his PhD on that project, looking at the interaction between counter-terrorism laws and countering violent extremism (CVE) programs. Keiran has published in leading Australian and international journals on counter-terrorism law and policy, and has made frequent submissions to parliamentary inquiries on new counter-terrorism laws introduced by the Australian government. He has also commented on these laws in the media, including for the ABC, SBS, *The Guardian*, and *The Sydney Morning Herald*. Keiran's research focuses on counter-terrorism laws, CVE programs, intelligence whistleblowing, counter-insurgency, big data and privacy law, and cyber-terrorism.

Tim Legrand is a Lecturer at the National Security College, Crawford School of Public Policy at the ANU, Canberra. His research is concerned with international policy transfer, evidence-based policy-making, and the domestic and transnational dimensions of security policy governance in the Anglosphere with particular focus on counter-terrorism and critical infrastructure protection. His research has been published in leading international journals including *Public Administration, Policy Studies, British Politics, European Political Science* and the *Journal of Comparative Policy Analysis.* He is also the co-editor (with Professor Allan McConnell) of *Emergency Policy* (Ashgate: 2012) and has contributed a number of chapters to edited collections. Dr Legrand currently holds adjunct positions as Associate Professor at the Institute for Governance and Policy Analysis at the University of Canberra and Research Fellow at Griffith University.

Bernadette McSherry is the Foundation Director of the Melbourne Social Equity Institute at the University of Melbourne and an Adjunct Professor in the Melbourne Law School and the Faculty of Law, Monash University. She has degrees in Arts and Law, as well as Psychology. Her PhD in Law was obtained from York University in Canada and her doctoral thesis focused on concepts of criminal responsibility and mental impairment. Professor McSherry is the sole author of a book on preventive detention and risk assessment for Routledge, New York, and has published widely in the fields of mental health law and criminal law. She is a legal member of the Victorian Mental Health Tribunal and the President of the Australian and New Zealand Association of Psychiatry, Psychology and Law. In 2011, she was elected a Fellow of the Academy of Social Sciences in Australia and a Fellow of the Australian Academy of Law.

Sarah Murray is an Associate Professor at the University of Western Australia where she teaches Constitutional Law and researches in the areas of Public Law and legal institutional change. Her PhD thesis, 'Less-Adversarial Practice and the Constitutional Role of the Judiciary in Australia', was awarded the 2011 Mollie Holman Doctoral Medal for Law by Monash University and was published as a monograph, *The Remaking of the Courts – Less-Adversarial Practice and the Constitutional Role of the Judiciary in Australia*, by Federation Press in 2014. She was the editor of *Constitutional Perspectives on an Australian Republic: Essays in Honour of Professor George Winterton* (Federation Press, 2014) and is a co-author of *Winterton's Australian Federal Constitutional Law* (Thomson, 2014) and *The Constitution of the Commonwealth of Australia: History, Principle and Interpretation* (CUP, 2015). She was the 2015 Institute of Advanced Studies Distinguished UWA Early Career Research Fellow for the Humanities and has published public law scholarship across a range of Australian and international journals.

Helen Punter is currently a Doctoral Candidate at the University of Queensland, Australia. She completed her undergraduate studies and honours, in Criminology and Criminal Justice, at Griffith University, Queensland. Helen holds positions as sessional tutor at the School of Criminology and Criminal Justice, and holds multiple Research Assistant positions, working on projects such as the Intimate Partner Homicide Project (Griffith University) and the Alcohol and Harm Minimisation Project (University of Newcastle). As a research assistant, Helen was a contributing author to a publication on restorative justice conferencing titled 'Agreements in restorative justice conferences: Exploring the implications of agreements for post-conference offending behaviour'. Also as part of a professional placement program with the ARC Centre of Excellence in Policing and Security (CEPS) in 2010, Helen published an article on police move-on powers in Queensland titled 'Move-on powers: New paradigms of public order policing in Queensland'.

Jocelyn Stacey is an Assistant Professor of Law at the Peter A. Allard School of Law at the University of British Columbia, where she researches and teaches in the areas of environmental law, public law and administrative law. She has published on these topics in leading Canadian law journals including the *Supreme Court Law Review*, *Osgoode Hall Law Journal* and *Journal of Environmental Law and Policy*. She has a doctorate in law from McGill University, an LLM from Yale Law School and an LLB from the University of Calgary. She has a BSc from the University of Alberta and worked in climate change research for the Canadian government before beginning her career in law. Prior to undertaking her graduate work, she clerked for the Honourable Justice Marshall Rothstein at the Supreme Court of Canada.

Dallal Stevens is a Reader and Director of Research at the School of Law, University of Warwick. Her research interests focus on refugee and asylum law and policy. She has published numerous books, peer-reviewed journal articles, book chapters and reports, including *UK Asylum Law and Policy: Historical and Contemporary Perspectives* (Sweet & Maxwell, 2004), *Refugee Protection and the Role of Law: Conflicting Identities* (Routledge, 2014, ed. with Susan Kneebone and Loretta Baldassar) and *States, the Law and Access to Refugee Protection: Fortresses and Fairness* (ed. with Maria O'Sullivan, Hart, forthcoming 2017). Recently, she has been considering the impact of globalisation on asylum and her current research is concerned with the protection of refugees and forced migrants in the Middle East, and the movement of people across the Mediterranean to Europe. Dallal's work has been supported by external grants from the British Academy, the Arts and Humanities Research Board and the ESRC. She is Associate Editor of the *Journal of Immigration, Asylum and Nationality Law*.

Tamara Tulich is a Lecturer in the Faculty of Law at the University of Western Australia. Tamara researches and publishes in the areas of preventive justice, anti-terror lawmaking and indefinite detention regimes. Tamara's current research, with Professor Harry Blagg and supported by a grant from the Australian Institute of Criminology, examines diversionary pathways for Indigenous Youth with Foetal Alcohol Spectrum Disorders in the West Kimberley region of Western Australia. Tamara completed her PhD as part of the Laureate Fellowship project 'Anti-Terror Laws and the Democratic Challenge' in the Gilbert + Tobin Centre of Public Law, and was also a Nettheim Doctoral Teaching Fellow at the University of New South Wales. She has practised as a solicitor at the Mental Health Advocacy Service at NSW Legal Aid.

Svetlana Tyulkina is an Associate of the Gilbert + Tobin Centre of Public Law and was formerly a Postdoctoral Research Fellow on the Australian Research Council Laureate Fellowship: Anti-Terror Laws and the Democratic Challenge Project in the Centre. Prior to joining the UNSW Faculty of Law, she was a PhD student at the Central European University, where she has completed the doctoral thesis entitled 'Militant Democracy'. Svetlana's recent work focuses on comparative counter-terrorism and constitutional law, and she has published articles and presented at a number of Australian and international conferences on topics of her research interests. Svetlana's book *Militant Democracy: Undemocratic Political Parties and Beyond* was published by Routledge in January 2015.

George Williams AO is the Dean, the Anthony Mason Professor, a Scientia Professor and the Foundation Director of the Gilbert + Tobin Centre of Public Law at the Faculty of Law, University of New South Wales. He has written and edited many books, including *Australian Constitutional Law and Theory* and *The Oxford Companion to the High Court of Australia*, and has appeared as a barrister in the High Court in cases over the past two decades. He has served on a number of public inquiries, and as chair of the Victorian Human Rights Consultation Committee in 2005 helped bring about Australia's first State bill of rights, the Victorian Charter of Human Rights and Responsibilities. He is a columnist for the *Sydney Morning Herald*.

Acknowledgements

This volume was provoked by Andrew Ashworth and Lucia Zedner's incisive work *Preventive Justice* (Oxford University Press, 2014), which, among other things, sought to generate debate on the extent and limitations of preventive justice. The project derives from a collaboration between researchers at the TC Beirne School of Law at the University of Queensland and the University of Western Australia Law School, and a stimulating workshop at the University of Queensland on 24 April 2015. The workshop drew together academics from Australia and overseas to discuss the new questions and challenges that preventive justice poses for governments (and the international community) that have not yet received sustained focus in the literature.

We wish to thank the University of Western Australia Law School and the TC Beirne School of Law for generously funding the workshop and supporting our project. We are indebted to the TC Beirne School of Law events team of Jane Gay, Nadine Davidson-Wall and Therese Yat for their efforts in hosting the workshop. We are tremendously grateful to everyone who participated in the workshop, the authors who contributed chapters to this collection and Professor Lucia Zedner for writing her generous foreword. We thank the editorial team at Routledge for their support and guidance in publishing this book. Very Special thanks are owing to our wonderful team of research assistants, Sarah Mauriks, Yannis Vrodos and Balawyn Jones. And, of course, we are grateful to the individual participants, discussants and authors without whom this project would not have been prosecuted to successful completion.

Partnerships in academic life are rarely as fulfilling as this project has been. We have departed from alphabetical ascendancy in the ordering of surnames to acknowledge the leadership, driving passion and unfailing commitment of Tamara Tulich, who has steered this project from its earliest days, assuming key roles in negotiations with prospective authors and publishers alike, and maintained a keen eye on those critical deadlines.

Tamara Tulich
Rebecca Ananian-Welsh
Simon Bronitt
Sarah Murray
June 2016

Taking the preventive justice project forward

Lucia Zedner[*]

The concept of preventive justice

Preventive justice is a concept with over two hundred years of history. It is also a concept with ever greater salience in a world in which the increasing demands of security lead governments to extend their policing and preventive powers. The rich array of contributions to this volume makes clear both the complexities and challenges of preventive justice. They also explore its potential as a means by which to understand contemporary developments and to guide and limit them. Preventive justice has many manifestations. It describes a substantive domain of governmental lawmaking and public policy. It connotes a burgeoning area of academic scholarship that is variously exploratory, analytical, taxonomic and critical. And it seeks to articulate a normative framework of values and principles by which justice might be done in a field too often characterised by injustice, arbitrariness and the overreaching of state power.

As an area of scholarship, the ambit of preventive justice is contested, and its aims are diverse, and while there are growing areas of agreement and common interest, it is as yet an emergent enterprise in which much work remains to be done before it can be described as a settled field. So this volume is a particularly welcome addition to the literature because it advances the project of identifying, classifying, understanding and evaluating preventive endeavours wherever they occur. The book's organisational structure first introduces the reader to the concept of preventive justice, its history, development and implications. Second, its central chapters furnish a fascinating series of case studies of preventive justice – and injustice. Throughout, and particularly in Part III, its contributors critically appraise preventive laws, policies and measures to address vital questions of legitimacy, fairness, accountability and efficacy. In so doing, the chapters in this volume explore the promise and potential pitfalls of preventive justice scholarship and pay critical attention to questions of what should constitute the content and scope (see Chapter 1 by Tamara Tulich) of attempts to regulate preventive justice.

In any discussion of preventive justice, the tragic events of 9/11 inevitably loom large. Although preventive endeavour obviously predates these and subsequent

* Lucia Zedner is Senior Research Fellow at All Souls College, Oxford, Professor in the Faculty of Law, University of Oxford, and Conjoint Professor in the Faculty of Law, University of New South Wales.

terrorist attacks across the globe, their impact massively amplified and intensified demands for security. As Tulich rightly observes, 9/11 has been pivotal in shaping the subsequent development of preventive justice scholarship. She is careful to acknowledge the historical continuities with earlier practices to show that what is new is not so much risk itself but our growing preoccupation with the inevitable uncertainty surrounding precautionary action.

Many of the contributions to this volume focus on the realm of counter-terrorism. The potentially catastrophic threats posed by contemporary terrorism license the introduction of emergency powers and the enactment of exceptional measures. Often these are time-limited only by ineffectual 'sunset clauses', which are all too easily renewed into de facto permanency. Post 9/11, prevention became the art of the possible. The then United States Attorney General, John Ashcroft, declared the United States administration willing to use any available legal, and significant extra-legal, measures to combat terrorism.[1] In many jurisdictions, including Australia, the ease with which new laws and measures were introduced on grounds of protecting the public, maintaining order or defending national security is startling. Collectively, the contributions to this volume make clear that the wider task of prevention has, in effect, been 'terrorised' as the threat of terrorist attack places governments under intense pressure to identify the dangerous and take exceptional measures to avert catastrophic harms.[2] New laws permit procedural shortcuts and sidestep the protections that normally attach to the criminal process. In earlier times, such derogations might have been resisted as overreaching the legitimate limits of state preventive power. Today, a landscape that would have been unrecognisable a generation ago is simply accepted as the 'new normal'.

Of course, 9/11 and the continuing threat of terrorism is only one (albeit a large) part of the picture. The move to prevention precedes 9/11 and has multiple drivers – for example, the development of actuarial risk assessment technologies, the rise of prudentialism, risk management and, not least, the influence of the precautionary principle.[3] First established in environmental law, the precautionary principle has had enormous influence across the entire preventive terrain. Although the precautionary principle has been articulated in differing strong and weak formulations, its early enunciation in the UN Environment Programme

1 Attorney General Ashcroft, 'Outlines Foreign Terrorist Tracking Task Force' (Speech delivered on 31 October 2001), available at www.justice.gov/archive/ag/speeches/2001/agcrisisremarks10_31.htm (accessed 5 September 2016).

2 Bruce Ackerman, *Before the Next Attack* (Yale University Press, 2007); Lucia Zedner, 'Terrorizing Criminal Law' (2014) 8(1) *Criminal Law and Philosophy* 99.

3 Malcolm Feeley and Jonathan Simon, 'The New Penology: Notes on the Emerging Strategy of Corrections and its Implications' (1992) 30(4) *Criminology* 449; Malcolm Feeley and Jonathan Simon, 'Actuarial Justice: The Emerging New Criminal Law', in David Nelken (ed.), *The Futures of Criminology* (Sage, 1994) 173; Pat O'Malley, 'Risk, Crime and Prudentialism Revisited', in Kevin Stenson and Robert Sullivan (eds), *Crime, Risk and Justice: The Politics of Crime Control in Liberal Democracies* (Willan Publishing, 2001) 89; Elizabeth Fisher, 'Precaution, Precaution Everywhere: Developing a "Common Understanding" of the Precautionary Principle in the European Community' (2002) 9(1) *Maastricht Journal of European and Comparative Law* 7.

(1992) *Rio Declaration* captures the fundamental idea: 'Where there are threats of serious or irreversible damage, lack of full scientific certainty shall not be used as a reason for postponing cost-effective measures to prevent environmental degradation.'[4] This formulation establishes a laudable presumption against governmental inaction when there is uncertainty about a potentially catastrophic risk. However, as Susan Donkin makes clear in Chapter 3, the idea of precaution has escaped its principled limits to become an insistent driver of a very much less principled precautionary 'approach' that demands intervention or suggests the inexorable logic of radical action. The injunction that, in the face of risk of 'serious or irreversible' damage, lack of full scientific certainty shall not be used as a reason for inaction is consciously twisted by politicians and policy-makers into a positive licence for action. Resort to the language of precaution – pointedly made without reference to principle – becomes a rhetorical flourish with which to justify new emergency laws and measures.

Nevertheless, there is much to be said for a retrieval of the precautionary principle from the panning it commonly receives by preventive justice scholars. In Chapter 2, Jocelyn Stacey persuasively demonstrates that the precautionary principle also has the capacity to limit and constrain decision-making under the rule of law. Stacey suggests, therefore, that there is more commonality between the precautionary principles and the normative project of preventive justice than its advocates have allowed. That said, whereas in the environmental field its deployment may have serious consequences for the interests of big business and their profit margins, in the security domain the resultant costs are primarily to fundamental human rights.[5] So even if the precautionary principle could be mobilised as a restraining principle in respect of counter-terrorism and national security policies, its implications are very different in respect of security than in respect of environmental protection.

Although Part I of this volume focuses principally on the concept of preventive justice, the authors make clear that this conceptual analysis cannot safely be divorced from concrete questions of practice. For example, Donkin's chapter compares the control order regime in Australia with its antecedent counterpart, the former United Kingdom control order (now the United Kingdom Terrorism Prevention and Investigation Measure (TPIM)). This comparative analysis reveals that concepts, and the substantive measures that instantiate them, may take very different forms in different countries. Whereas in the United Kingdom the present form and scope of the control order/TPIM is largely a product of its domestic history (not least as a result of successive legal challenges on human rights

4 United Nations Conference on Environment and Development, *Rio Declaration on Environment and Development*, UN Doc A/CONF.151/26 (vol I); 31 ILM 874 (1992).

5 Peter Ramsay, 'Imprisonment under the Precautionary Principle', in G Robert Sullivan and Ian Dennis (eds), *Seeking Security: Pre-Empting the Commission of Criminal Harms* (Hart Publishing, 2012) 194; Heidi Mork Lomell, 'Punishing the Uncommitted Crime: Prevention, Pre-Emption, Precaution and the Transformation of the Criminal Law', in Barbara Hudson and Synnøve Ugelvik (eds), *Justice and Security in the 21st Century: Risks, Rights and the Rule of Law* (Routledge, 2012) 83.

grounds), in Australia the control order has different targets and is subject instead to constitutional constraints. The comparison also reveals that although control orders bear the same name in both countries, their purpose and use (or non-use) derives from the peculiarities of local conditions. Comparative analysis such as this makes clear that preventive justice, and the measures to which it gives rise, are increasingly widespread and yet remain localised in form and function.

Preventive (in)justice: case studies

Serious scholars of preventive justice must range widely if they are to map out the preventive impetus in domains as diverse as counter-terrorism, dangerous violent and sexual offences, organised crime, and immigration offences.[6] This volume boldly extends the remit further still by considering the application of preventive laws and measures in new areas, including the treatment of those with mental illness (Chapter 4 by Bernadette McSherry, and Chapter 5 by Helen Punter), those seeking protection as refugees or asylum seekers (Chapter 6 by Peter Billings and Dallal Stevens), and in respect of procedural arrangements such as deferred prosecution agreements (Chapter 12 by Simon Bronitt).

Much existing preventive justice scholarship, informed as it is by the Harm Principle first articulated by J S Mill,[7] has focused on what states may do to prevent harm to others. Whether and to what extent the state may legitimately intervene to prevent individuals from committing harms to themselves is a staple of jurisprudential debate. It is also central to contemporary controversies such as the abuse of illegal drugs and 'legal' highs, and the rights and wrongs of assisted suicide. Although they raise many of the same issues as laws and measures designed to prevent harms to others, these controversies have not yet attracted the attention of preventive justice scholars. An important exception lies in the field of mental health law, where measures to prevent harm to self, in particular those at risk of suicide, are highly developed. And yet, as McSherry observes, risk predictive tools remain inaccurate and provide little evidence of a firm link between mental illness and criminal harms. Patients are subject to what McSherry incisively terms 'coercive care' in the name of preventing future harm to self or others.[8]

Equally worrying is Punter's observation that the mere fact of mental disability is taken as sufficient ground to invoke police apprehension powers on grounds of public protection. Punter deplores this contravention of the human rights provision that the fact of disability alone shall not justify deprivation of liberty (Article 14 of the *Convention on the Rights of Persons with Disabilities*).[9] Interestingly, however,

6 Andrew Ashworth and Lucia Zedner, *Preventive Justice* (Oxford University Press, 2014).
7 John Stuart Mill, *On Liberty* (Penguin, 1859/1979).
8 Bernadette McSherry and Ian Freckelton (eds), *Coercive Care: Rights, Law and Policy* (Routledge, 2013).
9 *Convention on the Rights of Persons with Disabilities*, GA Res 61/106, UN GAOR, 61st sess, 76th plen mtg, Agenda Item 67(b), UN Doc A/RES/61/106 (13 December 2006).

Punter concludes that police intervention can also provide the opportunity to divert those with mental illness away from the criminal justice system and toward mental health services. In this much, it represents both a potential intrusion on liberties and also a 'therapeutic opportunity'. This duality of benefit and burden is one that bedevils much preventive endeavour: the key difference here is that the individual bearing the burden of intervention and enjoying its benefits is one and the same person.

A particularly important contribution, made by many chapters, is the sustained exploration of underlying drivers and causal mechanisms, as well as the supposed justifications offered, for new preventive measures. Such is the impact of globalisation that these influences can be international. So, for example, in Chapter 8, Svetlana Tyulkina and George Williams recognise that the London bombings in 2005 provided a major stimulus to the introduction of control orders in Australia and the preventative detention orders (PDOs) that permit a person to be held, without arrest or charge, by the police for up to 14 days. The impact of the London bombings, together with specific intelligence said to give serious grounds for concern about future terrorist threats, proved decisive in persuading the legislature of the need for new measures. Strikingly, though, Tyulkina and Williams argue that in Australia 'no attempt was made to identify what gap in the existing law would be filled by the PDO nor why it was necessary'. Rather, the arguments made for introducing PDOs appear to have been largely rhetorical devices designed to make the government look 'tough'. In short, whereas control orders were a direct import from the United Kingdom, the authors argue that the preventative detention order was *sui generis*: its justification did not rely upon existing models elsewhere and its exceptional violation of rights finds few parallels.

Likewise, Billings and Stevens explore the grounds proffered for preventive immigration detention in Australia and the United Kingdom, to consider its role in facilitating incapacitation, deterrence, adjudication and deportation. Although they similarly employ comparative research to explore the uses of preventive immigration detention, in the Australian context Billings and Stevens find its use is tailored to the identifiably local demands of managing those seeking protection, whether as refugees or asylum seekers. These diverse case studies raise important questions about the origins, conditions of deployment and variations in local practices of preventive justice. They also reveal that while some preventive measures fulfil clearly defined (if not wholly unproblematic) needs, others appear to be driven more by knee-jerk political responses to world events.

To date, preventive justice research has tended to focus primarily on coercive measures.[10] That focus is admirably broadened by Keiran Hardy's contribution, in Chapter 7, which looks at developments in the realm of so-called 'soft power'.[11]

10 Andrew Lynch, Edwina Macdonald and George Williams (eds), *Law and Liberty in the War on Terror* (The Federation Press, 2007); G Robert Sullivan and Ian Dennis (eds), *Seeking Security: Pre-Empting the Commission of Criminal Harms* (Hart Publishing, 2012); Ashworth and Zedner, above n 6.

11 Keiran Hardy, *Ruthlessness and Sympathy: Smart Power Thinking in Counter-Terrorism and Counter-Insurgency* (PhD in law 2014), UNSW; Joseph Nye, *Soft Power: The Means to Success in World Politics* (Public Affairs, 2004).

Hardy examines the United Kingdom government's *Prevent* strategy that seeks to counter violent extremism by targeting those at risk of radicalisation through community-based interventions. Although one might expect such 'soft' measures to generate fewer problems and to entail less serious incursions on civil liberties, Hardy's chapter amply demonstrates their capacity to be just as intrusive and problematic as other more obviously coercive interventions. His chapter rightly asks whether coercion is a 'necessary element' or whether preventive justice scholarship could profitably extend its reach to consider ostensibly non-coercive measures, policies and programs to show that many of the ills of preventive measures apply no less to these less obviously coercive endeavours. Whether a clear line between the nature and impact of coercive and non-coercive measures can be distinguished is open to question, particularly if one accepts that coercion lies as much in the subjective perception of those who feel themselves to be coerced as in the avowed intention of the perpetrator.

Evaluating preventive justice: legitimacy and effectiveness

Although the four chapters in Part III are explicitly tasked with 'evaluating preventive justice', the commitment to assess and appraise the legitimacy and the effectiveness of these laws and measures is shared by all contributors. The question of legitimacy relates to the validity of laws and measures, to the means by which they are enacted and enforced, as well as to public perception.[12] Collectively, the contributions reveal multiple injustices that occur when the grounds for new laws and measures are inadequate; when oversight of preventive decision-making is ineffective (see Chapter 9 by Tim Legrand and Teneille Elliott); when measures are implemented by means that do not meet standards of procedural fairness; when effective judicial oversight of preventive orders is lacking (see Chapter 11 by Sarah Murray) and when scope for judicial review is limited (see Chapter 6 by Billings and Stevens). The absence of adequate legal constraints and of sufficient checks leads to practices that are more accurately identified as instances of preventive *injustice*. In the security domain, the lack of openness and transparency further inhibits scrutiny (see Chapter 9 by Legrand and Elliott). Other chapters also raise important questions about how far due process protections owed by the state are tied to citizenship. As Billings and Stevens show, where preventive measures are predicated upon protecting a community comprised only of citizens, the threat posed by non-citizens is too easily asserted or assumed rather than proven. This obviously has adverse implications for those who are not yet and may never be citizens.

Preventive justice scholarship has tended to focus on the normative issues it throws up and has paid much less attention to the question of whether measures are actually effective, partly because what constitutes efficacy is 'ambiguous and

12 Anthony Bottoms and Justice Tankebe, 'Beyond Procedural Justice: A Dialogic Approach to Legitimacy in Criminal Justice' (2012) 102 *Journal of Criminal Law and Criminology*, 119; David Beetham, *The Legitimation of Power* (Macmillan, 1981).

contested'.[13] Evaluating efficacy returns us to the fraught, but often overlooked, question of why preventive measures are introduced in the first place. The readiness with which jurisdictions seek to import measures, particularly in times of crisis,[14] has already been noted. Transplants occur regardless of immediate need, fit with local legal culture or conditions, and with scant regard to how measures were used – or abused – in the originating jurisdiction. The transplant of the control order from the United Kingdom to Australia (discussed above) is just one such example. In Chapter 10, Rebecca Ananian-Welsh observes that the migration of orders occurs not only between countries but also internally across states and territories, as well as across different genres of risk. Ananian-Welsh notes how the model of the control order was adapted to help police organised crime; after the Serious and Organised Crime Control Order was introduced in South Australia, it was copied by every other state and territory. As this and several other chapters reveal, preventive measures are attractive to policy-makers partly because they satisfy a determination to make use of all available means to tackle threats and partly because they allow leaders to appear tough on crime and serious about security. Even if they are not in fact used, their very existence conveys 'an image of a responsive government concerned with taking strong action to protect citizens'.[15]

The recognition that rhetorical efficacy may be as important as practical efficacy is an important insight and may help explain why orders, introduced with so much political hullabaloo, are not subsequently used. As we have seen, the United Kingdom control order was copied in Australia although the need for it was far less evident. That its introduction was uncalled for is arguably evidenced by the fact that, of the original control order regime, only two orders were ever imposed and, even since reform in 2014, only six counter-terrorism control orders have been imposed.[16] Likewise, PDOs were introduced in 2005 but remained completely unused until 2014.[17] And although the Serious and Organised Crime Control Order was adopted across Australia to target 'bikie' gangs, it too was never used.[18] It is a moot question how we should think about measures placed upon the statute book in moments of crisis, perhaps by governments anxious to be seen to be 'doing something'. One possible explanation lies in the concept of 'security theater', developed by Bruce Schneier, which deftly captures the practice of developing measures that ostentatiously promote security but which actually do little to achieve it.[19]

It would be wrong, however, to suggest that the contributors are unremittingly sceptical about the efficacy or potential of preventive measures. Bronitt, for

13 See Chapter 9 by Legrand and Elliott.
14 Oren Gross and Fionnuala Ní Aoláin, *Law in Times of Crisis: Emergency Powers in Theory and Practice* (Cambridge University Press, 2006).
15 See Chapter 10 by Ananian-Welsh.
16 See Chapter 3 by Donkin and Chapter 10 by Ananian-Welsh.
17 See Chapter 8 by Tyulkina and Williams.
18 See Chapter 10 by Ananian-Welsh.
19 Bruce Schneier, *Beyond Fear: Thinking Sensibly About Security in an Uncertain World* (Springer, 2006).

example, analyses deferred prosecution agreements (DPAs) in cases involving large corporations as a means to avert the risk of corporate failure, consequent harm to third parties, loss of confidence in local markets or even the global economy. Although Bronitt is rightly careful to delineate the potential pitfalls of this controversial device (not least risks to due process, constitutional values, transparency and fairness), he flags up the potential of DPAs to engage offenders in the preventive project by imposing upon them the duty to take steps to mitigate losses and prevent future harms. The idea of the criminal actor as an agent of his own redemption is not new,[20] but the notion that individuals, organisations and corporations might be called upon actively to mitigate or avert future harms certainly merits further exploration.

Measuring effectiveness also depends on how clearly the originating aims and goals are articulated. Where there is no clearly defined purpose, it is very much harder to say with confidence whether a measure has fulfilled its objectives or not.[21] As several chapters make clear, security laws and counter-terrorism measures remain remarkably immune to evidence-based evaluation of whether they successfully identify and target the greatest risks, and empirical research into their effectiveness is lacking.[22] Nor has sufficient attention been paid to the attendant moral hazards and opportunity costs of counter-terrorism policies, not least the political costs of measures that alienate communities and undermine trust in ways that may actually exacerbate risk and run counter to the interests of security.

Preventive justice at the crossroads: some reflections

It should by now be clear that this volume makes a particularly timely contribution, coming as it does as preventive justice scholarship moves from an emergent to an established field of enquiry. At its best, such scholarship enables us to see linkages and similarities between developments in widely differing domains from crime,[23] to terrorism,[24] immigration,[25] mental health[26] and even the management of environmental risks.[27] In so doing, it creates the possibility of generating explanatory frameworks that apply across different laws and measures[28] and of elaborating normative frameworks that can be applied across otherwise apparently unrelated domains.[29]

20 Antony Duff, *Punishment, Communication and Community* (Oxford University Press, 2001).
21 See Chapter 8 by Tyulkina and Williams and Chapter 10 by Ananian-Welsh.
22 See e.g. Chapter 9 by Legrand and Elliott.
23 See Chapter 10 by Ananian-Welsh and Chapter 12 by Bronitt.
24 See Chapter 3 by Donkin, Chapter 7 by Hardy, Chapter 8 by Tyulkina and Williams, and Chapter 9 by Legrand and Elliott.
25 See Chapter 6 by Billings and Stevens.
26 See Chapter 4 by McSherry and Chapter 5 by Punter.
27 See Chapter 2 by Stacey.
28 See Chapter 11 by Murray.
29 As Steiker insightfully observed: Carol S Steiker, 'Foreword: The Limits of the Preventive State' (1998) 88(3) *Journal of Criminal Law and Criminology* 771.

Yet, in so doing, preventive justice faces two countervailing hazards. First, there is a risk of seeing prevention everywhere so that preventive imperatives are ascribed to laws and measures in ways that distort their real character and aims. Whether the widely varying instances of preventive practice are in fact amenable to identification and treatment as constituent parts of a unified problem is a question that needs tackling head-on if the risk of over-extension is to be avoided. Tulich justifiably invites us to consider whether the range of preventive practices is capable of being classified as a cohesive entity or whether their shared characteristics are less salient than their differences.

Second, in the bid to carve out their terrain, have preventive justice scholars been less attentive to the question of boundaries than they should? In any field of scholarship, and particularly one not yet well established, academics need to draw lines in order to place limits on the scope and ambitions of their endeavour. But deciding what is in and what is out can lead to arbitrariness unless close attention is paid to the determinative principles and categorical distinctions by which boundaries are drawn. For example, if one decides to focus only on coercive measures that impinge upon individual liberties,[30] it might be objected that to insist upon coercion as a defining characteristic is to exclude much of relevance and importance.[31] It might also be said that the effects of preventive endeavour cannot properly be understood by focusing on measures aimed at individuals alone. The revelations by Edward Snowden of mass surveillance and mass data retention by the United States National Security Agency make clear that preventive measures need be neither coercive nor targeted at individuals to provoke enormous controversy about the overreaching of the preventive state.[32]

Another important issue is the risk that by focusing on the normative questions thrown up by preventive justice and even conceiving it as 'justice', we overlook the many injustices entailed. This is a particular risk where religion, race, class and gender play a decisive role in determining who is subject to intrusive, coercive measures and who is not.[33] The case studies in this volume suggest the enormous value of close inquiry into how laws and measures are targeted and against whom they are deployed. Tulich alerts us to the fact that the selective focus of preventive measures on marginalised groups is such that the burdens may fall in uneven and inherently unjust ways. Perhaps we need now to move beyond the conceptual, analytical and normative deliberations, called for by Steiker,[34] to encourage a new

30 As I did in my book with Andrew Ashworth: Ashworth and Zedner, above n 6; see also Andrew Ashworth and Lucia Zedner, 'Preventive Orders: A Problem of Under-Criminalization?' in Antony Duff, Lindsay Farmer, S E Marshall, Massimo Renzo, and Victor Tadros (eds), *The Boundaries of the Criminal Law* (Oxford University Press, 2010).

31 See Chapter 4 by McSherry and Chapter 7 by Hardy.

32 Russell Miller (ed.) *Privacy and Power: A Transatlantic Dialogue in the Shadow of the NSA-Affair* (Cambridge University Press, 2017).

33 Alpa Parmar, 'Stop and Search in London: Counter-Terrorist or Counter-Productive?' (2011) 21(4) *Policing and Society* 369.

34 Steiker, above n 29.

generation of scholars to carry out empirical research into the practices of preventive measures. This would allow us to develop a more fine-grained picture of the impact of preventive measures along lines of race, religion, gender, socio-economic and citizenship status. Exploring the intersectionality of these different classifications would enable us to see how the burdens of prevention are in fact distributed and by whom they are principally borne.

This idea of preventive justice as critique can profitably be taken further. While principles of preventive justice have largely been conceived as a means of guiding and restraining the application of preventive measures, some contributors to this volume suggest that where a measure is not compatible with key principles of preventive justice, it should, quite simply, be abolished.[35] Their challenge invites serious debate about what principles should apply, when the case for abolition is made, or whether a principled approach can, even in egregious cases, open the way for modification and amendment until justice is achieved.

Fundamentally, preventive justice scholarship is motivated by concern about the extension of state coercive power in the name of protection and it seeks to critique instances of overreaching. But, as the contributions to this volume make clear, the preventive justice project generates a new hazard – that by articulating principles and values by which to regulate, it may render legitimate that which should be subject to continuing critique. Whether preventive justice can fulfil the aims set out by Tulich in her insightful introductory chapter – namely, to guide state action without also blindly justifying it – is perhaps the biggest challenge going forward. Failure to meet this challenge may lead preventive justice scholars to inadvertently furnish a justificatory veneer to laws and measures that are inherently problematic. Certainly, the evidence provided by the contributions to this volume is that emergency and other exceptional preventive measures become 'normalised', win public acceptance and gain constitutional legitimacy[36] – paradoxically even as a result of constitutional challenge – with worrisome ease. The legitimacy of their place within a liberal legal order becomes accepted and doubts about their necessity or effectiveness are quickly overborne. Whereas earlier scholars looked upon preventive justice as a source and means of regulation, the powerfully argued contributions to this volume provide forceful reasons to consider whether we would do better to talk about regulating preventive justice.

35 See Chapter 8 by Tyulkina and Williams.
36 See Chapter 11 by Murray.

Part I

The preventive justice concept

1 Critical reflections on preventive justice

Tamara Tulich

Introduction

'Preventive Justice' was coined by Blackstone, in the late eighteenth century, to describe an area of law devoted to preventing future crime by intervening where there exists 'a probable suspicion, that some crime is intended or likely to happen'.[1] Governments have long employed 'preventive justice' measures that restrain an individual's liberty on the basis of an estimation of future harm, rather than past acts (even if past acts form part of the prediction of future harm). In England, preventive measures have been traced to the twelfth century, with the power granted to Justices of the Peace to bind over subjects to keep the peace.[2] This preventive jurisdiction was well established by the time Australian colonies enacted 'Bushranger' legislation in the 1830s, which permitted the apprehension and detention without charge of a person suspected of being a felon until the suspected felon established, to the reasonable satisfaction of a Justice of the Peace, that he or she was not a felon.[3]

The events of September 11, 2001, and the ensuing 'war on terror', magnified the role that law and policy can play in preventing harm. The breadth and intensity of the preventive response to terrorism embarked upon by many nations, in line with United Nations Security Council Resolutions, brought to the fore questions

1 William Blackstone, *Commentaries on the Laws of England* (R Bell, 1772), book IV, 248. Blackstone's comments have been cited with approval by members of the High Court of Australia: see e.g. *Devine v R* (1967) 119 CLR 506; *Griffiths v R* (1977) 137 CLR 293.

2 A binding-over order restrained future breaches of the peace, requiring the person to promise (with or without a sureties or bond) to be of good behaviour in the future for a defined period of time. Today, good behaviour or peace bonds have been placed on a statutory footing, and like their predecessors these powers do not depend upon conviction of any offence: Simon Bronitt and Bernadette McSherry, *Principles of Criminal Law* (Thomson Reuters, 3rd edn, 2010) 795ff. Dershowitz traces the Office of Justice of the Peace to the time of Richard I in the twelfth century (then called the Office of Conservator of the Peace, to become Guardian of the Peace, Keeper of the Peace and, finally, Justice of the Peace): Alan M Dershowitz, *Preemption: A Knife that Cuts Both Ways* (W W Norton & Co, 2006) 43, 50.

3 Bernadette McSherry, *Managing Fear: The Law and Ethics of Preventive Detention and Risk Assessment* (Routledge, 2014) 12–15.

of preventive governance.[4] Post-September 11 anti-terrorism lawmaking has also highlighted the paradoxical nature of 'preventive justice' measures: preventing the occurrence of anticipated harm through law has consequences – including for accepted legal principles and protections – that can weaken the fabric of the society that the measures seek to protect.[5] Preventive anti-terror measures risk creating a template for the expansion of preventive incursions on liberty more generally and for the creation of an alternative system of justice that is devoid of, or contains an attenuated version of, the normal civil liberty protections afforded.[6]

Preventive justice scholarship suggests a way to address this paradox. Collectively, this scholarship conducts a wide-ranging and multi-jurisdictional study of preventive policies and practices. Its aim is to develop principles and values – a preventive jurisprudence – to guide and limit action by governments to prevent future harm. This academic focus on the preventive role of the state is deliberate and normative: to illuminate the problematic treatment of preventive measures as unrelated and discrete, and the need for the articulation of legal limitations on preventive governmental action. Importantly, this scholarship acknowledges the significance of the duty to protect the public, but contests its prioritisation above all else.[7] Rather, preventive justice scholarship stresses that preventive measures in furtherance of this duty ought to be justified and subject to principled limits.[8]

This chapter critically engages with the emerging body of preventive justice literature, tracing its history and examining its utility as a framework for conceptualising and normatively limiting preventive governmental action. It argues that preventive justice scholarship has much to offer: it promotes critical engagement with the multifarious forms of prevention employed by governments, and exposes common issues in the operation of preventive measures. However, questions remain about the utility and coherency of preventive justice, instrumentally and conceptually.

4 Carol S Steiker, 'Proportionality as a Limit on Preventive Justice: Promises and Pitfalls' in Andrew Ashworth, Lucia Zedner and Patrick Tomlin (eds), *Prevention and the Limits of the Criminal Law* (Oxford University Press, 2013) 194. See e.g. SC Res 1368, UN SCOR, 57th sess, 4370th mtg, UN Doc S/RES/1368 (12 September 2001); SC Res 1373, UN SCOR, 57th sess, 4385th mtg, UN Doc S/RES/1373 (28 September 2001); SC Res 1455, UN SCOR, 58th sess, 4686th mtg, UN Doc S/RES/1455 (17 January 2003); SC Res 1456, UN SCOR, 58th sess, 4688th mtg, UN Doc S/RES/1456 (20 January 2003); SC Res 1566, UN SCOR, 60th sess, 5053rd mtg, UN Doc S/RES/1566 (8 October 2004). These resolutions are binding on Member States under Part VII of the United Nations Charter. See generally Eric Rosand, 'The Security Council as "Global Legislator": Ultra Vires or Ultra Innovative?' (2004–5) 28 *Fordham International Law Journal* 542.

5 These are not new costs; as Finnane and Donkin remind us, the liberal state has, in its pursuit of security, long departed from accepted legal principles and protections: Mark Finnane and Susan Donkin, 'Fighting Terror with Law? Some Other Genealogies of Pre-emption' (2013) 2(1) *International Journal for Crime and Justice* 3.

6 Eric S Janus, *Failure to Protect: America's Sexual Predator Laws and the Rise of the Preventive State* (Cornell University Press, 2006) 94.

7 Andrew Ashworth and Lucia Zedner, *Preventive Justice* (Oxford University Press, 2014) 266.

8 Ibid.

This chapter argues that this is emblematic of a developing literature that has, in line with international events, focused predominantly on prevention in the anti-terror and sex offender contexts. It argues that the core project of preventive justice scholarship – to examine the various contexts in which preventive measures are used so that guiding principles and justifications may be developed – can make an important contribution to identifying and abating the costs of prevention in terms of burdens on state budgets and civil liberties.

The emergence of preventive justice scholarship

There are various and competing conceptions of 'prevention' in contemporary lawmaking. Many accounts that explain or analyse the current prevalence of preventive measures are couched in terms of a 'marked shift in political emphasis'[9] (albeit that the extent and newness of this shift is often contested).[10] For some, this shift is articulated in terms of the 'emergent phenomenon' of the 'new penology' or 'actuarial justice';[11] for others, the emergence of 'the risk society' and 'world risk society';[12] others yet identify that risk has now been surpassed by uncertainty, giving rise to questions of precautionary justice.[13] Jocelyn Stacey, in Chapter 2 of this collection, critically examines the treatment of precaution in these accounts. Preventive justice scholarship is another way in which this apparent shifting emphasis in law and policy has been articulated and conceptualised.

Preventive justice scholarship builds on the work of Carol Steiker who, in the late 1990s, invoked the idea of the 'preventive state' to describe a host of measures introduced in various jurisdictions in the United States which sought to

9 Andrew Ashworth, 'Criminal Law, Human Rights and Preventative Justice' in Bernadette McSherry, Alan Norrie and Simon Bronitt (eds), *Regulating Deviance: The Redirection of Criminalisation and the Futures of Criminal Law* (Hart Publishing, 2009) 87, 87. See also Bernadette McSherry and Patrick Keyzer, *Sex Offenders and Preventive Detention: Politics, Policy and Practice* (Federation Press, 2009) 20–3.

10 See e.g. in relation to the new penology: David Garland, 'Penal Modernism and Postmodernism' in Thomas G Blomberg and Stanley Cohen (eds), *Punishment and Social Control* (Transaction Publishers, 3rd edn, 2012) 45, 65; Jonathan Simon and Malcolm M Feeley, 'The Form and Limits of the New Penology' in Thomas G Blomberg and Stanley Cohen (eds), *Punishment and Social Control* (Transaction Publishers, 3rd edn, 2012) 75, 76. See also Lucia Zedner, 'Policing Before and After the Police: The Historical Antecedents of Contemporary Crime Control' (2006) 46 *British Journal of Criminology* 78.

11 Malcolm M Feeley and Jonathan Simon, 'The New Penology: Notes on the Emerging Strategy of Corrections and Its Implications' (1992) 30 *Criminology* 449; Malcolm M Feeley and Jonathan Simon, 'Actuarial Justice: the Emerging New Criminal Law' in David Nelken (ed.), *The Futures of Criminology* (Sage, 1994) 173; Simon and Feeley, 'The Form and Limits of the New Penology', above n 10, 77.

12 Ulrich Beck, *Risk Society* (Sage Publications, 1992); Ulrich Beck, *World Risk Society* (Polity Press, 1999); Ulrich Beck, *World at Risk* (Polity Press, 2009).

13 Richard V Ericson, *Crime in an Insecure World* (Polity Press, 2007); François Ewald, 'The Return of the Crafty Genius: An Outline of a Philosophy of Precaution' (1999) 6(1) *Connecticut Insurance Law Journal* 47, reproduced in Pat O'Malley (ed.), *Governing Risks* (Ashgate, 2005) 538; Lucia Zedner, *Security* (Routledge, 2009).

prevent crime by incapacitating or treating those deemed dangerous.[14] Steiker was referring to a disparate collection of new or expanded 'preventive' laws and policing initiatives, ranging from pre-trial preventive detention of juveniles and adults to post-sentence indefinite detention of serious violent sex offenders, and the expansion of police powers to conduct suspicionless searches.[15] Steiker traced the genesis of the preventive state to the nineteenth century, and its growth to favourable conditions in the twentieth century: the creation of the modern police force and institutions such as prisons and psychiatric hospitals in the former was bolstered by the growth of the regulatory state in the latter. These developments enabled and promulgated diverse preventive practices by governments.[16]

For Steiker, the emergence of the preventive state demanded further and different scrutiny. Preventive policies and practices were being treated as discrete and unrelated, rather than, as Steiker argued they should be, as part of a 'unified problem' – 'a facet of a larger question in need of a more general conceptual framework'.[17] Without a holistic approach, jurisprudence relating to preventive measures would remain undernourished; 'salient similarities' between preventive measures and the concerns they raise would evade discovery.[18] Importantly, focusing attention on the collection of preventive practices employed by governments would enable the articulation and policing of the limits of the preventive state.

Steiker highlighted that unlike 'the punitive state', in respect of which the constitutional and due process limitations on state action were well established and maintained, the limits of state action to prevent harm remained largely unchecked.[19] This was, Steiker noted, in part a function of the timing of the drafting of the American Constitution. The dangers of the punitive state were well known to the Founders and thus constraints on the state as punisher were included in the American Constitution.[20] The emergence of the preventive state, however, came later, as a function of the coalescing of events in the nineteenth and twentieth centuries. As a result, preventive state practices and institutions were 'cabined' within the existing constitutional framework, making it 'harder to see the preventive state as a category than it is to so view the punitive state'.[21]

14 Carol S Steiker, 'Forward: The Limits of the Preventive State' (1998) 88(3) *Journal of Criminal Law and Criminology* 771, 774.
15 Ibid. 774–5.
16 Ibid. 778–9.
17 Ibid. 778.
18 Ibid. 779.
19 Ibid. 773–4.
20 Ibid. 778.
21 Ibid. 779. See also Markus Dubber's excellent work on the emerging concept in the nineteenth century of preventive policing: Markus Dubber, *The Police Power: Patriarchy and the Foundations of American Government* (Columbia University Press, 2005); Markus Dubber, 'Preventive Justice: The Quest for Principle' in Andrew Ashworth, Lucia Zedner and Patrick Tomlin (eds), *Prevention and the Limits of the Criminal Law* (Oxford University Press, 2013) 69.

Steiker, and many after her, have distinguished between the preventive state and the punitive or reactive state to illustrate both the growing collection of preventive measures and the lack of consideration given to the question of the limits of governmental action to prevent harm.[22] The distinct temporal viewpoints of state action to prevent and punish are also often compared. The focus of the preventive state is prospective: state intervention occurs prior to harm by, for instance, incapacitating those deemed dangerous. The focus of the punitive state is retrospective: the state conducts after-the-fact investigation and punishes criminal acts. This contradistinction, while useful, should not be understood as suggesting that these two objectives, prevention and punishment, are easily distinguishable or mutually exclusive. Nor should it be inferred that the preventive state is displacing the punitive state. Rather, it has been argued that preventive measures are rising in prominence and being used to extend as opposed to supplant the criminal justice system.[23]

In invoking the preventive state concept, Steiker presented a normative model. Steiker argued that the limits of the preventive state ought to be articulated and policed, as are those of the punitive state (such as the principle of finality of sentence).[24] There are a number of guises through which the limits of state action to prevent harm may be articulated, including the principles of criminalisation, public law or human rights law.[25] Steiker focused on the constitutional and due process limits of the preventive state. She identified that the question of the limits of preventive action had been sidelined because, among other reasons, the courts were preoccupied with whether a measure amounted to punishment, and therefore whether the enhanced protections of the criminal justice system ought to apply.[26] This leaves what Steiker argued is the 'mistaken impression that if the state is not punishing, it is not doing anything objectionable at all, constitutionally speaking or otherwise'.[27] The general conceptual framework of

22 See e.g. Dershowitz, *Preemption*, above n 2; Alan M Dershowitz, 'The Preventive State: Uncharted Waters after 9/11' in Matthew J Morgan (ed.), *The Impact of 9/11 and the New Legal Landscape: The Day that Changed Everything?* (Macmillan, 2009) 7; Lucia Zedner, 'Preventive Justice or Pre-Punishment? The Case of Control Orders' (2007) 60 *Current Legal Problems* 174.

23 Ashworth, 'Criminal Law, Human Rights and Preventative Justice', above n 9, 87–8.

24 Steiker, 'The Preventive State', above n 14, 773–4.

25 See e.g. Ashworth, 'Criminal Law, Human Rights and Preventative Justice', above n 9, 87; Andrew Ashworth and Lucia Zedner, 'Just Prevention: Preventive Rationales and the Limits of the Criminal Law' in Antony Duff and Stuart Green (eds), *Philosophical Foundations of Criminal Law* (Oxford University Press, 2011) 279; Andrew Ashworth and Lucia Zedner, 'Prevention and Criminalization: Justifications and Limits' (2012) 15(4) *New Criminal Law Journal* 542; Steiker, 'The Preventive State', above n 14. See also Steiker, 'Proportionality' above n 4; Peter Ramsay, 'Democratic Limits to Preventive Criminal Law' in Andrew Ashworth, Lucia Zedner and Patrick Tomlin (eds), *Prevention and the Limits of the Criminal Law* (Oxford University Press, 2013) 214.

26 Steiker, 'The Preventive State', above n 14, 783–4.

27 Ibid. 784.

the preventive state provided one way to begin the project of identifying and establishing limits on preventive state action.

Steiker deliberately pitched the preventive state at a high 'level of conceptual generalization' in order that it may capture the diverse set of preventive measures employed by governments.[28] This may, Steiker suggested, facilitate the drawing of fresh insights about particular preventive practices. By moving beyond the 'exceptionally particularized way in which the law has been developed on these issues up to this point', it may also produce greater predictability for those generating policy and subject to it.[29] Steiker further identified benefits of drawing attention to, and recognising connections between, the practices of the preventive state: it may engender a constructive dialogue about the proper limits of preventive state action,[30] and also that the concerns raised in respect of 'certain preventive practices may shed light on what may (or may not) be cause for concern about other preventive practices'.[31] Identifying similarities between the diverse set of preventive measures may avoid dangers discovered in one measure being blindly reproduced in another.[32]

The September 11 terrorist attacks and the so-called 'war on terror' have been pivotal in shaping the development and focus of preventive justice scholarship. Prevention of terrorism has been a defining feature of post-September 11 lawmaking, with Australia, the United Kingdom, Canada and the United States introducing anti-terror measures targeting individuals deemed 'dangerous' – namely, but not limited to, suspected terrorists – and restraining their liberty before they cause harm.[33] This anti-terror lawmaking has, more than ever before, brought to the forefront the question of preventive governmental action, raising, Steiker writes, 'profound questions about how we should delineate the substantive and procedural limits of the state's power to prevent harmful or undesirable conduct'.[34] At the same time, anti-terror lawmaking has reinforced the absence of a conceptual framework to embody and guide the use of preventive restraints by the state.[35] As Andrew Ashworth, Lucia Zedner and Patrick Tomlin have remarked:

28 Ibid. 779–80.
29 Ibid.
30 In particular, without needing to refer back to, or construct arguments in terms of, the punitive state: ibid. 779.
31 Ibid. 779.
32 Zedner, 'Pre-Punishment?', above n 22, 189. See also Dershowitz, *Preemption,* above n 2.
33 Victor V Ramraj, Michael Hor, Kent Roach and George Williams (eds), *Global Anti-Terrorism Law and Policy* (Cambridge University Press, 2nd edn, 2012); Kent Roach, *The 9/11 Effect: Comparative Counter-Terrorism* (Cambridge University Press, 2011).
34 Steiker, 'Proportionality', above n 4, 194.
35 See e.g. Zedner, 'Pre-Punishment?', above n 22, 189–90; Dershowitz, *Preemption*, above n 2; Andrew Ashworth, Lucia Zedner and Patrick Tomlin, 'Introduction' in Andrew Ashworth, Lucia Zedner and Patrick Tomlin (eds), *Prevention and the Limits of the Criminal Law* (Oxford University Press, 2013) 1.

> There are good reasons to justify state use of coercion to protect the public from harm. And yet, although the rationales for and justifications of state punishment have been explored extensively, the scope, limits, and principles of what we term preventive justice – the use of the criminal law and related coercive measures in a directly preventive way – have attracted little doctrinal or conceptual analysis (save in respect of counterterrorist measures).[36]

Ashworth and Zedner have sought to rectify this deficit, developing an account of the justifications for, and principles to guide and limit, preventive justice in England and Wales.[37] Ashworth and Zedner trace the history and examine the operation of coercive preventive measures in a number of contexts, including policing, anti-terrorism, immigration and health, and develop justifications for and principles to guide and limit state action in these areas. From this study, they also identify the 'most prominent rights and principles' that ought to guide the use of coercive preventive measures more generally, such as the principle of the least restrictive alternative.[38] In Australia, Bernadette McSherry has explored the human rights and ethical implications of risk assessments for preventive detention and supervision regimes in a number of contexts, including mental health and anti-terrorism.[39]

However, in line with the breadth and intensity of the preventive response to terrorism embarked upon by many nations, preventive scholarship has, over the last decade, largely focused on terrorist suspects.[40] Preventive measures in respect of sex offenders have featured in American, and to a lesser extent Australian, scholarship.[41] Outside of the United States, scholarship has principally concentrated

36 Ashworth, Zedner and Tomlin, 'Introduction', above n 35.
37 Ashworth and Zedner, *Preventive Justice*, above n 7.
38 Ibid. 253–4.
39 McSherry, *Managing Fear*, above n 3.
40 However, there are examples of the comparative treatment of preventive measures after September 11, 2001: see e.g. Andrew Ashworth and Lucia Zedner, 'Defending the Criminal Law: Reflections on the Changing Character of Crime, Procedure, and Sanctions' (2008) 2 *Criminal Law and Philosophy* 21; Andrew Ashworth and Lucia Zedner, 'Preventive Orders: A Problem of Undercriminalization' in Antony Duff, Lindsay Farmer, S E Marshall, Massimo Renzo, and Victor Tadros (eds), *The Boundaries of the Criminal Law* (Oxford University Press, 2010) 59; Andrew Ashworth, Lucia Zedner and Patrick Tomlin (eds) *Prevention and the Limits of the Criminal Law* (Oxford University Press, 2013); Dershowitz, *Preemption*, above n 2; Finnane and Donkin, above n 5; McSherry, *Managing Fear*, above n 3; Bernadette McSherry and Patrick Keyzer (eds), *Dangerous People: Policy, Prediction, Practice* (Routledge, 2011); Christopher Slobogin, *Minding Justice: Laws that Deprive People with Mental Disability of Life and Liberty* (Harvard University Press, 2006).
41 See e.g. for sex offenders: Wayne Logan, 'Liberty Interests in the Preventive State: Procedural Due Process and Sex Offender Community Notification Laws' (1999) 89 (4) *Journal of Criminal Law and Criminology* 1167; Michelle Olson, 'Putting the Brakes on the Preventive State: Challenging Residency Restrictions on Child Sex Offenders in Illinois under the Ex Post Facto Clause' (2010) 5(2) *Northwestern Journal of Law and Social Policy* 403; McSherry and Keyzer, *Sex Offenders*, above n 9; McSherry and Keyzer, *Dangerous People*, above n 40. See e.g. for terrorists: Robert

on preventive anti-terrorism measures and the concerns they raise for the roles of the state and the criminal justice system.[42] Recently, however, the focus of scholarship has sharpened on the principles and parameters of preventive justice, with particular emphasis on the role and rationales of coercive preventive measures.[43] Preventive scholarship has also adopted a more reflective and critical posture, challenging the categories and assumptions upon which it is based.[44]

With the notable exceptions of Ashworth, Zedner and McSherry, preventive scholarship has largely concentrated the relationship between prevention and the criminal law, demonstrating both the long presence and profusion of prevention in the criminal justice system, and its influence on conceptions of crime, punishment and the criminal law.[45] Concerns have been raised about prevention driving the unprincipled development of the criminal law and subverting its protections,[46] giving rise to significant questions about the proper role of the criminal law, and

Chesney and Jack Goldsmith, 'Terrorism and the Convergence of Criminal and Military Detention Models' (2008) 60 *Stanford Law Review* 1079; David Cole and Jules Lobel, *Less Safe, Less Free: Why America is Losing the War on Terror* (The New Press, 2007); David Cole, 'Terror Financing, Guilt by Association and the Paradigm of Prevention in the "War on Terror"' in Andrea Bianchi and Alexis Keller (eds), *Counterterrorism: Democracy's Challenge* (Hart Publishing, 2008) 233. For terrorists and sex offenders, see: Eric S Janus, 'The Preventive State, Terrorists and Sexual Predators: Countering the Threat of a New Outsider Jurisprudence' (2004) 40 *Criminal Law Bulletin* 576; Janus, *Failure to Protect*, above n 6.

42 Ashworth and Zedner, 'Just Prevention', above n 25; Francesca Galli, 'The War on Terror and Crusading Judges: Re-establishing the Primacy of the Criminal Justice System' in Aniceto Masferrer (ed.), *Post 9–11 and the State of Permanent Legal Emergency* (Springer, 2012) 153; Susanne Krasmann, 'The Right of Government: Torture and the Rule of Law' in Ulrich Bröckling, Susanne Krasmann and Thomas Lemke (eds), *Governmentality: Current Issues and Future Challenges* (Routledge, 2011) 115; Jude McCulloch, 'Australia's Anti-Terrorism Legislation and the Jack Thomas Case' (2006) 18(2) *Current Issues in Criminal Justice* 357; Jude McCulloch and Bree Carlton, 'Preempting Justice: Suppression of Financing of Terrorism and the "War on Terror"' (2006) 17(3) *Current Issues in Criminal Justice* 397; Jude McCulloch and Sharon Pickering, 'Pre-Crime and Counter-Terrorism: Imagining Future Crime in the War on Terror' (2009) 49(5) *British Journal of Criminology* 628; Heidi Mork Lomell, 'Punishing the Uncommitted Crime: Prevention, Pre-emption, Precaution and the Transformation of Criminal Law' in Barbara Hudson and Synnøve Ugelvik (eds), *Justice and Security in the 21st Century: Risks, Rights and the Rule of Law* (Routledge, 2012) 83; András Sajó, 'From Militant Democracy to the Preventive State?' (2006) 27(5) *Cardozo Law Review* 2255; Zedner, 'Pre-Punishment?', above n 22; Lucia Zedner, 'Terrorizing Criminal Law' (2014) 8(1) *Criminal Law and Philosophy* 99.

43 See e.g. Ashworth and Zedner, 'Preventive Orders', above n 40; Ashworth and Zedner, 'Just Prevention', above n 25; Ashworth, Zedner and Tomlin, *Prevention and the Limits of the Criminal Law*, above n 40.

44 See e.g. Markus Dubber, 'Preventive Justice: The Quest for Principle', above n 21, 47; Finnane and Donkin, above n 5.

45 See e.g. the contributions to the edited collection: Ashworth, Zedner and Tomlin, *Prevention and the Limits of the Criminal Law*, above n 40; Dershowitz, *Preemption*, above n 2.

46 Ashworth and Zedner, 'Just Prevention', above n 25, 9.

its jurisprudence, in the face of burgeoning prevention.[47] Within this context, important work has been done on the difficult questions of what values, constraints and justifications ought to guide and support coercive preventive measures[48] and preventive and pre-emptive decision-making.[49] However, what has been lacking in the literature to date is a critical appraisal of the utility and coherency of preventive justice. The following two sections of this chapter begin this task by examining the potential promise and pitfalls of the preventive justice scholarship.

The promise of preventive justice scholarship

Preventive justice scholarship promises to develop a more cohesive preventive jurisprudence, and to articulate the principles that ought to govern state action that seeks to prevent harm in the future.[50] Ashworth and Zedner remind us:

> The duty to protect the public is always liable to be laid down as a trump card. Preventive justice does not contest this duty, but it does contest its claim to outplay all other values and insists that preventive measures should be subject to restraining principles.[51]

By focusing attention on, and promoting critical engagement with, the collection of preventive measures employed by governments, preventive justice scholarship has the potential to highlight broader issues of the discriminatory and disproportionate application of preventive measures: that is, who is – and isn't – subject to preventive measures and how different types of preventive measures compare with each other; including whether and why, for instance, there are preconditions, such as past harm, or principles, such as the least restrictive alternative, for some measures and not others.

The answers to these questions have broader implications. Eric Janus, for example, has argued that 'risk' has now replaced 'race, gender, sexual orientation and disability' as the 'marker of otherness' and the 'foundation of outsider jurisprudence'.[52] He highlights that anti-terrorism and sexual predator laws in the United States provide a deleterious road map for the expansion of preventive incursions on liberty more generally. Importantly, Janus argues that these legislative schemes 'reintroduce and relegitimize the concept of the degraded other' and

47 Zedner, 'Pre-Punishment?', above n 22; Christopher Slobogin, 'The Civilization of the Criminal Law' (2005) 58(1) *Vanderbilt Law Review* 121; Zedner, 'Terrorizing Criminal Law', above n 42; Jeremy Waldron, 'Responses to Zedner, Haque and Mendus' (2014) 8(1) *Criminal Law and Philosophy* 135.

48 See e.g. the contributions to the edited collection: Ashworth, Zedner and Tomlin, *Prevention and the Limits of the Criminal Law*, above n 40.

49 See e.g. Dershowitz, *Preemption*, above n 2.

50 Zedner, 'Pre-Punishment?', above n 22.

51 Ashworth and Zedner, *Preventive Justice*, above n 7, 266 (citation omitted).

52 Janus, *Failure to Protect*, above n 6, 103–4.

create an alternative system of justice that is devoid of, or contains an attenuated version of, the normal civil liberties protections afforded.[53]

These concerns resonate beyond the United States where preventive measures predominantly affect marginalised and excluded members of society, such as the mentally ill, serious sex offenders and terrorist suspects. For example, the overwhelming majority of persons charged with terrorism-related offences in Australia have been Muslim men and all but one of Australia's listed terrorist organisations have been Muslim groups.[54] Similarly, almost all of those incarcerated for terrorism-related offences in the United Kingdom identify as Muslim.[55] These civil liberties concerns are amplified in Australia, due to the absence of a national Bill or Charter of Rights.[56]

Preventive justice scholarship can assist in drawing out these issues by promoting the comparative study of preventive practices and consideration of common issues that they raise.[57] As Zedner has identified, recognising that 'there are similar issues at stake in respect of' various preventive measures, from pre-trial, mental health and immigration detention to preparatory offences, 'might also permit the articulation of larger principles and values by which preventive justice might legitimately be pursued without the need for reference back to the entrenched and often inappropriate provisions of civil and criminal procedure'.[58] Indeed, safeguards or protections devised in respect of one preventive law may be used to improve others – providing an opportunity to enhance the integrity of preventive measures employed by governments.[59]

While speaking to contemporary preventive practices, preventive justice scholarship is not ahistorical. As Steiker noted, the current role of the state as preventer of harm and disorder was made possible by the creation of the modern police force and institutions such as prisons and hospitals for the mentally ill in the nineteenth century, and the growth of the regulatory state in the twentieth

53 Ibid. 94.
54 As at May 2016, there are 20 listed terrorist organisations; one – the Kurdistan Workers' Party (PKK) – is not a Muslim organisation: Attorney-General's Department, Commonwealth Government, *Listed Terrorist Organisations* (May 2016), available at www.nationalsecurity.gov.au/Listedterroristorganisations/Pages/default.aspx (accessed 5 September 2016). For the experience of Muslims in Australia after September 11, 2001, see: Scott Poynting and Barbara Perry, 'Climates of Hate: Media and State Inspired Victimisation of Muslims in Canada and Australia Since 9/11' (2007) 19(2) *Current Issues in Criminal Justice* 151.
55 United Kingdom Home Office, *Operation of police powers under the Terrorism Act 2000 and subsequent legislation: Arrests, outcomes, and stop and search, Great Britain, quarterly update to September 2015* (10 December 2015) 5.1.
56 Only two jurisdictions in Australia have a general regime of statutory rights protection: the Australian Capital Territory and Victoria: *Human Rights Act 2004* (ACT); *Charter of Human Right and Responsibilities Act 2006* (Vic). See generally Nicola McGarrity and George Williams, 'Counter-Terrorism Laws in a Nation without a Bill of Rights: The Australian Experience' (2010) 2 *City University of Hong Kong Law Review* 45.
57 Steiker, 'The Preventive State', above n 14; Zedner, 'Pre-Punishment?', above n 22.
58 Zedner, 'Pre-Punishment?', above n 22, 190.
59 See e.g. ibid. 189.

century.[60] It is only relatively recently, Steiker observes, that modern states have 'amassed the power, knowledge and institutions to undertake large-scale preventive projects'.[61] What distinguishes the contemporary preventive state is, Ashworth and Zedner suggest, a 'preoccupation with risk and public protection' coupled with consequentialist reasoning that 'privileges efficacy, economy and outcome over justice'.[62]

Many accounts of the contemporary preoccupation with managing – and averting – future harm subscribe, however, to a view that there has been a recent transformation in governance and society.[63] Many suggest that the fixation on risk, (in)security and uncertainty dating from around the middle of the twentieth century, or even from this century's 'war on terror', has radically transformed how we govern and are governed. The latter view is often expounded by politicians. In 2004, then Australian Prime Minister John Howard, for example, stated that 'the events of the 11th of September . . . changed forever the world in which we live. And it changed the way in which we must . . . respond'.[64]

However, accounts that subscribe to the view that there has been a transformation in governance and society run a real danger of missing critical continuities – or relevant discontinuities – with historical practices and overlooking enduring or recurring preoccupations in governance, such as uncertainty and dangerous persons.[65] This is not to suggest that no change has occurred socially, culturally, economically or politically since the middle of the last century.[66] Nor is it to suggest that the preoccupation with risk, uncertainty and (in)security that has characterised the later part of the twentieth century has not shaped and been shaped by the particular circumstances in which it arose.[67] Influential accounts have demonstrated that the current preoccupation with risk and (in)security

60 Although it can be noted that it does not seek to provide a more detailed account of the emergence or trajectory of the preventive state. For this, see Dubber, *The Police Power*, above n 21.

61 Steiker, 'Proportionality', above n 4, 194.

62 Ashworth and Zedner, 'Defending the Criminal Law', above n 40, 40–1.

63 See e.g. Beck's risk society thesis: Beck, *Risk Society*, above n 12; Dershowitz, 'Uncharted Waters after 9/11', above n 22, 7; Ericson, above n 13, 20. See also David Garland, *The Culture of Control: Crime and Social Order in Contemporary Society* (University of Chicago Press, 2001).

64 Prime Minister John Howard, 'Closing Address' (Speech delivered at the Liberal Party National Convention, Adelaide, 8 June 2003) extracted in Jenny Hocking, 'Protecting Democracy by Preserving Justice: Even for the Feared and Hated' (2004) 27(2) *University of New South Wales Law Journal* 319, 335 (citations omitted). See also Finnane and Donkin, above n 5.

65 See e.g. Dershowitz, *Preemption*, above n 2; Ewald, 'The Return of Descartes's Malicious Demon: An Outline of a Philosophy of Precaution', above n 15, 273.

66 See e.g. Garland, *The Culture of Control*, above n 63, ch 4; John Pratt, *Governing the Dangerous* (Federation Press, 1997).

67 Beck, *Risk Society*, above n 12; Ericson, above n 13; Bill Hebenton and Toby Seddon, 'From Dangerousness to Precaution: Managing Sexual and Violent Offenders in an Insecure and Uncertain Age' (2009) 49 *British Journal of Criminology* 343, 345; Zedner, *Security*, above n 13.

has altered how crime is governed,[68] how governance is rationalised through crime,[69] the calibration of dangerousness,[70] and the categorisation of criminological behaviour from categorisations of dangerousness to risk, and then to precaution.[71] Many commentators have observed a new precautionary logic influencing contemporary governance practices and lawmaking.[72] Aradau and van Munster, for example, have argued that:

> What is new is not so much the advent of a risk society as the emergence of a 'precautionary' element that has given birth to new configurations of risk that require that the catastrophic prospects of the future be avoided at all costs.[73]

Rather, it is to suggest that accounts that neglect the relevance of history are invariably myopic. O'Malley, for example, has sketched a genealogy of risk to illustrate how risk and prevention have featured strongly, but with variance, in liberal governance since the nineteenth century.[74] Importantly, O'Malley illustrates that risk is neither a recent phenomenon nor static: risk has played 'many different roles, and appears in many different guises and institutional forms, over this long period'.[75] Similarly Ewald postulates that precaution represents the mechanism by which society responds to and frames uncertainty under contemporary political, social and economic circumstances, which he describes as governed by an attitude or behaviour framed as the paradigm of security or safety.[76] Different paradigms are in existence at different historical moments, with different mechanisms for framing state or regulatory responses to uncertainty.

Preventive strategies have long been part of the regulatory arsenal of liberal states. Finnane and Donkin have studied three historical examples of pre-emption

68 See e.g. scholarship on the new penology, n 11.

69 Jonathan Simon, *Governing Through Crime: How the War on Crime Transformed American Democracy and Created a Culture of Fear* (Oxford University Press, 2007).

70 Pratt, *Governing the Dangerous*, above n 66; John Pratt, 'Dangerousness, Risk and Technologies of Power' (1995) 28(1) *Australian and New Zealand Journal of Criminology* 3.

71 Robert Castel, 'From Dangerousness to Risk' in Graham Burchell, Colin Gordon and Peter Miller (eds), *The Foucault Effect: Studies in Governmentality* (University of Chicago Press, 1991) 281; Hebenton and Seddon, above n 67.

72 Ericson, above n 13; Zedner, *Security*, above n 13.

73 Claudia Aradau and Rens van Munster, 'Governing Terrorism Through Risk: Taking Precautions, (un)Knowing the Future' (2007) 13 *European Journal of International Relations* 89, 91.

74 Pat O'Malley, 'Risk societies and the government of crime' in Mark Brown and John Pratt (eds), *Dangerous Offenders: Punishment and Social Order* (Routledge, 2000) 17.

75 Ibid. 18.

76 Ewald described this new paradigm as having 'not yet found its true name'. The translations from French to English differ on what moniker Ewald used to refer to this new paradigm – it is a 'paradigm of security' in the Utz translation and a 'paradigm of safety' in the version published in the *Connecticut Insurance Law Journal*. See Ewald, 'The Return of the Crafty Genius', above n 13, 48; Ewald, 'The Return of Descartes's Malicious Demon: An Outline of a Philosophy of Precaution', above n 15, 538.

drawn from times of war and peace and from within and beyond the criminal law context: the preventive detention of persons with mental illness, the preventive detention of habitual and dangerous offenders, and wartime internment.[77] They argue that the continuities between present and historical practices cast doubt upon concerns that anti-terror measures will be normalised and corrosive of the criminal justice system, as such measures having long been adopted. Finnane and Donkin write:

> Rather than counter-terrorist measures having the potential to leach into the normal criminal process, we suggest, instead, that it makes as much sense, if not more, to consider that the counter-terrorist measures enact strategies that have long been pursued by the modern liberal state's vision of securing its citizens in the interests of order and security, very often at the cost of individual liberty.[78]

In this way, preventive justice scholarship has much to contribute to understandings of prevention in contemporary lawmaking: identifying and tracing the use of preventive measures by governments, highlighting common issues that they raise and considering how legal systems are responding and should respond. This scholarship can make an important contribution by promoting and articulating legal principles to guide and constrain legislatures when crafting preventive laws. However, harnessing the potential of preventive justice scholarship to enhance public policy and law reform is not an easy task – nor is it a certain one. The next section explores criticisms and limitations of preventive justice.

The limits of preventive justice scholarship

The complexity and diversity of preventive measures, and uncertainty as to the content and scope of preventive justice, raise a number of questions about the utility and coherence of preventive justice scholarship. This section outlines these questions and challenges, which will be further explored in other chapters of this book. It argues that these challenges are not insurmountable. Rather, they are emblematic of an emerging area of scholarship and one that has, in line with international events, focused predominantly on prevention in the anti-terror and sex offender contexts. This focus has diverted attention from the broader project of preventive justice scholarship and tied questions of prevention to the criminal justice system, rather than civil or administrative systems. In doing so, many questions about the utility, coherency and contours of preventive justice have remained unanswered.[79]

77 Finnane and Donkin, above n 5.
78 Ibid. 13.
79 Ashworth and Zedner have, among other things, created a taxonomy of preventive measures ('Preventive Orders', above n 40) and considered the contours of the preventive state (*Preventive Justice*, above n 7).

A unified problem?

A question remains about whether preventive practices and policies are amenable, as Steiker suggests, to categorisation as part of a single, unified legal construct (namely, preventive justice) or whether the dissimilarities between them defy such a classification – that is, whether on closer inspection, specific and relevant differences emerge that render impossible the conception of preventive practices as part of a unified problem. It may be, rather, that this is a question of the relationship between the different 'preventive justice' measures, as opposed to the futility of their categorisation as a unified problem. The different contexts in which preventive regimes operate no doubt forms part of the reason why preventive practices have often been treated as *sui generis* – hindering, as Steiker contends, rather than aiding understandings of preventive governance.

The quest for a single organising construct of this emerging form of justice – *preventive* justice – draws parallels with the quest for general principles for a universal and uniform idea of responsibility that apply to all offences.[80] Critical scholars have doubted the utility of such rationalising enterprises. Bronitt and McSherry, for example, have pointed out that 'resolving incoherence through conceptual analysis often masks the internal contradictions within the law and limits the normative choices available for reform'.[81] Whether preventive practices are amendable to categorisation as a unified problem cannot be answered in the abstract. This collection will further explore this question through its case studies in mental health, national security and immigration.

Ambit and scope

A challenge facing preventive justice scholarship is articulating what falls within its purview – and why. For example, should everything deemed or labelled 'preventive' be included? Is it possible to distinguish between prevention and other objectives, such as punishment? Must the measure involve physical coercion, in the sense of infringing liberty, or might non-coercive preventive measures be included?[82]

Steiker, as noted, deliberately pitched the preventive state at a high 'level of conceptual generalization' in order that it may serve as a canopy under which to collate and investigate the diverse set of preventive measures employed by governments. This was to counteract the treatment of preventive measures as discrete and unrelated, and to thereby generate fresh insights into preventive

80 See generally Bronitt and McSherry, above n 2, 86ff. I thank Simon Bronitt for drawing my attention to this point.

81 Ibid. 86. See also Simon Bronitt, 'Toward a Universal Theory of Criminal Law: Rethinking the Comparative and International Project' 27 (2008) *Criminal Justice Ethics* 53.

82 I note that this question is not unique to this context. The same question arises for criminal law theorists, who tend to dismiss, gloss or exclude as exceptional, regulatory crime as being not 'true' criminal law. See generally Colin Scott 'Regulatory Crime: History, Functions, Problems, Solutions' in Ursula Kilkelly and Shane Kilcommins (eds) *Regulatory Crime in Ireland* (First Law, 2010).

governance and its limits. However, a veritable panoply of measures may be said to fall within preventive justice: from the various species of preventive detention (such as pre-trial, immigration, mental health, quarantine or post-sentence detention) to preventive restraints on liberty (such as control orders and other civil preventive orders, community supervision of sex offenders or apprehended violence orders), preventive offences (for example, precursor, inchoate or preparatory offences) and preventive police practices (such as warrants, suspicionless searches or surveillance). This breadth risks undermining not only the utility of the concept as reflective of a concentration of preventive governmental practices, but also the project of articulating principles to guide and limit state action to prevent harm.

Prevention and punishment

It may be neither possible nor desirable to identify a rationale that is preventive in order to demarcate preventive measures. Prevention is, it might be recalled, a rationale of the criminal justice system.[83] The relationship between relevant objectives, such as prevention and punishment, is often intricate and complex, and an adequate distinction between objectives may be difficult to strike. Punishment, imbued as it is with a confluence of purposes, is a helpful example.[84] Members of the High Court of Australia remarked in *Veen v The Queen (No 2)*:

> The purposes of criminal punishment are various: protection of society, deterrence of the offender and of others who might be tempted to offend, retribution and reform. The purposes overlap and none of them can be considered in isolation from the others when determining what is an appropriate sentence in a particular case.[85]

Even if an adequate distinction may be drawn, the effect of a law may negate or undermine the label. A preventive label or objective does not insulate a law from being 'stigmatic, burdensome or punitive' in substance or effect,[86] or from incurring a punitive sanction. The following extract from Whealy J's sentencing remarks in *R v Elomar*,[87] which relate to the offence of conspiracy to do acts in preparation for a terrorist act under the *Criminal Code Act 1995* (Cth), encapsulates these difficulties:

> The broad purpose of the creation of offences of the kind involved in the present sentencing exercises is to prevent the emergence of circumstances which may render more likely the carrying out of a serious terrorist act. Obviously enough, it is also to punish those who contemplate action of the prohibited kind. Importantly, it is to denounce their activities and to

83 Ashworth and Zedner, 'Just Prevention', above n 25.
84 And one used by many others. See e.g. Ashworth and Zedner, 'Defending the Criminal Law', above n 40.
85 (1988) 164 CLR 465, 476 (Mason CJ, Brennan, Dawson and Toohey JJ).
86 Ashworth and Zedner, 'Defending the Criminal Law', above n 40, 41.
87 (2010) 264 ALR 759.

> incapacitate them so that the community will be protected from the horrific consequences contemplated by their mindset and their actions.[88]

Preventive measures may be, and often are, experienced as punishment.[89] For example, the experience of involuntary mental health detention was recently described as 'overwhelming', and 'like a prison sentence'.[90] Delineating prevention and punishment is a difficult, if not fraught, task and it may be that attempts to quantify characteristics of laws that might fall within the conceptual framework of preventive justice along these lines simply generates something of a 'tick the box' guide to the preventive justice rather than a useful heuristic.

Many attempts to define preventive measures have sought to avoid this difficulty. Ashworth and Zedner have defined preventive measures according to three features:

- i restrictions on individual liberty of action
- ii in order to prevent harm or a risk of harm and
- iii are backed by threats of coercive sanctions.[91]

They distinguish preventive measures on the basis that 'their primary justifying aim is to restrict individual liberty in order to prevent future harm and not to punish wrongdoing (even where the measure is imposed as a consequence of past wrongdoing)'.[92] In Chapter 3 of this collection, Susan Donkin proposes an axis of prevention to distinguish between the different types of prevention and preventive measures. This raises two further issues for consideration regarding the ambit and scope of preventive justice: coercion and harm.

Coercive v non-coercive preventive measures

To date, preventive justice scholarship has focused on coercive preventive measures, predominantly in the anti-terror context, which involve liberty restraint. Ashworth and Zedner, for example, deliberately limit their study to coercive preventive measures, given the impact of such measures on individual autonomy.[93] In doing so, Ashworth and Zedner rely on Lamond's conception of coerciveness in law – that is, 'law uses coercion when it prescribes a sanction that is intended to impose sufficient pressure on a person to force or make that person act in a certain way'.[94] Coercion may involve a restraint on liberty – that is, physical coercion, or a threat

88 Ibid. [79].
89 Bernadette McSherry, 'Sex, Drugs and "Evil" Souls: The Growing Reliance on Preventive Detention Regimes' (2006) 32(2) *Monash University Law Review* 237, 271–2.
90 Communio, *Evaluation of Efficacy and Cost of the Mental Health Inquiry System – Final Report* (30 January 2012) NSW Health, 55.
91 Ashworth and Zedner, 'Preventive Orders', above n 40, 62.
92 Ibid.
93 Ashworth and Zedner, *Preventive Justice*, above n 7, 6.
94 Ibid. 6, citing Lamond.

that compels someone to act, or not act, in a particular way due to the consequences of non-compliance ('rational compulsion').[95]

Non-coercive preventive measures, such as situational crime prevention, countering violent extremism programs, rehabilitation and confiscation regimes, can also impact individual autonomy. Non-coercive preventive measures are noted by preventive justice scholars but have not as yet attracted sustained commentary. Whether and how non-coercive preventive measures engage with preventive justice warrants scrutiny, and is explored in greater detail by Keiran Hardy in Chapter 7 of this collection.

Prevention of which harm?

Blackstone viewed preventive justice as a means of avoiding *criminal* harm.[96] Are there good reasons to limit preventive justice scholarship to measures designed to avoid criminal harm? Or should it extend to harm that, if it eventuated, would not be criminal? Ashworth and Zedner have taken a broader view of preventive justice, including in their study measures designed for public protection.[97] Similarly, McSherry explores preventive measures drawn from within and beyond the criminal justice system.[98]

This approach acknowledges that measures designed to prevent harm to others, as well as harm that might be caused to oneself, have long featured on statute books, most notably in public health regulation. In the United Kingdom, for example, legislation was first introduced in 1800 to enable the preventive detention of persons found not guilty by reason of mental illness, and to provide for the preventive confinement of a person prior to the commission of an offence.[99] In Australia, the colonial Parliament of New South Wales first legislated with respect to persons with mental illness in 1843. The *Dangerous Lunatics Act 1843* (7 Vic No 14), which drew upon the United Kingdom's *Criminal Lunatics Act of 1800* (39 & 40 Geo 3, c 94),[100] provided for the preventive detention in gaol of persons regarded as a 'dangerous lunatic' or 'dangerous idiot',[101] and for the

95 Ibid.

96 William Blackstone, *Commentaries on the Laws of England* (R Bell, 1772), book IV, 248.

97 Ibid.

98 McSherry, *Managing Fear*, above n 3.

99 Richard Moran, 'The Origin of Insanity as a Special Verdict: The Trial for Treason of James Hadfield (1800)' (1985) 19(3) *Law and Society Review* 487, 513–4.

100 See e.g. Mark Finnane, 'From Dangerous Lunatic to Human Rights? The Law and Mental Illness in Australian History' in Catharine Coleborne and Dolly MacKinnon (eds), *'Madness' in Australia: Histories, Heritage and the Asylum* (University of Queensland Press, 2003) 23, 26–7; J H McClemens and J M Bennett, 'Historical Notes on the Law of Mental Illness in New South Wales' (1962) 4 *Sydney Law Review* 49, 60–1; Phillip Powell AM QC, *The Origins and Development of the Protective Jurisdiction of The Supreme Court of New South Wales* (The Francis Forbes Society for Australian Legal History, 2003) 15.

101 *Dangerous Lunatics Act 1843* (7 Vic No 14) s I.

preventive detention in a 'lunatic asylum' of persons found to be insane, 'but not dangerously so', and in need of 'care and maintenance'.[102]

Preventive measures in public health legislation facilitate intervention where the anticipated harm is not criminal. Although the preventive focus of anti-terror lawmaking has raised the visibility of preventive regulation, it has also diverted preventive scholarship. Scholarship on preventive measures has largely been yoked to questions of prevention and punishment, and the proper role of the criminal justice system. This has obscured inquiry into prevention beyond the criminal justice system, overlooking important continuities with preventive practices outside of this context and thereby stymieing the development of a broader preventive jurisprudence. Preventive scholarship has thereby continued, with notable exceptions, to elide a comparative and multi-jurisdictional approach to preventive measures as proposed by Steiker.

Recognising continuities and discontinuities between different preventive practices might assist in the articulation of principles to guide and constrain preventive action, unshackled by the strict academic separation of civil and criminal law and procedure. This collection will examine instances in which preventive measures are used in the mental health and immigrations contexts where the harm to be averted may not be criminal harm. Chapters 4 and 5, by Bernadette McSherry and Helen Punter respectively, provide case studies of prevention in the area of mental health, and Chapter 6 by Peter Billings and Dallal Stevens examines prevention in the immigration context. McSherry also considers, in Chapter 4, whether mental health laws are justified on the basis of risk of harm to self or others. This collection also explores, in Chapter 8 by Svetlana Tyulkina and George Williams, and Chapter 3 by Susan Donkin, preventive innovations in the anti-terrorism context.

Can prevention ever be just?

A final issue to consider is the desirability of regulating prevention. In particular, does preventive justice risk legitimising laws and practices that offend rights and liberties? Are state attempts to regulate prevention feasible and legitimate? Part III of this collection engages with these questions and explores how to assess effectiveness and legitimacy in the preventive justice context. In Chapter 9, Tim Legrand and Teneille Elliott argue that it is normatively desirable that government move beyond questioning effectiveness to capture broader questions concerned with appropriateness. In Chapter 10, Rebecca Ananian-Welsh examines the role that proven effectiveness may play in guiding the evolution of a preventive measure. In Chapter 11 of this collection, Sarah Murray questions whether the legitimacy of the courts is compromised by their involvement in the preventive justice enterprise.

102 *Dangerous Lunatics Act 1843* (7 Vic No 14) s XI.

Preventive justice and the other forms of justice

In their work on preventive justice, Ashworth and Zedner employ 'justice' in two senses. First, in the sense it is used in 'criminal justice system' to 'convey that it is part of an official framework of measures aimed at dealing with certain issues'.[103] In this respect, they draw attention to the fact that preventive justice is not an official framework, but that measures may occur within and beyond the criminal justice system. Second, they invoke justice in the substantive sense: that the set of values they articulate for preventive justice can generate both justifications and principled limits on state action to prevent harm. These values recognise both the state's duty to protect and the concomitant duty to do justice – to respect the rights of individuals. Ashworth and Zedner provide:

> If liberty is to be duly respected, the state's powers – justified as the minimum necessary powers to achieve an acceptable degree of prevention – should be so adjusted as to ensure that the liberty of all persons involved is preserved so far as possible.[104]

This highlights a further issue about the relationship between preventive justice and the other forms of justice – namely, retributive and restorative justice – which is examined by Simon Bronitt in Chapter 12 in the context of deferred prosecution agreements, an emerging regulatory tool that straddles the intersection of civil (private) and criminal (public) law.

Conclusion

Preventive justice scholarship provides one way to conceive of prevention in law-making. It promises a conceptual framework through which to engage critically with the assortment of preventive practices employed by governments and to examine continuities and discontinuities between preventive practices, both past and present. Preventive justice literature traces the use of preventive measures by governments, to identify issues this raises, and to consider how legal systems are responding and should respond. In this context, important work has been done on the difficult questions of what values, principles and justifications ought to guide preventive measures.[105] In this way, preventive justice scholarship can make an important contribution by articulating legal principles to guide and constrain legislatures when crafting preventive laws.

What has been lacking in the literature to date is a critical appraisal of the utility of preventive justice scholarship, in particular as to its coherency and scope. This chapter has identified a number of potential limitations, including the lack of precision regarding the content and scope of preventive justice, and uncertainty as to whether preventive practices are capable of being classified as part of a unified

103 Ashworth and Zedner, *Preventive Justice*, above n 7, 6.
104 Ibid. 257.
105 See e.g. ibid.

project. It has been argued that, following September 11, much of the currency of the preventive scholarship has related to anti-terror laws, and to a lesser extent sex offender laws. As a result, potential continuities with preventive practices beyond these contexts have been overlooked, and questions of prevention have been yoked to the criminal justice system. The broader utility and coherency of preventive justice has therefore remained under-examined. This is, as this chapter has argued, emblematic of a developing literature that has, understandably, grappled with a prolific preventive legislative agenda in response to the ongoing and evolving threat of terrorism.

The reliance on preventive measures in anti-terrorism law has raised the visibility of prevention in domestic lawmaking, and with it an 'outsider jurisprudence' that focuses attention on the vulnerable groups targeted for prevention. 'At risk' is increasingly being used as a stigmatic label for those deemed threatening to security.[106] This is of particular concern, Sunstein remarks, because, when faced with security threats, governments 'often impose selective rather than broad restriction on liberty'.[107] Preventive justice scholarship stresses that the state's duty to do justice – to respect the rights of individuals – exists alongside the state's duty to protect. It emphasises that the duty to protect the public does not outweigh all others, but that preventive measures ought to be subject to justification and restraining principles.[108] In this way, preventive justice scholarship contributes an account of prevention that addresses the paradox of prevention and provides a way to minimise the costs associated with preventive measures to individual liberty and rights.

106 Ericson, above n 13, 157, 159.
107 Cass Sunstein, *Laws of Fear: Beyond the Precautionary Principle* (Cambridge University Press, 2005) 204.
108 Ashworth and Zedner, *Preventive Justice*, above n 7, 266.

2 Preventive justice, the precautionary principle and the rule of law

Jocelyn Stacey

Modern public environmental law is a field largely premised on prevention. From the 1970s onward, international and domestic environmental law has been shaped by the recognition that strictly remedial approaches to environmental issues are not adequate for deterring environmental harm and stemming serious environmental degradation.[1] The United Nations General Assembly 1992 Rio Declaration on Environment and Development (Rio Declaration) helped to solidify four guiding principles for public environmental law: polluter pays, prevention, sustainable development and precaution.[2] Of these four principles, only polluter pays – the idea that she or he who causes the pollution should bear its costs – is retributive. Prevention is the idea that we should take steps to prevent or mitigate foreseeable harm to the environment. It is often implemented through the requirement of conducting an environmental impact assessment prior to undertaking any regulatory activity. Sustainable development, an emerging and complex body of international law, has a significant preventive component.[3] It captures the idea

1 The 1972 United Nations Stockholm Conference on the Human Environment was the first global conference on environmental issues and was followed by the creation of the United Nations Environment Programme. Environmental assessment legislation proliferated around the world during this period, beginning with the United States *National Environmental Policy Act of 1969*, 42 USC § 4321. Countries around the world began to enact preventive environmental legislation: *Canadian Environmental Protection Act*, SC 1988, c 22; *Control of Pollution Act* 1974 (UK) c 40; *Environmental Assessment and Planning Act 1979* (NSW); *Fisheries Management Act 1991* (Cth); *Clean Air Act 1972* (NZ); *Environment Act 1986* (NZ).

2 These principles can be found in the *Declaration of the United Nations Conference on the Human Environment*, A/RES/2994, 27th sess (15 December 1972) in Report of the United Nations Conference on the Human Environment, Stockholm, 5–16 June 1972, UN Doc A/CONF.48/14/Rev.1, ch 1, reprinted (1972) 11 ILM 1416 and the United Nations Conference on Environment and Development, *Rio Declaration on Environment and Development*, UN Doc A/CONF.151/26 (vol I); 31 ILM 874 (1992). See also Philippe Sands and Jacqueline Peel, *Principles of International Environmental Law* (Cambridge University Press, 3rd edn, 2012); A Dan Tarlock, 'Is There a There There in Environmental Law' (2003) 19 *Journal of Land Use and Environmental Law* 213, 219.

3 See e.g. Marie-Claire Cordonier Segger and Ashfaq Khalfan, *Sustainable Development Law: Principles, Practices, and Prospects* (Oxford University Press, 2004).

that the present generation has an obligation to future generations not to push the Earth's ecological capabilities to their limits. The fourth principle – and the focus of this chapter – is the precautionary principle,[4] which posits that a lack of scientific certainty should not pose a barrier to state action in the face of serious or irreversible threats to the environment.

Despite its largely preventive orientation, environmental law has, with one exception, remained distinct from the burgeoning field of preventive justice. The exception is the precautionary principle, which has become a subject of interest and frequent scepticism among preventive justice scholars.[5] The precautionary principle is a central principle in environmental law. Its centrality arises from the pervasiveness of scientific uncertainty in environmental regulation – that is, our inability to reliably predict the consequences of our policy choices on environmental and human health.[6] The precautionary principle squarely addresses the question of how we ought to proceed in the face of unavoidable uncertainty. For example, the most widely accepted version[7] of the precautionary principle is that contained in the Rio Declaration:

> Where there are threats of serious or irreversible damage, lack of full scientific certainty shall not be used as a reason for postponing cost-effective measures to prevent environmental degradation.[8]

Preventive justice scholars have noted the temptation, particularly in the national security context, to rely on a kind of 'precautionary logic'[9] by which extreme measures are taken in an effort to avoid future, but uncertain, security threats. Counter-terrorism strategies that include anticipatory or pre-emptive military strikes, civil control orders and indefinite detention all aimed at preventing future terrorist attacks have been characterised as part of a precautionary approach to counter-terrorism.[10] Although no government has outright attempted to adopt

4 'Precaution', 'the precautionary principle' and 'precautionary approach' are used synonymously in this chapter. On the semantics of precaution, see Jacqueline Peel, 'Precaution – A Matter of Principle, Approach or Process?' (2004) 5 *Melbourne Journal of International Law* 483.
5 See, in particular, the first part of this chapter.
6 For my own take on uncertainty in environmental law, see Jocelyn Stacey, 'The Environmental Emergency and the Legality of Discretion in Environmental Law' (2015) 52(3) *Osgoode Hall Law Journal* (forthcoming) (arguing this uncertainty requires us to approach environmental issues as an ongoing emergency).
7 Sands and Peel, above n 2, 228; Daniel Bodansky, 'Deconstructing the Precautionary Principle' in David D Caron and Harry N Scheiber (eds), *Bringing New Law to Ocean Waters* (Martinus Nijhoff Publishers, 2004) 381, 381 (one of the ten commandments of environmental law).
8 Rio Declaration, above n 2.
9 Andrew Goldsmith, 'The Governance of Terror: Precautionary Logic and Counterterrorist Law Reform After September 11' (2008) 30 *Law and Policy* 141; Lucia Zedner, *Security* (Routledge, 2009) 84–5.
10 Tamara Tulich, 'A View Inside the Preventive State: Reflections on a Decade of Anti-Terror Law' (2012) 21(1) *Griffith Law Review* 209, 211; Jessica Stern and Jonathan B

the precautionary principle as a basis for security measures, public officials have relied on precautionary rhetoric. In the environmental context, the precautionary principle operates to justify state action even in the face of uncertainty. Preventive justice scholars thus worry that, in the security context, the precautionary principle would justify severe liberty-infringing measures.

This chapter explores the connection between the precautionary principle in environmental law and preventive justice scholarship, from the perspective of environmental law. It has two aims. First, the chapter traces the claims about the precautionary principle in the preventive justice literature back to their environmental roots. In doing so, it situates the precautionary principle within broader environmental law debates about how the principle ought to operate. Second, the chapter argues that the precautionary principle and principles of preventive justice ought to be understood as part of the same rule of law project – that is, the project of ensuring that all public decisions are publicly justified on the basis of core constitutional principles.[11] Understood in this way, both the precautionary principle and principles of preventive justice seek to respect and enable the autonomy of individuals, understood as their capacity to reason with the law. It is thus a mistake to think that the precautionary principle can be transposed from the environmental context to the national security context. What the rule of law requires in each context is distinct and these respective principles ought to be understood as attempts to maintain our commitment to the rule of law even under the challenging conditions in which we face uncertain future harm.

This chapter proceeds in three parts. The first part introduces the characterisation of the precautionary principle portrayed in the preventive justice scholarship. It argues that preventive justice scholars view the precautionary principle as a particularly potent decision-making logic with serious, negative consequences for the security context. The second part situates this partial characterisation of the precautionary principle within its environmental context. Drawing on examples from Australia and Canada, it argues that, while there is some support for this characterisation, the principle's influence has been far tamer in environmental law than is represented by preventive justice scholars. The third, and final, part argues that the connection between the precautionary principle and preventive justice comes at the foundational level of a commitment to democratic governance under the rule of law. What this foundational commitment requires in practice is necessarily context-dependent, such that both the precautionary principle and principles

Wiener, 'Precaution Against Terrorism' (2006) 9 *Journal of Risk Research* 393, 394–5; Simon Bronitt, 'Balancing Security and Liberty: Critical Perspectives on Terrorism Law Reform' in Miriam Gani and Penelope Matthews (eds), *Fresh Perspectives on the 'War on Terror'* (Australia National University ePress, 2008) 65. Cf. Alan Patterson and Craig McLean, 'Misleading and Dangerous: The Use of the Precautionary Principle in Foreign Policy Debates' (2010) 26(1) *Medicine, Conflict and Survival* 48 (on the need to rescue the precautionary principle from its misuse in the counter-terrorism context).

11 David Dyzenhaus, 'Preventive Justice and the Rule-of-Law Project' in Andrew Ashworth, Lucia Zedner and Patrick Tomlin (eds), *Prevention and the Limits of the Criminal Law* (Oxford University Press, 2013) 91.

articulated and defended by preventive justice scholars should be understood as complementary, but not transferrable, attempts to maintain our commitment to the rule of law even under conditions of uncertainty.

Precaution and preventive justice

Preventive justice scholars have noted the rhetorical parallels between the precautionary principle in environmental law and the explanations that government officials have offered for sweeping counter-terrorism measures.[12] It is therefore understandable that preventive justice scholars approach the precautionary principle with deep scepticism. They have come to characterise the precautionary principle in the security context in particularly strong and monolithic terms. For example, Carol Steiker writes of:

> 'the precautionary principle', which holds that if an action or policy *might* cause severe and irreversible harm to the public or the environment, the proponents of the action should bear the burden of proof of no harm, in the absence of a scientific consensus that the harm will *not* occur. The implications of widespread adherence to an analogous principle in the preventive detention context are sobering: we should expect to see large numbers of low-level terrorist suspects detained, coupled with surveillance and/or detention of large numbers of people who are simply members of ethnic or religious groups or organizations from whom terrorists are commonly recruited.[13]

Similarly, Ashworth and Zedner write:

> The benefit of [the precautionary] approach is that it licenses officials to take preventive measures, particularly in cases where the potential harm is life-threatening or gravely damaging to human safety or health. The problem is that the precautionary principle may license arbitrary and unfounded decision-making with serious adverse consequences for individual liberties.[14]

Steiker, Ashworth and Zedner identify three potentially problematic aspects of the precautionary principle: *threat, command* and *measures*. First, they are concerned about the nature of the *threat* that will trigger state action. Steiker highlights the necessarily speculative nature of the future harm. And while Ashworth and Zedner focus on grave threats, others worry that the precautionary principle will be invoked against trivial threats, far below the threshold of serious and irreversible

12 Stern and Weiner, above n 10, 398–401; Tulich, above n 10, 212–5.

13 Carol S Steiker, 'Proportionality as a Limit on Preventive Justice: Promises and Pitfalls' in Andrew Ashworth, Lucia Zedner and Patrick Tomlin (eds), *Prevention and the Limits of the Criminal Law* (Oxford University Press, 2013) 194, 208 (citations omitted).

14 Andrew Ashworth and Lucia Zedner, *Preventive Justice* (Oxford University Press, 2014) 120.

harm that is required in the environmental context.[15] Elsewhere, Zedner worries about the indiscriminate application of precaution, stating that, unlike risk assessment, precaution 'treats all as possible sources of suspicion or threat'.[16] Steiker rightly notes the discriminatory ramifications of implementing sweeping counter-terror measures ostensibly based on a precautionary approach.

Preventive justice scholars also emphasise the *command* imposed on the decision-maker. They are especially concerned that the precautionary principle seems to compel or 'licence' the decision-maker to take preventive action.[17] For Steiker, the decision-maker discharges his or her obligations by reversing the burden of proof – that is, by requiring the affected party to show the absence of harm, rather than requiring the government to show the possibility of harm.[18] If the burden is not met, then the decision-maker, on this view, has no option but to take action by, for example, implementing heightened surveillance or increased detention practices.

This attention to the obligatory nature of the precautionary principle leads to further concerns about the *measures* that follow from its implementation. Preventive justice scholars are rightly concerned about 'serious adverse consequences for individual liberties'. Measures are analysed and criticised on the basis of their proximity to the perceived threat or their epistemological basis.[19] Having determined that certain measures are precautionary – and thus dubious – the next task for many preventive justice scholars is to determine whether such measures can be justified on the basis of their effectiveness.[20] Some preventive justice scholars worry that precautionary measures are 'arbitrary and unfounded'[21] or 'error prone'.[22] Others note the internal contradiction that the absence of evidence of effectiveness can serve as justification for further and more invasive precautionary measures.[23]

Preventive justice scholars present the precautionary principle as a linear, compulsory decision-making tool, one with striking ramifications in the national

15 François Ewald, 'The Return of Descartes's Malicious Demon: An Outline of a Philosophy of Precaution' in Tom Baker and Jonathan Simon (eds), *Embracing Risk: The Changing Culture of Insurance and Responsibility* (University of Chicago Press, 2002) 273, 283–4 (writing on our new 'security era' and the problems with extending the precautionary principle beyond the environmental context); Tulich, above n 10, 215 (adopting Ewald's concern); Zedner, *Security*, above n 9, 84.

16 Zedner, *Security*, above n 9, 84. See also Stern and Weiner, above n 10, 396; Genevieve Lennon, 'Precautionary Tales: Suspicionless Counter-Terrorism Stop and Search' (2015) 15(1) *Criminology and Criminal Justice* 44, 48 (specifically on suspicionless stop and search procedures).

17 See also Stern and Wiener, above n 10, 397; Zedner, *Security*, above n 9, 84.

18 Stern and Wiener, above n 10, 400–1.

19 Stern and Wiener, above n 10, 397, 403–4; Lennon, above n 166, 48–50; Tulich, above n 10, 232.

20 Stern and Wiener, above n 10, 415 ff.

21 Ashworth and Zedner, above n 14.

22 Tulich, above n 10, 231.

23 Zedner, *Security*, above n 9, 84–5; Goldsmith, above n 9, 159. See also Chapter 10 by Rebecca Ananian-Welsh in this collection.

security context. As we shall now see, this characterisation has some basis in environmental law, but the principle's implementation and its potential are far more nuanced.

The practice and potential of precaution in environmental law

In the environmental context, uncertainty about future environmental harm is often used as an excuse for maintaining the status quo. By eliminating uncertainty as a legitimate basis for inaction, the precautionary principle promises to help overcome a lack of political will to protect the environment.[24] In the security context, by stark contrast, there is seemingly no such lack of political will. It is thus understandable that preventive justice scholars approach the precautionary principle with serious reservations. At the same time, however, the precautionary principle has generated a vast and rich environmental jurisprudence and scholarship that is not represented in the preventive justice literature. The aim of this section is to trace the preventive justice characterisation of the precautionary principle back to its environmental law origins, to better understand the debates that the principle has generated and to set the stage for the argument that the precautionary principle is fundamentally connected to the rule of law.

The widely accepted formulation of the precautionary principle contained in the Rio Declaration, quoted above, simply requires that decision-makers attend to the scientific uncertainty inherent in their regulatory decisions. Consistent with the preventive justice characterisation, the Rio Declaration requires a *threat* of serious or irreversible harm for the principle to apply.[25] Notably, however, the *command* imposed by the Rio Declaration version of precaution is that decision-makers cannot use uncertainty as a basis for inaction.[26] Far from the strong, compulsory version of precaution articulated by preventive justice scholars, the Rio Declaration version of the precautionary principle does not compel decision-makers to take any action. It is simply an admonition to attend to the unavoidable limits of our ability to predict the effects of our actions on the environment. Nor does the Rio Declaration mention any connection to reversing the burden of proof. Finally, the Rio Declaration notes the need for cost-effective *measures*, although it is silent on the details. Indeed, a huge range of measures can flow from the precautionary

24 In the original German context, the precautionary principle was a justification for interventionist state action: Timothy O'Riordan and James Cameron, 'The History and Contemporary Significance of the Precautionary Principle' in Timothy O'Riordan and James Cameron (eds), *Interpreting the Precautionary Principle* (Routledge, 1994) 12, 16.

25 There are some versions of the precautionary principle that set a lower threat; see e.g. *Convention on the Ban of the Import of Hazardous Wastes into Africa and on the Control of their Transboundary Movements within Africa*, opened for signature 30 January 1991, 30 ILM 773 (entered into force 22 April 1998) art 3(f), but these are rare.

26 Again, there are some variations that impose stronger requirements on decision-makers: see e.g. *Convention for the Protection of the Marine Environment of the Baltic Sea Area*, opened for signature 22 September 1992, 32 ILM 1069 (entered into force 17 January 2000) art 2(2)(a), but these are less common than the Rio Declaration version.

principle: for example, delaying a decision to allow potentially environmentally harmful actions in order for more study or monitoring to occur, requiring certain mitigation measures on activities or prohibiting certain activities or pollutants.

It is this Rio Declaration version of the precautionary principle that has been widely incorporated into domestic law around the world.[27] This chapter cannot offer a comprehensive account of the vast practice and implementation of the precautionary principle worldwide. What it can do, however, is use two example countries – Australia and Canada – as snapshots for the practice and academic debates over the potential for the precautionary principle.[28] In both Canada and Australia, the Rio Declaration version of the precautionary principle has been incorporated into environmental law and policy. The countries provide useful comparator examples: on the one hand, the precautionary principle in Australia has generated sustained jurisprudential and academic engagement.[29] By way of contrast, there is a strong sense that the principle has yet to do any meaningful work in shaping environmental law in Canada.[30]

Canada

The Canadian legal perspective demonstrates the temptation to view the precautionary principle in black-and-white, all-or-nothing terms. On the one hand, some

27 Jacqueline Peel, *The Precautionary Principle in Practice* (The Federation Press, 2005) 17 (on the Rio Declaration as marking the 'arrival' of the precautionary principle); Elizabeth Fisher, 'Review: Laws of Fear: Beyond the Precautionary Principle' (2006) 69(2) *Modern Law Review* 288, 289–90 (on the widespread incorporation of the Rio Declaration of the principle).

28 Australia and Canada both present hard cases for environmental law and policy in that they have similar frontier mentalities where wilderness protection and natural resource exploitation often clash.

29 See Department of the Environment, *Inter-Governmental Agreement on the Environment* (IGAE) (1 May 1992), and Ecologically Sustainable Development Steering Committee, *National Strategy for Ecologically Sustainable Development* (Australian Government Publishing Service, Canberra, December 1992); *Environmental Protection Act 1970* (Vic); *Gene Technology Act 2000* (Cth); *Protection of the Environment Administration Act 1991* (NSW); *Ozone Protection Act 1989* (Cth). For academic commentary on the extensive engagement with the principle in Australia, see Elizabeth Fisher, *Risk Regulation and Administrative Constitutionalism* (Hart Publishing, 2007) ch 4.

30 This is despite an early and strong statement by the Supreme Court of Canada that the precautionary principle, as approaching a principle of customary international law, is a background norm for interpreting domestic environmental law: *114957 Canada Ltée (Spraytech, Société d'arrosage) v Hudson (Town)* [2001] SCC 40. Chris Tollefson, 'A Precautionary Tale: Trials and Tribulations of the Precautionary Principle' (Paper presented at Environment in the Courtroom: Key Environmental Concepts and the Unique Nature of Environmental Damage Symposium, Canadian Institute of Resources Law, University of Calgary, 23–4 March 2012) 17. Fisher notes related concerns about the justiciability of the principle in the United Kingdom courts: Elizabeth Fisher, 'Is the Precautionary Principle Justiciable?' (2001) 13(3) *Journal of Environmental Law* 315.

Canadian courts take a similar view to that of preventive justice scholars – that is, they think that the precautionary principle compels particular action. In the context of judicial review of environmental assessment decisions, for example, the Canadian Federal Court and Federal Court of Appeal repeatedly state that the precautionary principle would have 'paralyzing effects' because it would require prohibiting development.[31] This claim is not supported by the Rio Declaration,[32] the language of Canadian environmental assessment legislation[33] or by any sophisticated scholarship on the precautionary principle.[34] By assuming a 'compulsory' or a strong version of precaution and refusing to invoke it in this context, the Canadian Federal Courts have stifled the judicial development of the principle.

At the same time, Canadian courts have also assumed the opposite interpretation of the precautionary principle: that the principle is simply the application of common sense.[35] For example, in *Morton v Minister of Fisheries and Oceans and Marine Harvest Canada Inc*,[36] a concerned scientist sought judicial review of a licence that permitted the transfer of potentially diseased salmon from a hatchery to a fish farm located in coastal waters. The scientific uncertainty pertained to the causal relationship between a particular disease agent, for which the transferred salmon tested positive, and a well-documented fatal disease in western Canada's iconic wild salmon populations. The Federal Court noted the scientific debate over the issue, but argued that the relevant Regulation's prohibition on activities that 'may be harmful' to wild fish populations should be interpreted generously, in line with the precautionary principle.[37] The Federal Court held that the condition of the licence that allowed the transfer of 'low risk' fish was inconsistent with the Regulation and, by issuing the licence, the Minister did not 'err[] on the side of caution'.[38] Although the decision is precautionary in the ordinary sense of the

31 *Canadian Parks and Wilderness Society v Canada (Minister of Canadian Heritage)* [2003] FCJ 703 [24]; *Pembina Institute for Appropriate Development v Canada (Attorney General)* [2008] FCJ 324 [32]; *Greenpeace Canada v Canada (Attorney General)* [2014] FCJ 515 [83] (repeating the quote, although the court in this case actually does properly apply the precautionary principle despite its reluctance to name it as such). The decision, however, is overturned on appeal with no reference to the precautionary principle: *Ontario Power Generation Inc v Greenpeace Canada* [2015] FCA 186.

32 Rio Declaration, above n 2.

33 *Canadian Environmental Assessment Act*, SC 2012, c 19, s 52, s 4.

34 Influential regulatory scholar Cass Sunstein has perpetuated this characterisation of the principle, but it is a caricature. See Cass R Sunstein, *Laws of Fear* (Cambridge University Press, 2005) 457; Jaye Ellis, 'Overexploitation of a Valuable Resource? New Literature on the Precautionary Principle' (2006) 17 *European Journal of International Law* 445; Fisher, 'Review', above n 27.

35 This understanding of the precautionary principle persists in the Australian context as well: see e.g. *Leatch v National Parks and Wildlife Service and Shoalhaven City Council* (1993) 81 LGERA 270.

36 [2015] FC 575.

37 Ibid. [97].

38 Ibid. [46].

word, it is far from obvious that the precautionary principle itself played any distinctive role in the decision. Ordinary principles of statutory interpretation could have led the Federal Court to the same conclusion that a low-risk transfer 'may be harmful'. Moreover, it is noteworthy that the Federal Court invoked the precautionary principle to help adjudicate known scientific risks. The issue about the causal connection between the disease agent and disease was known, documented and supported, if not conclusively, by scientific evidence. In other words, though a precautionary success story, *Morton* is remarkably tame.

Australia

The lack of serious Canadian judicial development of the principle has led environmental law scholars to turn to Australia where the courts have contemplated a distinctive role for the principle.[39] The key Australian decision on the precautionary principle is *Telstra Corporation Limited v Hornsby Shire Council*,[40] a decision by Preston CJ of the New South Wales Land and Environment Court. *Telstra* was a review of the merits of a local council's refusal to grant Telstra a development approval to install mobile phone antennae on a building. Concerns were raised before the local council about the possible public health effects of radiofrequency and electromagnetic energy from the proposed mobile phone towers. Preston CJ attempted to synthesise precautionary principle jurisprudence and articulate a specific and comprehensive test for applying the precautionary principle in the domestic context.[41]

In His Honour's view, the precautionary principle requires the application of a three-part test. The first step, set out in the decision, is to determine whether two threshold criteria are met for the principle to be invoked: (i) the existence of a threat; and (ii) the existence of scientific uncertainty about such a threat.[42] While Preston CJ set out broad-ranging considerations for the determination of the existence of a threat, His Honour maintained that '[t]he threat of environmental damage must be adequately sustained by scientific evidence'.[43] Similarly, Preston CJ stated that the scientific uncertainty must be grounded in 'reasonable scientific plausibility'.[44] Once the threshold is met, Preston CJ reasoned, the burden shifts to the proponent of the activity to demonstrate that the threat does

39 See, in particular, Chris Tollefson and Jamie Thornback, 'Litigating the Precautionary Principle in Domestic Courts' (2008) 19(1) *Journal of Environmental Law and Practice* 33.
40 (2006) 67 NSWLR 256 (*Telstra*).
41 For detailed analysis of this case, see Fisher, *Risk Regulation*, above n 29, 155–60; Jacqueline Peel, 'When (Scientific) Rationality Rules: (Mis)Application of the Precautionary Principle in Australian Mobile Phone Tower Cases' (2007) 19(1) *Journal of Environmental Law* 103.
42 *Telstra* [128].
43 Ibid. [134].
44 Ibid. [148], relying on Nicolas de Sadeleer, *Environmental Principles: From Political Slogans to Legal Rules* (Oxford University Press, 2005).

not exist or is negligible. Assuming the proponent cannot discharge this burden, the final step is for the judge to treat the threat as a reality and determine the appropriate precautionary measures through a proportionality analysis.[45] His Honour held that, in this case, the requirement of serious or irreversible environmental damage was not met and thus there was no basis for applying the precautionary principle.[46]

These brief snapshots of the precautionary principle in practice in Canada and Australia confirm that many of the claims of preventive justice scholars are grounded in environmental law. The principle is often portrayed as *commanding* specific and severe precautionary *measures*: for example, a ban on development. The *Telstra* framework commands a reversed burden of proof that, should it not be met, requires precautionary action.[47] At the same time, however, the decisions reflect a narrow understanding of *threat* and *uncertainty*. Far from the vast world of unknown threats that can arise in both environmental and security contexts, the influence of the precautionary principle in environmental law has focused on filling relatively narrow and identifiable gaps within science.[48] The precautionary principle, as applied, does not currently operate to challenge the limits of scientific expertise, introduce different worldviews or sources of knowledge, or take seriously the possibility of unknown-unknowns.

The 'tame'[49] version of the precautionary principle articulated in *Telstra* gives rise to two questions about the limits and potential for the precautionary principle in environmental law. The first is a question about the principle's apparent requirement of reversing the burden of proof, and the second is a question about the relationship between the precautionary principle and risk assessment. As we shall now see, environmental law scholars have argued that the precautionary principle has the potential to be much more than either a reversed burden of proof or a modification to risk assessment. Perhaps it is this potential that is the source of anxiety for preventive justice scholars.

45 *Telstra* [150].
46 Ibid. [184]–[185].
47 The consensus among Canadian legal academics is that the principle requires a reversed burden of proof: Jamie Benidickson, Nathalie J Chalifour, Yves Prévost, Jennifer A Chandler, André Dabrowski, Scott Findlay, Annik Déziel, Heather C McLeod-Kilmurray and Dan Lane, *Practicing Precaution and Adaptive Management: Legal, Institutional and Procedural Dimensions of Scientific Uncertainty* (June 2005), Institute of the Environment, University of Ottawa (online); Nathalie J Chalifour, 'A (Pre) Cautionary Tale About the Kearl Oil Sands Decision: The Significance of *Pembina Institute for Appropriate Development et al. v. Canada (Attorney-General)* for the Future of Environmental Assessment' (2009) 5(2) *McGill International Journal of Sustainable Development Law and Policy* 251; David L VanderZwaag, 'The Precautionary Principle in Environmental Law and Policy: Elusive Rhetoric and First Embraces' (1998) 8 *Journal of Environmental Law and Practice* 355.
48 Peel, *Precautionary Principle*, above n 27, 219.
49 Tollefson and Thornback, above n 39, 38; John S Applegate, 'The Taming of the Precautionary Principle' (2002–2003) 27 *William and Mary Environmental Law and Policy Review* 13.

Burden of proof

The idea that the precautionary principle can be operationalised by reversing the burden of proof reflects a judicial or quasi-judicial understanding of the principle. Yet front-line environmental decisions are generally implemented in an administrative or regulatory context that is quite unlike a criminal trial, with its comparatively clear onus and standard of proof.[50] In an administrative context, various 'burdens' arise with respect to providing specific information and conducting analyses. It may be that, in some cases, the precautionary principle will operate to reverse or influence a burden of proof, but whether it does so requires careful attention to the specific regulatory context.[51] The notion that the precautionary principle requires the same thing in every instance does not reflect the enormous range of environmental issues to which the principle is relevant, or the diverse regulatory processes and decisions taken in response to these issues.

Moreover, the 'reversed burden of proof' approach unduly narrows the innovative possibilities for precautionary decision-making. Precautionary principle scholars have argued that 'the reversal of the burden of proof, "abusively associated with the principle of precaution, is more sensational than representative of reality"'.[52] Most international environmental agreements do not specify a reversed burden of proof,[53] nor do many instances of domestic implementation of the precautionary principle require a strict burden of proof approach.[54] Some scholars have noted the existence of far more creative institutional design, such as citizens' assemblies and independent public watchdogs, as examples of precautionary measures that bear little relationship to a reversed burden of proof interpretation.[55] In short, for all its merits in the context of judicial decision-making, it is far from

50 Judith Jones and Simon Bronitt, 'The Burden and Standard of Proof in Environmental Regulation: The Precautionary Principle in an Australian Administrative Context' in Elizabeth Fisher, Judith Jones and René von Schomberg (eds), *Implementing the Precautionary Principle: Perspectives and Prospects* (Edward Elgar Publishing, 2006) 137.

51 Peel, *Precautionary Principle*, above n 27, 154–5. For example, *Wier v Canada (Minister of Health)* [2011] FC 1322 (on the specific requirements of the *Pest Control Products Act*, SC 2002, c 28, s 17 which requires the Minister to make a determination of whether there are 'reasonable grounds to believe that the health or environmental risks of the product are, or its value is, unacceptable'); *Environmental Defence Canada v Canada (Minister of Fisheries and Oceans)* [2009] FC 878 (on the *Species at Risk Act*, SC 2002, c 29 requirement that government officials act on whatever scientific information is available at the time).

52 Ellis, above n 34, 459 (including her translation of Julien Cazala, 'Principe de précaution et procédure devant le juge international', in *Le principe de précaution*).

53 Ibid.

54 See e.g. *Canadian Environmental Assessment Act*, SC 2012, c 19; *Environment Protection and Biodiversity Conservation Act 1999* (Cth); *Environment Protection Act* 1970 (Vic).

55 Kerry H Whiteside, *Precautionary Politics: Principle and Practice in Confronting Environmental Risk* (MIT Press, 2006) 132ff.; Genevieve Cartier, 'Le principe de précaution et la déférence judiciaire en droit administratif' (2002) 43 *Les Cahiers de droit* 79, 99–100.

clear that a reversed burden of proof approach reflects the administrative reality of environmental decision-making.

Precaution and risk

Preventive justice scholars understand the precautionary principle as an exception to the norm of risk assessment. Yet, as we have seen, in many instances the precautionary principle has not supplied a distinctive decision-making framework. Rather, it is viewed as operating within a risk assessment paradigm:[56] for example, recognising a margin of error in risk assessment or '[w]eighting the risk of error in favour of the environment'.[57] Yet defenders of the precautionary principle argue that it has far greater potential to challenge status quo decision procedures and to challenge dominant assumptions about our capacity to 'manage' risk.[58] Commentators point out that there are multiple sources of uncertainty in environmental decision-making.[59] Some of these sources can be identified, measured and quantified with actuarial data and probabilistic analysis. But some of these sources are inherent in the scientific process itself. There are questions that we do not yet know to ask and these have particular salience when regulators are confronted with novel innovations and potentially novel risks.[60] From this perspective, the precautionary principle is an 'exception' to risk assessment only in that it forces us to confront the inevitable incompleteness of any attempt to comprehensively quantify perceived risks. The important question, then, is what a decision-maker ought to do with a necessarily partial risk assessment in hand.[61]

It is this vision – as a departure from risk assessment – that understandably makes preventive justice scholars nervous about the precautionary principle. But what happens in this gap between risk assessment and ultimate decision is precisely what can link the two projects of preventive justice and the precautionary principle under the much more fundamental project of maintaining the rule of law. In particular, it is the importance of procedure and reason-giving that links the precautionary principle with preventive justice. For example, Fisher and Harding write that:

> The principle regulates the reasons for a decision and the process by which a decision is made . . . This is because regulating outcomes (beyond requiring

56 Privy Council Office of Canada, *A Framework for the Application of Precaution in Science-Based Decision Making About Risk* (25 July 2003) Government of Canada (online).

57 *Telstra* [162].

58 Whiteside, above n 55; Ellis, above n 34, 456.

59 See e.g. Peel, *Precautionary Principle*, above n 27, ch 3; Fisher, *Review*, above n 27, 317–8.

60 Malcolm McGarvin, 'Science, Precaution, Facts and Values' in Tim O'Riordan, James Cameron and Andrew Jordan (eds), *Reinterpreting the Precautionary Principle* (Cameron May, 2001) 35, 42–3 (discussing ignorance and indeterminacy); Peel, *Precautionary Principle*, above n 27, ch 3.

61 Ellis, above n 34, 453.

decision makers to pursue broad statutory goals) is logically impossible in cases of scientific uncertainty.[62]

In other words, the rationale for the precautionary principle does not lie in its substantive legitimacy.[63] The very conditions of uncertainty that require the precautionary principle preclude us from evaluating the principle solely on its ability to generate effective outcomes.[64] It would be difficult, if not impossible, to know when an unforeseen catastrophe has been avoided. Instead, defenders of the principle look to its potential to instantiate procedures through which a community can collectively decide how to proceed in the face of uncertainty. Most defenders of the precautionary principle therefore argue that it requires a more inclusive decision-making process, which formalises non-expert citizen participation and collective decision-making.[65] This enables the consideration of factors that do not fit into the language of risk assessment – factors such as voluntariness, or whether potential risks may affect already marginalised populations – and it opens up the process of risk assessment to critical analysis from a variety of perspectives. Although the specific procedural requirements of the precautionary principle are vastly different from what principles of preventive justice require in situations where serious liberty infringement is at stake, we shall now see that both ought to be understood as essential to maintaining and enabling the autonomy of individuals. In other words, both are attempts to maintain our fundamental commitment to democratic governance under the rule of law, even when faced with conditions of uncertainty.

Precaution, prevention and the rule of law project

The rule of law, as is often noted, is an 'essentially contested concept'.[66] The conception of the rule of law advanced here is the idea that public officials must publicly justify their decisions on the basis of core constitutional principles. It is a conception elaborated by Dyzenhaus, who states that its basic content is that:

62 Elizabeth Fisher and Ronnie Harding, 'The Precautionary Principle and Administrative Constitutionalism: The Development of Frameworks for Applying the Precautionary Principle' in Elizabeth Fisher, Judith Jones and René von Schomberg (eds), *Implementing the Precautionary Principle: Perspectives and Prospects* (Edward Elgar Publishing, 2006) 113, 115.

63 See Whiteside, above n 55, ch 5 (in particular at 123) for a notable exception.

64 This means that frequent charges against the principle – such as Cass Sunstein's claim that it is irrational – miss the mark: Sunstein, above n 34. Indeed, Sunstein finds the Rio Declaration definition of precaution 'unobjectionable' (23) and endorses an 'Anti-Catastrophe Principle', which in his view is narrower than precaution but necessary because of worst-case scenario threats whose probability cannot be assessed (109).

65 Whiteside, above n 55, 119; Peel, *Precautionary Principle*, above n 27, 222–7; Fisher, *Risk Regulation*, above n 29, 43 (describing the deliberative constitutive interpretation of the principle).

66 W B Gallie, 'Essentially Contested Concepts' (1955) 56 *Proceedings of the Aristotelian Society* 167, 169.

> [L]egislation must be capable of being interpreted in such a way that it can be enforced in accordance with the requirements of due process; the officials who implement it can comply with a duty to act fairly, reasonably and in a fashion that respects the equality of all those who are subject to the law and independent judges are entitled to review the decisions of these officials to check that they do so comply.[67]

On this view, what makes law *law* – and not merely an act of political power – is its compliance with the rule of law. And it is this compliance that creates its own kind of legal legitimacy.[68] This is why public officials, such as those defending 'advanced interrogation tactics' in the aftermath of the September 11 terrorist attacks, seek to justify their actions by pointing to their prior legal authorisation. Dyzenhaus calls this *rule by law*, the notion that an action is governed by law in the formal sense that it is authorised by positive law.[69] But Dyzenhaus argues that we cannot have rule by law without *rule of law*, such that the failure of public actions to comply with the rule of law calls into question its status as law.[70]

Preventive measures, notably in the counter-terrorism context, are often examples of attempts to rule *by* law without the rule *of* law. Individuals facing significant infringements of their liberty are deprived of basic rights of due process – for example, the right to know the case against them, or the opportunity to properly contest this case before an independent tribunal.[71] To the extent that these measures fail to comply with the rule of law, they lose their claim to legal legitimacy that comes with the status of law.

Dyzenhaus defends this conception of the rule of law project on the basis that it respects underlying values of liberty and equality. Although the underlying rationales for the rule of law are much debated, I have argued elsewhere that it respects and enables the autonomy of law's subjects, understood as their rational and self-determining capacity.[72] In other words, law is something worth having, not only because compliance protects individuals from arbitrary public decisions, but also because compliance with the rule of law is what enables legal subjects to reason with the law: to understand it and obey it, or to contest it and thereby participate in further deliberations about what the law is and ought to be. When legislation

67 David Dyzenhaus, *The Constitution of Law: Legality in a Time of Emergency* (Cambridge University Press, 2006) 12–13.

68 See, further, Chapter 11 by Sarah Murray.

69 Dyzenhaus, *Constitution of Law*, above n 67, 6, 206.

70 Dyzenhaus, *Preventive Justice*, above n 11, 97.

71 For an example, see Chapter 8 by Svetlana Tyulkina and George Williams in this collection which looks at preventative detention orders – a measure which departs significantly from the ordinary requirements of due process – under Australia's national anti-terrorism regime.

72 Jocelyn Stacey, *The Constitution of the Environmental Emergency* (DCL Thesis, McGill University, 2015). See also Hoi Kong, 'Election Law and Deliberative Democracy: Against Deflation' (2015) 9 *Journal of Parliamentary and Political Law* 35, pt I; Kristen Rundle, *Forms Liberate: Reclaiming the Jurisprudence of Lon L Fuller* (Hart Publishing, 2012).

complies with well-known formal indicia of the rule of law (public, general, prospective, etc.), is implemented congruently with the stated rule and is subject to review by independent judges, the autonomy interests of those subject to law are respected.[73]

However, not all issues can be adequately addressed exclusively through legislative provisions that meet these formal criteria. Complex environmental decisions require the exercise of administrative discretion in response to technical and constantly evolving environmental decisions. Public officials may need to move swiftly and decisively to protect individuals and environmental health from pollutants, to halt activities that undermine our ecological support systems, or to respond to an environmental catastrophe. Sound environmental decisions may further require a solid grasp of scientific and ecological knowledge to recognise how environmental issues – and our understanding of them – are constantly evolving. Similarly, responding to national security issues requires security expertise, decisive and coordinated action, and often secrecy. All of these features militate against governing exclusively through prospective and general legislative rules. Rather, responding to environmental issues and security issues in order to prevent future harm requires considerable administrative infrastructure that raises deep questions about how administrative decision-making can nonetheless comply with the rule of law.[74]

But when we understand the rule of law as serving the end of autonomy – that is, protecting individuals from arbitrary decisions and allowing them to reason with the law – then it is possible to understand how both administrative decisions and emergency response decisions can comply with the rule of law.[75] When these decisions are publicly justified on the basis of core constitutional principles, such as fairness and reasonableness, they will comply with the rule of law.[76] This conception of the rule of law gives rise to the familiar requirements of due process powerfully defended by preventive justice scholars, but, importantly, it can only be realised within a deliberative democracy.[77] While there are many theories of deliberative democracy, all share a fundamental understanding of the individual as a responsible agent capable of reasoning with the law.[78]

73 Lon Fuller, *The Morality of Law* (Yale University Press, revised edn, 1969); Rundle, above n 72.

74 Stacey, *Legality of Discretion*, above n 6. The status of administrative law as *law* is a perennial question. See e.g. E L Rubin, 'Law and Legislation in the Administrative State' (1989) 89 *Columbia Law Review* 369; Philip Hamburger, *Is Administrative Law Unlawful* (University of Chicago Press, 2014).

75 This is the central argument of Dyzenhaus: Dyzenhaus, *Constitution of Law*, above n 67.

76 The public justification conception of the rule of law also opens up the possibility of using creative institutional design, such as specialised tribunals, to ensure that especially challenging decisions are nonetheless publicly justified, as long as these tribunals are ultimately subject to review by the court.

77 Dyzenhaus hints at this with his 'culture of justification': Dyzenhaus, *Preventive Justice*, above n 11, 114.

78 See e.g. Amy Gutmann and Dennis Thompson, *Why Deliberative Democracy?* (Princeton University Press, 2004) 3.

It is at this intersection – of the rule of law and deliberative democracy – that the precautionary principle comfortably rests. The precautionary principle, in its best light, ought to be understood as an attempt to preserve this reasoning capacity of legal subjects even under conditions of uncertainty that challenge our ability to make fully informed public decisions. The details of what the precautionary principle will require in order to fulfil the requirement of public justification are necessarily context-dependent. In broad strokes, however, they consist of three features. These features better capture the nature of the relationship between the state and legal subject than any attempt to equate the precautionary principle with a reversed burden of proof or any attempt to square the precautionary principle with a risk assessment framework. On this view, the principle requires a decision-making procedure that enables collective reasoning about how to proceed in the face of uncertainty, one that ensures that expert information is exposed to public scrutiny. In other words, the process must be justified on the ground that it promotes democratic deliberation. It requires detailed reasons by the decision-maker that identify sources of uncertainty and the assumptions used to factor that uncertainty into the decision. And it requires proper institutional channels for independent review. The result of these features is that the precautionary principle operates to inform ordinary administrative law requirements of fairness and reasonableness to ensure they reflect the reality of environmental decision-making. These are simple, but demanding, requirements. In many instances they are met. But the examples offered in this chapter demonstrate that public officials often fall short by failing to offer reasons[79] or setting an untenable threshold for non-experts with legitimate concerns about uncertain consequences.[80]

Although these features might look quite different from what we would expect in the preventive justice context when significant liberty interests are at stake, they nonetheless share the essential characteristics of the rule of law. In their respective contexts, principles of preventive justice and precaution ensure there is an open process in which those affected by the decision have meaningful opportunities to be heard; they ensure affected individuals can contest a decision that is of questionable legality before an independent tribunal. Moreover, these principles operate to make democratic participation internal to the requirements of the rule of law. This conception respects the legal subject's capacity to reason with the law, namely to participate in the ongoing project of articulating and rearticulating the content of the law.

Conclusion

This chapter has explored the connections between the precautionary principle in the preventive justice context and the precautionary principle in environmental law. It traced the roots of the preventive justice characterisation of the

79 *Morton v Minister of Fisheries and Oceans and Marine Harvest Canada Inc* [2015] FC 575.

80 *Telstra.*

precautionary principle through its operation in the environmental context. It argued that, at least in Australia and Canada, the reality of the precautionary principle is somewhat tamer than that imagined by preventive justice scholars. The precautionary principle has not operated to address instances of true uncertainty in the environmental context, it has not operated to displace a risk assessment paradigm, and it does not typically compel any particular course of preventive action. At the same time, however, the hopes of environmental law scholars remain high. They argue that the precautionary principle has far more potential than is currently realised.

While a broader, reinvigorated precautionary principle may be a source of anxiety among preventive justice scholars, this chapter has sought to assuage these concerns. It has advanced an understanding of the precautionary principle that is wholly consistent with the normative project of preventive justice, a project, as I understand it, of articulating how we can maintain our commitment to the rule of law even under conditions of uncertainty about future harm. It is thus misguided to claim that the precautionary principle can provide a basis for sweeping preventive action in the national security context. The precautionary principle, in its best light, is an essential part of realising commitment to democratic governance under the rule of law in the environmental context. And, in this sense, it and preventive justice are complementary efforts to both protect and enable the autonomy of those subject to the law.

3 Amendments to the Australian terrorism control order scheme

A precautionary tale?

Susan Donkin

Introduction

As highlighted by many chapters in this collection,[1] preventive justice has left an indelible mark on the legal framework of several jurisdictions, particularly in the post-September 11 era. Much has been written about the shift away from traditional reactive criminal justice principles and safeguards in favour of preventive, precautionary or pre-emptive measures introduced in response to terrorism.[2] Terrorism control orders, introduced in both the United Kingdom and Australia in 2005, are one such preventive measure. Control orders (COs) were designed to prevent anticipated future offending rather than punish past offences by imposing various prohibitions, obligations and restrictions on individuals *suspected* of posing a terrorist threat. It is this pre-emptive or precautionary element, among others, that led to criticism from scholars and practitioners alike.[3] By imposing sanctions on non-convicted individuals in the civil realm, the intervention occurs either prior to the commission of a crime or in cases where there is insufficient evidence to

1 See e.g. this chapter, Chapter 8 by Svetlana Tyulkina and George Williams, and Chapter 10 by Rebecca Ananian-Welsh.

2 See e.g. David Dyzenhaus and Rayner Thwaites, 'Legality and Emergency – The Judiciary in a Time of Terror' in Andrew Lynch, Edwina MacDonald and George Williams (eds), *Law and Liberty in the War on Terror* (The Federation Press, 2007) 9; Andrew Lynch, Nicola McGarrity and George Williams, 'The emergence of a "culture of control"' in Nicola McGarrity, Andrew Lynch and George Williams (eds), *Counter-Terrorism and Beyond: The Culture of Law and Justice after 9/11* (Routledge, 2010) 3; Alan M Dershowitz, *Preemption: A Knife That Cuts Both Ways* (W W Norton & Co, 2006); Lucia Zedner, 'Pre-Crime and Post-Criminology?' (2007) 11(2) *Theoretical Criminology* 261; Lucia Zedner, 'Preventive Justice or Pre-Punishment? The Case of Control Orders' (2007) 60(1) *Current Legal Problems* 174 ('Preventive Justice or Pre-Punishment').

3 See e.g. Lucia Zedner, 'Fixing the Future? The Pre-emptive Turn in Criminal Justice' in Bernadette McSherry, Alan Norrie and Simon Bronitt (eds), *Regulating Deviance: The Redirection of Criminalisation and the Futures of Criminal Law* (Hart Publishing, 2009); Joint Committee on Human Rights, *Twelfth Report of Session 2005–06: Counter-Terrorism Policy and Human Rights: Draft Prevention of Terrorism Act 2005 (Continuance in force of sections 1 to 9) Order 2006.*

prosecute. Described as coercive preventive measures,[4] COs are thus problematic due to the timing of the intervention, as well the absence of well-established criminal procedural safeguards overseeing the civil process giving rise to them.

The British CO scheme was eventually replaced with Terrorism Prevention and Investigation Measures (TPIMs) in 2012. Although very similar to COs, TPIMs have a higher threshold for issuance and less restrictive obligations – a direct result of the legal challenges to its predecessor. In contrast, despite the conclusion of the Australian Independent National Security Legislation Monitor (INSLM) that the Australian scheme was ineffective, inappropriate and unnecessary,[5] that scheme was not abolished. Instead, amendments to the Australian CO scheme were introduced in November 2014 that, among other things, lowered the threshold for issuance and expanded instances in which COs could be sought. These amendments signalled a renewed determination to make use of an existing, albeit underutilised, preventive measure. In the first nine years of the CO scheme, Australia only issued two COs, both of which were against individuals who had allegedly trained with terrorist organisations.[6] Within a few months of the 2014 amendments, however, four new COs had been applied for. Whereas the original COs were primarily issued in response to past actions[7] which, at the time, could not be prosecuted retrospectively, the most recently issued COs are facilitated by the lower threshold for issuance and appear to constitute a shift towards precautionary prevention.

As highlighted by Tamara Tulich[8], the state has both a punitive or reactive mandate as well as a preventive one. Although the criminal justice system typically intervenes after an offence has been committed, preventive measures targeting risky individuals are, for the most part, accepted interventions of the preventive state. Since the risk of future offending is calculated based on previous events, this can be described as reactive prevention. Anti-terrorism measures, such as the COs examined in this chapter, are based on a precautionary logic, which aims to prevent potential offending at some point in the future, without requiring past offending or evidence in the traditional sense due to the potentially catastrophic events which may ensue if not prevented. Based on the precautionary principle,

4 Andrew Ashworth and Lucia Zedner, *Preventive Justice* (Oxford University Press, 2014).
5 Independent National Security Legislation Monitor, 'Declassified Annual Report' (Commonwealth of Australia, 2012) 4.
6 For a more detailed account of the COs issued against Jack Thomas and David Hicks, see Susan Donkin, *Preventing Terrorism and Controlling Risk: A Comparative Analysis of Control Orders in the UK and Australia* (Springer Science and Business Media, vol 1, 2013); Andrew Lynch, 'Thomas v Mowbray: Australia's "War on Terror" Reaches the High Court' (2008) 32(3) *Melbourne University Law Review* 1182; Kent Roach, *The 9/11 Effect: Comparative Counter-Terrorism* (Cambridge University Press, 2011).
7 Thus justifying the preventive ground for issuance. Independent National Security Legislation Monitor, above n 5.
8 See Chapter 1 by Tamara Tulich in this collection.

examined in more detail by Jocelyn Stacey,[9] imposing restrictions on the basis of intelligence without any prior finding of guilt is referred to as precautionary prevention. Reactionary and precautionary prevention are at opposite ends of the axis of prevention, which symbolises the reach of the preventive state.[10]

Whereas Britain replaced COs with a less onerous measure aiming to improve evidence-gathering and subsequent prosecutions, Australia's most recent amendments have moved in the opposite direction. This chapter examines the diverging evolution of the CO schemes in both jurisdictions. By comparing the rationale behind Australia's original two COs with the most recent cases, this chapter considers both the necessity and the likely impact of the recent amendments to the Australian CO scheme. Finally, it makes the case that the changes to the scheme have widened the net of state control, shifting from a reactively preventive application of COs towards a more precautionary approach, characterised by increased reliance on intelligence rather than evidence.

British CO origins

To contextualise the Australian CO developments, it is instructive to first examine the scheme's origins. The Australian implementation was based on the British CO scheme introduced the same year. COs aimed to protect the general public from a risk of terrorism by imposing obligations on individuals who were suspected of involvement in terrorism-related activities so as to restrict or prevent these individuals from further involvement in said activities.[11] British COs severely restricted an individual's liberty by imposing various restrictions on the controlee's associations, place of residence (including forced relocation), travel and employment, as well as the imposition of lengthy curfews, to name but a few. The Secretary of State for the Home Department (Home Secretary) described them as a mechanism to contain and disrupt individuals who could not be prosecuted or deported.[12]

Although the *Prevention of Terrorism Act 2005* (UK) (PTA) set out two types of CO, derogating and non-derogating,[13] only the latter was ever issued. Initiated by the Home Secretary in cases where there was insufficient evidence to prosecute individuals for terrorism-related offences, the standard of proof for the non-derogating CO was not the traditional civil standard of *the balance of probabilities*,

9 See Chapter 2 by Jocelyn Stacey in this collection.

10 The axis of prevention and the distinction between reactive and precautionary prevention is further detailed in Donkin, above n 6.

11 *Prevention of Terrorism Act 2005* (UK) (PTA) c 2 ss (1)(1) and (3) (note: the PTA was repealed in 2011 by the *Terrorism Prevention and Investigative Measures Act 2011* (UK)).

12 United Kingdom, *Parliamentary Debates*, House of Commons, 26 January 2005, vol 430, col 307 (Charles Clarke).

13 The distinction related to Article 5 of the European Convention on Human Rights (ECHR), which prohibits the detention of an individual without the due process of law. The derogating control order (DCO) was a custodial measure, which would have *deprived* the individual of his or her liberty.

but an even lesser standard of *reasonable ground for suspicion*. The Home Secretary had grounds for issuance if he or she:

a ha[d] reasonable grounds for suspecting that the individual is or has been involved in terrorism-related activity; and
b consider[ed] that it [was] necessary, for purposes connected with protecting members of the public from a risk of terrorism, to make a control order imposing obligations on that individual.[14]

However, the Home Secretary was required to liaise with the police to determine whether there was sufficient evidence against that individual to be used for the purposes of prosecution both prior to issuance and throughout the duration of a CO.[15]

Although the two CO schemes were similar in purpose, the Australian and British approaches differed significantly in their application. The United Kingdom made greater use of the CO scheme, issuing a total of 52 non-derogating COs in the seven-year period of the British scheme's existence. Some observers noted the 'commendable restraint and composure' with which the British government has decided to implement the scheme, especially compared with the actual number of apparently known terrorist suspects.[16]

COs have been widely criticised by politicians, civil liberties organisations and academics alike, with much of the criticism related to procedural issues and civil liberties arising as a result of their precautionary nature.[17] The British CO scheme was shaped, and its eventual overhaul triggered, by multiple legal challenges, most of which pertained to the obligations, prohibitions and restrictions outlined in the orders.[18]

14 PTA c 2, s 2(1).
15 PTA c 2, s 8(2).
16 David Bonner, 'Checking the Executive? Detention Without Trial, Control Orders, Due Process and Human Rights' (2006) 12(1) *European Public Law* 45, 71; Lord Carlile of Berriew QC, *Fifth Report of the Independent Reviewer pursuant to Section 14 (3) of the Prevention of Terrorism Act 2005* (1 February 2010) Gov UK (online), available at www.gov.uk/government/uploads/system/uploads/attachment_data/file/243571/9781849871518.pdf (accessed 5 September 2016); Clive Walker, *Terrorism and the Law* (Oxford University Press, 2011).
17 Andrew Goldsmith, 'The Governance of Terror: Precautionary Logic and Counterterrorist Law Reform After September 11' (2008) 30(2) *Law and Policy* 141; Patrick Keyzer and Sam Blay, 'Double Punishment – Preventive Detention Schemes Under Australian Legislation and Their Consistency with International Law: the Fardon Communication' (2006) 7(2) *Melbourne Journal of International Law* 407; Simon Bronitt, 'Balancing Security and Liberty: Critical Perspectives on Terrorism Law Reform' in Miriam Gani and Penelope Mathew (eds), *Fresh Perspectives on the 'War on Terror'* (ANU E Press, 2008) 65; Ashworth and Zedner, above n 4; Joint Committee on Human Rights, *Counter-Terrorism Policy and Human Rights (Thirteenth Report): Counter-Terrorism Bill*, House of Lords Paper no 172, House of Commons Paper 1077, Session 2007–08 (2008).
18 Bronwen Jaggers, 'Anti-terrorism Control Orders in Australia and the United Kingdom: A Comparison' (Research Paper No 28, Parliamentary Library, Parliament of Australia, 2007–08). The most significant challenges centred around the length of the curfew and whether it constituted a breach under Article 5 of the ECHR, and the

The three key themes to emerge from the British legal challenges related to issues around the length of the potential curfew, the extent to which measures designed to achieve a preventive aim resembled punishment, and the procedural fairness of the process. Much of the civil liberties criticism of COs related to an apparent derogation from well-established criminal law safeguards. Yet it is important to reiterate that, technically, COs are civil measures and thus not subject to the same standards as a criminal trial. Many of these issues arose due to the hybrid nature of COs.[19] COs were designed to prevent the individual from engaging in the type of behaviour giving rise to the CO in the first place. However, a breach of any of the conditions set out in the CO without reasonable excuse has the potential to elevate the measure to the criminal realm, and the controlee would face up to five years' imprisonment. Given that some controlees' CO conditions were loosely worded, and some were apparently not viable,[20] it is perhaps not surprising that some controlees ended up breaching conditions outlined in their COs. In total, 14 of the 52 controlees were prosecuted for breaching CO obligations. However, prosecuting breaches proved fairly difficult and only two individuals were ever convicted as a result. The Independent Reviewer of Terrorism Legislation, David Anderson QC,[21] explained that several factors contributed to the difficulties of prosecuting breaches, including the Crown Prosecution Service's resource-intensive task to review multiple sources of evidence for relatively minor transgressions, an inability to present certain evidence due to potentially exposing the source of the intelligence, and delayed hearings and jury trials resulting in a sense of insignificance, especially if the controlee had subsequently improved his compliance and if the jury deemed certain requirements trivial. That being said, prosecutions were typically not sought unless the individual had committed a considerable number of breaches of their conditions.[22] Although some breaches of CO conditions were prosecuted over

controlee's right to receive a fair trial under Article 6 of the ECHR, given the use of Special Advocates and that much of the supporting information was kept from the controlee.

19 Andrew Ashworth, 'Criminal Law, Human Rights and Preventative Justice' in Bernadette McSherry, Alan Norrie and Simon Bronitt (eds), *Regulating Deviance: The Redirection of Criminalisation and the Futures of Criminal Law* (Hart Publishing, 2009) 87. Bonner, above n 16; Simon Bronitt and Susan Donkin, 'Australian Responses to 9/11: New World Legal Hybrids?' in Aniceto Masferrer (ed.), *Post 9/11 and the State of Permanent Legal Emergency* (Springer Netherlands, vol 14, 2012) 223.

20 Zedner, 'Preventive Justice or Pre-Punishment', above n 2.

21 David Anderson, *Terrorism Prevention and Investigation Measures in 2012: First Report of the Independent Reviewer on the Operation of the Terrorism Prevention and Investigation Measures* (March 2013) Gov UK (online), available at https://terrorismlegislationreviewer.independent.gov.uk/wp-content/uploads/2013/04/first-report-tpims.pdf (accessed 5 September 2016).

22 David Anderson, *Control Orders in 2011: Final Report of the Independent Reviewer on the Prevention of Terrorism Act 2005* (March 2012) Gov UK (online), available at https://terrorismlegislationreviewer.independent.gov.uk/wp-content/uploads/2013/04/control-orders-2011.pdf (accessed 5 September 2016).

the years in the United Kingdom,[23] not a single individual placed on a CO was subsequently prosecuted for terrorism-related offences. The lack of ensuing prosecutions may either be indicative of the effectiveness of COs in deterring controlees from engaging in terrorist acts or, alternatively, the upshot of restrictions preventing evidence-gathering capable of supporting subsequent prosecution.

In January 2012, seven years after the scheme's introduction, the British government replaced the controversial terrorism control order with TPIMs.[24] Hailed as addressing a number of criticisms voiced against COs, the replacement TPIMs are intended to provide a less controversial solution to those individuals thought to pose a risk to security, but, like its predecessor, against whom insufficient evidence to prosecute or deport exists. A greater range of safeguards, including a higher threshold for issuance and a two-year maximum duration of COs, were introduced as a result of civil liberty concerns. As well as avoiding some of the more politically divisive measures, such as curfews and forced relocation, the government highlighted that TPIMs were created to facilitate prosecution of suspects,[25] a process often hindered by the restrictions and obligations set out in COs.[26] As a result, the restrictions contained in the new measure were described as being less severe than that of their predecessor. Kent Roach argued that the abolition of COs signalled 'renewed confidence in the criminal process and a fading sense of emergency'.[27] On the other hand, opponents criticised TPIMs for being almost identical to COs,[28] doing nothing to remedy the legal limbo in which controlees find themselves. Certainly, the issuing procedure remains much the same, in that they originate with the executive. Although the burden of proof has been increased to the civil standard, arguably appropriate for a civil measure, it still falls short of the criminal standard. While perhaps less onerous than COs, TPIMs are still able to impose significant restrictions on individuals without a finding of guilt, meaning TPIMs remain hybrids between civil and criminal law.

Australia's CO scheme

Based on the now overhauled British scheme, Australian COs were originally introduced as part of Australia's extensive anti-terrorism measures in the *Anti-Terrorism Act (No. 2) 2005* (Cth). The Australian Federal Police (AFP) could

23 The longest punishment was a 15-month custodial sentence for contravening control order obligations: Lord Carlile of Berriew QC, *Sixth Report of the Independent Reviewer Pursuant to Section 14(3) of the Prevention of Terrorism Act 2005* (3 February 2011) Gov UK (online), available at www.gov.uk/government/uploads/system/uploads/attachment_data/file/97989/lord-carlile-sixth-report.pdf (accessed 5 September 2016).

24 *Terrorism Prevention and Investigation Measures Act 2011* (UK).

25 United Kingdom, *Parliamentary Debates*, House of Commons, 26 January 2011, col 308 (Theresa May).

26 Lord Macdonald of River Glaven QC, *Review of Counter-terrorism and Security Powers* (January 2011) Gov UK (online) 9.

27 Roach, above n 6, 287.

28 Leading some critics to rename them 'control orders lite'.

apply to a federal court for an interim CO (ICO) if they considered it would assist in preventing a terrorist attack, or if the individual in question was suspected of having received or provided training to a listed terrorist organisation.

In Australia, COs are subject to a two-stage process, an interim and a confirmed CO. Originally, a senior member of the AFP would request the Attorney-General's written consent to apply for an ICO against a suspect if he or she either:

a consider[ed] on reasonable grounds that the order in the terms to be requested would substantially assist in preventing a terrorist act; or
b suspect[ed] on reasonable grounds that the person has provided training to, or received training from, a listed terrorist organisation.[29]

Unlike the United Kingdom, Australia exercised restraint in issuing COs, with only two issued between 2005 and 2014. Both COs were issued against Australian citizens who had either been acquitted of or had served their sentence for terrorism-related offences. The first Australian ICO was issued against Joseph Thomas in August 2006,[30] despite Thomas being acquitted of two counts of providing support to a terrorist organisation, and having his conviction of intentionally receiving funds from a terrorist organisation overturned on appeal.

The first ground on which the ICO was made – that the order would 'substantially assist in preventing a terrorist act' – relied upon Thomas' admission in his interview with AFP officers in Pakistan that he had received weapons and explosives training with Al-Qa'ida in 2001. Because of his acquired knowledge, Thomas was considered 'an available resource that can be tapped [into] to assist commit terrorist acts'.[31] Also, his training with Al-Qa'ida could serve as a potential source of inspiration and training to aspiring extremists. The obligations were imposed to protect the public and substantially assist in the prevention of a terrorist attack by preventing Thomas from passing on his knowledge and skills to others. As part of his ICO conditions, Thomas was obliged to observe a five-hour overnight curfew, report to named police stations three times a week, not leave the country, not communicate or associate with named individuals, and have his communications limited and monitored.[32]

Thomas subsequently challenged the constitutional validity of the CO scheme in the High Court of Australia.[33] Thomas contended that issuing COs was antithetical to the judicial function.[34] Thomas also argued that the courts were only able to impose a deprivation or restriction on liberty following a determination of criminal guilt. In other words, the judiciary's role is to rule on infractions already committed rather than on the basis of what might be done at some point in the future. By majority, the High Court held that restrictions or deprivation of liberty

29 *Anti-Terrorism Act (no. 2)* 2005 (Cth) s 104.2(2).
30 *Jabbour v Thomas* (2006) 165 A Crim R 32.
31 Ibid. [42], [59] (Mowbray FM).
32 *Jabbour v Thomas* [2006] FMCA 1286
33 *Thomas v Mowbray* (2007) 233 CLR 307.
34 Ibid. 329 [17] (Gleeson CJ).

that are punitive in character may only be imposed following a judicial determination of criminal guilt. However, the Court held that COs were not considered punishment, rather a form of preventive restraints against future conduct. In a majority 5:2 ruling, the High Court found that issuing COs was indeed a valid exercise of judicial power and rejected Thomas' appeal. Thomas' ICO was never confirmed[35] and he was eventually cleared of all terrorism-related charges.[36]

The second Australian CO was issued against David Hicks upon his release from prison in 2007. Having already spent over six years in Guantanamo Bay, he was eventually returned to Australia in May 2007, where he served the remainder of his sentence. Hicks' ICO, issued to coincide with his release from prison, was justified on the basis of Hicks having received training from a listed terrorist organisation and, as such, the Court was satisfied, on the balance of probabilities, that the ICO would substantially assist in the prevention of a terrorist attack. The reasons for issuing the ICO against Hicks were grounded in his having trained with two listed terrorist organisations over an approximately 12-month period in 2000/2001 in Pakistan and Afghanistan.[37] This knowledge allegedly provided both Hicks and others with the ability to carry out a terrorist attack, as well as potentially serving as a source for other extremists. The ICO stated that the obligations were conceived to protect the public, reintegrate Hicks into Australian society and culture, protect him from being manipulated, and prevent his knowledge from helping others to commit terrorist acts. Hicks' ICO was confirmed in February 2008.[38]

Australia's two original COs in Australia were issued on the basis of Thomas and Hicks having trained with proscribed terrorist organisations, thus supporting findings that the COs would substantially assist in the prevention of a terrorist act. It is important to note that the alleged training for both Thomas and Hicks took place prior to September 11, before training with a proscribed terrorist organisation became an offence under s 102.5 of the *Criminal Code Act 1995* (Cth) (*Criminal Code*).

Australia's original COs enabled the government to fill a legal void. Not having any legal recourse to prosecute retrospectively, the government was able to issue both COs on the basis of the training clause – that is, the reactive clause for issuance. This in turn justified the preventive clause for issuance: that the CO would

35 Although the statute stipulates the confirmation of the ICO within a reasonable time frame, in this case the parties had agreed that the ICO would extend until the constitutional challenge had been heard. The AFP did not proceed with confirming the CO, and instead entered into a simple agreement with Thomas along the same lines as his ICO; Lynch, above n 6.

36 David Anderson described using COs on acquitted individuals as 'a troubling feel', but believes it is a by-product of the disparity between the criminal standard of proof and the threshold for issuance.

37 Lashkar-e-Tayyiba (LeT) and Al-Qa'ida.

38 Hicks' confirmed control order (CCO) contained some amendments to the original obligations set out in the ICO, including having the curfew reduced from six to four hours overnight, and reducing the reporting requirements.

substantially assist in preventing a terrorist act. As such, Thomas' and Hicks' COs are examples of a reactively preventive measure.[39]

Whereas the British CO scheme faced several legal challenges, resulting in various amendments and, ultimately, the replacement of COs with TPIMs in 2012,[40] to date the Australian regime has faced but one, albeit unsuccessful, constitutional challenge. Seven years after COs were first introduced, the long overdue reviews by Australia's first INSLM, and the Council of Australian Governments Review of Counter-Terrorism Legislation (COAG Review) echoed at least some concerns raised earlier by scholars and practitioners. In his 2012 Annual Report, the INSLM, Bret Walker SC, highlighted that as training with a listed terrorist organisation is now an offence in its own right, as opposed to requiring a CO to address the previous legal black hole, using a CO to deal with individuals who have done so is a 'historical problem' and thus no longer relevant.[41] The INSLM concluded that COs in their original format were 'not effective, not appropriate and not necessary'.[42] He went on to suggest that the only way COs could be any of the above would be if they were issued to individuals with previous terrorist convictions upon their release from prison if those individuals continued to pose a danger to the public due to unsatisfactory rehabilitation.[43] Ultimately, however, the INSLM recommended repealing the CO regime altogether.

The COAG Review, on the other hand, recommended retaining the regime, albeit with some amendments. One of the recommendations was to *raise* the threshold of the second basis for issuing a CO – that is, the training clause, to *'considers' on reasonable grounds* that a person has provided or received training from a listed organisation.[44] Although the government was unwilling to abolish the CO scheme altogether as proposed by the INSLM, it did incorporate some of the recommendations made by the INSLM and COAG reviews in its 2014 amendments to the CO scheme.

Australian amendments

Unlike its British predecessor, amendments made to the Australian CO regime in 2014 were neither in response to legal challenges nor as a direct result of the two

39 The axis of prevention distinguishes between interventions that occur after the commission of an (alleged) offence – that is, reactive prevention – and those that occur prior to the offence – that is, precautionary prevention. For a detailed explanation, see Donkin, above n 6.

40 TPIMs have encountered similar legal challenges to their predecessor – for instance, the duration of overnight restrictions; see e.g. *Secretary of State for the Home Department v BM* [2012] EWHC 714 (Admin) (27 March 2012) [4] and *Secretary of State for the Home Department v CC* [2012] EWHC 2837 (Admin) (19 October 2012) [64].

41 Independent National Security Legislation Monitor, above n 5, 31.

42 Ibid. 4.

43 Similar to *Fardon v Attorney-General (Qld)* (2004) 223 CLR 575 type provisions.

44 Council of Australian Governments, *Review of Counter-Terrorism Legislation* (2013) Australian Government (online), recommendation 27.

reviews.[45] Rather, they were in response to the perceived new threat of returning foreign fighters. In 2014, the Australian government made its first amendments to the CO scheme.[46] Adding yet further weight to Australia's 'hyper-legislative' approach,[47] the *Counter-Terrorism Legislation Amendment (Foreign Fighters) Act 2014* (Cth) (FFA) was introduced in response to the increased threat posed to Australia by individuals returning from conflict zones in the Middle East. The FFA introduced four significant amendments involving the issuance of COs:

1 It lowered the threshold for issuing a CO from *considering* on reasonable grounds that the CO would substantially assist in preventing a terrorist act, to *suspecting*.[48]
2 The training clause now includes individuals who have engaged in hostile activity in a foreign country. The threshold remains as *suspecting*.[49]
3 Individuals convicted of a terrorism-related offence, act or organisation in Australia or abroad may now also be subject to a CO.[50]
4 An interim CO (ICO) may now also be sought if there is reasonable suspicion that the order would substantially assist in preventing support for or facilitation of a terrorist act,[51] or that an individual has supported or facilitated engagement in a hostile activity abroad.[52]

The government reiterated that although the initial threshold for application may have been lowered, the issuing court still must be satisfied that the CO would substantially assist in preventing a terrorist act on the balance of probabilities, and that each of the restrictions, prohibitions and obligations set out in any CO are reasonably necessary and appropriate.[53] However, there are concerns associated with lowering the threshold for issuance to mere suspicion that a CO would substantially assist in preventing a terrorist act. The main concern is that COs could be more readily justified in cases where insufficient evidence to prosecute exists. Some may argue that this is not a problem, especially given that one of the reasons for the creation of the British CO scheme was precisely to deal with suspects against whom insufficient evidence to prosecute existed. Moreover, we know that there have been multiple cases in which the AFP have considered applying for a CO where insufficient evidence to prosecute existed.[54] However, until recently, the AFP chose not to apply for a CO in these instances. Indeed, the INSLM

45 The INSLM's fourth report was, however, referred to in more detail.
46 Valid until September 2018.
47 Roach, above n 6.
48 FFA s 70 amended *Criminal Code* s 104.2(2)(a).
49 FFA s 71 amended *Criminal Code* s 104.2(2)(b)(ii).
50 Ibid.
51 *Criminal Code* s 104.2(2)(c).
52 *Criminal Code* s 104.2(2)(d).
53 Revised Explanatory Memorandum, Counter-Terrorism Legislation Amendment (Foreign Fighters) Bill 2014 (Cth) 131 [753]–[754].
54 Other reasons for considering applying for a CO include: post-conviction, following the withdrawal of criminal charges, during a criminal trial against the contingency of

highlighted that surveillance and investigation appeared to have been more effective at dealing with terrorist suspects.[55] Ultimately, prosecution should remain the preferred option for dealing with individuals suspected of terrorist involvement.

A further cause for concern is that lowering the threshold of issuance of the second ground from *considering* to *suspecting* removes an additional safeguard and expands the target pool of potential controlees. One of the COAG Review's recommendations was to raise the threshold of the former training clause for issuance, which was at *suspecting*, to *considering*.[56] Rather than following this recommendation, the government has lowered the threshold of a key clause for issuance, one that has been used to justify the issuance of COs.

The expansion of the training clause to include individuals who have engaged in hostile activity in a foreign country is a direct reflection of the government's aim of dealing with returning fighters. Moreover, it reduces the onus on the government to substantiate any claim that the activity engaged in was indeed for training purposes, as well as ensuring that an omission or delay in adding an organisation to the proscribed terrorist organisation list does not result in the CO being rejected. That being said, both of the ICOs against Thomas and Hicks were issued on the basis of having trained with organisations that were proscribed only after the alleged training had taken place. Moreover, the threshold for issuance has remained a lower level of proof based on mere *suspicion* that said training or activity took place, ignoring the COAG Review's recommendation to raise it to the civil standard.

The amendments to the training clause are somewhat disconcerting for two reasons. First, the historical necessity of this clause due to the absence of a training offence has been rectified with the introduction of s 102.5 to the *Criminal Code*. Second, engaging in hostile activity in a foreign country is also an offence in its own right under s 119.1 of the *Criminal Code*. Given that simply entering and remaining in so-called declared areas[57] as an Australian citizen, resident or visa-holder can incur a lengthy sentence,[58] the retention and expansion of the training clause would indicate that the government wants an additional measure available in cases where there is insufficient evidence to prosecute.

The third amendment explicitly states that COs can be issued against individuals convicted of a terrorism-related offence in Australia or abroad. Implementing one of the INSLM's recommendations, the inclusion of the post-conviction clause

acquittal, during a criminal investigation before charges were brought. Independent National Security Legislation Monitor, above n 5, 13.

55 This is likely a result of covert telecommunications interception being admissible in 'prescribed' legal proceedings in Australia (*Telecommunications (Interception and Access) Act 1979* (Cth)), unlike the United Kingdom.

56 Council of Australian Governments, above n 44.

57 The Foreign Affairs Minister has the power to declare certain areas in foreign countries 'if he or she is satisfied that a listed terrorist organisation is engaging in a hostile activity in that area of the foreign country' per s 119.3(1) of the *Criminal Code*.

58 Exceptions are made for individuals travelling with legitimate purposes, such as providing humanitarian aid, visiting family members, journalism or performing official government duties per s 119.2(3) of the *Criminal Code*.

ensures that COs remain an option for convicted terrorists upon their release. As the government stated, this additional criterion fills a gap in the CO regime, allowing law enforcement to place controls on individuals convicted of terrorism offences who are suspected of still presenting a risk to the community.[59] Yet, even under the original CO regime, David Hicks' CO was issued upon his release from prison.[60] This suggests that the original wording was sufficient, and the amendment was not technically necessary, in order to issue COs to convicted terrorists upon their release from prison. As such, including a post-conviction clause might suggest that the government is pre-empting potential legal challenges in future CO cases issued against recently released individuals, or that the AFP or the Australian Security Intelligence Organisation are aware of intelligence relating to the presence of individuals who fall into the category of being convicted abroad; thus requiring the tools to deal with such cases.

The final amendments further expand the grounds upon which a CO can be issued. The two additional grounds for issuance – that is, that the CO would substantially assist in preventing the provision of support for or the facilitation of a terrorist act, and that a person has provided support or otherwise facilitated the engagement in a hostile activity abroad – are broadly worded provisions, both of which only require reasonable suspicion. The first clause could be interpreted as an expansion of the regime's primary catch-all justification grounds for issuance – that is, suspecting that the CO would substantially assist in preventing a terrorist act, which presumably is directed at individuals thought to pose a direct risk – to individuals who may in some way be associated with or related to a person of interest. This amendment thus has the ability to significantly expand the pool of potential controlees. The second additional ground for issuance includes actions classed as offences under the FFA, but at a lower threshold,[61] once again making a CO applicable in cases with insufficient evidence to prosecute under the *Criminal Code*.

The amendments made to the CO regime by the FFA have undoubtedly increased the pool of potential controlees; however, it is important to note that legislative changes do not necessarily lead to greater use of a particular measure. Although some statutes appear to have a more symbolic rather than practical impact, the government appears to be sending a clear message that the recent amendments to the CO scheme were conceived with practical application in mind. The next section of this chapter examines whether the recent amendments were cited in the grounds for issuance of the most recent CO cases in Australia.

59 Revised Explanatory Memorandum, Counter-Terrorism Legislation Amendment (Foreign Fighters) Bill 2014 (Cth) 132 [758].

60 After serving a seven-year sentence for the newly introduced, retrospective offence of 'providing material support to terrorism' issued by a Military Commission in Guantanamo Bay. Hicks recently had his conviction for providing material support for terrorism set aside after successfully challenging his terrorism conviction by a military court/tribunal at Guantanamo. In February 2016, the United Nations Human Rights Council found his detention both at Guantanamo Bay and in Australia to have been arbitrary and unlawful.

61 Similar to the expanded training provision.

Post-amendment COs

Despite Australian COs being on the statute books for ten years, the issuance of COs has been restrained, especially in comparison with their British counterpart. However, whereas there were only two COs issued in the first nine years of the Australian scheme, four ICOs were issued just a few months after the amendments came into force in November 2014.[62] Indeed, it took just over a month for the first two ICOs to be issued. Due to the non-publication order on the first two ICO cases under the new scheme,[63] it is currently not possible to speculate about the grounds upon which these were issued. What is known is that they were served to coincide with raids and searches at the suspects' residences in Sydney. One of the suspects was subsequently arrested for breaching the conditions of the ICO just a few days later. Although the breaches were reportedly fairly minor,[64] that suspect has been remanded in custody since.[65] Unlike the British authorities, it appears that their Australian counterparts are quick off the mark to act on minor breaches of COs, resurrecting important concerns around the hybrid nature of COs. Ultimately, however, neither of the two ICOs were ever confirmed, and the AFP permitted the COs to lapse after 12 months.[66]

Fortunately, the two subsequent cases are more accessible, and thus shed some light on the grounds for issuance. The third post-amendment ICO was issued to Ahmad Saiyer Naizmand, a 20-year-old from Sydney.[67] Naizmand was originally arrested in anti-terrorism raids in September 2014, but was released without charge. In the summary of grounds on which the ICO was made, Naizmand was mentioned in an intercepted phone call as a person who would be willing to carry out a random killing of non-believers in Australia. Moreover, it was alleged that Naizmand is part of a Sydney-based group supporting Islamic State, some members of which had been arrested. Due to Naizmand's frequent association with these individuals, and Naizmand's alleged attempts to source firearms, the ICO was issued on the grounds that the Court was satisfied the ICO would substantially assist in preventing a terrorist act, and that each obligation, prohibition

62 As of February 2016.
63 Issued in December 2014.
64 For allegedly making two unauthorised phone calls, one to his mother, the other to an associate: Paul Farrell, 'Man arrested in counter-terrorism operation "breached control order"', *The Guardian* (online) 24 December 2014, available at www.theguardian.com/australia-news/2014/dec/24/two-arrested-counter-terrorism-sydney-appleby (accessed 5 September 2016).
65 At the time this chapter was written in February 2016, this was over a year.
66 Paul Farrell, 'AFP drops control orders placed on two Sydney men in 2014', *The Guardian* (online) 28 December 2015, available at www.theguardian.com/australia-news/2015/dec/28/afp-drops-control-orders-placed-on-two-sydney-men-in-2014?CMP=share_btn_tw (accessed 5 September 2016).
67 *Neil Gaughan v Ahmad Saiyer Naizmand* (Unreported (file number SYG562/2015), Federal Circuit Court of Australia, Driver J, 5 March 2015–30 November 2015). For completeness, on 30 November 2015, the Federal Court confirmed and varied the ICO that was issued on 5 March 2015, with the result that the ICO became a CO that was to remain in force until 6 March 2016.

and restriction was reasonably necessary, appropriate and adapted for the purposes of protecting the public from a terrorist act.

As part of his obligations under the ICO, Naizmand was required to comply with a seven-hour overnight curfew and to report to the police three times a week. The ICO also prohibited Naizmand from communicating or associating with named individuals, communicating via any unapproved form of communication (phone, VOIP, email, ISP or computer) and visiting certain areas and places (including international airports, ports, correctional facilities, specified individuals' residences). The most controversial obligation was the restriction on his place of worship to one particular mosque in Parramatta,[68] with Naizmand arguing that this prohibited the free exercise of his religion. Naizmand was also required to participate in weekly counselling and educational programs.[69] It has since emerged that Naizmand had connections to the Parramatta shooting in October 2015. Naizmand's ICO was eventually confirmed in November 2015, with the AFP agreeing to the removal of the contentious restriction of attending a particular mosque, as well as loosening some of the restrictions around access to communication.[70]

The fourth ICO was issued against 18-year-old Harun Causevic in September 2015.[71] Causevic was first held under a preventative detention order in April 2015 for his alleged involvement in plotting a terrorist act planned for ANZAC day, before being charged two days later.[72] However, the terrorism-related charges against him were dropped in August 2015, as there was insufficient evidence to prosecute him. While Causevic's ICO acknowledged the inability to prove his involvement beyond reasonable doubt, it highlighted that this alone was not sufficient to determine the necessity of an ICO to protect the public.[73] Moreover, Causevic's apparent lack of remorse and behaviour exhibited while on remand showed that Causevic continued to exhibit the same extremist ideology, thus making him a risk to public safety. Therefore, the ICO was issued on the basis that it would substantially assist in preventing a terrorist act, and that the Federal Circuit Court was satisfied that each of the obligations, prohibitions and restrictions was reasonably necessary, appropriate and adapted to protect the public from a

68 *Neil Gaughan v Ahmad Saiyer Naizmand* (Unreported (file number (P)SYG562/2015). Federal Circuit Court of Australia, Driver J, 19 October 2015) Control 4.
69 Ibid. Control 10.
70 Paul Farrell, 'Judge confirms first control order in more than eight years on man, 20', *The Guardian* (online) 1 December 2015, available at www.theguardian.com/australia-news/2015/dec/01/judge-confirms-first-control-order-in-over-eight-years-on-man-20 (accessed 5 September 2016).
71 *Neil Gaughan v Harun Causevic* (Unreported (file number MLG2056/2015), Federal Circuit Court of Australia, Hartnett J, 9 September 2015). For completeness, the ICO was issued on 10 September 2015 and the proceeding was adjourned for hearing on 20 June 2016 in the Federal Circuit Court of Australia.
72 Causevic was also charged with weapons offences.
73 Summary of grounds on which the order was made: *Neil Gaughan v Harun Causevic* (Unreported (file number MLG2056/2015), Federal Circuit Court of Australia, Hartnett J, 9 September 2015), schedule 2, [8].

terrorist act.[74] Although the majority of Causevic's conditions are very similar to those imposed on Naizmand, Causevic is required to wear a tracking device at all times. In addition to a five-hour overnight curfew, Causevic is also prohibited from communicating or associating with six named individuals, and is required to participate in counselling or education on his spiritual, emotional and physical wellbeing for at least an hour every week. Causevic's ICO was confirmed, with some amendments to his conditions, in July 2016.

Both of the most recently issued ICOs appear to make use of the lowered threshold for issuing a CO – that is, suspecting that the CO would substantially assist in preventing a terrorist act. The summary of grounds on which Causevic's ICO was made makes reference to insufficient evidence to prosecute him for terrorism offences.[75] Together with an apparent lack of remorse and continued belief in an extremist ideology, Causevic was deemed a risk to the safety of the public,[76] thus constituting sufficient grounds to justify issuing an ICO. As such, at least one ICO has now been sought and issued in a case with insufficient evidence to prosecute.

The evidence against Naizmand appeared to be equally scarce. Naizmand's ICO was issued on the basis of information obtained via interception of a phone call, such as Naizmand being named in that conversation as a person willing to kill, Naizmand's association with individuals known to support Islamic State, as well as alleged attempts to source firearms, all of which ultimately were cited as support for the reduced threshold for issuance. However, Naizmand's alleged association with Islamic State supporters would also give rise to reasoning for the new clause in s 104.2(2)(c) of the *Criminal Code* to be utilised as it would assist in preventing support or facilitation of a terrorist act. Yet this clause is not stated in Naizmand's ICO as a ground for issuance, which instead relies on the expanded justification provision of assisting in preventing a terrorist attack.

The most recent cases have emphasised the Australian government's intention to implement the amendments expanding the CO regime, and, with it, its willingness to place increased reliance on intelligence over evidence and prosecution, the hallmark of precautionary prevention. The final section of this chapter argues that these amendments have widened the net of control, shifting Australia's CO scheme towards one characterised by precautionary prevention.

The shift towards precautionary prevention

This chapter has explored the recent amendments to the Australian CO scheme, beginning with a comparison with the developments of the now overhauled British scheme, before examining the instances of CO issuances in Australia since the

74 Ibid.

75 Summary of grounds on which the order was made: *Neil Gaughan v Harun Causevic* (Unreported (file number MLG2056/2015), Federal Circuit Court of Australia, Hartnett J, 9 September 2015) 8.

76 Ibid. 9 and 10.

scheme's inception in 2005. Comparing the evolution of the Australian and British CO schemes underscored the opposing directions taken in each jurisdiction. In the United Kingdom, the TPIM threshold for issuance was increased compared with its CO origins, additional safeguards were introduced, and restrictions and obligations were made less onerous. All of these amendments occurred despite several assertions of the necessity of the CO scheme. In contrast, the Australian threshold for issuance was reduced, and the instances in which a CO can be sought significantly expanded. Moreover, the two Australian reviews of the CO scheme were barely acknowledged.

Australian COs were conceived as a preventive measure against anticipated future offending. In its original iteration, there were two grounds for issuance: one is reactively preventive – that is, based on having trained with a proscribed organisation – and the other is pre-emptively preventive[77] – that is, it aims to substantially assist in preventing a terrorist attack. Both Thomas' and Hicks' COs were primarily issued on training grounds, thus justifying the preventive one – in other words, reactively preventive.[78]

The recent amendments to the CO scheme's grounds for issuance add a further reactive ground by explicitly including individuals with prior terrorism-related offences, as well as two more preventive ones with the inclusion of individuals suspected of providing support or facilitating terrorism in Australia or abroad. However, issuing COs on a low threshold of suspicion alone casts a wide net of precaution over an expanded pool of potential controlees, signalling a shift from the previously reactively preventive application of COs towards precautionary prevention if applied to individuals against whom there is insufficient evidence to prosecute.

Indeed, the four most recent CO cases appear to support this trend. Although we do not know much about the two orders issued in December 2014, the very fact that they are subject to non-publication orders may indicate the more precautionary nature of these ICOs. If the grounds for issuance are based on sensitive intelligence about an anticipated act or event, disclosure in an open court may jeopardise the investigation. The aim of a CO in such cases would be prevention via disruption. Even though the source of the intelligence is protected, however, the individuals in question are aware that their alleged act has been detected, and the restrictions contained within the CO would be tailored towards preventing them from further engaging in said activity. Although the alleged act may have been foiled, presumably so are any further opportunities of gathering valuable evidence with a view to prosecuting the controlees in the future. In Naizmand's case, an intercepted phone call between two other named individuals was listed in the reasons for issuance, thus exposing the state's surveillance of said individuals. Yet this was obviously not deemed problematic in terms of affecting an ongoing investigation. In both Naizmand's and Causevic's cases, the lack of evidence to prosecute them, even for preparatory offences, is not only a further indication of a

77 An example of precautionary prevention.
78 Donkin, above n 6.

shift towards precautionary prevention, but also an indication of the government's willingness to apply the new CO provisions.

Taking into account the lowered threshold for issuance, as well as the additional clauses for issuance, the government has expanded COs' possible applications – in other words, it has widened the net. Although these amendments clearly expand the potential use of COs, some additional safeguards have also been incorporated.[79] At this point, it is important to reiterate the government's justification for the introduction of the amendments contained within the FFA, namely that these have been made in response to the threat of fighters returning from engaging in hostile activity abroad – that is, training or fighting. However, while the FFA serves an important rationalisation for the amendments to the CO scheme, the underlying aim may not necessarily be to apply COs to returned fighters. Indeed, the current lack of issuance against returned fighters would support this hypothesis. Rather, the heightened awareness around radicalised Australians fighting in Syria and Iraq, and the potential danger of returning individuals may serve as the government's justification to widen the net.

In addition to expanding the grounds for issuance and thus the potential pool of controlees, recent amendments also signalled an expansion in both directions along the axis of prevention. Not only has the inclusion of convicted terrorists further cemented Australia's reactively preventive issuance of COs, but the reduced threshold for issuance of the justification clause marks the advent of precautionary prevention, characterised by an increased reliance on intelligence, as opposed to evidence. Indeed, the most recent CO cases are indicative of this shift.

Although the arguments for net-widening appear fairly compelling, the federal Attorney-General, George Brandis QC, initially asserted that the Australian government was not interested in expanding the regime. Less than a year later, however, additional amendments to the CO scheme have been put before Parliament. The current proposals under the *Counter-Terrorism Legislation Amendment Bill (No.1) 2015* (Cth) not only further expand the potential pool of controlees by lowering the age at which at CO can be issued to 14,[80] but also place restrictions on information and retrospectively allow secret evidence in CO hearings. One of the justifications for the lowering of the age has to do with the mental capacity to commit crimes, which is currently 14 for many other crimes, and is in line with other jurisdictions. However, proponents of this approach appear to be confusing the mental capacity of individuals who have committed crimes and been found guilty of them with applying severely restrictive obligations on a teenager as a precautionary measure. The age of the current controlees ranges from 18 to 21, which is younger than Thomas and Hicks were. Moreover, the fact that the

79 For instance, an individual served with an interim control order will now be more comprehensively informed of his or her rights of review, representation and appeal (s 104.12(1)(b)(iv–ix)).

80 Currently, there are already provisions to issue CO to suspects as young as 16 years old. Rather than being valid for up to one year, these COs can only be issued for up to three months.

October 2015 Parramatta shooter, Farhad Khalil Mohammad Jabar, was only 15 years old appears to have given further support for lowering the age of issuance.

Brandis argued that the increased use of COs could be helpful to law enforcement. However, Brandis would do well to revisit the British experience. Not only were COs not conducive to police investigations, but no former controlee was ever subsequently prosecuted for a terrorism-related offence. Certainly, the Australian government has demonstrated its willingness to issue COs more frequently in the first few months of the amended provisions than in the previous nine years. Indeed, given that the amendments were introduced as part of the FFA, one might expect the government to use COs as part of its legal arsenal in the fight against returning foreign fighters. That being said, several dozen fighters are known to have returned from declared areas, none of whom have, as far as we know, been issued with a CO. Time will tell whether increased issuance of COs in Australia will lead to legal or constitutional challenges capable of shaping the future of the scheme. Ultimately, however, future issuances will reveal whether Australia decides to pursue a precautionary or reactively preventive approach to terrorism COs.

Part II

Preventive (in)justice: case studies in mental health, security and migration

4 Preventive justice, risk of harm and mental health laws

Bernadette McSherry

Introduction

The term 'preventive justice', as Tamara Tulich has pointed out in this collection,[1] was first used in the late eighteenth century and linked to laws aimed at preventing future crime by intervening where there exists 'a probable suspicion, that some crime is intended or likely to happen'.[2] Many of the chapters in this collection are concerned with preventive justice in the form of 'pre-crime' measures, particularly in relation to suspected terrorists.

There is also a range of 'post-crime' and 'post-sentence' schemes that enable indefinite or continued detention or supervision aimed at preventing reoffending, particularly in relation to those viewed as high-risk offenders such as sex offenders. These schemes have been extensively discussed elsewhere.[3]

In a similar fashion to Helen Punter's chapter on police powers under mental health legislation,[4] this chapter is concerned with preventive justice in a sense that goes beyond the traditional link between the concept and the criminal law. Using Australia as a case study, it examines civil laws that enable the involuntary detention and supervision of persons with mental impairments[5] on the basis of their risk to self or others. Such civil laws are widespread across common law jurisdictions, with a 2009 study by Elizabeth Fistein and colleagues comparing 32 such laws.[6]

1 See Chapter 1 by Tamara Tulich in this collection.
2 William Blackstone, *Commentaries on the Laws of England* (R Bell, 1772), book IV, 248.
3 See e.g. Bernadette McSherry, *Managing Fear: The Law and Ethics of Preventive Detention and Risk Assessment* (Routledge, 2014); Bernadette McSherry and Patrick Keyzer, *Sex Offenders and Preventive Detention – Politics, Policy and Practice* (Federation Press, 2009); Bernadette McSherry and Patrick Keyzer (eds), *'Dangerous' People: Policy, Prediction and Practice* (Routledge, 2011).
4 See Chapter 5 by Helen Punter in this collection.
5 I will use the term 'persons with mental impairments' throughout this chapter as this is the term agreed upon and used in Article 1 of the *Convention on the Rights of Persons with Disabilities*, opened for signature 30 March 2007, 2515 UNTS 3 (entered into force 3 May 2008).
6 Elizabeth C Fistein, Anthony J Holland, Isabel C H Clare and Michael J Gunn, 'A Comparison of Mental Health Legislation from Diverse Commonwealth Jurisdictions' (2009) 32(3) *International Journal of Law and Psychiatry* 147.

Andrew Ashworth and Lucia Zedner place such preventive laws within a public health law context.[7] They write: '[P]ublic health law provides for the taking of liberty-restricting coercive measures against individuals in various contexts, including compulsory treatment and deprivation of liberty.'[8]

Thus, as well as compulsory detention for certain infectious diseases, a number of schemes bring into play the evidence of health practitioners such as the detention of those with cognitive impairments, alcohol and other drug dependency, or severe mental impairments. Most of these schemes are predicated on the risk of harm to others due to problem behaviours as well as possible harm to self.

Preventive justice in relation to these schemes adds an extra layer of treatment and/or behaviour modification to the rationale of the prevention of future harm. It has a 'coercive care'[9] component in addition to extending the notion of preventing future crime to preventing future harm to self or others.

Involuntary detention for the purpose of treatment of those with severe mental impairments has been, and remains, controversial. The first stand-alone mental health statute was England's *Lunacy Act 1890* which created a formal legal structure designed to allow legal oversight and restriction of medical discretion.[10] Since then, there have been different versions of mental health legislation, with rights discourse appearing in different manifestations.[11] In 1994, Tom Campbell referred to laws which enable such detention as 'institutionalised discrimination' because they target one specific group based on prejudicial assumptions.[12] In addition, such laws appear to target a group within a group, namely those who are of low socioeconomic status and often with non-Caucasian backgrounds.[13] Anthony O'Brien has pointed out, for example, that the 'relationship between use of compulsion and social deprivation is ethically troubling because it suggests that those already deprived of social and material resources face an additional loss of personal liberties'.[14] As will be explored later in this chapter, the coming into force of the

7 Andrew Ashworth and Lucia Zedner, *Preventive Justice* (Oxford University Press, 2014).
8 Ibid. 196.
9 See Bernadette McSherry and Ian Freckelton (eds), *Coercive Care: Rights, Law and Policy* (Routledge, 2013).
10 Kathleen Jones, *Mental Health and Social Policy 1845–1959* (Routledge and Kegan Paul, 1960).
11 Philip Fennell, 'Institutionalising the Community: The Codification of Clinical Authority and the Limits of Rights-Based Approaches' in Bernadette McSherry and Penelope Weller (eds), *Rethinking Rights-Based Mental Health Laws* (Hart Publishing, 2010) 13, 15.
12 Tom D Campbell, 'Mental Health Law: Institutionalised Discrimination' (1994) 28 (4) *Australian and New Zealand Journal of Psychiatry* 554, 554.
13 See e.g. Hinemoa Elder and Rees Tapsell, 'Maori and the Mental Health Act' in John Dawson and Kris Gledhill (eds), *New Zealand's Mental Health Act in Practice* (Victoria University Press, 2013) ch 14; Anthony J O'Brien, 'Social Deprivation and the Use of the Mental Health Act' in John Dawson and Kris Gledhill (eds), *New Zealand's Mental Health Act in Practice* (Victoria University Press, 2013) ch 17.
14 Anthony J O'Brien, 'Social Deprivation and the Use of the Mental Health Act' in John Dawson and Kris Gledhill (eds), *New Zealand's Mental Health Act in Practice* (Victoria University Press, 2013).

Convention on the Rights of Persons with Disabilities (CRPD) has given added impetus to calls for the abolition of mental health laws. For example, the Committee on the Rights of Persons with Disabilities has emphasised that 'mental health laws that permit forced treatment . . . must be abolished in order to ensure that full legal capacity is restored to persons with disabilities on an equal basis with others'.[15] Nevertheless, government mental health policy and practice concerning the necessity for laws that enable the involuntary detention of those with mental impairments for the purpose of treatment remains firmly entrenched.

Currently, each of the six Australian states and two territories has mental health legislation that enables the involuntary detention and treatment of persons with mental impairments.[16] In general, the provisions in Australian mental health acts enabling involuntary treatment require there to be some form of 'mental illness' which is largely based on the existence of certain symptoms. There is also a 'need for treatment' criterion such that the treatment must be linked to the mental illness in addition to a criterion relating to risk, dangerousness or harm to self or others.[17]

Section 40(e) of the *Mental Health Act 2013* (Tas) and ss 25(1)(c) and (2)(c) of the *Mental Health Act 2014* (WA) include a criterion that 'the person does not have decision-making capacity' and s 12(1) of the *Mental Health Act 2016* (Qld) refers to a person not having 'capacity to consent to be treated for the illness'. This creates a 'hybrid' risk and capacity civil commitment model. This means that in Tasmania, Western Australia and Queensland, a person diagnosed with mental illness who has decision-making capacity may not be detained and treated without consent, even where there is considered to be a risk to his or her own health and safety, or the safety of others.[18] Because this hybrid model is so

15 Committee on the Rights of Persons with Disabilities, *General Comment No 1 (2014) – Article 12: Equal Recognition before the Law*, 11th sess, UN Doc CRPD/C/GC/1 (19 May 2014) [7].

16 *Mental Health (Care and Treatment) Act 1994* (ACT); *Mental Health Act 2007* (NSW); *Mental Health and Related Services Act 2004* (NT); *Mental Health Act 2016* (Qld); *Mental Health Act 2009* (SA); *Mental Health Act 2013* (Tas); *Mental Health Act 2014* (Vic); *Mental Health Act 2014* (WA).

17 For a full description of these laws, see Bernadette McSherry and Kay Wilson, 'The Concept of Capacity in Australian Mental Health Law Reform: Going in the Wrong Direction?' (2015) 40 *International Journal of Law and Psychiatry* 60, 63.

18 While capacity to consent to treatment is not a criterion for involuntary treatment under s 5 of the *Mental Health Act 2014* (Vic), s 70 requires informed consent to treatment to be sought prior to treatment being given. Section 71 then deals with the situation where a person 'has the capacity to give informed consent, but does not give informed consent to the treatment proposed by the authorised psychiatrist': s 71(1)(a)(ii). It requires the authorised psychiatrist to consult with a range of stakeholders and make enquiries to try to understand why the person does not wish to consent to treatment and to consider a range of less restrictive treatment options before giving involuntary treatment. Section 71(3) enables the psychiatrist to override a person's refusal to give informed consent by stating that '[t]he authorised psychiatrist may make a treatment decision for the patient if the authorised psychiatrist is satisfied that there is no less restrictive way for the patient to be treated other than the treatment

new, it is unknown whether anyone has not been detained and treated on this basis.

What is important to note is that evidence of some form of risk of harm remains a key criterion for the deprivation of liberty under these laws. The next section considers some of the empirical evidence on risk in relation to persons with mental impairments and notes that the literature is equivocal as to any correlation between certain forms of mental impairment and harm to self or others. It may be that this justification for the risk criterion relies more on prejudice than empirical evidence. This point is taken up later.

Evidence of risk of harm to self or others

In relation to risk of self-harm, the general premise would seem to be that those with severe mental impairments are at a higher risk of suicide than others, yet there is surprisingly little written about predictors of suicide. Alex Pokorny conducted a large-scale prospective trial of the prediction of suicide made at the point of admission of 4,800 individuals to the inpatient psychiatric services of a Veterans Administration Medical Center in Houston.[19] Pokorny was unable to find any combination of clinical or other factors that could be used in practice and concluded that '[a]lthough we may reconstruct causal chains and motives after the fact, we do not possess the instruments to predict particular suicides before the fact'.[20] There have been few subsequent studies of predictors of suicide and there is some evidence to suggest that suicides often occur during periods when the risk of self-harm appears to be low.[21]

Much more attention has been paid to the risk of harm to others posed by persons with severe mental impairments. Christopher Ryan argues that it is inappropriate to base mental health laws on the risk of harm to others given that those with mental impairments are 'by and large, no more dangerous' than other members of society, and because the low base rate of violence among those with mental impairments makes it almost impossible to predict who will become violent in the future.[22] Similarly, Matthew Large, Christopher Ryan, Olav Nielssen and Robert Hayes argue that because there are problems associated with predicting the risk of harm to others and there is a tendency of psychiatrists to err on the side of safety, '[t]he dangerousness criterion effectively condones the detention of

proposed by the authorised psychiatrist'. This indicates that s 71 sets up a 'process right' or a right to participate in decision-making rather than a substantive right to refuse treatment.

19 Alex D Pokorny, 'Prediction of Suicide in Psychiatric Patients: Report of a Prospective Study' (1983) 40(3) *Archives of General Psychiatry* 249.

20 Ibid. 257.

21 J Y S Dong, T P Ho and C K Kan, 'A Case-Control Study of 92 Cases of In-Patient Suicides' (2005) 87(1) *Journal of Affective Disorders* 91.

22 Christopher J Ryan, 'Capacity as a Determinant of Non-Consensual Treatment of the Mentally Ill in Australia' (2011) 18(2) *Psychiatry, Psychology and Law* 248, 248.

many mentally ill people who will never become dangerous, so that it might capture the few who will'.[23]

The association between violence and certain forms of severe mental impairments remains unclear. Michael Norko and Madelon Baranoski reviewed a number of studies on correlations of violence, focusing particularly on mental illness as a key correlate, and concluded that the 'research on violence has not produced a clearly uniform picture of the most important mental health variables associated with risk of violent behaviour'.[24] They also reviewed the accuracy of predictions of future harm primarily in relation to those studied in psychiatric emergency departments and concluded that '[c]linical assessments of risk achieve better-than-chance accuracy, although clinicians may not be particularly good at identifying specific conditions under which violence will occur'.[25]

It does appear that members of a small subgroup of those with severe mental impairments may be arrested because their hallucinations or delusions are associated with violence or because they cause public disturbance.[26] Paul Mullen has suggested that most of the violence among those diagnosed with schizophrenia is perpetrated by members of relatively small subgroups, who probably constitute no more than 10–15 per cent of all those diagnosed with schizophrenia.[27] This is a small number given that it is estimated that approximately 0.5 per cent of Australians – around 115,000 people – have some form of psychotic disorder, just under half of which is diagnosed as schizophrenia.[28] Mullen posits that such subgroups will generally include young men with a history of disadvantage in childhood, antisocial and violent behaviour in adolescence, substance misuse, unemployment and a disorganised lifestyle. Thus, severe mental impairment may be best viewed as one of many criminogenic factors for violent behaviour.[29]

23 Matthew Large, Christopher Ryan, Olav Nielssen and Robert Hayes, 'The Danger of Dangerousness: Why We Must Remove the Dangerousness Criterion from Our Mental Health Acts' (2008) 34 *Journal of Medical Ethics* 877, 879.

24 Michael A Norko and Madelon V Baranoski, 'The State of Contemporary Risk Assessment Research' (2005) 50(1) *Canadian Journal of Psychiatry* 18, 24.

25 Ibid. 23.

26 J Junginger, K Claypoole, R Laygo and A Crisanti, 'Effects of Serious Mental Illness and Substance Abuse on Criminal Offenses' (2006) 57(6) *Psychiatric Services* 879; J K Petersen, J L Skeem, E Hart, S Vidal and F Keith, 'Comparing the Offense Patterns of Offenders with and without Mental Disorder: Exploring the Criminalization Hypothesis' (2012) 61(12) *Psychiatric Services* 1217.

27 Paul E Mullen, 'Schizophrenia and Violence: From Correlations to Preventive Strategies' (2006) 12(4) *Advances in Psychiatric Treatment* 239. See also Paul E Mullen, 'A Reassessment of the Link between Mental Disorder and Violent Behaviour, and its Implications for Clinical Practice' (2007) 31 *Australian and New Zealand Journal of Psychiatry* 3.

28 Vera A Morgan, Anna Waterreus, Assen Jablensky, Andrew Mackinnon, John J McGrath, Vaughan Carr, Robert Bush, David Castle, Martin Cohen, Carol Harvey, Cherrie Galletly, Helen J Stain, Amanda Neil, Patrick McGorry, Barbara Hocking, Sonal Shah and Suzy Saw, *People Living with a Psychotic Illness* (Commonwealth of Australia, 2010).

29 See also Matt Vogel, 'Mental Illness and Criminal Behavior' (2014) 8(4) *Sociology Compass* 337.

The one factor that does seem to be universally associated with a significantly increased risk of violence is substance abuse.[30] In a series of studies conducted on a sample of individuals with severe mental impairments in Victoria, Mullen and colleagues found that the highest rates of violence occurred for those diagnosed with schizophrenia in conjunction with a substance abuse problem.[31] Mental health laws, however, are keen to focus on 'mental illness' as a discrete category, and substance use is generally seen as irrelevant to a diagnosis.[32]

Jennifer Skeem, Jillian Peterson and Eric Silver point out that there is a widely held belief among the public and thus policy-makers that 'mental illness' causes criminal behaviour.[33] They state that 'there is little compelling evidence that (a) mental illness directly causes criminal behaviour for this population, or (b) that effective mental health services meaningfully reduce new crimes and new victims'.[34] If the evidence is so unclear in relation to the risk of harm to self or others and diagnoses of 'mental illness', why then do mental health laws seem to assume there is a link? Social psychology may provide some answers in this regard and this is taken up in the next section.

The role of public perception and the marginalisation of certain groups

Arthur Crisp and colleagues have argued that public perceptions of severe mental impairments – in particular schizophrenia – reflect media reports linking these conditions to violence.[35] Although it appears that the portrayal of mental health issues in the Australian media in general is improving,[36] many media stories still

30 Junginger et al., above n 26; Petersen et al., above n 26.

31 Paul Mullen, Philip Burgess, Cameron Wallace, Simon Palmer and David Ruschena, 'Community Care and Criminal Offending in Schizophrenia' (2000) 355 *Lancet* 614; Cameron Wallace, Paul Mullen and Philip Burgess, 'Criminal Offending in Schizophrenia over a 25 Year Period Marked by Deinstitutionalization and Increasing Prevalence of Comorbid Substance Use Disorders' (2004) 161(4) *American Journal of Psychiatry* 716; Cameron Wallace, Paul Mullen, Philip Burgess, Simon Palmer, David Ruschena and Chris Browne, 'Serious Criminal Offending and Mental Disorder' (1998) 172(6) *British Journal of Psychiatry* 477.

32 Some mental health statutes specifically exclude substance use from consideration in determining whether the person concerned has a mental illness. For example, s 4(2) of the *Mental Health Act 2014* (Vic) states that '[a] person is not to be considered to have mental illness by reason only of any one or more of the following . . . (l) that the person uses drugs or consumes alcohol'.

33 Jennifer Skeem, Jillian Petersen and Eric Silver, 'Toward Research-Informed Policy for High-Risk Offenders with Severe Mental Illnesses' in Bernadette McSherry and Patrick Keyzer (eds), *Dangerous People: Policy, Prediction and Practice* (Routledge, 2011) 111.

34 Ibid. 113.

35 A H Crisp, M Gelder, S Rix, H I Metzler and O J Rowlands, 'Stigmatisation of People with Mental Illnesses' (2000) 177 *British Journal of Psychiatry* 4.

36 Catherine Francis, Jane Pirkis, Richard Warwick Blood, David Dunt, Philip Michael Burgess, Belinda Morley Andrew Stewart and Peter Putnis, 'The Portrayal of Mental

link violence with severe mental impairments such as schizophrenia.[37] In England, for example, Arun Chopra and Gillian Doody analysed newspaper articles in Nottingham and Dorset referring to schizophrenia and found that they had a negative tone five times as often as a positive tone and 80 per cent of the negatively toned stories related to crime and violence.[38] Similarly, a study of Australian online and print news media stories referring to schizophrenia found that 47.3 per cent featured violence in some way and 46 per cent were viewed as 'stigmatizing'.[39] This study found that 'stigmatizing stories appeared at higher rates in tabloid newspapers, in stories referring to foreign events, and in stories where the affected person was young, male, and linked to substance use'.[40] The foreign events referred to here are often mass killings such as the murders that occurred in Norway in mid-2011.

Theories of social exclusion may help explain why those with severe mental impairments are portrayed as categorically different to the majority and prone to violence even when there is not a strong evidentiary basis for this. The concepts of 'prejudice', 'stigma' and 'discrimination' are central to explanations as to why certain groups are marginalised.

Prejudice means prejudgment (from the Latin '*prae*' and '*judicium*'), and although the term is generally linked to derogatory social attitudes or beliefs, there are many studies indicating that most individuals are prejudiced in the sense of making assumptions about certain groups.[41] Susan Fiske refers to 'gut level' prejudices that stem from anticipated threats, thus affecting the ways in which a certain group is seen to threaten the goals or interests of the person concerned. Such prejudices may provoke emotions such as fear or anger.[42] Most research on prejudice has focused on sexism and racism rather than disability or sexual orientation.[43] Instead, the concept of 'stigma' has been used primarily in studies focusing on exclusion and mental impairments.[44]

Health and Illness in Australian Non-Fiction Media' (2004) 38(7) *Australian and New Zealand Journal of Psychiatry* 541.

37 Belinda Cain, Roseanne Currie, Eleanor Danks, Fiona Du, Erica Hodgson, Jennifer May, Kirsty O'Loghlen, Yen Phan, Jennifer Powter, Nayab Rizwan, Shazmi Shahim, Dominique Simsion, Steve Loughnan and Nick Haslam '"Schizophrenia" in the Australian Print and Online News Media' (2014) 6(2) *Psychosis: Psychological, Social and Integrative Approaches* 97.

38 Arun K Chopra and Gillian A Doody, 'Crime Rates and Local Newspaper Coverage of Schizophrenia' (2007) 31 *Psychiatric Bulletin* 206.

39 Cain et al., above n 37.

40 Ibid. 102.

41 See Graham M Vaughan and Michael A Hogg, *Social Psychology* (Pearson Australia, 6th edn, 2011) 376 ff.

42 Susan T Fiske, 'Stereotyping, Prejudice and Discrimination' in Daniel T Gilbert, Susan T Fiske and Gardner Lindzey (eds), *The Handbook of Social Psychology* (McGraw-Hill, 4th edn, 1998) 357.

43 See Vaughan and Hogg, above n 41, 378–9.

44 Graham Thornicroft, *Shunned: Discrimination Against People with Mental Illness* (Oxford University Press, 2006).

The term 'stigma' derives from the Greek for 'mark' or 'tattoo'. In Ancient Greece, the term referred to the mark placed on those worthy of contempt by burning with a hot iron. The plural form 'stigmata' in the Christian tradition referred to the marks that were said to appear on the devout which resembled the wounds of the crucified Christ. Erving Goffman used the term to refer to an attribute that discredited an individual, reducing him or her 'from a whole and usual person, to a tainted, discounted one'.[45] Goffman set out three categories of stigmatising conditions: 'blemishes of individual character' that are assumed to reflect immoral or deviant behaviour; 'abominations of the body' arising from physical disfigurements or deviations from what is considered 'normal'; and 'tribal stigmas' that are based on the membership of a despised racial, ethnic or religious group. Goffman states that there is a belief that 'the person with a stigma is not quite human'.[46]

Social exclusion is closely related to stigmatisation. Carol Miller and Cheryl Kaiser observe that stigma is so interconnected with rejection and exclusion that prejudice towards members of stigmatised groups is often measured by asking people to indicate the social distance they want to keep between themselves and the stigmatised group.[47] Stigmatisation and social exclusion are so pervasive that some researchers have posited that these processes serve to enhance personal or group self-esteem for those doing the excluding,[48] as well as serving to alleviate discomfort and anxiety. There is some research suggesting that those diagnosed with mental illness have been subjected to social exclusion because people tend to feel uncomfortable around those who they know or believe to have a mental impairment in part because they are perceived as unpredictable and 'dangerous'.[49]

Robert Brooks has pointed out that 'almost all cultures have viewed mental illness as a deviant form, subject to negative social sanctions'.[50] In this regard, Michael Perlin has coined the term 'sanism' to describe 'an irrational prejudice of the same quality and character of other irrational prejudices that cause (and are

45 Erving Goffman, *Stigma: Notes on the Management of Spoiled Identity* (Prentice-Hall, 1963) 3.

46 Ibid. 4–6.

47 Carol Miller and Cheryl Kaiser, 'Implications of Mental Models of Self and Others for the Targets of Stigmatization' in Mark R Leary (ed.), *Interpersonal Rejection* (Oxford University Press, 2001).

48 T A Wills, 'Downward Comparison Principles in Social Psychology' (1981) 90(2) *Psychiatric Bulletin* 245; H Tajfel and J C Turner, 'The Social Identity Theory of Inter-group Behavior' in S Worchel and W G Austin (eds), *The Psychology of Intergroup Relations* (Nelson-Hall, 2nd edn, 1986) 7.

49 Amerigo Farina and Kenneth Ring, 'The Influence of Perceive Mental Illness on Interpersonal Relations' (1965) 70(1) *Journal of Abnormal Psychology* 47; Amerigo Farina, 'Stigma' in K T Mueser and N Tarrier (eds), *Handbook of Social Functioning in Schizophrenia* (Allyn and Bacon, 1998) 247.

50 Robert Brooks, 'Official Madness: A Cross-Cultural Study of Involuntary Civil Confinement Based on Mental Illness' in Jane Hubert (ed.), *Madness, Disability and Social Exclusion: The Archaeology of 'Difference'* (Routledge, 2000) 9, 11–12.

reflected in) prevailing social attitudes of racism, sexism, homophobia, and ethnic bigotry'.[51]

In recent years, there has been a move away from the concept of stigma towards that of discrimination to explain the experiences of those who are excluded. Discrimination here is used in the sense of treating a person with mental impairment differently to others, thus violating the principle of equality before the law. This preference for the use of the word discrimination results from the term 'stigma' being seen as locating the problem within the individual who is excluded rather than focusing on the negative attitudes of those carrying out exclusory practices. Graham Thornicroft argues that much of the work on stigma 'has been beside the point' because it has concentrated on the attitudes of 'normal' people to certain groups of individuals and has focused on hypothetical situations, rather than examining the actual experiences of those who have been 'shunned'.[52] Thornicroft states that shifting the focus from *stigma* to *discrimination* has the advantage of focusing on actual behaviour rather than just attitudes and can lead to much-needed research on interventions to change discriminatory behaviour.

Social psychological theories of social exclusion can thus assist in explaining why certain groups have been singled out for preventive detention. The work on prejudice, stigma and, more recently, discrimination also helps to explain why the perceived link between violence and severe mental impairments remains a part of public perceptions.

Human rights as a framework for change

Risk as a central criterion for the involuntary detention of persons with mental impairments appears intractable given the tendency to link severe mental impairments with violence despite a lack of strong evidence in this regard. Social psychology helps explain why this link remains in place. This section now turns to a consideration of how human rights may be able to provide a framework for change despite the intractable nature of risk as a criterion for detention of those with mental impairments.

The Convention on the Rights of Persons with Disabilities

The CRPD currently has some 160 signatories, with Australia ratifying it on 17 July 2008. Australia is therefore bound to comply with its provisions.[53] However,

51 Michael L Perlin, *International Human Rights and Mental Disability Law: When the Silenced Are Heard* (Oxford University Press, 2012) 34.

52 Graham Thornicroft, *Shunned: Discrimination Against People with Mental Illness* (Oxford University Press, 2006) 191.

53 *Vienna Convention on the Law of Treaties*, opened for signature 23 May 1969, 1155 UNTS 331 (entered into force 27 January 1980): Article 26 sets out that '[e]very treaty in force is binding upon the parties to it and must be performed by them in

the Articles set out in the CRPD do not form part of Australian law unless they are specifically incorporated by Parliament into domestic law.[54]

Neither 'disability' nor 'persons with disabilities' is defined in the CRPD, but Article 1 states that the latter term includes 'those who have long-term physical, *mental*, intellectual or sensory *impairments* which in interaction with various barriers may hinder their full and effective participation in society on an equal basis with others' (emphasis added). The Preamble recognises that disability is 'an evolving concept' and results from the interaction between individuals with impairments and societal barriers.

When Australia ratified the CRPD, it included a declaration which is a form of 'interpretative' statement.[55] This differs from a reservation which may serve to limit the legal effect of certain provisions in a treaty.[56] Australia's declaration attempts to clarify its understanding of certain provisions. It states:

> Australia recognizes that persons with disability enjoy legal capacity on an equal basis with others in all aspects of life. Australia declares its understanding *that the Convention allows for fully supported or substituted decision-making arrangements*, which provide for decisions to be made on behalf of a person, only where such arrangements are necessary, as a last resort and subject to safeguards;
>
> Australia recognizes that every person with disability has a right to respect for his or her physical and mental integrity on an equal basis with others. Australia further declares its understanding that *the Convention allows for compulsory assistance or treatment of persons*, including measures taken for the treatment of mental disability, where such treatment is necessary, as a last resort and subject to safeguards.[57]

good faith'; Article 27 provides that '[a] party may not invoke the provisions of its internal law as justification for its failure to perform a treaty'; Article 29 provides that '[u]nless a different intention appears from the treaty or is otherwise established, a treaty is binding upon each party in respect of its entire territory'. This means that when a federation enters into a treaty, it binds all of the individual states within that federation and the federation cannot use the internal laws that create its federal structure to argue that the treaty is not binding on one part of its territory. This is supported by s 61 (executive power) of the *Australian Constitution* which gives the Commonwealth Executive the power to enter treaties on behalf of Australia and to bind the states, although in practice the Executive consults with the Commonwealth Parliament and the Treaties Council, part of the Council of Australian Governments, prior to entering into a treaty: www.dfat.gov.au/treaties/making; www.coag.gov.au/treaties_council (accessed 5 September 2016). In addition, Article 4(5) of the CRPD provides that '[t]he provisions of the present Convention shall extend to all parts of federal states without any limitations or exceptions'.

54 *Kioa v West* (1985) 159 CLR 550, 570 (Gibbs CJ).

55 *Convention on the Rights of Persons with Disabilities: Declarations and Reservations (Australia)*, opened for signature 30 March 2007, 999 UNTS 3 (entered into force 3 May 2008).

56 A Kaczorowska, *Public International Law* (Routledge, 4th edn, 2010) 106.

57 *Declarations and Reservations*, above n 55 (emphasis added).

Article 14(1)(b) of the CRPD states that 'the existence of a disability shall in no case justify a deprivation of liberty'. The United Nations Office of the High Commissioner for Human Rights has stated that:

> [I]t is contrary to article 14 to allow for the detention of persons with disabilities based on the perceived danger of persons to themselves or to others. The involuntary detention of persons with disabilities based on presumptions of risk or dangerousness tied to disability labels is contrary to the right to liberty.[58]

Nevertheless, some member states, including Australia, have interpreted Article 14 as meaning that although people with a disability cannot be involuntarily detained 'solely' because of their disability, a deprivation of liberty can be justified if there is a risk of harm to self or others.[59] This approach appears to be supported by paragraph 19 of the United Nations Human Rights Committee's General Comment on the right to liberty set out in Article 9 of the *International Covenant on Civil and Political Rights*.[60] Paragraph 19 states that:

> [t]he existence of a disability shall not in itself justify a deprivation of liberty but rather any deprivation of liberty must be necessary and proportionate, *for the purpose of protecting the individual in question from serious harm or preventing injury to others.*[61]

To further complicate matters, it has been argued that Article 14 may permit involuntary detention provided it is 'de-linked' from disability and is drafted in terms that are 'disability neutral'. This would potentially undermine the right to liberty more generally, as it would permit member states to implement preventive detention regimes for all people whom it considers dangerous.[62]

The way forward for post-CRPD mental health laws

Some scholars have argued that risk should be replaced by 'capacity' as the key criterion for compulsory treatment, either through 'fused' guardianship and

58 United Nations Office of the High Commissioner for Human Rights, *Statement on article 14 of the Convention on the Rights of Persons with Disabilities* (September 2014), available online at www.ohchr.org/EN/NewsEvents/Pages/DisplayNews.aspx?NewsID=15183&LangID=E (accessed 5 September 2016).

59 United Nations Enable, *Daily summary of discussions related to Article 10: Liberty and Security of the Person* (26 May 2004)United Nations, available online at www.un.org/esa/socdev/enable/rights/ahc3sum10.htm (accessed 5 September 2016).

60 United Nations Human Rights Committee, *General Comment No 35: Article 9 (Liberty and Security of Person)*, UN Doc CCPR/C/GC/35 (16 December 2014).

61 Ibid. [19] (emphasis added).

62 Peter Bartlett, 'The United Nations Convention on the Rights of Persons with Disabilities and Mental Health Law' (2012) 75(5) *The Modern Law Review* 752, 773.

mental health laws[63] or, at the very least, through revised mental health laws[64] based primarily on a lack of 'mental' or decision-making capacity.

This, however, also conflicts with recent interpretations of the CRPD. Article 12(2) of the CRPD recognises that 'persons with disabilities enjoy legal capacity on an equal basis with others in all aspects of life'. Such a recognition of universal 'legal capacity' has been interpreted as meaning that there should be no allowance for substituted decision-making on the grounds of a perceived lack of 'mental' capacity. The United Nations Committee on the Rights of Persons with Disabilities' General Comment on Article 12 points out that:

> the concepts of mental and legal capacity have been conflated so that where a person is considered to have impaired decision-making skills, often because of a cognitive or psychosocial disability, his or her legal capacity to make a particular decision is consequently removed . . . a person's disability and/or decision-making skills are taken as legitimate grounds for denying his or her legal capacity and lowering his or her status as a person before the law. Article 12 does not permit such discriminatory denial of legal capacity.[65]

Laws that enable involuntary treatment on the basis of a loss of decision-making capacity on this view are therefore discriminatory. Mental capacity should no longer be intrinsically linked to legal capacity. In Genevra Richardson's words, '[i]n its purest form there is no point beyond which legal capacity is lost. There is no binary divide'.[66]

63 John Dawson and George Szmukler, 'Fusion of Mental Health and Incapacity Legislation' (2006) 188 *British Journal of Psychiatry* 504; George Szmukler, Rowena Daw and John Dawson, 'A Model Law Fusing Incapacity and Mental Health Legislation' (2010) 20 *Journal of Mental Health Law* 11; Rowena Daw, 'The Case for a Fusion Law: Challenges and Issues' in Bernadette McSherry and Ian Freckelton (eds), *Coercive Care: Rights, Law and Policy* (Routledge, 2013) 93; George Szmukler, Rowena Daw and Felicity Callard, 'Mental Health Law and the UN Convention on the Rights of Persons with Disabilities' (2014) 37(3) *International Journal of Law and Psychiatry* 245.

64 Matthew Large, Christopher Ryan, Olav Nielssen and Robert Hayes, 'The Danger of Dangerousness: Why We Must Remove the Dangerousness Criterion from our Mental Health Acts' (2008) 34(12) *Journal of Medical Ethics* 877; Christopher Ryan, 'Capacity as a Determinant of Non-Consensual Treatment of the Mentally Ill in Australia' (2011) 18 *Psychiatry, Psychology and Law* 248; Christopher Ryan, Olav Nielssen, Michael Paton and Matthew Large, 'Clinical Decisions in Psychiatry Should Not be Based on Risk Assessment' (2010) 18(5)*Australasian Psychiatry* 398; Sascha Mira Callaghan and Christopher Ryan, 'Is There a Future for Involuntary Treatment in Rights-based Mental Health Law?' (2014) 21(5) *Psychiatry, Psychology and Law* 747.

65 United Nations Committee on the Rights of Persons with Disabilities, *General Comment Article 12: Equal Recognition before the Law*, 11th sess, UN Doc CRPD/C/GC/1 (25 November 2013) [13].

66 Genevra Richardson, 'Mental Capacity in the Shadow of Suicide: What Can the Law Do?' (2013) 9(1) *International Journal of Law in Context* 87, 92.

A few scholars have taken a 'purist' approach in arguing that the complete abolition of mental health laws would be in line with the CRPD.[67] However, with the current state of mental health service delivery, many who would benefit from treatment would go untreated. There is the danger of increased imprisonment and, from a practical perspective, no government has signalled a desire to go down this track.

Perhaps the 'least worst' solution is to try to shift the focus away from involuntary to voluntary treatment wherever possible. The CRPD is unique in combining positive and negative rights, placing obligations on member states to provide adequate services in the community.[68] The development and wider availability of a broad range of treatment options is necessary for the realisation of the rights to legal capacity and liberty. For example, it is difficult to view the right to liberty for persons with disabilities in isolation from the supports that are available for them in the community. This is especially the case where the reality is that de-institutionalisation has not been implemented, or has only been partially implemented, in many states and therefore many persons still spend all or large parts of their lives in institutions.[69]

The right to liberty cannot be realised where it effectively leads to a choice between homelessness, squalid and unsafe rooming-houses, prison or accommodation otherwise unsuitable for individual needs. Compliance with the CRPD, as Terry Carney and Fleur Beaupert note, goes well beyond law reform, to reforms in service provision and social attitudes.[70]

Andrew Ashworth and Lucia Zedner have called for 'a concerted effort to articulate appropriate guiding values and limiting principles' in relation to preventive justice measures.[71] One important limiting principle is that liberty-restricting mental health laws should operate very much as a last resort. Recent mental health acts contain provisions to the effect that before compulsory treatment can be ordered, there must be no less restrictive means reasonably available to enable the person to receive treatment.[72] However, if psychiatric and support

67 See e.g. Tina Minkowitz, 'The United Nations Convention on the Rights of Persons with Disabilities and the Right to be Free from Non Consensual Psychiatric Interventions' (2007) 34(2) *Syracuse Journal of International Law and Commerce* 405; Tina Minkowitz, 'Abolishing Mental Health Laws to Comply with the Convention on the Rights of Persons with Disabilities' in Bernadette McSherry and Penelope Weller (eds), *Rethinking Rights-Based Mental Health Laws* (Hart Publishing, 2010) 151.

68 See Bernadette McSherry and Kay Wilson, 'Detention and Treatment Down Under: Human Rights and Mental Health Laws in Australia and New Zealand' (2011) 19(4) *Medical Law Review* 548.

69 Arie Rimmerman, *Social Inclusion of People with Disabilities: National and International Perspectives* (Cambridge University Press, 2013) 138.

70 Terry Carney and Fleur Beaupert, 'Public and Private Bricolage – Challenges Balancing Law, Services and Civil Society in Advancing "CRPD" Supported Decision-Making' (2013) 36(1) *University of New South Wales Law Journal* 175.

71 Ashworth and Zedner, above n 7, 250.

72 See e.g. s 5(d) *Mental Health Act 2014* (Vic); s 25(2)(e) *Mental Health Act 2014* (WA); s 13 *Mental Health Act 2016* (Qld).

services are either inadequate or non-existent, then there will be no less restrictive means other than compulsory treatment. Limiting principles for preventive justice in relation to compulsory treatment are not enough. Guiding values should also be prominent and focus on providing options for good-quality community mental health services and supports to ensure voluntary treatment wherever possible.

Conclusion

The notion of the prevention of risk of harm to self or others is entrenched in mental health laws. This reflects social psychology research indicating that certain groups are marginalised because of prejudiced assumptions, stigma and discrimination. As George Szmukler and Nikolas Rose have observed, '[r]isk factors might inadvertently offer new markers for discrimination and social exclusion'.[73] Empirical research and human rights arguments which challenge the detention of persons with mental impairments on the basis of risk have thus far had little impact.

Ultimately, it may be better to concentrate on improving treatment, care and support systems for those with mental impairments in general, than arguing for the abolition of mental health laws based on risk. Using the CRPD to emphasise the obligations placed on member states to provide adequate services and accommodation may in the long run prove more effective than waiting for laws enabling involuntary detention and treatment of persons with severe mental impairments to disappear. Only then will preventive 'justice' in relation to those with severe mental impairments not only be done but also be seen to be done.[74]

73 George Szmukler and Nikolas Rose, 'Risk Assessment in Mental Health Care: Values and Costs' (2013) 31(1) *Behavioral Sciences and the Law* 125, 135.

74 Paraphrasing Lord Hewart CJ in *R v Sussex Justices,* Ex parte *McCarthy* [1924] 1 KB 256, 259.

5 Policing persons with mental illness

Preventive justice or preventing injustice?

Helen Punter

Introduction

Recent years have seen the proliferation of various laws, policies and procedures to address the over-representation of persons with mental disorders, or 'PMI',[1] within criminal justice systems internationally. A widespread strategy used to reduce harm to, or harm by, PMI and to prevent unnecessary contact with the criminal justice system has been the embedding of police powers in mental health legislation.[2] Such laws authorise police officers to apprehend or detain a person and take him or her to mental health services for assessment (usually involuntarily) if they reasonably believe the person has a mental illness and there is a significant risk of harm to the person or others.

Rapid growth has occurred in the area of specialised intervention programs.[3] These types of programs focus on establishing collaborative relationships between police services and mental health services. Their overall aim is to enhance police officers' interactions with PMI, with a focus on ensuring the wellbeing of all participants involved in mental health crises.[4]

1 It is recognised that terminology is contested in this area. For the purposes of this chapter, the term 'persons with mental illness' (PMI) is used throughout. The term 'mental illness' is used, as this is the terminology utilised throughout Australian mental health legislation. However, it should be recognised that Canadian and United Kingdom mental health laws use the term 'mental disorder'. 'Mental illness' is considered treatable whereas 'mental disorder' can include non-treatable disorders: John Ellery Gray, Bernadette Maree McSherry, Richard L O'Reilly and Penelope June Weller, 'Australian and Canadian Mental Health Acts Compared' (2010) 44(12) *Australian and New Zealand Journal of Psychiatry* 1126, 1129. For this chapter, the terminology of 'persons with mental illness' (PMI) encompasses both categories, of treatable and non-treatable.

2 For the purposes of this chapter, the term 'police apprehension powers' will be used to describe provisions that exist in most mental health legislation in Australia, Canada and the United Kingdom.

3 The term 'specialised intervention programs' is being used to describe the police-led and co-response models used for dealing with mentally ill persons. See Amanda Butler, 'Mental Illness and the Criminal Justice System: A Review of Global Perspectives and Promising Practices' (Research Report, International Centre for Criminal Law Reform, 2013).

4 See Martha Williams Deane, Henry J Steadman, Randy Borum, Bonita M Veysey and Joseph P Morrissey, 'Emerging Partnerships Between Mental Health and Law Enforcement' (1999) 50(1) *Psychiatric Services* 99.

The first section of this chapter will analyse police practices such as police apprehension powers and specialised intervention programs as instances of preventive justice. The second section considers whether police apprehension powers and specialised intervention programs are compatible with human rights such as the right to liberty and protection against arbitrary detention; raising questions as to whether the powers made available through these types of laws create discrimination against PMI. The third section will consider whether such laws and programs can be beneficial to PMI, such as through facilitating access to treatment and mental health services and reducing contact with the criminal justice system, thus reducing the 'criminalisation' of PMI. From this perspective, this form of policing may be envisaged as *preventing injustice*, thus promoting greater autonomy, social engagement and quality of life for PMI. Overall, this chapter aims to analyse the place of police apprehension powers and specialised intervention programs within a preventive justice framework and elucidate some of the ways in which they can both limit and promote individual liberty for those individuals who are subject to such legal rules and procedures.

Police apprehension powers and specialised intervention programs

In common law jurisdictions such as Australia, Canada, the United Kingdom and the United States, mental illness is a high-profile issue, and the interaction between the police and PMI has gained particular attention. These common law jurisdictions have similar histories regarding the movement of PMI from institutions into the community for treatment and care. Deinstitutionalisation was the process whereby state mental health facilities, established to care for the mentally ill, were closed or reduced and patients moved to community-based care.[5] Deinstitutionalisation of the mental health care system, the treatment of mental illness via pharmaceuticals[6] and reduced financial support of mental health services have resulted in high numbers of PMI living within the community, increasing public visibility, often resulting in increased contact with police.[7]

Although the role of police in responding to PMI undergoing mental health crises is a contentious issue, this role is now an embedded part of police officers' routine duties. This means that police are 'gatekeepers' not only to the criminal justice system but also to mental health services.[8] There has been an increase in the awareness that the policing of PMI needs to be done differently, and for that reason different initiatives have been developed, aimed at enhancing police

5 George Paulson, *Closing the Asylums: Causes and Consequences of the Deinstitutionalization Movement* (McFarland and Company, 2012).

6 Ibid. The advent of pharmaceuticals to treat mental health issues facilitated the treatment of mentally ill individuals within the community.

7 See e.g. H Richard Lamb and Leona L Bachrach, 'Some Perspectives on Deinstitutionalization' (2001) 52(8) *Psychiatric Services* 1039.

8 Victoria Herrington and Katrina Clifford, 'Policing Mental Illness: Examining the Police Role in Addressing Mental Ill-Health' in Isabelle Bartkowiak-Theron and Nicole L Asquith (eds), *Policing Vulnerability* (Federation Press, 2012) 117.

officers' interactions with PMI and improving the safety of both police and persons involved in mental health crises. Provisions such as police apprehension powers are embedded in mental health legislation across Australia, Canada and the United Kingdom, and initiatives such as specialised intervention programs have been adopted internationally; the Crisis Intervention Team (CIT) program originally developed in the United States is now utilised in both Australia and Canada.[9]

Mental health legislation: police apprehension powers

Mental health statutes are widely used in developed countries:

> to address the issue of how a person with a severe mental illness which is likely to cause harm to the person or others and which makes voluntary admission [to a mental health facility] impossible, can be admitted and treated while protecting the person's legal rights.[10]

Provisions within these statutes provide police officers with powers to apprehend individuals if the officer is satisfied or reasonably believes that a person has, or appears to have, a mental illness. Further, the apprehension of the person must be necessary to prevent harm to self or others. Generally, the purpose of the detention is to facilitate the transportation of the person to a mental health facility to undergo assessment (often involuntarily). It is these powers, provided within mental health legislation, that are the focus of this chapter.[11]

9 See e.g. Amanda Butler, 'Mental Illness and the Criminal Justice System: A Review of Global Perspectives and Promising Practices' (Research Report, International Centre for Criminal Law Reform, 2013).

10 John Ellery Gray, Bernadette Maree McSherry, Richard L O'Reilly and Penelope June Weller, 'Australian and Canadian Mental Health Acts Compared' (2010) 44(12) *Australian and New Zealand Journal of Psychiatry* 1126, 1126.

11 Legislation reviewed for this chapter: Australia: *Mental Health (Treatment and Care) Act 1994* (ACT) s 37; *Mental Health Act 2007* (NSW) s 22; *Mental Health and Related Services Act 2000* (NT) s 32A; *Mental Health Act 2000* (Qld) ss 33–36; At the time of writing this chapter, the *Mental Health Act 2000* (Qld) was under review, and police apprehension powers were flagged for removal from the Act. *Mental Health Act 2009* (SA) s 57; *Mental Health Act 2013* (Tas) ss 17–22; *Mental Health Act 2014* (Vic) s 351; *Mental Health Act 2014* (WA) s 156. Canada: *Mental Health Act*, RSA 2000, c M-13, s 12; *Mental Health Act*, RSBC 1996, c 288, s 28; *Mental Health Act*, SM 1998, c M-110, s 12; *Mental Health Act*, RSNB 1973, c M-10, s 10; *Mental Health Care and Treatment Act*, SNL 2006, c M-9.1, s 20; *Mental Health Act*, RSNWT 1988, c M-10, s 11; *Involuntary Psychiatric Treatment Act*, SNS 2005, c 42, s 14; *Mental Health Act*, RSNWT (Nu) 1988, c M-10, s 11; *Mental Health Act*, RSO 1990, c M-7, s 17; *Mental Health Act*, RSPEI 1988, c M-6.1, s 8; *An Act Respecting the Protection of Persons Whose Mental State Presents a Danger to Themselves or to Others*, RSQ c P-38.001, s 8; *Mental Health Services Act*, SS 1984-85-86, c M-13.1, s 20; *Mental Health Act*, RSY 2002, c 150, s 8. United Kingdom: *Mental Health Act 1983* (UK) c 20, s 136; *Mental Health (Northern Ireland) Order 1986* (NI) s 130; *Mental Health (Care and Treatment) (Scotland) Act 2003* s 297.

Most mental health legislation in Australia, Canada and the United Kingdom contain provisions that empower police to apprehend PMI that are usually known as police apprehension powers. The key goals of mental health legislation are to provide for the involuntary assessment, treatment and protection of PMI.[12] In line with this overall aim, police apprehension powers ultimately provide police with an alternative to a criminal justice response. The New South Wales legislation is explicit in this respect, stating that apprehension under the relevant section 'would be beneficial to the person's welfare to be dealt with in accordance with this Act, rather than otherwise in accordance with law'.[13] Although there are similarities in approaches between the jurisdictions, there are some distinct differences. The various approaches and criteria found in the Australian, Canadian and the United Kingdom mental health laws are briefly described in the next section.

Harm criteria

All jurisdictions in Australia, Canada and the United Kingdom set out harm criteria, which outline the type and degree of harm to self or others (and in some cases property)[14] that justifies apprehension. Although most refer to physical harm, broad harm criteria are adopted in most jurisdictions which do not limit harm to physical and/or bodily harm. For example, the Tasmanian provision is that '[t]he person's safety or the safety of other persons is likely to be at risk if the person is not taken into protective custody'.[15] A number of Canadian provinces also include a 'deterioration' criterion. Newfoundland and Labrador's legislation provides the power to apprehend a person where a police officer believes that a person 'as a result of the mental disorder . . . is likely to suffer substantial physical or mental deterioration'.[16]

Mental illness criteria

All jurisdictions in Australia, Canada and the United Kingdom require police officers to have at least some suspicion that the individual who has come to their attention has a mental illness.[17] The requirement of mental illness was explicit in all but one[18] of the mental health statutes reviewed. The threshold that a police officer must meet before utilising the powers outlined in these sections varies between jurisdictions. The criteria range from a low threshold of 'it appears to the

12 See e.g. Genevra Richardson, 'Balancing Autonomy and Risk: A Failure of Nerve in England and Wales?' (2007) 30(1) *International Journal of Law and Psychiatry* 71.
13 *Mental Health Act 2007* (NSW) s 22(1)(b).
14 *Mental Health Act 2009* (SA) s 57(c)(ii); *Mental Health Act 2014* (WA) s 156(1)(b)(ii).
15 *Mental Health Act 2013* (Tas) s 17(1)(c); see also *Mental Health Act 2014* (WA) s 156(1)(b)(i).
16 *Mental Health Care and Treatment Act*, SNL 2006, c M-9.1, s 20(b); see e.g. *Mental Health Act*, SM 1998, c M-110, s 12.
17 Some mental health legislation indicates that police officers are not required to exercise clinical judgment. See e.g. *Mental Health and Related Services Act 2000* (NT) s 32A(6)(1)(a).
18 *Mental Health and Related Services Act 2000* (NT) s 32A.

police officer that . . . the person has a mental illness'[19] to the police officer 'suspects on reasonable grounds'[20] or 'reasonably believes'[21] that the person has a mental illness. Suspicion carries less conviction than belief;[22] therefore, reasonable suspicion is a lower threshold than 'reasonable belief'.[23]

Transportation and assessment

In all Australian, Canadian and United Kingdom jurisdictions, the purpose of police apprehension powers is to take PMI to a health facility or mental health facility (usually involuntarily) for assessment by a doctor or a mental health practitioner. Although legislation in most jurisdictions only makes mention of health, or mental health, facilities for detainment for the purpose of assessment, s 136 of the English and Welsh Act notes that a person can be removed to a 'place of safety', meaning 'any police station, prison or remand centre' or a hospital if management is willing to receive the person.[24] A person apprehended pursuant to these sections should be transported 'as soon as practicable'[25] or 'without delay'.[26] Although not all jurisdictions specify time frames for detention, for those that do these times frames range from four hours to 72 hours. For example, in Australia the Tasmanian Act provides that a person must not be detained in an authorised facility for assessment, under particular circumstances, for longer than four hours.[27] In Canada, the Nova Scotia Act provides that a person may be detained in an appropriate place for examination for up to 24 hours.[28] Under s 136(2) of the *Mental Health Act 1983* (UK), a person may be detained at a place of safety for a maximum period of 72 hours for the purpose of being 'examined by a registered medical practitioner and to be interviewed by an approved mental health professional and of making any necessary arrangements for his treatment or care'.

Use of force

In approximately half of the jurisdictions reviewed, from Australia, Canada and the United Kingdom, mental health legislation explicitly mentions police use of force, including restraints, or use of conferred police powers in order to exercise the

19 See *Mental Health Act 2009* (SA) s 57(1)(c)(i).
20 See e.g. *Mental Health Act 1996* (WA) s 156.
21 See e.g. *Mental Health Act 2000* (Qld) s 33.
22 *Tuc v Manley* (1985) 19 A Crim R 310.
23 *George v Rockett* (1990) 170 CLR 104.
24 *Mental Health Act 1983* (UK). See also *Mental Health (Northern Ireland) Order 1986* (NI) s 129(7) which also includes 'any police station' as a 'place of safety' among other places.
25 See e.g. *Mental Health and Related Services Act 2000* (NT) s 32A(3); *Mental Health Services Act,* SS 1984-85-86, c M-13.1, s 20(2).
26 See e.g. *Mental Health Act*, RSNWT (Nu) 1988, c M-10, s 11; *Mental Health Act*, RSNWT 1988, c M-10, s 11(1)(f).
27 *Mental Health Act 2013* (Tas) s 20(b), 20(2).
28 *Involuntary Psychiatric Treatment Act*, SNS 2005, c 42, s 15(1).

functions outlined in the police apprehension powers. For example, the Northern Territory provision states that a police officer may 'use any reasonable force and assistance' in order to apprehend and take the person to a place for assessment.[29] Although use of force and restraints is not explicitly mentioned in the other jurisdictions reviewed, it is reasonable to assume that police officers would have all the usual powers conferred on them under normal circumstances to apprehend a person of interest or to maintain public order and peace. In general, it is lawful for a police officer to use reasonable necessary force when exercising or attempting to exercise powers outlined in criminal or policing legislation in the administration and enforcement of the law.[30]

Specialised intervention programs

As noted above, for those individuals experiencing mental health crises, police have become the 'gatekeepers' to mental health services. With police acting in such a pivotal role, police services internationally have sought new approaches toward police interactions with PMI. Since the 1980s, and influenced by the shift from an enforcement policing model to a community policing model,[31] many police services, particularly in the United States, have developed strategies for enhancing interactions between police officers and PMI, especially when PMI are experiencing mental health crises.[32] A key component of the various specialised intervention programs is the development of partnerships between police services and mental health services and professionals, with the expectation that better services and outcomes can be achieved for PMI in crisis.

Three distinct models of collaboration between law enforcement and mental health professionals have been identified;[33] however, over recent years the most rapidly implemented model has been the 'police-based specialised response model'. This model 'involve[s] sworn officers who have special mental health training, serving as the first-line police response to mental health crises in the community and acting as liaisons to the formal mental health system'.[34] The CIT programs are typical of this model.[35]

29 *Mental Health and Related Services Act 2000* (NT) s 32A(7)(a); see *Mental Health (Northern Ireland) Order 1986* (NI) s 131(2) for an example of provisions for the use of the usually conferred police powers.
30 See e.g. *Criminal Code*, RSC 1985, c C-46, s 25.
31 Randy Borum, Martha Williams Deane, Henry J Steadman and Joseph Morrissey, 'Police Perspectives on Responding to Mentally Ill People in Crisis: Perceptions of Program Effectiveness' (1998) 16(4) *Behavioral Sciences and the Law* 393.
32 Judy Hails and Randy Borum, 'Police Training and Specialized Approaches to Respond to People with Mental Illnesses' (2003) 49(1) *Crime and Delinquency* 52.
33 Ibid.
34 Ibid. 54.
35 See Randolph Dupont and Sam Cochran, 'Police Response to Mental Health Emergencies: Barriers to Change' (2000) 28(3) *Journal of the American Academy of Psychiatry and the Law Online* 338; see generally Michael T Compton, Mauma Bahora, Amy C Watson and Janet R Oliva, 'A Comprehensive Review of Extant Research on

In 1987, in Memphis, Tennessee, a young black man armed with a knife in the midst of a mental health crisis was shot and killed by police when he failed to disarm himself.[36] Accusations of police brutality and racism followed and the Memphis community appealed for new approaches to police involvement with persons in mental health crises.[37] By 1988, the Memphis Police Department's CIT was established and was a partnership formed between the Memphis Police Department, the Alliance of the Mentally Ill (AMI), mental health providers, the University of Memphis and the University of Tennessee.[38]

The Memphis CIT model was established to create a more 'intelligent, understandable, and safe approach to mental [health] crisis events'.[39] Two basic goals are set out: first, to improve officer and consumer safety and, second, to redirect individuals with mental illness from the judicial system to the health care system.[40] At its core, the Memphis CIT model represents a pre-arrest diversionary program for PMI. CIT officers undertake 40 hours of specialised training from mental health providers, to provide officers with appropriate skills, for identifying PMIs and thus reacting appropriately. On completion of training, these officers act as 'specialised front-line responders', where their job is 'to redirect PMI, when appropriate, to treatment services instead of the judicial system'.[41]

The Memphis CIT model's key component is that the psychiatric emergency departments are required to take all referrals, thus ensuring efficiency for the police officers and, importantly, reducing stress for PMI.[42] Evaluations of CIT programs have shown that CIT trained officers are more likely to resolve police and PMI interactions through diversion to the mental health system than through arrest.[43]

Crisis Intervention Team (CIT) Programs' (2008) 36(1) *Journal of the American Academy of Psychiatry and the Law Online* 47.

36 CIT Centre, *The CIT Program: Background* University of Memphis, available online at www.cit.memphis.edu/overview.php?page=1 (accessed 5 September 2016). Within the Australian context, how Victorian and Queensland police services handle people with mental illness has been similarly influenced by fatal police shootings; see Jude McCulloch, 'Policing the Mentally Ill' (2000) 25 *Alternative Law Journal* 241.

37 Ibid.

38 The City of Memphis, *Crisis Intervention Team* (2016), available online at www.memphistn.gov/Government/PoliceServices/CrisisInterventionTeam.aspx (accessed 5 September 2016).

39 Ibid.

40 Randolph Dupont, Sam Cochran and Sarah Pillsbury, *Crisis Intervention Team Core Elements* (September 2007), University of Memphis, available online at http://cit.memphis.edu/pdf/CoreElements.pdf (accessed 5 September 2016)

41 Compton et al., above n 35, 47.

42 Sam Cochran, Martha Williams Deane and Randy Borum, 'Improving Police Response to Mentally Ill People' (2000) 51(10) *Psychiatric Services* 1315.

43 Ibid.; Henry J Steadman, Martha Williams Deane, Randy Borum and Joseph P Morrissey, 'Comparing Outcomes of Major Models of Police Responses to Mental Health Emergencies' (2000) 51(5) *Psychiatric Services* 645; Jennifer Skeem and Lynne Bibeau, 'How Does Violence Potential Relate to Crisis Intervention Team Responses to Emergencies?' (2008) 59(2) *Psychiatric Services* 201.

Police apprehension powers and specialised intervention programs: a form of preventive justice?

The primary objective of both police apprehension powers and specialised intervention programs is to reduce harm to PMI, police officers and the public, and it is this element that frames them as a form of preventive justice. Ashworth and Zedner describe a coercive preventive measure as being preventive:

> if it is created in order to avert, or reduce the frequency or impact of, behaviour that is believed to present an unacceptable risk of harm. It is coercive if it involves state imposed restrictions on liberty of action, backed by a coercive response, or the threat of a coercive response, to the restricted individual.[44]

What is important to note is that PMI may be considered a distinctive group insofar as they can be both *a* risk (perceived to be creating a risk to others) and of being *at* risk (perceived to be a risk to self and to be vulnerable to victimisation).[45] Therefore, in one circumstance a PMI may be considered to be 'a risk', and therefore the police may act to prevent harm to others (community safety), and in another circumstance a PMI may be considered to be 'at risk', whereby the police may act to ensure the safety of a PMI who is at risk from self-harm and/or some form of victimisation. Either situation is thought to require some preventive action and this usually falls to the police by virtue of their positon in society, particularly their 24/7 availability[46] and their state-sanctioned ability to use force where necessary.

A further element that frames police apprehension powers and specialised intervention programs as preventive is the use of detention to take PMI to a facility for assessment and/or treatment. In many cases the removal of a PMI from a place to a mental health facility is done against the PMI's wishes and without consent. Nickel notes that '[p]reventive measures in law use coercive threats or forceful incapacitation in hopes of preventing some future harm, crime, nuisance, or obstruction of legitimate government activities'.[47] Slobogin refers to Bentham's perspective that liberty deprivation based on harm prevention is justified on a utilitarian basis, which 'permits deprivation of liberty if the benefits of doing so

44 Andrew Ashworth and Lucia Zedner, 'Introduction: The State and Coercive Preventive Measures' in Andrew Ashworth and Lucia Zedner (eds), *Preventive Justice* (Oxford University Press, 2014) 2, 22.

45 For a discussion on 'at risk' and 'a risk', see Sonja Stanford, 'Critically Reflecting on Being "at Risk' and "a Risk" in Vulnerable People Policing' in Isabelle Bartkowiak-Theron and Nicole L Asquith (eds), *Policing Vulnerability* (The Federation Press, 2012) 20.

46 See Maria Docking, Kerry Grace and Tom Bucke, *Police Custody as a 'Place of Safety': Examining the Use of Section 136 of the Mental Health Act 1983* (September 2008) Independent Police Complaints Commission, available online at www.ipcc.gov.uk/sites/default/files/Documents/section_136.pdf (accessed 5 September 2016).

47 James W Nickel, 'Restraining orders, Liberty, and Due Process' in Andrew Ashworth, Lucia Zedner and Patrick Tomlin (eds), *Prevention and the Limits of the Criminal Law* (Oxford University Press, 2013) 157, 159.

outweigh the harm caused'.[48] Slobogin notes that 'the criminal justice system is often aimed at achieving this goal',[49] and it appears that police apprehension powers, found in mental health legislation, and specialised intervention programs are in general also dedicated to this objective. These police powers offer a new procedural element to preventive justice; however, at their core these powers are diversionary in nature. Consequently, they sit between criminal and civil powers of prevention.

Are policing PMI interventions compatible with human rights?

The human rights of individuals in most countries, if not protected constitutionally or via a Bill or Charter of Rights, are protected by various international conventions aimed at ensuring all people's basic rights. The most recognisable of these conventions is the United Nations *Universal Declaration of Human Rights* (UDHR),[50] which outlines certain 'universal and inalienable'[51] human rights fundamental to all human beings. These rights are often protected through domestic and international law. However, it has been identified that human rights as specified in the UDHR have been failing to protect the rights of persons with disabilities.[52]

On 13 December 2006 the United Nations adopted the *Convention on the Rights of Persons with Disabilities* (CRPD) in order to address these failings. The CRPD entered into force on 3 May 2008[53] and has since become the paramount human rights document when considering the rights of PMI.[54] The CRPD incorporates rights found in other treaties, and expresses those rights in a way that is specific to PMI.[55] The CRPD's objective is 'to promote, protect and ensure the full and equal enjoyment of all human rights and fundamental freedoms by all

48 Christopher Slobogin, 'Eliminating Mental Disability as a Legal Criterion in Deprivation of Liberty Cases: The Impact of the Convention on the Rights of Persons with Disabilities on the Insanity Defense, Civil Commitment, and Competency Law' (2015) 40 *International Journal of Law and Psychiatry* 36, 37.

49 Ibid. 37.

50 *Universal Declaration of Human Rights*, GA Res 217A (III), UN GAOR, 3rd sess, 183rd plen mtg, UN Doc A/810 (10 December 1948).

51 Office of the High Commissioner, *Your Human Rights*, United Nations Human Rights, available online at www.ohchr.org/en/issues/pages/whatarehumanrights.aspx (accessed 5 September 2016).

52 See United Nations, *Convention on the Rights of Persons with Disabilities*: *Why a Convention?* (2006), available online at www.un.org/disabilities/convention/questions.shtml#one (accessed 5 September 2016); Annegret Kämpf, 'The Disabilities Convention and its Consequences for Mental Health Laws in Australia' (2008) 26(2) *Law in Context* 10.

53 *Convention on the Rights of Persons with Disabilities*, GA Res 61/106, UN GAOR, 61st sess, 76th plen mtg, Agenda Item 67(b), UN Doc A/RES/61/106 (13 December 2006).

54 See e.g. Bernadette McSherry and Penelope Weller (eds), *Rethinking Rights-Based Mental Health Laws* (Hart Publishing, 2010).

55 Peter Bartlett, 'The United Nations Convention on the Rights of Persons with Disabilities and Mental Health Law' (2012) 75(5) *The Modern Law Review* 752.

persons with disabilities, and to promote respect for their inherent dignity'.[56] Under the CRPD, persons with disabilities includes 'those who have long-term physical, *mental*, intellectual or sensory impairments which in interaction with various barriers may hinder their full and effective participation in society on an equal basis with others'.[57]

Australia, Canada and the United Kingdom have ratified the CRPD.[58] The United States signed the CRPD on 30 July 2009, but is yet to ratify it.[59] Ratification of the CRPD means that Australia, Canada and the United Kingdom 'take an obligation under international law to implement it'.[60] However, the Articles set out in the CRPD do not become part of domestic law by virtue of the ratification:[61] the CRPD must be incorporated into domestic law by legislation; otherwise it is not directly binding.[62]

In most jurisdictions the rights of PMI are reflected in mental health legislation. For example, s 8(1)(a) of the Queensland *Mental Health Act 2000* (Qld) states that a person who has a mental illness has the:

> Same human rights: the right of all persons to the same basic human rights must be recognised and taken into account; a person's right to respect for his or her human worth and dignity as an individual must be recognised and taken into account.[63]

Section 9 of the *Mental Health Act 2000* (Qld) further notes that any care or treatment should be the least restrictive on the person's liberty, and pose the least interference with his or her rights.

The following section considers whether police apprehension powers and specialised intervention programs used by police in response to persons in mental health crises comply with human rights as outlined in the CRPD. This, in turn, raises questions as to whether the powers made available through these types of

56 *Convention on the Rights of Persons with Disabilities*, GA Res 61/106, UN GAOR, 61st sess, 76th plen mtg, Agenda Item 67(b), UN Doc A/RES/61/106 (13 December 2006), Article 1.
57 Ibid. (emphasis added).
58 United Nations Treaty Collection, *Convention on the Rights of Persons with Disabilities* (2016) United Nations, available online at https://treaties.un.org/Pages/ViewDetails.aspx?src=TREATY&mtdsg_no=IV-15&chapter=4&clang=_en (accessed 5 September 2016).
59 Ibid.
60 United Nations High Commissioner for Human Rights, *Annual Report of the United Nations High Commissioner for Human Rights and Reports of the Office of the High Commissioner and the Secretary-General: Thematic Study by the Office of the United Nations High Commissioner for Human Rights on enhancing awareness and understanding of the Convention on the Rights of Persons with Disabilities* (26 January 2009) United Nations [21], available online at www2.ohchr.org/english/bodies/hrcouncil/docs/10session/A.HRC.10.48.pdf (accessed 5 September 2016).
61 Ibid. [22].
62 Ibid. [23].
63 See also *Involuntary Psychiatric Treatment Act*, SNS 2005, c 42, s 64.

laws operate in a discriminatory way against PMI. When considering whether these laws and programs are compliant with the rights as set out in the CRPD, there are three key components that require examination: (1) the assurance of individual liberty, and protection against arbitrary detention; (2) the linking of mental illness with risk of harm to self or others, as a standard for police action to apprehend PMI; and (3) the suitable accommodations for those being detained during what is essentially a health crisis, not a criminal matter or action.

Deprivation of liberty and mental illness

Contemporary police interaction with PMI has been augmented through the use of police apprehension powers and specialised intervention programs. The key power available in both of these approaches, when dealing with PMI during mental health crises, is the ability for police to detain the person and take him or her, involuntarily, to a health facility for assessment. It is this power that may violate the CRPD. Article 14 of the CRPD deals with the liberty and security of disabled persons, requiring that:

1. States Parties shall ensure that persons with disabilities, on an equal basis with others:

a Enjoy the right to liberty and security of person;
b Are not deprived of their liberty unlawfully or arbitrarily, and that any deprivation of liberty is in conformity with the law, and that the existence of a disability shall in no case justify a deprivation of liberty.[64]

Article 14(1)(b) of the CRPD suggests that police powers, as set out in mental health legislation and specialised intervention programs that include a deprivation of liberty based on the existence or suspected existence of mental illness, are in violation of the CRPD. The United Nations High Commissioner for Human Rights' report[65] identified measures for the effective implementation of the CRPD, highlighting where existing legislation might require amendment to ensure compliance. In the area of rights to liberty and security of person, the High Commissioner was clear in her stance on Article 14(1)(b) noting that:

> Article 14, paragraph 1 (b), of the Convention unambiguously states that 'the existence of a disability shall in no case justify a deprivation of liberty' . . .

64 *Convention on the Rights of Persons with Disabilities*, GA Res 61/106, UN GAOR, 61st sess, 76th plen mtg, Agenda Item 67(b), UN Doc A/RES/61/106 (13 December 2006), Article 14.

65 United Nations High Commissioner for Human Rights, *Annual Report of the United Nations High Commissioner for Human Rights and Reports of the Office of the High Commissioner and the Secretary-General: Thematic Study by the Office of the United Nations High Commissioner for Human Rights on enhancing awareness and understanding of the Convention on the Rights of Persons with Disabilities* (26 January 2009) United Nations.

> [U]nlawful detention encompasses situations where the deprivation of liberty is grounded in the combination between a mental or intellectual disability and other elements such as dangerousness, or care and treatment. Since such measures are partly justified by the person's disability, they are to be considered discriminatory and in violation of the prohibition of deprivation of liberty on the grounds of disability, and the right to liberty on an equal basis with others prescribed by Article 14.[66]

From this perspective, police powers that allow the apprehension or detention of an individual based on the criterion that an individual is mentally ill or appears to be mentally ill, renders that criterion incompatible with Article 14(1)(b) of the CRPD, which provides that a 'disability shall in no case justify a deprivation of liberty'.

Deprivation of liberty and mental illness connected to risk of harm

Another key component of these police powers that is open for scrutiny regarding compliance with the CRPD is the clear linking of preventive detention of PMI (or persons suspected of having a mental illness) with dangerousness or risk.[67] The High Commissioner voiced concerns about the linking of preventive detention with the risk of harm to self or others because of the person's mental illness, stating that:

> Legislation authorizing the institutionalization of persons with disabilities on the grounds of their disability without their free and informed consent must be abolished. This must include the repeal of . . . *provisions authorizing the preventive detention of persons with disabilities on grounds such as the likelihood of them posing a danger to themselves or others*, in all cases in which such grounds of care, treatment and public security are linked in legislation to an apparent or diagnosed mental illness. This should not be interpreted to say that persons with disabilities cannot be lawfully subject to detention for care and treatment or to preventive detention, but that the legal grounds upon which restriction of liberty is determined must be de-linked from the disability and neutrally defined so as to apply to all persons on an equal basis.[68]

This statement suggests that the police apprehension powers located within Australian, Canadian and United Kingdom mental health legislation breach

66 Ibid. [48] (citations omitted).
67 For further discussion, see Chapter 4 by Bernadette McSherry in this collection.
68 United Nations High Commissioner for Human Rights, *Annual Report of the United Nations High Commissioner for Human Rights and Reports of the Office of the High Commissioner and the Secretary-General: Thematic Study by the Office of the United Nations High Commissioner for Human Rights on enhancing awareness and understanding of the Convention on the Rights of Persons with Disabilities* (26 January 2009) United Nations, [49] (emphasis added), available at www2.ohchr.org/english/bodies/hrcouncil/docs/10session/A.HRC.10.48.pdf (accessed 5 September 2016).

Article 14(1) of the CRPD by including both *mental illness* and *risk of harm to self or others* in the criteria for detention.[69] The most consistent criteria set for the use of police apprehension powers, found in mental health legislation, is that a police officer may apprehend or detain a person if a police officer reasonably suspects that the person has a *mental illness* and there is some indication of a *risk of harm to self or others.*[70] However, from a preventive justice perspective it is the risk of harm to others and the obligation of the state to keep its citizens safe[71] that justifies the use of such powers.

Further, Article 14(2) of the CRPD requires that:

> States Parties shall ensure that if persons with disabilities are deprived of their liberty through any process, they are, on an equal basis with others, entitled to guarantees in accordance with international human rights law and shall be treated in compliance with the objectives and principles of the present Convention, including by provision of reasonable accommodation.

Of particular interest in this Article is the 'provision of reasonable accommodation'. All mental health legislation, in both Australia and Canada, specifies that PMI apprehended by police should be taken to a health facility or mental health facility for assessment. However, s 136 of the *Mental Health Act 1983* (UK) requires apprehended person to be taken to a 'place of safety'. A 'place of safety' under the United Kingdom Act 'means any police station, prison or remand centre, or any hospital the managers of which are willing temporarily to receive him'.[72]

The use of police custody as a 'place of safety' is one of the most contentious elements of s 136 of the United Kingdom Act. Codes of Practices for both England and Wales state that police stations as a 'place of safety' should only be used 'on an exceptional basis'.[73] However, there is evidence suggesting that police custody is being frequently used as a 'place of safety'. A joint inspection undertaken by Her Majesty's Inspectorate of Constabulary, the Care Quality Commission, Healthcare Inspectorate Wales and Her Majesty's Inspectorate of Prisons to review the degree to which police custody was used as a 'place of safety' found that during 2011/2012 in excess of 9,000 persons were detained in police custody compared with 16,035 taken to a hospital.[74] In an earlier study by Docking, Grace and Bucke,

69 See e.g. *Mental Health Act 2014* (Vic) s 351(1); *Mental Health Act*, RSA 2000, c M-13, s 12(1); *Mental Health Act 1983* (UK) c 20, s 136(1).

70 See e.g. *Mental Health Act 2014* (Vic) s 351; *Mental Health Act*, RSO 1990, c M-7, s 17.

71 Ashworth and Zedner, above n 44, 2; Klaus Grunther, 'Responsibility to Protect and Preventive Justice' in Andrew Ashworth, Lucia Zedner and Patrick Tomlin (eds), *Prevention and the Limits of the Criminal Law* (Oxford Scholarship Online, 2013).

72 *Mental Health Act 1983* (UK) c 20, s 55(1).

73 Her Majesty's Inspectorate of Constabulary, Her Majesty's Inspectorate of Prisons, the Care Quality Commission and Healthcare Inspectorate Wales, *A Criminal Use of Police Cells?* (20 June 2013) Justice Inspectorates ('*A Criminal Use of Police Cells?*'), available online at www.justiceinspectorates.gov.uk/hmic/media/a-criminal-use-of-police-cells-20130620.pdf (accessed 5 September 2016).

74 Ibid.

during a 12-month period in 2005/2006 police custody was identified as the main 'place of safety', with 11,500 people detained in police custody compared with 5,900 people detained in hospital for the same reason.[75]

Both of these findings indicate that police custody as a 'place of safety' is being utilised more often than 'on an exceptional basis'. Additionally, the circumstances for those persons detained under s 136 are materially different to those detained for a criminal offence. Those detained under s 136, who are suspected of having a mental illness, may be held for a maximum of 72 hours and with no requirement of review,[76] whereas those detained for a criminal offence may not be detained for more than 24 hours[77] and reviews of detention are undertaken at regular intervals.[78] It is this excessive contact with police and often unnecessary contact and exposure to the criminal justice system that can result in increased negative stigma for the detained person.

Police apprehension powers and specialised intervention programs: preventing injustice

Police apprehension powers and specialised intervention programs can be critiqued as a deprivation of basic human rights, as outlined in the CRPD, and for creating disadvantage for those exposed to them. However, injustice can occur in many different ways for PMI, not only through actions taken that are non-compliant with the CRPD but also through neglect of their specific needs. Therefore, these powers may also be examined to explore the ways in which they might facilitate greater autonomy, quality of life and social engagement for PMI. From this perspective these forms of police powers, used for policing PMI, could be envisaged as *preventing injustice.*

PMI may be at a disadvantage when they come into contact with various elements of the criminal justice system. Generally, there can be a power imbalance that exists between police and the community that requires safeguards for human rights.[79] This power imbalance may be heightened when the community member interacting with the police has a mental illness. However, PMI are often considered by the community to be violent or dangerous,[80] and therefore 'a risk'. It is this perspective that justifies subjecting PMI to coercive preventive measures such as police apprehension powers and specialised intervention programs that aim to

75 Docking, Grace and Bucke, above n 46.
76 *A Criminal Use of Police Cells?*, above n 73, 5–6.
77 *Police and Criminal Evidence Act 1984* (UK), c 60, s 41.
78 Ibid. s 40.
79 See e.g. Tamar Hopkins, 'Policing in an Era of Human Rights' (2007) 32(4) *Alternative Law Journal* 224.
80 See Bruce G Link, Jo C Phelan and Michaeline Bresnahan, 'Public Conceptions of Mental Illness: Labels, Causes, Dangerousness, and Social Distance' (1999) 89(9) *American Journal of Public Health* 1328; Patrick W Corrigan, Amy C Watson, Amy C Warpinski and Gabriela Gracia, 'Implications of Educating the Public on Mental Illness, Violence, and Stigma' (2004) 55(5) *Psychiatric Services* 577.

prevent harm to members of society. Instead of 'a risk', PMI should be considered 'at risk'. As a group, PMI are particularly vulnerable to criminalisation,[81] victimisation[82] and stigmatisation,[83] all of which can impact on their ability to participate fully in society. These issues are discussed in the next section.

Risks for PMI through contact with the criminal justice system

Criminalisation

The criminalisation of PMI may be viewed as a consequence of the disproportionate interaction that PMI have with the police. The criminalisation of PMI was first advanced by Marc Abramson.[84] Abramson observed that more stringent criteria set out in a new mental health Act enacted in California in 1969 had an impact on the rate at which mental health professionals were accepting involuntary patients for detention and treatment. The effect of this was that police had to utilise criminal sanctions as a way to ensure involuntary detention. Abramson noted that this shift in dealing with PMI resulted in the 'criminalization of disordered behavior'. While the criminalisation of PMI is a contentious concept,[85] an early study testing the 'criminalisation hypothesis'[86] found that suspects that showed symptoms of mental illness were 20 per cent more likely to be arrested compared with suspects who did not appear to be mentally ill. Further, data indicates that PMI are overrepresented within prison populations.[87]

81 See Marc F Abramson, 'The Criminalization of Mentally Disordered Behavior: Possible Side-Effect of a New Mental Health Law' (1972) 23(4) *Psychiatric Services* 101; Linda A Teplin, 'Criminalizing Mental Disorder: The Comparative Arrest Rate of the Mentally Ill' (1984) 39(7) *American Psychologist* 794.

82 Vaginia Aldigé Hiday, Marvin S Swartz, Jeffrey W Swanson, Randy Borum and H Ryan Wagner, 'Criminal Victimization of Persons with Severe Mental Illness' (1999) 50(1) *Psychiatric Services* 62; Linda A Teplin, Gary M McClelland, Karen M Abram and Dana A Weiner, 'Crime Victimization in Adults with Severe Mental Illness: Comparison with the National Crime Victimization Survey' (2005) 62(8) *Archives of General Psychiatry* 911; For a varied discussion on the role of public perception and the marginalisation of certain groups, see Chapter 4 by Bernadette McSherry in this collection.

83 Sarah Clement, O Schauman, T Graham, F Maggioni, S Evans-Lacko, N Bezborodovs, C Morgan, N Rüsch, J S L Brown and G Thornicroft, 'What is the Impact of Mental Health-Related Stigma on Help-Seeking? A Systematic Review of Quantitative and Qualitative Studies' (2015) 45(01) *Psychological Medicine* 11; Bruce G Link and Jo C Phelan, 'Conceptualizing Stigma' (2001) 27 *Annual Review of Sociology* 363; see Link et al., *Public Conceptions*, above n 80; Teplin, *Criminalizing Mental Disorder*, above n 81, 799.

84 Abramson, above n 81.

85 See e.g. Robin Shepard Engel and Eric Silver, 'Policing Mentally Disordered Suspects: A Reexamination of the Criminalization Hypothesis' (2001) 39(2) *Criminology* 225.

86 Teplin, *Criminalizing Mental Disorder*, above n 81, 799.

87 Australian Institute of Health and Welfare (AIHW), *The Mental Health of Prison Entrants in Australia 2010* (June 2012), available online at www.aihw.gov.au/publication-detail/?id=10737422201 (accessed 5 September 2016); World Health

Victimisation

The prevalence of victimisation for PMI is generally greater than for the general population. Studies have indicated that the rates of violent crime victimisation[88] for PMI have ranged from two and a half times greater[89] to more than 11 times greater[90] than the general population. A systematic review of nine studies found criminal victimisation rates of 4.3 per cent to 35.04 per cent; these rates of victimisation were 2.3 to 104.4 times greater than for the general population.[91]

Stigmatisation

The behaviours exhibited by some PMI, particularly those diagnosed with severe psychotic disorders, may unduly contribute to the uneasiness that many people experience around PMI, often resulting in the involvement of the police to deal with situations.[92] Therefore, much of the police–PMI contact and PMI over-representation in the criminal justice system may not be the result of an individual's participation in criminal activity, but because they have a mental illness which creates behavioural differences that can be amplified due to their public visibility.[93] Further, police interactions with PMI can escalate and result in more punitive responses because of inappropriate responses by PMI due to symptomatic behaviours such as verbal abuse, aggression and lack of respect directed at persons in authority.[94]

An extreme outcome from police and PMI contact are fatal police shootings, usually occurring during mental health crises. Police shootings serve to reinforce stereotypes, particularly that PMI are violent and dangerous,[95] which creates further stigmatisation of PMI in the eyes of the public. However, some research

Organisation (WHO), *Trenčín Statement on Prisons and Mental Health* (2008), available online at www.euro.who.int/__data/assets/pdf_file/0006/99006/E91402.pdf?ua=1 (accessed 5 September 2016).

88 Types of violent crimes referred to include rape, other forms of sexual assault, robbery, mugging and assault (aggravated, simple).

89 Hiday et al., above n 82.

90 Teplin et al., *Crime Victimization*, above n 82.

91 Roberto Maniglio, 'Severe Mental Illness and Criminal Victimization: A Systematic Review' (2009) 119(3) *Acta Psychiatrica Scandinavica* 180.

92 See Linda A Teplin, 'Managing Disorder: Police Handling of the Mentally Ill' in Linda A Teplin (ed.), *Mental Health and Criminal Justice* (Sage Publications, 1984) 157.

93 Victoria Herrington and Katrina Clifford, 'Policing Mental Illness: Examining the Police Role in Addressing Mental Ill-Health' in Isabelle Bartkowiak-Theron and Nicole L Asquith (eds), *Policing Vulnerability* (The Federation Press, 2012) 117; Joel W Godfredson, Stuart D M Thomas, James R P Ogloff and Stefan Luebbers, 'Police Perceptions of Their Encounters with Individuals Experiencing Mental Illness: A Victorian Survey' (2011) 44(2) *Australian and New Zealand Journal of Criminology* 180.

94 Teplin, *Criminalizing Mental Disorder*, above n 81, 799.

95 See Link et al., *Public Conceptions*, above n 80.

suggests that PMI are in fact no more violent or dangerous than the average person.[96] Stigma is particularly harmful for PMI, deterring individuals from seeking help,[97] which results in delays in receiving treatment. Delays in treatment can, in turn, result in worse outcomes than if treatment had been given earlier.[98] Without adequate treatment, there can also be a particular risk of deterioration while in the community.[99]

Preventing injustice

Many PMI are vulnerable to various adverse circumstances and outcomes. Police apprehension powers and specialised intervention programs help to redirect PMI from the criminal justice system to the mental health care system for care and treatment, diminishing some of the risks for PMI, thus preventing injustices occurring, such as criminalisation, stigmatisation or not having access to treatment.[100] Treatment is particularly important due to the stability it can create in an individual's life, creating better opportunities for employment, education and housing.

Although the key criteria of these police powers may be incompatible with provisions in the CRPD, there is some recognition that the need exists to be able to treat PMI involuntarily, without consent, for their own wellbeing and the wellbeing of others. For example, the United Nations High Commissioner for Human Rights[101] indicated that the CRPD does not completely exclude the need for

96 Ibid. However, this is contested, see e.g. Cameron Wallace, Paul E Mullen, and Philip Burgess, 'Criminal Offending in Schizophrenia Over A 25-Year Period Marked by Deinstitutionalization and Increasing Prevalence of Comorbid Substance Use Disorders' (2004) 161(4) *American Journal of Psychiatry* 716.

97 Clement et al., above n 83.

98 Nynke Boonstra, Rianne Klassen, Sjoerd Sytems, Max Marshall, Lieuwe De Haan, Lex Wunderink and Durk Wiersma, 'Duration of Untreated Psychosis and Negative Symptoms: A Systematic Review and Meta-Analysis of Individual Patient Data' (2012) 142(1) *Schizophrenia Research* 12; Bernardo Dell'Osso, Ira D Glick, David S Baldwin and Carlo A Altamura, 'Can Long-Term Outcomes Be Improved by Shortening the Duration of Untreated Illness in Psychiatric Disorders? A Conceptual Framework' (2013) 46(1) *Psychopathology* 14.

99 Kay Wilson, 'Law Reform or Systemic Reform? Stakeholder Perceptions of Resource Constraints in Mental Health in Australia, New Zealand and Canada' (2013) 20(4) *Psychiatry, Psychology and Law* 553. For further discussion of stigma, see Chapter 4 by Bernadette McSherry in this collection.

100 For a discussion of coercion in treatment, see Chapter 4 by Bernadette McSherry in this collection.

101 United Nations High Commissioner for Human Rights, *Annual Report of the United Nations High Commissioner for Human Rights and Reports of the Office of the High Commissioner and the Secretary-General: Thematic Study by the Office of the United Nations High Commissioner for Human Rights on enhancing awareness and understanding of the Convention on the Rights of Persons with Disabilities* (26 January 2009) United Nations, [49], available online at www2.ohchr.org/english/bodies/hrcouncil/docs/10session/A.HRC.10.48.pdf (accessed 5 September 2016).

preventive detention or detaining a person for the purpose of care or treatment.[102] Szmukler, Daw and Callard suggest that to do so:

> would be seriously at variance with a widespread moral intuition (expressed in rights to life and health) that there are certain circumstances (including, for example, coma) in which treatment should be provided to a person who as a result of an impairment of mental functioning cannot make treatment decisions for himself or herself.[103]

This view was also highlighted by a report delivered by the Expert Committee tasked with reviewing the *Mental Health Act 1983* (UK), in order to provide recommendations to the government regarding new legislation and how best to 'protect the rights of individual patients and the need to ensure public safety'.[104] The Expert Committee stated that they were 'convinced that whatever the precise scope of a mental health act it must primarily be seen as a health measure and must be consistent with the professional ethics of the health services'.[105]

In addition to this, and consistent with Article 14 of the CRPD, the Expert Committee considered the links between detention, risk and mental illness within the context of consent and capacity. In response to the Expert Committee's draft proposal, a small minority believed that 'a mental health act should authorise treatment in the absence of consent only for those who lack capacity'.[106] Further, '[i]f a person with a mental disorder who refused treatment was thought to pose a serious risk to others then he or she should be dealt with through the criminal justice system, not through a health provision'.[107] However, there was a much larger group that took the opposing view and were willing 'to accept the over-riding of a capable refusal in a health provision on grounds of public safety in certain circumstances'.[108] The Expert Committee weighted its support toward the majority view, noting:

> most of those who commented accepted that *the safety of the public must be allowed to outweigh individual autonomy where the risk is sufficiently great and, if the risk is related to the presence of a mental disorder for which a health intervention of likely benefit to the individual is available, then it is appropriate that such intervention should be authorised as part of a health provision.* Mental

102 This area is contested. For a discussion on more recent comments by the United Nations Committee on the Rights of Persons with Disabilities regarding mental and legal capacity, see Chapter 4 by Bernadette McSherry in this collection.

103 George Szmukler, Rowena Daw and Felicity Callard, 'Mental Health Law and the UN Convention on the Rights of Persons with Disabilities' (2014) 37(3) *International Journal of Law and Psychiatry* 245, 248.

104 Department of Health, 'Review of the Mental Health Act 1983' (Report of the Expert Committee, Department of Health, 1999), 1.

105 Ibid. 18, [2.3].

106 Ibid. 18, [2.6].

107 Ibid. 19, [2.6].

108 Ibid. 19, [2.7].

> disorder unlike most physical health problems may occasionally have wider consequences for the individual's family and carer, and very occasionally for unconnected members of the public affected by the individual's behaviour, acts and omissions.[109]

These imperatives to ensure that PMI receive care and treatment, and to ensure safety to self and others, when an individual is clearly unable to make decisions about his or her own care, constitute a form of preventive justice. That is, these imperatives provide a clear opportunity to *prevent injustice.* Police officers, through the use and application of apprehension powers and specialised intervention programs, are uniquely placed to use their discretion in ensuring that these individuals are diverted from contact with the criminal justice system to mental health services, thus granting PMI the opportunity to receive appropriate services. Access to appropriate treatment diminishes the chance of mental health crises, which in turn decreases the risk of unnecessary contact with the police and the potential for arrest and entry into the criminal justice system. Szmukler, Daw and Callard 'suggest that very few would support the idea that the State never, even as a last resort, has a duty to protect those who are clearly unable to make crucial treatment decisions for themselves'.[110]

Early, or earlier, identification and intervention is where the police powers discussed throughout this chapter could be of greatest importance to the outcomes for PMI who come into contact with the criminal justice system by virtue of either criminal behaviour or mental health crises. Again, police apprehension powers and specialised intervention programs provide the potential for *preventing injustice* for this population.

Conclusion

Overall, this chapter has aimed to analyse the place of police apprehension powers and specialised intervention programs within preventive justice and elucidate some of the ways in which they can both limit and promote individual liberty for those individuals who are subject to such laws and procedures. Police apprehension powers and specialised intervention programs contain criteria that violate the requirements of the CRPD. For example, police apprehension powers can be deployed when an officer merely suspects a person is mentally ill and is a risk to self or others. To link mental health in any way with dangerousness as a criterion for detention is incompatible with Article 14 of the CRPD.[111]

As a form of preventive justice, these powers may well be violating provisions of the CRPD as they place individual autonomy and liberty second to the public good in order to prevent harm. However, preventive police powers in this area may promote positive outcomes for PMI, or at the very least diminish the negative

109 Ibid. 19, [2.7] (emphasis added).
110 Szmukler, Daw and Callard, above n 103, 250.
111 See Chapter 4 by Bernadette McSherry in this collection.

effects for PMI, particularly at the crucial moment of their initial contact with police. For PMI who come into contact with police due to a mental health crisis, police apprehension powers and specialised intervention programs provide police officers an opportunity to divert these individuals from the criminal justice system to mental health services for assessment, treatment and care. Additionally, for those PMI whose contact with police involves violations of the law, police can also use these powers to divert PMI to mental health services to be assessed and accurately identify any existing mental disorder at entry to the criminal justice system. Diagnosis at this point may provide a therapeutic opportunity.[112]

Ultimately, the application of diversionary powers may reduce the level of criminalisation, victimisation and stigmatisation for some PMI. This would have a direct impact in the short and long term. To date, little research has been conducted on how these laws and programs impact PMI, and there is a need for research to fill this gap in knowledge.

112 See e.g. James Ogloff, Michael R Davis, George Rivers and Stuart Ross, 'The Identification of Mental Disorders in the Criminal Justice System' (2007) (334) *Trends and Issues: In Crime and Criminal Justice.*

6 Protection seekers and preventive justice

Immigration detention in Australia and the United Kingdom

Peter Billings and Dallal Stevens*

Introduction

This chapter critically explores the justifications, scope and limits of immigration detention in Australia and the United Kingdom, and makes a distinctive contribution to the developing preventive justice scholarship alongside the established studies focused on criminal law/procedure and counter-terrorism.[1] We critically reflect on the combination of preventive and administrative rationales for immigration detention, and consider the anticipated harms that states claim both require and validate prolonged periods of incarceration as a valid regulatory tool of immigration control. We examine how conventional, public law-based, constraints on executive action are absent, ineffective or present in attenuated forms in this regulatory space. Without orthodox and effective checks and balances that promote substantive and procedural justice, protracted and even indefinite periods of detention for many protection seekers have eventuated.[2] We conclude the chapter by indicating how administrative and/or judicial review processes might be reformed in each context so that the necessity and proportionality of immigration detention, including preventive rationales for detention, can be more effectively scrutinised.

Australian perspectives

Regulating administrative detention

This section focuses on the Australian government's use of detention for 'unlawful non-citizens' – in particular, irregular maritime arrivals seeking refuge who are

* Peter Billings gratefully acknowledges the research assistance of Ms Eloise Gluer.

1 E.g. Andrew Ashworth and Lucia Zedner (eds), *Preventive Justice* (Oxford University Press, 2014) ch 10. For a critical introduction to preventive justice scholarship, see Chapter 1 by Tamara Tulich in this collection.

2 Prolonged detention can be properly characterised as arbitrary (or 'disproportionate' under human rights law) when viewed in the light of the general justifications supporting detention. See Carol S Steiker, 'Proportionality as a Limit on Preventive Justice: Promises and Pitfalls' in Andrew Ashworth, Lucia Zedner and Patrick Tomlin (eds), *Prevention and the Limits of the Criminal Law* (Oxford University Press, 2013) ch 10.

governed through prolonged deprivation of liberty. This practice occurs onshore and also offshore – at sea and in third countries pursuant to bilateral regional processing agreements.[3]

Onshore detention

In 1992, immigration detention was conceived of as an extraordinary measure 'aimed at boat people', temporary in nature and time-limited.[4] The measure was justified in two ways: on an administrative basis linked to effective processing and determination of entry claims and for preventive reasons aimed at the deterrence of irregular maritime migration from South East Asia.[5]

Subsequently, the *Migration Reform Act 1992* (Cth) removed important temporal constraints and established a uniform scheme of mandatory detention for all unlawful non-citizens divorced from the detainee's personal circumstances. Under the *Migration Act 1958* (Cth), detention of unlawful non-citizens[6] by the executive, without judicial order or warrant, is authorised.[7] Relevantly, where 'officers' know or suspect a person to be an unlawful non-citizen in the 'migration zone', or in an 'excised offshore place', then immigration detention is *mandatory*. For persons seeking to enter the 'migration zone' who would (upon effecting entry) be unlawful non-citizens, detention is *permitted*. Non-citizens liable to be detained for prolonged periods include protection visa claimants pending administrative decisions about their refugee status *and* visa eligibility, and 'declared' refugees (within the meaning of the 1951 *Convention Relating to the Status of Refugees* and 1967 *Protocol Relating to the Status of Refugees* – together, 'Refugees Convention')[8] whose visa claims are refused or cancelled on security or adverse character grounds, but who cannot be removed or deported.

In 2008, the Australian Labor government signalled a shift away from a presumption of secure detention for unlawful non-citizens pending resolution of their legal status.[9] This 'risk-based' policy framework was infused by 'human rights'

3 On offshore processing and detention, see *AG v Secretary of Justice* [2013] NRSC 10 (18 June 2013); *Plaintiff M68/2015 v Minister for Immigration and Border Protection* (2016) 327 ALR 369; and *Namah v Pato* [2016] PGSC 12; SC1496 (22 April 2016).

4 See the *Migration Amendment Act 1992* (Cth) that inserted s 54Q into the *Migration Act 1958* (Cth) and limited detention to 273 days; and, Commonwealth, *Parliamentary Debates*, House of Representatives, 5 May 1992, 2370 (Gerard Hand).

5 Commonwealth, *Parliamentary Debates*, House of Representatives, 5 May 1992, 2370 (Gerard Hand).

6 Generally, any person who is not a 'lawful non-citizen' (i.e. holds a valid visa) is an 'unlawful non-citizen': *Migration Act 1958* (Cth) ss 13(1), 14(1).

7 The key provision requiring (or permitting) detention is s 189, in conjunction with ss 196, 198.

8 Opened for signature 28 July 1951, 189 UNTS 137 (entered into force 22 April 1954) and opened for signature 31 January 1967, 606 UNTS 267 (entered into force 4 October 1967).

9 See Commonwealth, *Department of Immigration and Citizenship – Annual Report 2008–09*, Parl Paper No 351 (2009) 114.

ideals respecting individual liberty, and prohibiting arbitrary – or disproportionate – detention.[10] Unlawful non-citizens were to be initially detained for administrative reasons: health, identity and security checks. Government policy provided that *ongoing* detention was justifiable on specific, preventive, grounds, namely:

1 on *protective* grounds, for non-citizens posing an unacceptable risk to the community (be it on character, security or health grounds); and
2 on *non-compliance* grounds, to prevent future immigration offences in respect of non-citizens who repeatedly breach visa conditions.[11]

By 2011, the policy had been effectively abandoned with unlawful maritime arrivals being detained for the duration of their processing.[12] The discord between Labor's detention policy and practice is well illustrated by the arbitrary and discriminatory moratorium on the processing of Sri Lankan and Afghan asylum seekers' claims during 2010. This led to asylum seekers, who had arrived by boat, being warehoused in the Curtin Immigration Detention Centre in Western Australia, effectively left in limbo for months, while processing of their protection visa claims was suspended in a vain attempt to deter other Sri Lankan and Afghan asylum seekers from coming to Australia via unlawful means.[13]

Following the Coalition's federal election victory in September 2013, the numbers of detainees in secure detention has fallen markedly due to: (1) bridging visa grants facilitating community release; (2) use of community detention; (3) transfers of protection seekers to regional processing centres; and (4) rapid decline in irregular maritime arrivals who have been deterred or denied entry by maritime interdiction. But the average time spent in detention has risen sharply from 72 days in July 2013 to a peak of 445 days in December 2015.[14] Here, government policy and calculated executive inertia, rather than case complexity, may account

10 See Commonwealth, *Immigration Detention in Australia: A New Beginning (Criteria for Release from Immigration Detention): Joint Standing Committee on Migration*, Parl Paper No 571 (2008).

11 See Department of Immigration and Border Protection, *Procedures Advice Manual 3 (PAM3): Migration Act Detention Services Manual* (Canberra: The Dept, 1994) (PAM3) referencing the immigration detention values announced in July 2008.

12 Australian Human Rights Committee, Submission to the Joint Select Committee on Australia's Immigration Detention Network, *Joint Select Committee on Australia's Immigration Detention Network* (August 2011) 14 [25]. Labor's policy shifted again in November 2011 when detainees were released into the community on safe haven/ bridging visas (see *Plaintiff M79/2012 v Minister for Immigration and Citizenship* (2013) 252 CLR 336). Then, post 13 August 2012, Labor's 'no advantage' policy applied, reviving offshore regional (refugee) processing.

13 See Peter Billings, 'Juridical Exceptionalism in Australia: Law, Nostalgia and the Exclusion of Others' (2011) 20(2) *Griffith Law Review* 271, 296–7.

14 Department of Immigration and Border Protection, *Immigration Detention and Community Statistics Summary* (30 December 2015) Australian Government (online) 11; and Australian Human Rights Commission, *The Forgotten Children: National Inquiry into Children in Immigration Detention* (November 2014) (online) 56.

for the protracted periods of detention for unauthorised arrivals. For those detainees arriving before regional resettlement was introduced in July 2013,[15] caught up in the backlog of asylum cases, the Coalition government simply deferred resolution of protection visa claims until legislative amendments, reintroducing temporary protection visas, with retrospective effect, were passed in December 2014.[16]

In short, onshore immigration detention has been, officially, directed at protective purposes: public health and safety are said to be protected by *incapacitating* protection seekers who, upon arrival, may carry a contagious disease, or who officials consider pose an unacceptable risk to public safety/security. Detention also serves to manage those non-citizens who officials believe are a 'flight' risk, to prevent them absconding. Detention also serves ancillary *administrative* purposes relating to visa processing/adjudication and facilitating removal/deportation. General *deterrence* of irregular maritime migration has served as an, official rationale justifying detention onshore in the past. But, at present, deterrence only grounds maritime detention practices, to which attention now turns.

Maritime detention

Operation Sovereign Borders (OSB) commenced on 19 December 2013. A decisive aspect of OSB is a maritime border security operation directed squarely at preventive aims: namely, efficiently managing migration controls, deterring people smuggling operations, mitigating the risk of harm to protection seekers by deterring hazardous maritime ventures, and promoting compliance with migration law by preventing unauthorised maritime arrivals from entering Australia. Interdiction at sea was resuscitated following a sharp rise in unauthorised maritime arrivals during 2009–2012. The strategy has been executed via 'tow-backs' and 'take-backs', and entails interception, deprivation of liberty, conspicuously unfair screening procedures and limited judicial oversight.

Tow-backs have been executed by interception at sea, coupled with returns to neighbouring transit countries. For example, asylum seekers have been intercepted en route to Australia, detained for several days on border protection vessels and then coerced into cramped and hot carceral spaces on disposable lifeboats, and towed back to the edge of Indonesian territory. Worryingly, this has occurred without an assessment of whether Australia's international law obligations are engaged.[17]

15 The regional resettlement policy augmented regional processing arrangements by providing for resettlement, on Papua New Guinea and Nauru respectively, and prohibited resettlement in Australia for refugees.

16 See e.g. *Plaintiff S4/2014 v Minister for Immigration and Border Protection* (2014) 253 CLR 219: the plaintiff's detention was unlawfully prolonged for reasons related to the executive's policy of not granting permanent protection visas to irregular maritime arrivals.

17 See Michael Bachelard, 'Vomitous and terrifying: the lifeboats used to turn back asylum seekers', *Sydney Morning Herald* (online) 2 March 2014, available at www.smh.com.au/national/vomitous-and-terrifying-the-lifeboats-used-to-turn-back-asylum-seekers-20140301-33t6s.html (accessed 5 September 2016).

Equally troublesome, take-backs have involved interception at sea coupled with either direct repatriations following perfunctory screening procedures[18] or attempted 'safe third country' returns. In respect of the latter, there was a failed attempt to return Sri Lankan interdictees to India in July 2014. The legality of this preventive action was tested in *CPCF v Minister for Immigration and Border Protection*[19] (*CPCF*), considered below.

Exploring legal constraints on immigration detention: onshore

Immigration detention raises risks of executive overreach and human rights infringements, and presents a critical need for effective checks and balances. The High Court of Australia has, over many years, entertained several challenges to the legality of prolonged immigration detention. In a recent case, three judges expressed the view that immigration detention provisions are constitutionally valid only if they are for relevant statutory purposes and if they are subject to clear 'reasonable time' constraints.[20] So the bleak prospect that detention might endure for the term of a non-citizen's natural life (countenanced in *Al-Kateb v Godwin*)[21] is doubtful, due to implied constitutional constraints. However, these limits on immigration detention rest on the capacity of the court to identify and agree on valid statutory purposes, and an assessment of what is a 'reasonable time' to achieve those purposes.

Statutory purposes

'The common law does not recognise any executive warrant authorising arbitrary detention.'[22] And immigration detention is not arbitrary because the executive's power is constrained; it is directed to particular statutory purposes, coupled with temporal limits.[23] In *Plaintiff M76/2013 v Minister for Immigration, Multicultural Affairs and Citizenship*[24] (*M76*), Hayne J observed that mandatory detention provisions served the broad preventive purpose of immigration control, 'to control the arrival and presence of non-citizens in Australia'.[25] Whereas

18 See e.g. Matthew Knott, 'Asylum seekers screened at sea returned to Sri Lanka' *Sydney Morning Herald* (online) 7 July 2014, available at www.smh.com.au/federal-politics/political-news/asylum-seekers-screened-at-sea-returned-to-sri-lanka-20140706-3bh3x.html (accessed 5 September 2016).
19 (2015) 316 ALR 1.
20 *Plaintiff M76/2013 v Minister for Immigration, Multicultural Affairs and Citizenship* (2013) 251 CLR 322, 369 [139] (Crennan, Bell and Gageler JJ).
21 (2004) 219 CLR 562, 575 (Gleeson CJ), 651 (Hayne J).
22 (2013) 251 CLR 322, 369 [139] (Crennan, Bell and Gageler JJ).
23 Ibid. The temporal limits are not precisely fixed at the time detention commences, but statutory purposes must be fulfilled as soon as reasonably practicable (i.e. capable of achievement).
24 (2013) 251 CLR 322.
25 Ibid. 366 [127] (emphasis added).

in *Plaintiff S4/2014 v Minister for Immigration*[26] (*S4*) the High Court of Australia, having identified the broad regulatory objectives of the *Migration Act 1958* (Cth), stated that mandatory detention served purely administrative purposes, namely:

> the purpose of removal from Australia; the purpose of receiving, investigating and determining an application for a visa permitting the alien to enter and remain in Australia; or, in a case such as the present, the purpose of determining whether to permit a valid application for a visa.[27]

This passage can be read as fully identifying the statutory purposes underlying onshore mandatory detention, although the list of permissible purposes underpinning non-citizens' detention may not be closed.[28] In *S4* the High Court did not expressly reject or endorse alternative statutory purposes for detention suggested in earlier cases. For example, immigration detention has been interpreted as legitimately serving an *exclusionary* purpose, by *segregating* unlawful non-citizens from the wider community.[29] In *Al-Kateb*, two judges decided that preventing the entry of unlawful non-citizens into the community, pending an entry or removal decision, was an ancillary purpose underpinning detention.[30] Three other judges went further, observing that entry, removal *and* exclusion from the community could justify detention. Thus, exclusion was not merely ancillary; it could justify detention *absent* other statutory purposes (which might be exhausted) related to entry, or removal.[31] Exclusion was said to advance *protective* purposes, preventing undesired infiltration of, or presence in, the community, and the attainment of *de facto* citizenship.[32] Importantly – and despite the clear similarities between the lived experience of immigration detention and penal incarceration – there is no judicial recognition that immigration detention is imposed as punishment for an offence relating to unauthorised arrival.[33]

26 (2014) 253 CLR 219.
27 Ibid. 231 [26]. See also *Plaintiff M68/2015 v Minister for Immigration and Border Protection* (2016) 327 ALR 369, 310 [46] (French CJ, Kiefel and Nettle JJ), 317 [94] (Bell J), 332 [184] (Gageler J), 343 [260] (Keane J), and 362 [392] (Gordon J, dissenting) (concerning offshore refugee processing on Nauru and incidental executive detention).
28 *Plaintiff M68/2015 v Minister for Immigration and Border Protection* (2016) 327 ALR 369, 360–1 [382] (Gordon J).
29 E.g. *Re Woolley; Ex parte M276/2003* (2004) 225 CLR 1, 75–7 [222]–[228] (Hayne J).
30 *Al-Kateb*,576 [17] (Gleeson CJ), 609 [126]–[127] (Gummow J).
31 Ibid. 584–5 [45]–[46] (McHugh J), 644–5 [247] (Hayne J), 658–9 [289] (Callinan J).
32 Ibid. 584 [46] (McHugh J), 659 [289] (Callinan J). See also *Re Woolley; Ex parte M276/2003* (2004) 225 CLR 1, 46–7 [115] (McHugh J).
33 *Re Woolley; Ex parte M276/2003* (2004) 225 CLR 1, 14 [26] (Gleeson CJ); *M76*, 385 [207] (Kiefel and Keane JJ); *Jaffarie v Director-General of Security* (2014) 226 FCR 505, 532–3 [95] (Flick and Perram JJ) citing *Al-Kateb*, 584 [44]–[45] (McHugh J).

Another protective purpose was implied by Heydon J in *M47 /2012 v Director General of Security*[34] (*M47*): 'the detention of unlawful non-citizens who threaten the safety or welfare of the community because of the risks they pose to Australia's security'.[35] One of the difficulties with this justification (which reflects government policy) is that detainees may be incarcerated – on protective grounds – due to adverse security/character assessments, in circumstances where they pose no real danger to the community.[36] This circumstance is aggravated by the fact that non-citizens with adverse security assessments subject to removal do not enjoy due process via administrative merits review,[37] and judicial review is largely ineffectual.[38]

In *M76*, Kiefel and Keane JJ also identified exclusion as a discrete purpose underlying detention. Significantly, Their Honours observed that even if the legislative scheme were read as constrained by both a purposive (*removal*) and temporal limitation (*reasonably practicable) and* also an implied qualification that this be effected *within a reasonable time frame*, detention would, nonetheless, continue to be lawful. This was attributed to the 'evident purpose' (underlying s 189) of *preventing unauthorised entry* into the Australian community.[39]

In summary, the combination of preventive and administrative purposes underlying immigration detention, and the phrasing of these aims in expansive terms, sits uneasily alongside the unanimous judgment in *S4*, which clearly stated that detention serves specific statutory purposes: removal, investigation and determination of a visa application, and to determine whether to permit a valid visa. Suffice to say, it is far from easy to disentangle and identify the legitimate purpose(s) of immigration detention.

Temporal constraints

In *Al-Kateb*, the High Court of Australia determined that the *Migration Act 1958* (Cth) supplied a clear mandate requiring unlawful non-citizens to be detained until removed, deported or granted a visa. The law, it was held, authorised prolonged detention without a fixed end-point. The High Court was, subsequently,

34 (2012) 251 CLR 1.

35 Ibid. 136 [346]. This purpose correlates to government policy: see *PAM3*, above n 11.

36 Ibid. 194 [534] (Bell J). The Australian Security Intelligence Organisation's (ASIO) security assessments capture a larger cohort of refugees than those falling within the exclusionary provisions of the Refugees Convention.

37 In 2012 an Independent Reviewer of Adverse Security Assessments was appointed to provide periodic non-binding reviews of adverse security assessments relating to non-citizens who engage Australia's protection obligations (Attorney-General's Department (Cth), *Independent Reviewer of Adverse Security Assessments* (2012) Australian Government (online)). As a consequence of this process, 21 detainees were released from detention in 2014/15 (Commonwealth Ombudsman, *An analysis of reports under s 486O of the Migration Act 1958 sent to the Minister by the Ombudsman in 2014/15* (August 2015) (online) 13).

38 *Jaffarie v Director General of Security* (2014) 226 FCR 505, 521–2 [48] (Flick and Perram JJ).

39 *M76*, 379–80 [182]–[183].

invited to overrule *Al-Kateb* in *M47. M47* was officially declared a refugee but refused a visa to enter Australia because of an adverse security assessment. Accordingly, *M47* remained in detention pending removal. It was argued that there was no reasonable prospect or likelihood of another country agreeing to admit *M47* and, because there was no realistic prospect of removal, detention was unlimited and, therefore, unlawful.

A majority of the High Court of Australia disposed of the matter in favour of *M47*, but without the need to address the arguments directed at the correctness of *Al-Kateb*. However, Gummow and Bell JJ (dissenting) determined that *Al-Kateb* should not be followed.[40] Their Honours favoured the construction of s 198 of the *Migration Act 1958* (Cth) advanced by Gleeson CJ (in the minority in *Al-Kateb*) which 'better accommodates the basic right of personal liberty'.[41] Importantly, Gleeson CJ considered that if removal of a detainee ceased to be a practical possibility, then detention must cease, at least for as long as that situation continues. It followed that the statutory duty of removal imposed on an immigration officer subsists, but is in abeyance, where removal is impractical.[42]

Notably, in *M47*, Gummow and Bell JJ claimed that the majority reasoning in *Al-Kateb* was weakened by the absence of a discussion of the 'principle of legality',[43] which mandates that the legislature must manifest an intention to abrogate fundamental principles, infringe rights or depart from the general system of law (the 'clear statement' principle).[44] Subsequently, in *M76*, Kiefel and Keane JJ refuted that view, adding that there was no legislative lacuna and so no work for the principle of legality to do.[45] Their Honours highlighted the absence of *precise* temporal limitations on the duration of detention for removal purposes.[46] Accordingly, *Al-Kateb, M47* and *M76* show that the interpretation of temporal elements in the legislative scheme supporting immigration detention divides judicial opinion, and equally divisive is the applicability of the 'principle of legality'.

Constitutional constraints

A constitutional head of power – the naturalization and aliens power contained in s 51(xix) *Commonwealth Constitution* – supports the administrative confinement of unlawful non-citizens in detention.[47] However, the effect of Chapter III of the *Constitution* is that, certain exceptional categories aside, deprivation of liberty can

40 *M47*, 61 [120], 68 [145] (Gummow J), 193 [533] (Bell J).
41 Ibid. 61 [120] (Gummow J).
42 *Al-Kateb*, 578 [22] (Gleeson CJ).
43 *M47*, 60 [119] (Gummow J), 193 [532] (Bell J).
44 *Potter v Minahan* (1908) 7 CLR 277, 304 (O'Connor J).
45 Justice Hayne reaffirmed the interpretative approach His Honour adopted, as part of the majority, in *Al-Kateb: M76*, 366 [127].
46 *M76*, 379 [182] (Kiefel and Keane JJ). Cf. *Al-Kateb* (Gleeson CJ, Gummow and Kirby JJ).
47 *Chu Kheng Lim v Minister for Immigration, Local Government and Ethnic Affairs* (1992) 176 CLR 1.

only be made by judicial order on conviction for an offence after adjudication of guilt.[48] Among the recognised exceptions to this rule is that non-citizens' liberty may be constrained for the purpose of determining questions about the person's entry or removal or deportation. The constitutional issue is whether detention can lawfully continue when statutory purposes are exhausted (or frustrated) and are incapable of fulfilment within a reasonable time frame.

The legislative requirement that detention is required until 'removal is undertaken as soon as reasonably practicable' may be read as importing a 'reasonable time' qualification, or else risk infringing Chapter III constraints. This idea stems from the case of *Chu Kheng Lim v Minister for Immigration, Local Government and Ethnic Affairs*[49] (*Lim*) where a majority of the High Court of Australia held that immigration detention is constitutionally valid *only if* the laws that require and authorise administrative detention are 'limited to what is reasonably capable of being seen as necessary for the purposes of deportation or necessary to enable an application for an entry permit to be made and considered'.[50] In *M76*, Crennan, Bell and Gageler JJ revisited *Lim*, identifying a clear temporal limitation on detention:

> The necessity referred to in that holding in *Lim* is not that detention *itself* be necessary for the purposes of the identified administrative processes but that the *period* of detention be limited to the time necessarily taken in administrative processes directed to the limited purposes identified. The temporal limits and the limited purposes are connected such that the power to detain is not unconstrained.[51]

Whereas, in *M76* Hayne J, confirming *Al-Kateb*, stated that the power to detain unlawful non-citizens was not unbounded, pinpointing the statutory duty to remove 'as soon as reasonably practicable', and purposive constraints which must be 'ascertainable, and enforceable, [by the courts] at all times during its continuance'.[52] His Honour harboured no doubts about the validity of laws authorising indefinite detention until removal for unauthorised non-citizens, concluding that the question of the law's consistency 'with basic tenets of common humanity' was for Parliament and the polity to ponder.[53] Kiefel and Keane JJ agreed that the detention laws were valid; executive detention, where removal was currently unfeasible, did not violate Chapter III.[54]

48 Jeffrey Steven Gordon, 'Imprisonment and the Separation of Judicial Power: A Defence of a Categorical Immunity From Non-Criminal Detention' (2012) 36(1) *Melbourne University Law Review* 41.
49 (1992) 176 CLR 1.
50 Ibid. 33 (Brennan, Deane and Dawson JJ).
51 *M76*, 369 [139] (emphasis in original) (citation omitted). See also *S4*, 231 [26], where French CJ, Hayne, Crennan, Kiefel and Keane JJ referred to the cited passage from *Lim* with apparent approval, and *Plaintiff M68/2015 v Minister for Immigration and Border Protection* [2016] HCA 1, 55 [184]–[185] (Gageler J).
52 *M76*, 359 [98]–[99].
53 Ibid. 367 [130].
54 Ibid. 384–5 [205]–[208].

In summary, the High Court of Australia has recognised that detention laws have temporal limits that are necessary if the laws are to satisfy constitutional requirements. Where the judges differ is whether 'reasonable practicability of removal' must be read so as to require removal within a 'reasonable time-frame' in order to be valid. In *M76*, three judges (Crennan, Bell and Gageler JJ) offered support for the view that detention provisions are constitutionally valid laws if they are for relevant statutory purposes and if they are subject to clear 'reasonable time' constraints.[55] Otherwise powers of executive detention can be characterised as punitive laws and unconstitutional.

Exploring legal constraints on preventive detention: interdiction at sea

In *CPCF v Minister for Immigration and Border Protection*,[56] the legality of executive detention beyond Australia's borders, in the course of repelling protection seekers, was considered by the High Court of Australia. The Australian government relied on, *inter alia*, the *Maritime Powers Act 2013* (Cth) (MPA) to defeat the false imprisonment claim brought by the plaintiff. Significantly, s 72(4) MPA enabled a maritime officer to *detain and take* a person to a place outside the migration zone, including a place outside Australia, and s 72(5) provided for the restraint of a person on a vessel for the purposes of taking a person to another place.

By a slender majority the Court decided that there was statutory authority to detain and take the interdictees to India; it was not a 'speculative taking' and, therefore, constitutionally invalid. Pertinently, the Court rejected an alternative argument: that the actions of the maritime officers at sea were animated by an improper purpose – the *deterrence* of unauthorised maritime arrivals. The plaintiffs argued that the statutory scheme was only directed at preventing contravention of, or ensuring compliance with, the *Migration Act 1958* (Cth). Only two judges, Gageler and Keane JJ, addressed this argument and expressly rejected the claim that deterrence was an extraneous purpose vis-à-vis the MPA. Gageler J observed that the government's general policy of deterrence was consistent with the twin purposes of ensuring compliance with s 42(1) of the *Migration Act 1958* (Cth) and preventing contravention of s 42(1) from occurring in Australia.[57] In summary, two members of the Court accepted that the MPA enabled maritime officers to intercept and detain non-citizens in the contiguous zone, and remove them to another place, as an incident of preventing a contravention of migration law pursuant to a policy of deterrence.[58]

55 Cf. *Lim*, 73, where McHugh J doubted a long period of detention (over two years) could transform the character of immigration detention from administrative (non-punitive) to punitive.

56 (2015) 316 ALR 1.

57 *CPCF*, 80 [365], 96 [450] (Keane J) (concurring).

58 *Maritime Powers Act 2013* (Cth) s 41(1)(c)(ii) and *Maritime Powers Regulation 2014* (Cth) reg 8: specifically, to prevent a contravention of the *Migration Act 1958* (Cth) s 42(1).

Remarkably, with the High Court of Australia's decision pending, the government moved pre-emptively to reinforce executive maritime powers to undertake turn backs.[59] The *Migration and Maritime Powers Legislation Amendment (Resolving the Asylum Legacy Caseload) Act 2014* (Cth), schedule 1, evidences a legislative intent to neutralise the effects that any negative ruling in *CPCF* might have had for Australia's interdiction policy. Critically, the 'detain and taking power' was amended confirming that a detained vessel can be taken outside Australia and that the destination can repeatedly change.[60] Plainly, for preventive purposes, maritime interdictees face the real prospect of a prolonged period detained at sea, while 'taking' decisions are made, given effect, and arrangements are made for detainees' disembarkation elsewhere. The Australian government now enjoys exorbitant powers, generating uncertainty about the duration of maritime detention. Limiting such detention to 'reasonable' periods, while relevant statutory purposes are pursued, provides a veneer of legitimacy but negligible security from protracted detention.[61] This temporal constraint does not enable the deprivation of liberty at sea to be rigorously scrutinised by the courts, to guard against arbitrariness.[62] Indeed, the United Nations Special Rapporteur on Torture observed that Australia's maritime powers risk violating the *United Nations Convention Against Torture* 'because it allows for the arbitrary detention and refugee determination at sea, without access to lawyers'.[63]

United Kingdom perspectives

Regulating immigration detention

In the United Kingdom, the stated justification for immigration detention is 'the effective maintenance of immigration control' – the need to restrict the movement of people who have yet to persuade the state of their right to enter and remain, or whom the state wishes to remove. For those who support an unfettered sovereign right to control borders and admission to territory, detention – or *incapacitation* – is regarded as necessary to prevent a risk of harm, or an actual harm, from

59 Senate Legal and Constitutional Affairs Legislation Committee, *Migration and Maritime Powers Legislation Amendment (Resolving the Asylum Legacy Caseload) Bill 2014 [Provisions]* (2014) 7 [2.6], 18 [3.6].

60 *Maritime Powers Act 2013* (Cth), s 72(4)(a)–(b).

61 *Maritime Powers Act 2013* (Cth) s 72A. The most direct route to a destination does not need to be taken (s 72A(2)(b)).

62 Although limits on the power to detain and take can be judicially reviewed to ensure powers are not frustrated or spent, this is an ineffective safeguard against arbitrary detention, per art 9(1) ICCPR.

63 Human Rights Council, *Report of the Special Rapporteur on torture and other cruel, inhuman or degrading treatment or punishment, Juan E. Méndez – Observations on communications transmitted to Governments and replies received*, 28th sess, UN Doc A/HRC/28/68/Add.1 (6 March 2015) [30]–[31]. *Convention against Torture and Other Cruel, Inhumane or Degrading Treatment or Punishment*, opened for signature 10 December 1984, 1465 UNTS 85 (entered into force 26 June 1987).

occurring. 'Harm' is often related to the 'flight risk': the fear that the subject will abscond, disappear, commit or contribute to an undesirable act or a criminal offence.[64] Despite a low flight risk, and the requirement to use detention as a last resort, protection seekers are subject to detention for *preventive* reasons. They are increasingly likely to be detained for *administrative convenience*, rather than harm prevention – that is, their detention is argued to be facilitative for the state in some way.[65] The detention estate currently comprises ten designated immigration removal centres, which are operated by either the National Offender Management Service or private contractors. Between January and September 2015, 20,744 people entered detention.[66]

Powers to detain

The *Immigration Act 1971* (UK) contains the power to detain.[67] Before 1987, the detention of protection seekers was not routine.[68] Arguably, this was due to the perceived lack of a need to detain given the low number of asylum seekers. Until 1989, asylum claims remained below 4,500,[69] but as applications increased, reaching an all-time high of 84,130 in 2002, successive British governments introduced a range of new policies, with significant changes made to the detention regime for protection seekers.

Immigration officers and the Home Secretary possess a wide power to detain people.[70] Broadly, detention can occur pending refugee status determination, pending a decision to remove and pending removal. Immigration officers can also detain an individual at a port for up to three hours if the officer thinks the individual may be liable to arrest.[71] Two remarkable, if not unique, features pertain to

64 Detention is permissible where there is a reasonable suspicion that a crime has been committed or to prevent 'a concrete and specific offense': *M v Germany* (2010) 51 EHRR 976 [89].

65 See Cathryn Costello, 'Immigration Detention: The Grounds Beneath Our Feet' (2015) *Current Legal Problems* 1, 1–35, who differentiates between punitive, coercive and preventive detention.

66 Home Office, *Immigration Statistics July to September 2015 – Detention Tables* (26 November 2015) Gov.UK (online). These figures include children.

67 C 77, sch 2, para 16 and sch 3. Amendments have been made subsequently: *Immigration and Asylum Act 1999* (UK); *Nationality, Immigration and Asylum Act 2002* (UK); *Immigration, Asylum and Nationality Act 2006* (UK); *UK Borders Act 2007* (UK); *Immigration Act 2014* (UK).

68 Dallal Stevens, 'Asylum Seekers, Detention and the Law: Morality in Abeyance?' in Satvinder S Juss (ed.), *The Ashgate Research Companion to Migration Law, Theory and Policy* (Ashgate, 2013) 397.

69 Home Office, *Immigration Statistics April to June 2015*(27 August 2015) Gov.UK (online) (excluding dependants).

70 *Immigration Act 1971* (UK), c 77, sch 2, para 16 lists the circumstances where an immigration officer has authority to detain. The Home Secretary's powers to detain persons liable to deportation are contained in sch 3, and the *Nationality, Immigration and Asylum Act 2002* (UK) c 41, pt 4, ss 62(1)–(2) and 71(1)–(3).

71 *UK Borders Act 2007* (UK) c 30, s 2.

United Kingdom immigration detention: there is no automatic bail hearing[72] and no statutory time limit on the length of detention. To be lawful, detention must comply with domestic legislation and meet relevant human rights obligations arising, notably, under the *Human Rights Act 1998* (UK) and the *European Convention on Human Rights* 1950 (ECHR).[73]

Detention policy and guidance: the purpose of detention

The power to detain is *discretionary* so attention must focus on policy, operational instructions and detention centre rules for further direction on the power's implementation.[74] Operational guidance for immigration officers states that '[t]he power to detain must be retained in the interests of maintaining effective immigration control', but 'there is a presumption in favour of temporary admission or release and, wherever possible, alternatives to detention are used'.[75] Furthermore:

> Detention is **most** usually appropriate:
>
> - to effect removal;
> - initially to establish a person's identity or basis of claim; or
> - where there is reason to believe that the person will fail to comply with any conditions attached to the grant of temporary admission or release.[76]

The policy specifies numerous factors to be assessed when considering the need for initial or continued detention. The immigration officer's decision about immigration is informed by: the likelihood of and timescale for removal; a history of absconding/non-compliance/breach of immigration law; the subject's age, vulnerability and ties with the United Kingdom; whether the subject has a settled address and employment; whether there are outstanding legal processes that might incentivise keeping in touch with authorities; risk of offending or harm to the public; and any history of torture.[77] Furthermore, the officer or Home Secretary must inform the prospective detainee of the reasons for detention, and government policy currently details five: (1) the person is likely to abscond if given

72 *Immigration and Asylum Act 1999* (UK) c 33, ss 44–52 included routine bail hearings but these were never implemented and were removed by the *Nationality, Immigration and Asylum Act 2002* (UK) c 41, pt 4, s 68. The government has reduced the circumstances in which bail can be sought: *Immigration Act 2014* (UK) c 22, pt 1, s 7.

73 *Convention for the Protection of Human Rights and Fundamental Freedoms*, opened for signature 4 November 1950, 213 UNTS 221 (entered into force 3 September 1953), as amended by Protocol Nos 11 and 14.

74 The United Kingdom Visas and Immigration (Home Office) also disseminate practice information directly to practitioners, which is not widely published.

75 UK Visas and Immigration and Immigration Enforcement, *Chapters 46 to 62: detention and removals* (14 April 2016) Gov.UK (online) ch 55, 55.1.1.

76 Ibid. (emphasis in original).

77 Ibid. 55.3.1 and 55.14.

temporary admission or release; (2) there is insufficient reliable information to decide on whether to grant the person temporary admission or release; (3) the person's removal from the United Kingdom is imminent; (4) the person needs to be detained while alternative arrangements are made for their care; and (5) the person's release is not considered conducive to the public good.[78] Protection seekers can fall within one or more of these categories.

So detention can take place for a range of reasons, some of which are about preventing some unspecified harm – '[the persons'] release is not conducive to the public good'; '[the person is]likely to abscond' (and become untraceable/misbehave/become a burden) – while others are more elliptical – '[the person's] removal . . . is imminent; [the person] need[s] to be detained while alternative arrangements are made' (and they might become untraceable/misbehave/become a burden if given their liberty). The harm occasioned to the detainee is, unsurprisingly, not considered, despite the view that 'depriving a person of his or her liberty intentionally harms that person'.[79] Rather, as both law and policy make clear, the harm meted out to the subject of detention, through deprivation of liberty, is considered warranted, even in the case of the most vulnerable individuals on occasions.

Detained Fast Track

Previously, government policy stated another purpose underpinning detention: 'The application may be decided quickly using the fast track procedures' – otherwise known as the Detained Fast Track (DFT) system. Although this reason has now been removed following the suspension of the DFT in 2015 (see below), the fast-track detention of protection seekers is pertinent for our critique of preventive and administrative detention, to which our attention now turns.

Prior to the DFT process, some asylum seeker applicants were detained but the majority were not.[80] The idea of detention for mere 'administrative convenience' was unknown. In March 2000 this changed with the opening of the first 'reception centre' in Oakington, Cambridgeshire.[81] The adoption of a benign term 'reception centre' is striking; so too the use of detention for a new purpose – for applications that can be decided quickly – detention only for the duration of the initial decision, and for a limited period 'of about 7 days'. The rationale was that due to the high number of claimants (in 2000, this stood at 80,315),[82] the Home

78 Ibid. 55.6.3.
79 Victor Tadros, 'Controlling risk' in Andrew Ashworth, Lucia Zedner and Patrick Tomlin (eds), *Prevention and the Limits of the Criminal Law* (Oxford University Press, 2013) 133, 139.
80 Immigration Law Practitioners' Association, *The Detained Fast Track Process – A Best Practice Guide* (January 2008) (online) 1.
81 United Kingdom, *Parliamentary Debates*, House of Commons, 16 March 2000, vol 364, col 385 WS (Barbara Roche).
82 European Union Committee, *Handling EU asylum claims: new approaches examined – Report with evidence* (30 April 2004) House of Lords (online) 15.

Office needed protection seekers to be available for early interview and further representations. The scheme was extended, first to Harmondsworth Removal Centre in 2003 (note the shift in terminology to 'removal centre') for single young men, and then to Yarl's Wood Removal Centre in 2005, for women. Now, detention would be for the duration of initial decision *and* appeal. The Minister promised that 'we will detain straightforward claimants to enable a quick initial decision and swift removal after any appeal, providing they meet the criteria for detention'.[83] Although Oakington could be described as 'fast', the new scheme was intended to be 'superfast': induction and substantive interviews in two days, an in-country right of appeal within two days and the whole case, if refused, could be finalised in just five weeks.

This shift towards detention for administrative convenience can be characterised as preventive detention. The object is to ensure immediate access to individuals: to ensure they are available for examination, interview, decision, appeal and removal. Simply put, fast-track detainees were prevented from moving freely within the United Kingdom. From a harm perspective, the government argued that the asylum seeker system was under threat by the numbers, backlogs were growing, and people were waiting years for decisions. But this type of detention, ostensibly with an administrative or facilitative objective, poses a number of critical legal questions, the answers to which are complex, encompassing domestic, European Union and international law and policy.

Exploring (legal) constraints on preventive detention in the United Kingdom

Detention can be challenged in the High Court in England and Wales either by *habeas corpus* or judicial review, or by judicial review in Scotland. *Habeas corpus* applications are normally concerned with the power to detain, whereas judicial review might focus on the wider exercise of the discretion to detain.[84] The courts have a duty to guard the liberty of the person jealously, to construe broad statutory discretions narrowly and ensure they are exercised for solely for statutory purposes.[85] Where detention conditions are sufficiently poor, this may breach art 3 of the ECHR, which prohibits torture and inhuman or degrading treatment or punishment.[86] Pressure can also be brought to bear on the use and conditions of detention by independent oversight of the detention estate,[87] political intervention and campaigning by civil society.

83 United Kingdom, *Parliamentary Debates*, House of Commons, 18 March 2003, vol 401, col 42 WS (Beverley Hughes).

84 Ian Macdonald and Ronan Toal (eds), *Macdonald's Immigration Law and Practice* (Butterworths, 9th edn, 2015) [18.59].

85 Ibid. [18.44].

86 *R (on the application of AM) v Secretary of State for the Home Department* [2009] EWCA Civ 219.

87 E.g. HM Chief Inspector of Prisons, *Inspection* 2015, available online at www.justiceinspectorates.gov.uk/hmiprisons/inspections/?post_type=inspection&s&prison-inspection-type=immigration-removal-centre-inspections (accessed 5 September 2016).

Time in detention

European Union law imposes a maximum time limit of six months on detention during the return process (any extension thereafter is up to 12 months), but the United Kingdom has not implemented the Return Directive 2008/115/EC and is, therefore, not bound by it.[88] The, apparently, open-ended length of time an individual can be incarcerated is one of the most contentious aspects of immigration detention. However, the period in detention must be reasonable in the circumstances.[89] Many of the cases involving protracted detention relate to individuals imprisoned prior to removal or deportation, often following time served in prison for commission of a criminal offence. Protection seekers, whose claims have been refused, and who have been convicted of a criminal offence and served a prison sentence, also fall into this category. The leading case is *R (Hardial Singh) v Governor of Durham Prison*[90] (*Hardial Singh*) recently reaffirmed by the Supreme Court in *R (Lumba & Mighty) v Secretary of State for the Home Department*[91] (*Lumba & Mighty*).

In *Hardial Singh*, Woolf J stated that the power to detain was impliedly limited to a period that was reasonably necessary to achieve the purpose of the detention.[92] In *Lumba & Mighty*, Lord Dyson sought to clarify what have become known as the *Hardial Singh* principles.[93] Referring to his own judgment in *R (I) v Secretary of State for the Home Department*,[94] he stated that it was impossible and undesirable to produce an exhaustive list of the circumstances that are, or may be, relevant to the question of how long it is reasonable to detain a person pending deportation. However, relevant factors to consider included:

> the length of the period of detention; the nature of the obstacles which stand in the path of the Secretary of State preventing a deportation; the diligence, speed and effectiveness of the steps taken by the Secretary of State to surmount such obstacles; the conditions in which the detained person is being kept; the effect of detention on him and his family; the risk that if he is released from detention he will abscond; and the danger that, if released, he will commit criminal offences.[95]

Despite these judicial endeavours to determine what relevant factors inform a determination about the reasonableness of a period of detention period, without a

88 *Directive 2008/115/EC of The European Parliament and of The Council of 16 December 2008 on common standards and procedures in Member States for returning illegally staying third-country nationals* [2008] art 15.
89 Tom Bingham, 'Personal Freedom and the Dilemma of Democracies' (2003) 52(4) *International and Comparative Law Quarterly*, 841, 844–5.
90 [1984] 1 All ER 983; [1983] EWHC 1 (QB).
91 [2012] AC 245.
92 [1983] EWHC 1 (QB) [7].
93 [2012] 1 AC 245, 264–5 [22]. Lord Phillips dissented from this interpretation of Woolf J's judgment.
94 [2002] EWHC Civ 888.
95 [2012] 1 AC 245, 284 [104].

fixed time-limit there is always a risk that subjectivity will creep into any assessment of 'a reasonable period'.[96]

DFT

The DFT regime has been subject to sustained judicial scrutiny. First, *R (on the application of Saadi) v Secretary of State for the Home Department*[97] (*Saadi*) presented an opportunity for the House of Lords and then European Court of Human Rights (ECtHR), to reflect on the legality of seven-day detention in Oakington.[98] The House of Lords established that the right to detain asylum seekers existed, citing the *Immigration Act 1971* (UK).[99] Lord Slynn of Hadley decided that applicants could be held until the refugee determination was made; there was no need to show that there was a flight risk, nor was this type of detention limited to those who could not be granted temporary admission, for whatever reason.[100] He opined that the large number of applicants who had to be considered quickly justified detention for a short period in acceptable physical conditions. This did not mean that the Home Secretary could detain without any limits where no examination had taken place or decision had been made. Further, the Home Secretary must not act in an arbitrary manner, and an immigration officer must act reasonably in fixing the examination time and arriving at a decision in the light of the objective of promoting speedy decision-making.[101] For Lord Slynn the Oakington regime was reasonable and getting a speedy decision was 'in the interests not only of the applicants but of those increasingly in the queue'.[102]

The *Saadi* case also addressed the human rights implications of immigration detention. Article 5(1)(f) of the ECHR provides deprivation of liberty is permissible where 'the lawful arrest or detention of a person [is] to prevent his effecting an unauthorised entry into the country or of a person against whom action is being taken with a view to deportation or extradition'. The ECtHR agreed with the United Kingdom domestic courts that 'until a State has "authorised" entry to the country, any entry is "unauthorised"'.[103] The European Court of Human

96 The UN Working Party on Arbitrary Detention has recommended that 'an absolute maximum duration for the detention of asylum seekers should be specified in national law': United Nations Eco-Soc, Commission on Human Rights, *Report on the Visit of the Working Group on Arbitrary Detention to the United Kingdom on the issue of immigrants and asylum seekers*, 55th sess, E/CN. 4/1999/63/Add. 3 (18 December 1998) [35].
97 [2002] UKHL 41.
98 Ibid.; *Saadi v United Kingdom* (Application No 13229/03, European Court of Human Rights – Grand Chamber, 29 January 2008).
99 C 77, sch 2, para 16.
100 *Saadi*, [22].
101 Ibid. [24]–[25].
102 Ibid. [47].
103 *Saadi v United Kingdom* (Application No 13229/03, European Court of Human Rights – Grand Chamber, 29 January 2008) [65].

Rights Grand Chamber did not accept that as soon as an asylum seeker has surrendered him- or herself to the immigration authorities, he or she is seeking to effect an 'authorised' entry, with the result that detention cannot be justified under the first limb of article 5(1)(f).[104] The Grand Chamber decided that to interpret article 5(1)(f) as only permitting detention of a person who was trying to evade entry restrictions was far too narrow a construction.[105] What was important was that any deprivation of liberty had to be lawful – that is, 'a procedure prescribed by law' had been followed and the individual was protected from arbitrariness.[106] To avoid arbitrariness, detention must be carried out in good faith; it must be closely connected to the purpose of preventing unauthorised entry; the place and conditions of detention should be appropriate, bearing in mind that the measure is applicable to refugees who have fled from their own country; and the length of the detention should not exceed that reasonably required for the purpose pursued.[107] Bizarrely, the ECtHR concluded that the United Kingdom authorities acted in good faith in detaining the applicant because the policy animating the Oakington regime 'was generally to benefit asylum seekers', and a speedy decision was in the interests not only of the applicant but of those increasingly in the queue.[108] Furthermore, 'since the purpose of the deprivation of liberty was to enable the authorities quickly and efficiently to determine the applicant's claim to asylum, his detention was closely connected to the purpose of preventing unauthorised entry'.[109] But, as the ministerial statements justifying Oakington attest, the purpose of the regime was never conceived of, or articulated, in terms of 'benefitting' asylum seekers. Moreover, the argument that detention is needed to prevent unauthorised entry of someone who had already arrived at Heathrow airport, claimed asylum, was permitted to leave and to return in accordance with reporting instructions, was tortuous.

Further attempts to challenge the 'superfast' regime failed. In *R (on the application of the Refugee Legal Centre) v Secretary of State for the Home Department*,[110] the Court of Appeal held that the accelerated system did not deprive claimants of a fair

104 Ibid. [65].

105 Ibid. In any case, the United Nations High Commissioner for Refugees' (UNHCR) own Executive Committee Conclusion on detention permitted detention of asylum seekers and refugees where necessary to verify identity or to determine the elements on which the refugee status claim is based. See United Nations High Commissioner for Human Rights, *Detention of Refugees and Asylum Seekers – Ex Com Conclusion No 44 (XXXVII) – 1986* (13 October 1986) [b], available at www.unhcr.org/3ae68c43c0.html (accessed 5 September 2016). It also acknowledged that detention might be necessary 'to deal with cases where refugees or asylum-seekers have destroyed their travel and/or identity documents or have used fraudulent documents in order to mislead the authorities of the State in which they intend to claim asylum; or to protect national security or public order'.

106 *Saadi v United Kingdom* (Application No 13229/03, European Court of Human Rights – Grand Chamber, 29 January 2008) [67].

107 Ibid. [74].

108 Ibid. [77].

109 Ibid.

110 [2004] EWCA Civ 1481.

opportunity to put his or her case;[111] nor was there an unacceptable risk of unfairness.[112] Interestingly, the fact that some people might be detained for five weeks or longer (in excess of the 'reasonable' time of Oakington) was not under judicial review.

Questions about the legality, fairness, reasonableness and proportionality of fast-track detention were revisited in proceedings brought by Detention Action, a non-profit organisation.[113] These issues were being revisited due to significant changes arising since the *Saadi* case, which had validated the first incarnation of fast-track detention. There were now fewer asylum cases; the average time in detention was much longer than 7–10 days: 23.5 days from entry to exhaustion of appeal rights; the only criterion guiding decision-makers was whether a quick decision could be made; a very broad range of cases were included in the DFT, which had previously been considered too complex for a quick decision; there was limited scope for removal from the DFT; and a significant number of applicants were unrepresented.

In *R (on the application of Detention Action) v Secretary of State for the Home Department*,[114] Beatson LJ concluded that 'detention in the fast track by the application of the "quick processing" criteria, after the Secretary of State's decision and pending appeal is not objectionable in principle and does not breach the DFT Guidance'.[115] However, he judged that it did not satisfy the requirements of clarity and transparency established by the Supreme Court in *Lumba & Mighty*.[116] In *Lumba & Mighty*, Lord Dyson emphasised that the rule of law required a transparent statement of the circumstances in which the broad statutory criteria would be exercised to detain a person.[117] Lord Dyson stressed the importance of clear policy statements so that individuals knew the criteria being applied to them when detained by the executive.[118] Additionally, Beatson LJ would have concluded (had it been necessary to decide the matter) that, on the evidence before the Court, detention could not be said to be justified.[119] Following the case, the Home Office undertook to assess all asylum claimants in the DFT who were appealing and to release those who were not at risk of absconding. Very few were assessed as not presenting an absconding risk.

111 Ibid. [6].
112 Ibid. [20].
113 *R (on the application of Detention Action) v Secretary of State for the Home Department* [2014] EWHC 2245 (Admin); and *R (on the application of Detention Action) v Secretary of State for the Home Department* [2014] EWCA Civ 1634.
114 [2014] EWCA Civ 1634.
115 Ibid. [97].
116 [2012] 1 AC 245.
117 Ibid. [34].
118 Ibid. [36]. *Lumba & Mighty* dealt with unpublished policy whereas *R (on the application of Detention Action) v Secretary of State for the Home Department* [2014] EWHC 2245 (Admin) dealt with published policy and was, therefore, focused on breach.
119 Ibid. [97].

Subsequently, the Minister for Immigration and Security suspended the DFT scheme.[120] The government's application to appeal against the Court of Appeal judgment was refused in November 2015. The unravelling of fast-track detention for protection seekers in the United Kingdom leaves one wondering: what next? Strikingly, there has, as yet, not been any declaration by the courts that detention for asylum claimants for *administrative* reasons is objectionable *per se*. Immigration detention with all its preventive (and at times punitive) undertones is under threat but appears here to stay.[121]

Fairer regulation of immigration detention

The predicament analysed in this chapter is not novel[122] and it is fourfold. First, *executive officials* administer and apply the law and policy relating to deprivation of liberty absent effective oversight; that is, independent and impartial bodies (be they tribunals or courts) are not *routinely* required to check detention decision-making (for example, through periodic appeals, statutory reviews or bail proceedings). Second, substantive unfairness arises because the *necessity* of detention is not rigorously scrutinised by officials on an individual basis (as is required under international human rights law norms); habitually it stems, reflexively, from the state's characterisation of a person as unauthorised, unlawful or illegal. Third, and relatedly, prolonged detention often occurs in a context that is *procedurally unfair* to detainees who are assessed by officials as posing a risk to the community, because the substantive merits and/or legality of the risk assessment are not effectively reviewable. Fourth, the judiciary's capacity to promote the rule of law through judicial review, by policing legal limits on detention, is restricted because of (i) the expansive purposes officially underpinning and informing the statutory mandate governing detention, and (ii) due to the looseness/uncertainty afflicting 'reasonableness' as a normative constraint on the duration of detention.

In Australia, there is no access to an independent, impartial and effective review, entailing a *proportionality-based* analysis of detention for protection seekers, congruent with the views of the Australian Human Rights Commission and the United Nations Human Rights Committee.[123] Reform is urgently required to

120 United Kingdom, *Parliamentary Debates*, House of Commons, 2 July 2015, col 13WS, HCWS 83 (James Brokenshire).

121 In January 2016, Stephen Shaw (Stephen Shaw, *Review into the Welfare in Detention of Vulnerable Persons*, Cm9186 (2016)), was commissioned by the government, was critical of the regime and called on the Home Office to 'prepare and publish a strategic plan for immigration detention', recommendation 1. Shaw does not consider the need for immigration *per se* nor the indefinite nature of detention in the United Kingdom.

122 See Tulich's discussion of counter-terrorism studies in Chapter 1 of this collection.

123 See e.g. *Immigration detainees with adverse security assessments v Commonwealth of Australia (DIBP)* [2014] AusHRC 92; *FA, FB, FC and FD v Commonwealth of Australian (DIBP)* [2014] AusHRC 83; and UNHRC, *Draft General Comment 35 – Article 9: Liberty and security of person*,107th sess, UN Doc CCPR/C/107/R.3 (28 January 2013).

address the arbitrary detention of particular groups of protection seekers onshore. First, a statutory right to prompt periodic review before an independent and impartial body is warranted to guard against bureaucratic inertia and arbitrariness *pending* refugee status/visa determinations.[124] This would enable the detainee to check whether detention was merited (*qua*, necessary and proportionate) in individual circumstances. Importantly, a legal onus should rest on the immigration authorities to demonstrate, at regular intervals if required, the necessity and proportionality of detention after initial checks. Second, for '*failed*' protection seekers ('hard cases', including stateless people) who are detained *pending removal*, periodic access to external merits review to check the necessity and proportionality of ongoing detention where removal is sought but not directly realisable. Third, for those '*declared*' refugees subject to visa refusal or cancellation decisions on adverse security/character grounds,[125] access to periodic merits review to enable careful reconsideration of whether the risks posed to society by an individual can be managed in a less restrictive way other than resorting to indefinite detention in high-security facilities.[126]

Equally, in the United Kingdom, the necessity of detention has not been adequately scrutinised. Although recent case law has confirmed the unfairness and injustice inherent in the DFT regime, and questions have been raised regarding the detention of 'vulnerable people',[127] no decision has been taken declaring the use of (lengthy) detention for protection seekers (and other migrants) to be legally unacceptable. Nor has domestic human rights law or the ECHR obliged the United Kingdom to ground and justify, rigorously and transparently, the need for detention in individual cases. Arguably, the majority judges involved in the *Saadi* litigation, while declaring administrative detention at Oakington reception centre to be legal, did not anticipate that it would be used as extensively, and for as long, as it transpired. Immigration detention is also heavily politicised in the United Kingdom, and it is unlikely that the government will resist re-employing it in accelerated asylum cases; it may be a matter of time, therefore, before a replacement detained fast-track system is introduced. In the meantime, advocates must persist with legal, evidence-based, arguments to

124 The Administrative Appeals Tribunal is competent to carry out a *proportionality-based* review of detention decisions fairly and efficiently – in several respects it proceeds similarly to a curial hearing. An appropriately constituted division of the Tribunal could be empowered to determine, *inter alia*, whether secure/alternative detention, a residence determination (community detention), or visa grant subject to appropriate conditions was the *preferable* resolution in an individual's case.

125 A related problem is the limited access protection seekers have to merits review, and the limited utility of judicial review, over ASIO's adverse security assessments.

126 Joint Select Committee on Australia's Immigration Detention Network, *Final Report* (2012) chs 6 and 7; and Australian Human Rights Commission, *Immigration detention at Curtin: observations from visit to Curtin immigration detention centre and key concerns across the detention network* (2011).

127 Shaw, above n 121.

promote reforms, aimed at ensuring that immigration detention is only used as 'a measure of last resort'.[128]

Conclusions

This chapter has examined a particular form of preventive justice: immigration detention for protection seekers. These detainees are held for *general* preventive (including deterrent) and/or administrative purposes, often in circumstances where they have not committed crimes (although there may have been civil law violations or anticipated infractions). Rather, protection seekers' incarceration stems from their irregular movement and border crossings, and concomitant 'unauthorised' status under municipal laws. Their confinement may persist for months, years even, pending entry-related decisions or removal, deportation or exclusion.

Preventive immigration detention is highly problematical where it is applied indiscriminately and by reason of:

1 *harm prevention* (national security/public welfare/flight risk), in circumstances where the protection seeker is prevented from testing those grounds (and evidence) openly and effectively;
2 *administrative convenience* – an adjunct to (ostensibly, timely) adjudicative processes about protection seekers' claims and their legal status; and
3 *facilitating removal/deportation/exclusion* of individuals, in circumstances where there is no real prospect of expulsion to another state.

Additionally, judicial application of 'reasonableness', to delimit the lawful duration of detention, has not prevented prolonged and arbitrary periods of detention, while administrative processes are undertaken or removal/deportation/exclusion is realised. In view of the comparative case law explored in this chapter, and the punitive experiences of many detainees, a better label for the form of preventive justice examined here would be preventive injustice.[129]

128 United Nations High Commissioner for Human Rights, *Detention Guidelines – Guidelines on the Applicable Criteria and Standards relating to the Detention of Asylum-Seekers and Alternatives to Detention* (2012) (online).
129 See David Dyzenhaus, 'Preventive Justice and the Rule-of-Law Project' in Andrew Ashworth, Lucia Zedner and Patrick Tomlin (eds), *Prevention and the Limits of the Criminal Law* (Oxford University Press, 2013) 9, 92; and Bernadette McSherry, 'Sex, Drugs and Evil Souls' (2006) 32(2) *Monash University Law Review* 237, 271–2.

7 Preventive justice principles for countering violent extremism

Keiran Hardy

Introduction

In response to September 11 and later terror attacks, Western governments enacted a wide range of counter-terrorism laws which provided for coercive powers of arrest, temporary detention, imprisonment and other restrictions on liberty. Most recently, these laws have been supplemented with new offences and powers which are designed to address the threat of terrorism from individuals connected with or inspired by Islamic State.

For good reason, much of the academic literature on prevention in counter-terrorism has focused on these laws: mapping their scope, conceptualising them as a form of prevention, assessing their impact on individuals and communities, and considering how they might be appropriately limited. For example, other chapters in this collection address some of these questions in relation to the Australian control order legislation, which allows the state to impose significant restrictions on an individual's liberty without a finding of criminal guilt.[1]

Alongside these coercive laws, a second approach to preventing terrorism has developed as a key component of national counter-terrorism strategies. This second approach aims to address the underlying causes of terrorism rather than coerce or punish individuals. It developed most prominently in the United Kingdom after the 2005 London bombings, when the *Prevent* strategy became a core component of the United Kingdom's national strategy for countering terrorism.[2] *Prevent* and similar programs in other countries encompass various social policy initiatives which are designed to counter the spread of terrorist ideology and religious radicalisation. There have been renewed calls for such programs in response to the threat of Islamic State, particularly to reduce that organisation's influence through social media and the internet.

For ease of reference, these policy programs will be referred to collectively as countering violent extremism (CVE) programs. CVE programs have also been described as examples of 'soft power' (in contrast to the 'hard power' strategies

1 See, in particular, Chapter 3 by Susan Donkin, Chapter 10 by Rebecca Ananian-Welsh and Chapter 11 by Sarah Murray.

2 Secretary of State for the Home Department (UK), *Prevent Strategy*, Cm 8092 (2011) (Prevent Strategy 2011).

exemplified in counter-terrorism laws),[3] and efforts to win the 'hearts and minds' of communities (in contrast to coercing individuals).[4]

CVE programs are commonly viewed as part of the solution to the problems generated by counter-terrorism laws. For example, it is often recognised that the use of coercive counter-terrorism powers (such as stop and search) has contributed to a sense of alienation and discrimination in Muslim communities, and that this hampers efforts to prevent terrorism by undermining social cohesion and contributing to radicalisation.[5] CVE strategies which aim to improve social cohesion – such as outreach programs for improving relations between police and Muslim communities – are thus seen as an important counterweight to these kinds of problems. Jude McCulloch, Sharon Pickering and David Wright-Neville, for example, argue that non-punitive preventive measures are 'critical to a successful counter-terrorism strategy within societies that are defined by high levels of cultural and religious diversity'.[6] Similarly, David Cole and Jules Lobel argue that the 'best way forward' in counter-terrorism is to 'favour non-coercive preventive safeguards' and to 'develop close positive ties with Arab and Muslim communities'.[7]

This idea, that CVE programs balance out the problems with counter-terrorism laws, is attractive from a policy perspective, but its intuitive appeal is deceptive. A range of recurring issues with *Prevent* have been identified, including that the strategy's heavy focus on Islamist ideology compounds rather than mitigates the sense of discrimination felt in Britain's Muslim communities.[8] It is not yet clear whether similar problems will be experienced in other countries such as Australia and Canada, as those countries have less experience with CVE programs compared with the United Kingdom. Even so, the United Kingdom's problematic experience with *Prevent* certainly urges caution in advocating the benefits of CVE programs as a counterweight to the dangers of coercive preventive measures.

The many recognised problems with *Prevent* suggest that a principled discussion about CVE programs as a *preventive measure* in counter-terrorism is overdue. Too often, CVE programs are raised merely as a social policy alternative to problematic counter-terrorism laws. Yet these programs are also a core component of national

3 Martin Innes, 'Policing Uncertainty: Countering Terror Through Community Intelligence and Democratic Policing' (2006) 605 *The ANNALS of the American Academy of Political and Social Science* 22, 232–4; Sharon Pickering, Jude McCulloch and David Wright-Neville, *Counter-Terrorism Policing: Community, Cohesion and Security* (Springer 2008) 8.
4 Department for Communities and Local Government (UK), *Preventing Violent Extremism: Winning Hearts and Minds* (Communities and Local Government, April 2007).
5 Christina Pantazis and Simon Pemberton, 'From the "Old" to the "New" Suspect Community' (2009) 49(5) *British Journal of Criminology* 646.
6 Pickering, McCulloch and Wright-Neville, above n 3, 8.
7 David Cole and Jules Lobel, *Less Safe, Less Free: Why America is Losing the War on Terror* (New Press, 2007) 14, 265.
8 See especially Communities and Local Government Committee (UK), *Preventing Violent Extremism*, House of Commons Sixth Report, Session 2009–10 (2010) (CLG Committee) 9–10, 20–1.

counter-terrorism strategies, and they can also have a detrimental impact on relationships between police and Muslim communities.

The existing focus on coercive measures in preventive justice scholarship is understandable. Counter-terrorism laws pose obvious problems for human rights and the rule of law, and legal scholars have a range of concepts and principles at their disposal to analyse and critique these laws (including the harm principle, inchoate liability, and the rights to liberty and a fair trial). But CVE programs also raise a number of important issues which might be examined through a preventive justice lens, and they have not yet received any significant scholarly attention in this field.[9] There is indeed a voluminous literature on *Prevent*,[10] but that literature identifies policy problems with that particular strategy; it does not raise a more general discussion about the principles that should guide and limit the use of CVE programs as preventive measures in counter-terrorism.

This chapter aims to fill this important gap by considering whether it is appropriate to apply a preventive justice framework to CVE programs, and, if so, which preventive justice principles might guide and limit their use. It does so by examining Ashworth and Zedner's major study into preventive justice,[11] and questioning whether a similar conceptual framework would be justified in relation to the United Kingdom's *Prevent* strategy and like programs in other countries. In essence, the chapter asks whether existing approaches to preventive justice in counter-terrorism should be expanded to account for the use and operation of non-coercive preventive measures.

Part I of this chapter provides an overview of the United Kingdom's experience with *Prevent*. The aim of this section is not to set out the strategy and the issues it raises in detail, but rather to provide sufficient context to guide the remainder of the inquiry.

Part II explains Ashworth and Zedner's approach to preventive justice and identifies a number of their key principles. Part III considers whether it is appropriate to apply a preventive justice approach to CVE programs, and Part IV considers which principles might be relevant to those programs.

Within the confines of this chapter, it is not possible to develop a comprehensive framework for applying preventive justice principles to non-coercive preventive measures. Instead, Part IV is intended as the beginning of a discussion into what such a framework might look like. It asks: which of Ashworth and Zedner's

9 Ashworth and Zedner discuss briefly the relevance of CVE programs to preventive justice, but otherwise exclude these programs from consideration in their study: Andrew Ashworth and Lucia Zedner, *Preventive Justice* (Oxford University Press, 2014) 191–2.

10 See e.g. Paul Thomas, 'Failed and Friendless: The UK's "Preventing Violent Extremism" Programme' (2010) 12(3) *British Journal of Politics and International Relations* 442; Rachel Briggs, 'Community Engagement for Counterterrorism: Lessons from the United Kingdom' (2010) 86(4) *International Affairs* 971; Anthony Richards, 'The Problem with "Radicalization": The Remit of "Prevent" and the Need to Refocus on Terrorism in the UK' (2011) 87(1) *International Affairs* 143.

11 Ashworth and Zedner, above n 9.

principles are relevant to CVE programs, which are not, and which might be in need of some modification? Are any different or additional principles required to account for the particular problems generated by CVE programs?

Due to obvious and important differences between coercive laws and social policy, some modifications are clearly required when applying a preventive justice framework to CVE programs. However, it also becomes clear from this inquiry that preventive justice has much to offer when determining the values, limits and principles that should apply to non-coercive preventive measures in counter-terrorism.

Part I: The *Prevent* strategy and other CVE programs

The key example of a national program for countering terrorist ideology and radicalisation is the United Kingdom's *Prevent* strategy. *Prevent* is one of four strands in 'CONTEST', the United Kingdom's national strategy for countering terrorism.[12] A short version of *Prevent* initially appeared in the first publication of CONTEST in 2006,[13] although the more comprehensive document which came to be known as the '*Prevent* strategy' was published separately by the Labour government of Gordon Brown in 2008.[14] This strategy was revised by the Coalition government in 2011 after a range of problems and concerns were identified with the Labour government's approach.[15] The three aims of the current strategy are to:

1 counter terrorist ideology;
2 support vulnerable individuals; and
3 work with sectors and institutions where there are risks of radicalisation.[16]

Prevent work under the first objective largely centres around government efforts to counter terrorist propaganda, including through the media and online. Under the second objective, a police-supervised intervention program called 'Channel'

12 Secretary of State for the Home Department (UK), *CONTEST: The United Kingdom's Strategy for Countering Terrorism*, Cm 8123 (2011) (CONTEST 2011). The three other strands of CONTEST are 'Pursue', which roughly correlates with the United Kingdom's counter-terrorism laws but also includes an international dimension such as training foreign security services to combat terrorism; 'Protect', which focuses on protecting the United Kingdom's population and critical national infrastructure from terrorist acts; and 'Prepare', which focuses on developing emergency response procedures that can be used in the event of a successful attack.

13 Secretary of State for the Home Department (UK), *Countering International Terrorism: The United Kingdom's Strategy*, Cm 6888 (2006) 1–2, 9–12.

14 Home Office and Department for Communities and Local Government (UK), *The Prevent Strategy: A Guide for Local Partners in England – Stopping People Becoming or Supporting Terrorists and Violent Extremists* (Home Office and Department for Communities and Local Government, May 2008) (Prevent Strategy 2008).

15 Prevent Strategy 2011, above n 2.

16 Ibid. 7.

provides support to individuals who are determined to be at risk of radicalisation. Such support can include counselling, housing, employment and other services relevant to each individual. Under the third objective, employees in schools, hospitals and other public institutions are trained to identify individuals at risk of radicalisation. There is less of a focus on community-led projects under the Coalition government compared with Labour, although some 180 local authority projects (including education and internet safety programs) have been delivered under the new strategy.[17]

In 2015, elements of the *Prevent* strategy were put on a statutory footing.[18] There is now a duty on 'specified authorities' – including schools, universities and health services – to have 'due regard to the need to prevent people from being drawn into terrorism'.[19] Channel interventions are now also a statutory requirement, as each local authority area across the United Kingdom must ensure that a panel of persons is in place to assess the 'extent to which identified individuals are vulnerable to being drawn into terrorism'.[20]

Concerns with the *Prevent* strategy have largely centred around allegations of spying and discrimination against Britain's Muslim communities. This has resulted from a number of factors, including heavy police oversight, a lack of community control, and a disproportionate focus on combating extremist Islam compared with other forms of terrorism.[21] The Channel intervention program has caused particular concern about 'spying' on communities because United Kingdom police collected demographic data and sensitive personal details in order to determine which individuals required support under the program.[22] Since 2009, the *Prevent* strategy has also encompassed efforts to counter 'non-violent' extremism,[23] which threatens free speech on political and religious matters.

The Coalition government's revised strategy eased some of these concerns, although significant problems still remain. For example, while the Coalition government nominally expanded the scope of *Prevent* to include extreme right-wing and other forms of terrorism, it recognised that in practice the strategy will continue to focus on Islamist extremism.[24] This suggests that perceptions of discrimination against Muslim communities under the revised strategy are likely to persist. The Coalition government also maintained the Labour government's controversial approach to countering 'non-violent' extremism.[25] Consequently,

17 Secretary of State for the Home Department (UK), *CONTEST – The United Kingdom's Strategy for Countering Terrorism: Annual Report for 2014*, Cm 9048 (2015) 17.
18 *Counter-Terrorism and Security Act 2015* (UK) c 6, pt 5.
19 Ibid. s 26.
20 Ibid. s 36.
21 See generally CLG Committee, above n 8, 8–21, 44–62.
22 Vikram Dodd, 'Government Anti-Terrorism Strategy "Spies" on Innocent', *The Guardian* (London), 16 October 2009.
23 Secretary of State for the Home Department (UK), *Pursue Prevent Protect Prepare The United Kingdom's Strategy for Countering Terrorism*, Cm 7547 (2009) 13 (CONTEST 2009); Prevent Strategy 2011, above n 2, 6.
24 Prevent Strategy 2011, above n 2, 14–15, 25.
25 Ibid. 6.

the Home Affairs Committee reported in 2012 that there was still 'a lingering suspicion about the Prevent strategy amongst Muslim communities, many of whom continue to believe that it is essentially a tool for intelligence-gathering or spying'.[26]

The Coalition government's strategy also raised some new problems of its own, particularly as the statutory obligations placed on schools and universities to prevent people from being drawn into terrorism threatens free speech and academic freedom. Concerns have been expressed that these new duties will require university staff to inform and 'spy' on their Muslim students.[27]

This problematic experience with *Prevent* is not necessarily indicative of how CVE programs will operate in other countries. For example, it appears that Australia's community policing efforts in counter-terrorism have so far helped to improve relations between Muslim communities and police.[28] Nonetheless, the United Kingdom's experience with *Prevent* clearly demonstrates that CVE programs can compound the problems generated by coercive preventive measures in counter-terrorism. In particular, CVE programs have the capacity to compound rather than mitigate damaging perceptions of government spying and discrimination against Muslim communities. This gives ample reason to question whether preventive justice scholarship can speak to these social policy programs as well as to coercive counter-terrorism laws.

Part II: Ashworth and Zedner – preventive justice principles

In 2014, Ashworth and Zedner published the results of a three-year study into preventive justice.[29] The core aim of this study was to 'develop an account of the principles and values that should guide and limit the state's use of preventive techniques that involve coercion'.[30] Their key contribution is a list of 25 principles to guide and limit the state's use of coercive preventive measures.[31] These principles speak not only (or even primarily) to counter-terrorism, but to a wide range of contexts including immigration, mental health detention and the criminal law more generally.

26 Home Affairs Committee (UK), *Roots of Violent Radicalisation,* House of Commons Paper No 1446, Nineteenth Report of Session 2010–12 (2012) 31.
27 Ryan Gallagher and Rajeev Syal, 'University staff asked to inform on "vulnerable" Muslim students', *The Guardian* (online), 30 August 2011, available at www.theguardian.com/education/2011/aug/29/university-inform-vulnerable-muslim-students (accessed 5 September 2016); Home Affairs Committee, above n 26, Ev 104.
28 See e.g. Australian Human Rights Commission, Australian Multicultural Foundation and Australian Research Council Centre of Excellence in Policing and Security, *Building Trust: Working with Muslim Communities in Australia – A Review of the Community Policing Partnership Project* (AHRC and AMF, December 2010) 305 (Building Trust Review).
29 Ashworth and Zedner, above n 9.
30 Ibid.
31 Ibid. 254–64.

For the purposes of the sections below, it is important to define the key terms that frame Ashworth and Zedner's study. By 'preventive', they mean measures adopted by the state that are designed to reduce or avert a risk of harm.[32] By 'justice', they mean two things: first, that the preventive measures they address are part of an '*official framework* of measures aimed at dealing with certain issues'[33] and, second, that they develop a set of values and limiting principles 'that might be applied to concrete matters of lawmaking, policy, and practice'.[34] In other words, 'preventive justice' means that the measures adopted by the state in order to reduce or avert risks of harm are developed according to certain values and principles and confined within appropriate limits – as well as a conceptual framework which can be applied, in practice, to achieve these goals.

Ashworth and Zedner limit their study to *coercive* preventive measures, being preventive measures which involve 'state-imposed restrictions on liberty'.[35] They justify this focus first on the grounds that coercive preventive measures 'involve the authorized deprivation of basic rights', and second because the 'use of coercion stands contrary to a basic respect for the autonomy of individuals'.[36] These justifications for focusing on coercive measures are important for determining whether preventive justice has any relevance for CVE programs, and will be returned to in Part IV below.

Within the confines of this chapter, it is not possible to adequately recount or address each of Ashworth and Zedner's 25 principles. In order to consider the relevance of their framework for CVE programs, Part IV of this chapter will focus on a smaller number of principles which are key to Ashworth and Zedner's analysis. It will begin by considering their first six principles, which Ashworth and Zedner consider to be the 'most prominent'.[37] These are as follows:

- the right to liberty of the person;[38]
- the presumption of innocence;[39]
- the presumption of harmlessness;[40]
- The principle of the least restrictive appropriate alternative, which provides that individual liberty should not be interfered with if alternative means could appropriately achieve the same objective;[41]
- the principle of parsimony, which is based on a similar proportionality logic to the principle of the least restrictive appropriate alternative in requiring that

32 Ibid. 5, 20.
33 Ibid. 6 (emphasis added).
34 Ibid. 6.
35 Ibid. 20.
36 Ibid. 6, 250.
37 Ibid. 253.
38 Ibid. 52–3.*Convention for the Protection of Human Rights and Fundamental Freedoms*, opened for signature 4 November 1950, 213 UNTS 221 (entered into force 3 September 1953) art 5.
39 Ashworth and Zedner, above n 9, 53.
40 Ibid. 123, 131–2, 147, 168.
41 Ibid. 195.

'any interference with an individual's rights should be kept to a minimum consistent with security';[42]
- the necessity principle, which requires that any interference with individual liberty should be kept to the minimum necessary to achieve a preventive purpose.[43]

In order to determine whether preventive measures abide by the last three principles, the state must also consider the relative efficacy of alternative courses of action. Ashworth and Zedner are careful not to place too much weight on this idea, lest preventive measures be justified merely on the results they achieve, regardless of principled concerns.[44] However, they also argue that liberty-depriving powers should be supported by 'substantial evidential foundations' and that 'claims of operational necessity ought not to be accepted too readily or without *concrete evidence* that they are necessary'.[45] Due to the close connection between efficacy and the other key principles above, and because debates about effectiveness feature in other chapters in this collection,[46] Part IV will also consider the state's obligation to justify preventive measures on the grounds that they are effective in achieving their intended purposes.

In addition, Part IV will consider prominent rule of law values discussed by Ashworth and Zedner, as these are significant to any discussion of preventive measures in a modern democratic state. Although there are many different conceptions of the rule of law, the principle of maximum certainty and the prohibition against overbreadth are given particular emphasis in their study and are particularly relevant to counter-terrorism legislation. The principle of maximum certainty requires that criminal offences be 'drafted with as much certainty as possible, so as to clarify the boundaries of the criminal sanction, both for individuals and for courts'.[47] The prohibition against overbreadth provides that the criminal law should not 'provide for the criminalization and punishment of conduct that is significantly broader than the wrong it is aimed to prevent'.[48]

Finally, Part IV will consider the relevance of procedural safeguards. Ashworth and Zedner raise a number of more specific principles relating to courtroom procedure and evidence which are not immediately relevant to CVE programs.[49] However, these principles can be captured in a more general idea: individuals should be provided an 'opportunity to challenge'.[50] This would require that 'no

42 Ibid. 254.
43 Ibid.
44 Ibid. 195.
45 Ibid. 257 (emphasis added).
46 See Chapter 8 by Svetlana Tyulkina and George Williams, and Chapter 9 by Tim Legrand and Teneille Elliott in this collection.
47 Ashworth and Zedner, above n 9, 113.
48 Ibid.
49 Ibid. 261–2 (Principles R-V).
50 Ashworth and Zedner, above n 9, 169.

deprivation of a fundamental right be permitted without provision for the individual to challenge the decision upon which it is based'.[51]

This selection of principles does not exhaustively recreate Ashworth and Zedner's study, but it captures the essence of their framework in a form that is appropriate for a balanced analysis in the sections below. The principles that have been excluded are more specific to three areas: deprivations of liberty,[52] the drafting of criminal offences[53] and courtroom procedure.[54] These are not immediately relevant to CVE programs, and this of itself may say something about the relevance of preventive justice to social policy. However, these other principles have not been excluded merely to benefit this analysis. It will become clear in Part IV (and may already be apparent) that some of the principles identified above are relevant to social policy, while others are not, and some may be in need of modification if applied in other contexts.

The essence of these excluded principles has also been captured to some degree in those selected above. For example, those relating to courtroom procedure have been captured generally in the idea of an 'opportunity to challenge'.[55] The principles selected above may therefore serve as a useful distillation of Ashworth and Zedner's work which can be applied to other, non-legal contexts.

Part III: Applying a preventive justice approach to CVE programs

Ashworth and Zedner confine their study to coercive preventive measures,[56] so before determining the extent to which the principles identified above are relevant to CVE programs, we must first determine whether it is appropriate *at all* to analyse CVE programs through a preventive justice lens. This resonates with discussions in other chapters as to whether coercion is a necessary element of measures that are deemed an appropriate subject for preventive justice.[57]

The defining elements of Ashworth and Zedner's study suggest several reasons why it *is* justifiable to take a preventive justice approach to CVE programs. First, CVE programs are designed to reduce or avert the risk of a terrorist attack, so they are undoubtedly 'preventive' according to Ashworth and Zedner's definition.[58] More specifically, CVE programs are designed to prevent terrorist acts by

51 Ibid.
52 Ibid. 259–60 (Principles L–Q).
53 Ibid. 256 (Principles G–K).
54 Ibid. 261–2 (Principles R–Y).
55 See ibid. 169, 261–2. The essence of Principles L–Q (relating to deprivations of liberty) are captured to some degree by the first six key principles identified above, in part because Principles L–N largely repeat Principles A, C and D: see ibid. 256, 259. Those relating to the drafting of criminal offences (Principles G–K) are represented to a lesser degree, but the principles of maximum certainty and overbreadth have been included from this category: see ibid. 256.
56 Ibid. 6.
57 See e.g. Chapter 1 by Tamara Tulich and Chapter 4 by Bernadette McSherry in this collection.
58 Ashworth and Zedner, above n 9, 20.

countering the spread of terrorist ideology and radicalisation. In her foreword to the revised *Prevent* strategy, then Home Secretary Theresa May considered it 'vital that our counter-terrorism strategy contains a plan to prevent radicalisation and stop would-be terrorists from committing mass murder'.[59]

Second, CVE programs are part of the government's 'official framework' for preventing terrorist acts.[60] Since its inception, *Prevent* has remained one of four strands in CONTEST, the United Kingdom's national strategy for countering terrorism.[61] It might even be said, now that key elements of *Prevent* have been placed on a statutory footing,[62] that the lines between the state's legal responses to terrorism on the one hand and its social policy responses on the other are not as clear as they were when the *Prevent* strategy was first conceived.

Third, a key reason for Ashworth and Zedner's study was to articulate a set of values and limiting principles that could 'be applied to concrete matters of law-making, policy, and practice'.[63] The United Kingdom's problematic experience with *Prevent*, and particularly the damaging perceptions the strategy has generated in Britain's Muslim communities, suggests that developing a similar conceptual framework in relation to CVE programs would be a valuable contribution to counter-terrorism policymaking and practice.

Several other reasons for analysing counter-terrorism laws through a preventive justice lens are also present in the case of CVE programs. For example, in determining which individuals are vulnerable to radicalisation and likely to become involved in terrorism, early intervention programs like Channel also rely on problematic *predictions about future behaviour*.[64] CVE programs can suffer from *uncertainty*, as there is often a lack of clarity in these strategies as to the meaning of key terms such as 'extremism', 'violent' and 'radicalisation'.[65] They can also suffer from *overbreadth* in targeting non-violent and legitimate forms of expression.[66] Finally, they may impact on the *freedoms of speech* and *freedom from discrimination* by reducing the scope of speech acts considered acceptable by the state and by disproportionately targeting Muslim communities.

The major difference between counter-terrorism laws and CVE programs is, of course, that counter-terrorism laws involve *coercive* powers and sanctions, whereas the social policy initiatives found in CVE programs are (formally, at least) non-coercive. Community discussion groups and early intervention programs clearly do not involve 'state-imposed restrictions on liberty' such as arrest or imprisonment.[67]

59 Prevent Strategy 2011, above n 2, 1.
60 See e.g. Ashworth and Zedner, above n 9, 6.
61 CONTEST 2011, above n 12, 58–77.
62 *Counter-Terrorism and Security Act 2015* (UK) c 6 pt 5 ss 26, 36.
63 Ashworth and Zedner, above n 9, 6.
64 On the unreliability of such predictions, see Ashworth and Zedner, above n 9, 119–43.
65 See glossary in Prevent Strategy 2011, above n 2, 107–8 and discussion in Part V below.
66 CONTEST 2009, above n 23, 13; Prevent Strategy 2011, above n 2, 6.
67 Ashworth and Zedner, above n 9, 20.

This certainly needs to be factored into any analysis, but it is unclear whether it should be fatal to the current inquiry. On the one hand, a major founding reason for Ashworth and Zedner's study is not present.[68] As explained above, many of their more specific principles relating to coercive measures (namely, those relating to criminalisation, deprivations of liberty and courtroom procedures) have been excluded from this analysis as those principles are not immediately relevant to CVE programs. These important differences suggest that it is difficult to apply existing preventive justice frameworks beyond coercive legal measures.

On the other hand, the distinction that Ashworth and Zedner draw between coercive and non-coercive preventive measures in counter-terrorism may not be as clear as it first seems. The kinds of behaviours targeted by counter-terrorism laws and CVE programs, for example, can overlap. This is obvious in the list of risk factors relied upon by Channel coordinators to identify individuals at risk of radicalisation, which includes:

- spending increasing time in the company of other suspected extremists;
- changing their style of dress or personal appearance to accord with an extremist group
- attempts to recruit others to an extremist group
- expressing attitudes that justify offending on behalf of an extremist group
- plotting or conspiring with others.[69]

These behaviours are also clearly targeted by several offences in the *Terrorism Act 2000* (UK) (TA2000) and the *Terrorism Act 2006* (UK) (TA2006), including membership of a terrorist organisation, supporting a terrorist organisation, wearing the uniform of a terrorist organisation, encouragement of terrorism, and even the preparation of terrorist acts.[70] Indeed, the Coalition government recognised that conduct targeted under Channel 'may involve illegality', but noted merely that individuals who participate in the program will not receive a criminal record.[71]

It seems that counter-terrorism laws and CVE programs can also have similar aims – not only in the general sense that both strategies aim to prevent terrorism, but also more specifically with regard to *how* they aim to prevent terrorism. Like non-coercive policy measures in the *Prevent* strategy, the terrorist organisation offences in the TA2000 and speech offences in the TA2006 are also designed, in part, to prevent terrorist acts by countering the spread of terrorist ideology and radicalisation.[72]

It may even be possible to conceive of CVE programs as being coercive. As Ashworth and Zedner explain, coercion 'can be viewed from a subjective or

68 Ashworth and Zedner, above n 9, 6, 20, 250.

69 Home Office (UK), *Channel: Protecting Vulnerable from Being Drawn into Terrorism – A Guide for Local Partnerships* (Home Office, 2012) 12 (Channel Duty Guidance).

70 *Terrorism Act 2000* (UK) c 11, ss 11–13; *Terrorism Act 2006* (UK) c 11, ss 1, 5.

71 Channel Duty Guidance, above n 69, 11.

72 Prevent Strategy 2011, above n 2, 26.

objective point of view'.[73] That is, preventive measures are objectively coercive when the state intends that those measures will compel individuals to act in a particular way. However, an individual may still *feel* coerced, even if that is not the state's intention and the preventive measure does not involve formal sanction.[74] This is certainly the case under *Prevent*, as Britain's Muslim communities continue to perceive that strategy as a surveillance program which aims to bring their beliefs and behaviour in line with ill-defined 'British values'.[75] In particular, individuals may feel compelled to participate in intervention programs like Channel, even if they are not strictly required to do so.

The lack of formal or objective coercion, then, does not necessarily mean that CVE programs do not have a coercive impact on individuals and communities, or that they should be *a priori* excluded from the scope of preventive justice scholarship on those grounds. It may just mean that CVE programs are coercive in different ways to counter-terrorism laws. Although Ashworth and Zedner do not focus on CVE programs, they do recognise the potentially coercive nature of such strategies:

> [T]he use of 'soft' power under *Prevent* merges into more intrusive and liberty-eroding security strategies, such as surveillance, monitoring, intelligence gathering, and use of informants. . . . [D]espite the designation of *Prevent* as a form of 'soft' power, it is clear that it has coercive aspects and may render individuals more liable to coercive or, at least, intrusive measures.[76]

It may also be possible to justify a preventive justice approach to CVE programs on the grounds that those programs reduce individual autonomy.[77] If autonomy is defined as the capacity for individuals to determine the course of their own lives (that is, to *choose* different courses of action),[78] then it is clear that CVE programs like *Prevent* should also be included in principled discussions about preventive justice in counter-terrorism. *Prevent* restricts the range of beliefs and opinions that are considered acceptable by the state, and programs like Channel intervene into individuals' lives before those individuals have had sufficient opportunity to choose a different course of behaviour from that predicted by the state. In other words, like the United Kingdom's counter-terrorism laws,[79] Channel fails to treat individuals as rational, autonomous beings who are capable of choosing not to engage

73 Ashworth and Zedner, above n 9, 7.
74 Ibid.
75 CLG Committee, above n 8, Ev 102.
76 Ashworth and Zedner, above n 9, 191–2.
77 Ibid. 6.
78 Definitions of autonomy are contested, but key to most accounts is the idea that individuals should have the capacity to *choose* different courses of action: see e.g. John Christman and Joel Anderson (eds), *Autonomy and the Challenges to Liberalism: New Essays* (Cambridge University Press, 2009) 3.
79 Lucia Zedner, 'Preventive Justice or Pre-Punishment? The Case of Control Orders' (2007) 60(1) *Current Legal Problems* 174.

in unlawful conduct. This issue raises a complex debate about how to define autonomy and how to conceive of its relationship with personal *freedom*,[80] a much larger question which cannot be adequately addressed here. This could, however, provide a fruitful area for further research and debate.

The analysis above suggests that the traditional dichotomy between coercive and non-coercive measures does not sufficiently capture the complexity of preventive measures in counter-terrorism. Instead, it might be more accurate to think in terms of a spectrum of preventive measures in counter-terrorism, beginning at one end with substantive offences, and then moving 'back in time' to cover inchoate liability, pre-inchoate offences, Channel interventions, community projects and other social policy responses. The further back you move along this spectrum, the less coercive those preventive responses become, and the more they become targeted at the general population rather than individuals.

Even this spectrum, however, would not fully capture the complexity of preventive measures in counter-terrorism. As discussed above, for example, intervention programs and criminal offences can target the same conduct but lead to very different consequences. Coercive powers (such as stop and search) might also be used against large sections of the population,[81] whereas intervention programs like Channel are formally non-coercive but target individuals for engaging in conduct which might be unlawful.

However this spectrum of preventive responses might be conceived, it appears there are several reasons why it is appropriate and justifiable to apply a preventive justice framework to CVE programs. Given the many recognised problems with Prevent, it is also clear that counter-terrorism policymaking and practice would benefit from such an inquiry. The next section addresses this issue more closely, by considering what a preventive justice framework might look like if applied to CVE programs. It does so by considering the extent to which the principles set out in Part II are relevant to those programs.

Part IV: Which preventive justice principles?

If it is appropriate and justifiable to apply a preventive justice framework to CVE programs, the next important question is: what might such a framework look like? Despite some similarities in the issues raised by counter-terrorism laws and CVE communities (including uncertainty and overbreadth, and perceptions of discrimination against Muslim communities), there are clearly important differences.

80 Definitions of autonomy are usually distinguished from personal freedom, which describes the instrumental capacity to adopt different courses of action (such as to move wherever one chooses), as opposed to the mental capacity to *choose* how to act: John Christman, 'Constructing the Inner Citadel: Recent Work on the Concept of Autonomy' (1988) 99(1) *Ethics* 109, 111–12.

81 As was the case with the use of stop and search powers under s 44 of the TA2000 in Greater London before those laws were amended in 2012 by the *Protection of Freedoms Act 2012* (UK): see Ashworth and Zedner, above n 9, 55–8.

Most obviously, social policy programs do not involve formal punishment or restrictions on liberty.

It is not possible within the remaining scope of this chapter to set out a comprehensive framework for applying preventive justice principles to CVE programs. Indeed, the current inquiry raises a much larger question as to how preventive justice frameworks might be applied to non-coercive measures in areas other than counter-terrorism (including community policing more generally, and other forms of social and community crime prevention). What features below is intended as a brief sketch of what such a framework might look like in relation to CVE programs, to act as a catalyst for future debate. It will move through each of the key preventive justice principles identified in Part II, and assess the relevance of each in relation to the *Prevent* strategy and like programs.

Beginning with the first of Ashworth and Zedner's key principles, the right to liberty appears to have no relevance to CVE programs as it relates to formally coercive measures which result in deprivations of liberty. However, the presumptions of innocence and harmlessness appear to have some relevance for de-radicalisation and intervention programs like Channel. Given the unreliable nature of predictions about dangerousness and future behaviour, as well as the stigmatising effects of labelling individuals as dangerous,[82] the state should err on the side of assuming that individuals are *not* at risk of radicalisation for the purposes of such programs, rather than exposing them to unnecessary and stigmatising counter-terrorism interventions.

The principle of the least restrictive alternative should be applied when choosing between different approaches to CVE programs. If this principle dictates (as Ashworth and Zedner suggest) that CVE programs should be preferred over coercive counter-terrorism laws,[83] then it should also dictate that less intrusive social policy measures (such as community education projects) should be favoured over more intrusive social policy measures (such as Channel interventions).

The principles of parsimony and necessity are more relevant to coercive preventive measures, as they relate to whether sentencing decisions unduly impact on the right to liberty. However, these principles reveal a similar proportionality logic to the principle of the least restrictive alternative, in that any state action against the individual should be limited to the maximum extent possible, where two or more alternative courses of action are available.

The need for the state to demonstrate the efficacy of preventive measures is particularly relevant to CVE programs. There is very little direct evidence that CVE programs are effective in preventing terrorist acts,[84] and indeed it is not clear whether their effectiveness in this regard could ever be validly and accurately quantified. It is extremely difficult, for example, for a government to determine the extent to which a community discussion group about Islam contributed to a reduction in terrorism, or to adequately prove that a young individual on a

82 See Ashworth and Zedner, above n 9, 123.
83 Ibid. 255.
84 CLG Committee, above n 8, 52, Ev 4, Ev 21, Ev 67, Ev 73.

de-radicalisation program was otherwise going to become involved in terrorist activity.

There are no easy solutions to this problem. A common approach is to judge perceptions as to how these programs are received by communities,[85] but this says little about whether these programs are actually effective in preventing terrorist acts. Given the damaging perceptions that CVE programs can generate in Muslim communities, governments should conduct further research into whether these programs are having some beneficial effect in preventing terrorism – and produce such evidence to the wider public – before investing more funds and allowing these kinds of programs to expand.

The rule of law values discussed by Ashworth and Zedner have a particular legal meaning and significance, but the principle of maximum certainty and the prohibition against overbreadth should equally play an important role in principled discussions about CVE programs. Although the Coalition government included in its *Prevent* strategy a glossary of definitions which had not been provided by the Labour government,[86] this list of definitions remains vague and problematic. For example, 'extremism' is defined as 'vocal or active opposition to fundamental British values, including democracy, the rule of law, individual liberty and mutual respect and tolerance of different faiths and beliefs'.[87] This captures a range of speech acts which should be considered legitimate in a free democratic state, and it is difficult to see how individuals can adequately guide their conduct in relation to vague and problematic phrases such as 'fundamental British values'. Equally, the United Kingdom's government's continuing attempts to counter 'non-violent' extremism suggest that the scope of the *Prevent* strategy is framed more broadly than is necessary to prevent terrorism.

It might also be said that CVE programs undermine rule of law values by permitting significant state intervention into the lives of individuals and communities without legal authority and democratic approval. It is now a statutory requirement for local authorities to implement Channel across the United Kingdom,[88] but the details of this program (particularly the list of risk factors that are used to determine whether individuals are vulnerable to radicalisation) are determined by policy rather than law.[89]

There are indeed a range of recognised problems with the United Kingdom's counter-terrorism laws, but at least it can be said that those laws were passed by a democratically elected Parliament, and that the legislation itself and its use by police and other public officials is open to legal challenge. For example, decisions by the United Kingdom's House of Lords and Supreme Court and the European Court of Human Rights led to important changes to the United Kingdom's control order and stop and search legislation, which lessened the impact of those powers

85 See e.g. CLG Committee, above n 8; Building Trust Review, above n 28.
86 Prevent Strategy 2011, above n 2, 107–8.
87 Ibid. 107.
88 *Counter-Terrorism and Security Act 2015* (UK) c 6, pt 5, s 36.
89 See Channel Duty Guidance, above n 69, 12.

on individuals and communities.[90] In relation to de-radicalisation programs like Channel, no such avenues for legal challenge are available.

The procedural safeguards discussed by Ashworth and Zedner are also more directly relevant to counter-terrorism laws,[91] but it could be said that individuals who are wrongfully targeted with *Prevent*-style strategies should also be provided an 'opportunity to challenge' any decisions taken against their interests.[92] This is particularly relevant to de-radicalisation programs like Channel, which may wrongfully expose individuals to stigmatising counter-terrorism interventions. Where an individual is wrongfully assessed as requiring support under a de-radicalisation program, there should be some right to remedy (whether through damages or some other means) to account for the stigmatising effects of being associated with such a program.

In addition, CVE programs raise some particular concerns which may require some different or additional principles to be taken into account. This could include a greater discussion of how CVE programs impact on:

- The rights to freedom of speech and freedom from discrimination. This should include an assessment of the 'chilling' effect that such programs have on free discussion in schools and universities, and on public debate more generally.
- Institutional freedom. Now that the *Prevent* strategy is expanding into schools, universities, health services and other diverse parts of the public sector,[93] an assessment of how *Prevent* impacts on the culture and freedom of these institutions is required.
- The autonomy of communities. In particular, communities should be given a more significant role in developing their own projects for countering extremist ideology and radicalisation.[94] Imposing community-based strategies 'top-down' from a centralised government has contributed further to negative perceptions that *Prevent* is intended merely as a pretext for spying on communities.[95]

Finally, governments should clearly demarcate the lines between counter-terrorism laws and CVE programs. More specifically, governments should make clear which kinds of conduct may result in investigation by the authorities and possible sanction under the criminal law, which kinds of conduct will result in Channel interventions or other de-radicalisation initiatives, and which conduct is lawful and legitimate and will not justify a state response. Currently, the blurred boundaries between the United Kingdom's counter-terrorism laws and its *Prevent*

90 See Ashworth and Zedner, above n 9, 54–9, 185–9.
91 See ibid. 261–2.
92 Ibid. 169.
93 Prevent Strategy 2011, above n 2, 63–94; *Counter-Terrorism and Security Act 2015* (UK) c 6, pt 5 s 26.
94 See CLG Committee, above n 8.
95 Ibid. 49.

strategy continue to generate damaging perceptions that *Prevent* is simply a pretext for spying on Muslim communities.

A conceptual framework along these lines, which adapted existing approaches to preventive justice and accounted for the particular concerns of CVE programs, would be a valuable addition to counter-terrorism policymaking and practice. It would ensure that discussions about preventive justice in counter-terrorism take stock not only of problematic counter-terrorism laws, but also of non-coercive preventive measures which have a more subtle but no less damaging impact on community cohesion.

Conclusions

Determining the values and limiting principles that should apply to coercive counter-terrorism laws remains a key task, particularly as governments continue to develop new legal responses to the threat of foreign fighters returning from the conflicts in Iraq and Syria. At the same time, much greater attention should be paid to how social policy measures for countering terrorist ideology and radicalisation may compound the difficulties posed by these laws.

Too often, CVE programs are raised merely as a beneficial counterweight to coercive powers, when these programs can also generate damaging perceptions that the authorities are spying on and unfairly targeting Muslim communities. It is indeed possible that CVE programs may have a beneficial effect, but only if they are designed according to appropriate values and limiting principles. There is nothing inherent in the nature of these programs which makes them an unproblematic saviour to the many diverse problems of counter-terrorism laws.

The sections above have addressed two important questions: whether it is appropriate to apply a preventive justice framework to CVE programs, and the extent to which preventive justice principles are relevant to those programs. Part II identified a number of Ashworth and Zedner's preventive justice principles, and Parts III and IV assessed the relevance of their framework for CVE programs. This analysis focused on the United Kingdom's *Prevent* strategy, as *Prevent* clearly demonstrates the capacity for CVE programs to compound the problems with counter-terrorism laws. However, the above analysis could be used to help guide the development of CVE programs in other countries which have less experience in implementing formal strategies for countering radicalisation.

There are several reasons why it is justifiable to take a preventive justice approach to CVE programs. Like counter-terrorism laws, CVE programs are preventive measures designed to reduce the risk of terrorist acts and they are part of the state's official framework for countering terrorism. In particular, the many recognised problems with *Prevent* suggest that articulating a set of values and limiting principles for CVE programs would be a valuable contribution to counter-terrorism policymaking and practice.

The major conceptual hurdle in expanding existing preventive justice approaches to encompass CVE programs is that CVE programs are formally non-coercive.

However, this in itself should not deny the relevance of a preventive justice approach to CVE programs and the benefits such an approach could provide. This is, first, because the lines between coercive and non-coercive measures in counter-terrorism are not always clear. The Channel intervention program is a clear example of this, as the types of conduct it targets overlap to a significant degree with conduct criminalised under the United Kingdom's counter-terrorism laws. Second, if coercion is conceived as having both objective and subjective forms, then it is also possible to view CVE programs as having a coercive effect on individuals and communities, despite the lack of formal sanction. This is certainly the case with *Prevent*, as Britain's Muslim communities have perceived that strategy as a surveillance program which compels them to act in accordance with 'British values'.[96]

In considering which preventive justice principles are relevant to CVE programs, some modification of Ashworth and Zedner's framework is clearly required to account for important differences between coercive laws and social policy. Many of the more specific principles developed by Ashworth and Zedner are not directly relevant to CVE programs, as those programs do not involve deprivations of liberty, criminal offences or courtroom procedures.

Nonetheless, there is much reason to believe that preventive justice frameworks can speak to CVE programs as well as to coercive counter-terrorism laws. Drawing on the analysis in Part IV, a list of preventive justice principles for CVE programs could include the following:

- Individuals should be presumed *not* to be at risk of radicalisation unless there is compelling evidence to the contrary.
- Governments should favour community-based social policy initiatives (such as education programs) over targeted interventions (such as de-radicalisation programs).
- Governments should conduct further research into the effectiveness of CVE programs, and produce that research to the general public.
- CVE programs should contain clear definitions of important terms such as 'extremism', 'violence' and 'radicalisation'.
- CVE programs should only target violent extremism which poses a risk to security; 'non-violent extremism' should be addressed through other social policy avenues and public debate.
- Individuals who are wrongfully subjected to de-radicalisation programs should be provided with some opportunity to challenge those decisions and seek some remedy against the state.
- CVE programs should respect the freedoms of speech and discrimination.
- CVE programs should respect academic and institutional freedom.
- The lines between counter-terrorism laws and CVE programs, and the kinds of conduct targeted under each, should be clearly demarcated.

96 Ibid. Ev 102.

Further research could consider whether these principles are relevant to non-coercive preventive measures in areas other than counter-terrorism (such as community policing more generally, and other forms of social and community crime prevention). As they stand, these principles demonstrate that preventive justice has much to contribute in determining the values and limits that should apply to the use of non-coercive measures in the name of preventing terrorism.

8 Combating terrorism in Australia through preventative detention orders

Svetlana Tyulkina and George Williams

Introduction

Australia has introduced a range of extraordinary legal measures to combat the threat of terrorism.[1] One of these is preventative detention orders (PDO), which permits a person to be detained, without arrest or charge, by the police for up to 14 days. While in detention, the person's contact with the outside world, including family members, is strictly limited. PDOs can be issued to prevent an imminent terrorist act from occurring or to preserve evidence relating to a recent terrorist act.

PDOs were introduced into the *Criminal Code Act 1995* (Cth) (*Criminal Code*) in 2005. Since then, only four PDOs have been issued, including none at all in the first nine years of the regime. This sparing use of the power reflects a number of practical impediments and constraints, most notably the fact that a person subject to a PDO may not be questioned by the authorities. These are so significant as to have led people to describe the regime as being 'unworkable', 'impractical' and 'difficult . . . to use operationally'.[2]

The PDO regime has proved to be contentious due to its potential impact upon a number of human rights, including the right to a fair trial and freedom from arbitrary detention. This reflected in the fact that it is subject to a sunset clause.[3] The legislation was originally set to expire on 15 December 2015.[4] In the lead-up

1 See Andrew Lynch, Nicola McGarrity and George Williams, *Inside Australia's Anti-Terrorism Laws and Trials* (NewSouth Publishing, 2015).

2 Correspondence from the National Counter Terrorism Committee Secretariat to the New South Wales Ombudsman, 25 November 2010, quoted in New South Wales Ombudsman, *Review of Parts 2A and 3 of the* Terrorism (Police Powers) Act 2002 (2011) 29. Nevertheless, the view of the New South Wales Commissioner of Police is that '[r]emoving preventative detention powers would create a gap in law enforcement capability to prevent a suspected terrorist attack. . . . While it appears there is scope to improve the utility of these provisions . . . it would be imprudent to repeal this legislation': New South Wales Ombudsman, *Preventative detention and covert search warrants: Review of Parts 2A and 3 of the* Terrorism (Police Powers) Act 2002 (2014) 27.

3 See Nicola McGarrity, Rishi Gulati and George Williams, 'Sunset Clauses in Australian Anti-Terror Laws' (2012) 33(2) *Adelaide Law Review* 307.

4 *Criminal Code* s 105.53(2), as inserted by *Anti-Terrorism Act (No 2) 2005* (Cth), had provided: 'A preventative detention order, and a prohibited contact order, cannot be

to that date, the regime was reviewed by the Council of Australian Governments (COAG) Review of Counter-Terrorism Legislation[5] and the Independent National Security Legislation Monitor (INSLM).[6] Both recommended the abolition of the scheme.

The PDO regime was again the subject of debate in September 2014 when the Australian Government announced it would introduce measures to respond to the threat of terrorism posed by Australian 'foreign fighters' who participate in conflicts overseas. The *Counter-Terrorism Legislation Amendment (Foreign Fighters) Act 2014* (Cth) made minor changes to the PDO regime, and also extended its operation to 7 September 2018.[7]

This chapter first sets out how the PDO regime operates. It then assesses the regime in light of its goals, comparative approaches and principles of preventive justice, most notably the principles of necessity, least restrictive means, sufficient substantiating evidence and a right to fair trial. The chapter does not seek to explain or develop these principles of preventive justice. Rather, it is a case study that surveys how these principles can be applied to the PDO scheme to assess whether the regime is needed and justified.

Operation of the PDO regime

PDOs explained

Under Division 105 of the *Criminal Code*, a PDO can be made by an 'issuing authority' at the application of a member of the Australian Federal Police (AFP).[8] No preliminary consent is required from the Attorney-General. The issuing authority will differ depending on whether the AFP member is applying for an initial PDO (which allows detention for up to 24 hours)[9] or a continued PDO (which extends that detention up to 48 hours).[10] In the case of an initial PDO, the issuing authority can be a senior AFP member[11] who holds the rank of superintendent or higher.[12] In the case of a continued PDO, the issuing authority must be a serving or retired judge or the President or Deputy President of the Administrative Appeals Tribunal.[13]

applied for, or made, after the end of 10 years after the day on which this Division commences.'

5 Council of Australian Governments, 'Council of Australian Governments Review of Counter-Terrorism Legislation' (Report, 2013) (COAG Review).

6 Bret Walker, 'Declassified Annual Report' (Annual Report, Independent National Security Legislation Monitor, 20 December 2012) (INSLM Report).

7 *Criminal Code* s 105.53(2) as amended by *Counter-Terrorism Legislation Amendment (Foreign Fighters) Act 2014* (Cth).

8 *Criminal Code* s 105.7(1).

9 Ibid. s 105.8.

10 Ibid. s 105.11.

11 Ibid. s 105.7(1) note 1.

12 Ibid. s 100.1(1).

13 Ibid. s 105.2.

There are two grounds on which an issuing authority may make a PDO. First, an order may be made to prevent an imminent terrorist act from occurring,[14] meaning that the act is 'expected to occur . . . at some time in the next 14 days'.[15] For an order to be made on this ground, the issuing authority must be satisfied there are reasonable grounds to suspect that the subject:

- 'will engage in a terrorist act';
- 'possesses a thing that is connected with the preparation for, or the engagement of a person in, a terrorist act'; or
- 'has done an act in preparation for, or planning, a terrorist act'.[16]

The issuing authority must also be satisfied that making the PDO would substantially assist in preventing a terrorist act from occurring,[17] and that detaining the subject is reasonably necessary for this purpose.[18] The second ground for issuing a PDO is when a terrorist act has occurred in the last 28 days and it is reasonably necessary to detain a person in order to preserve evidence relating to that terrorist act.[19]

The PDO must set out the name, alias or description of the person affected, the period for which the person may be detained, the date and time the order is made and the date and time after which the person may no longer be taken into custody under the order.[20] Finally, it must set out a summary of the grounds on which the order was made.[21]

The grounds for issuing a PDO are the same for both initial and continued PDOs,[22] although an extension of 24 hours may be granted in regard to an initial PDO if the issuing authority is satisfied that further detaining the person is reasonably necessary for the purpose for which the order was made.[23] Each state and territory has enacted legislation enabling the further detention of individuals under a PDO for up to a total of 14 days.[24]

14 Ibid. s 105.1(a).
15 Ibid. s 105.4(5).
16 Ibid. s 105.4(4)(b).
17 Ibid. s 105.4(4)(c).
18 Ibid. s 105.4(4)(d).
19 Ibid. s 105.4(6).
20 Ibid. ss 105.8(6)(a)–(d).
21 Ibid. s 105.8(6)(e).
22 Ibid. s 105.10(1).
23 Ibid. ss 105.10(3)–(5).
24 *Terrorism (Extraordinary Temporary Powers) Act 2006* (ACT) pt 2; *Terrorism (Police Powers) Act 2002* (NSW) pt 2A; *Terrorism (Emergency Powers) Act 2003* (NT) pt 2B; *Terrorism (Preventative Detention) Act 2005* (Qld) pt 2; *Terrorism (Preventative Detention) Act 2005* (SA) pt 2; *Terrorism (Preventative Detention) Act 2005* (Tas) pt 2; *Terrorism (Community Protection) Act 2003* (Vic) pt 2A; *Terrorism (Preventative Detention) Act 2006* (WA) pt 2.

Effect on detainees

A police officer taking a person into custody or detaining a person under a PDO has the same powers and obligations as he or she would have if arresting or detaining the person for an ordinary offence.[25] Accordingly, the officer may enter and search the premises where the subject of the order is believed to be.[26] The officer is obliged to explain to the person at the first practical opportunity the effect of the PDO,[27] and the person must be supplied with a copy of the order.[28] A person detained under a PDO may be held in a state or territory prison or remand centre.[29]

The *Criminal Code* places limits on detainees contacting people and disclosing the fact of their being subject to a PDO. A detainee may contact one of his or her family members, one housemate, his or her employer, one employee, one business partner and any other person the police officer agrees to their contacting.[30] Communication with these people must occur in a way that can be monitored by the AFP.[31] The rights of the detainee to contact these people may also be removed by a prohibited contact order made by an issuing authority.[32] An application for such an order can be made on grounds such as that it is reasonably necessary to prevent serious harm to a person or to preserve evidence relating to a terrorist act.[33]

What can be said by the detainee to these specified, contactable people is strictly limited. A person detained under a PDO may contact another person by telephone, fax or email 'solely for the purposes of letting the person contacted know that the person being detained is safe but is not able to be contacted for the time being'.[34] The detainee may not disclose that they are being detained under a PDO or the period for which they are being detained.[35] Disclosing the existence of the PDO is a crime punishable by up to five years' imprisonment. This prohibition applies to the detainee, the detainee's lawyer, the police officer and the interpreter.[36]

Use made of PDOs

PDOs were introduced in Australia in late 2005, but the regime lay unused until September 2014. The first PDOs were issued in response to the concerns regarding 'foreign fighters', who took part in the conflicts in Iraq and Syria and then

25 *Criminal Code* s 105.19(2).
26 Ibid. s 105.22(1).
27 Ibid. s 105.29.
28 Ibid. s 105.32(1).
29 Ibid. s 105.27.
30 Ibid. ss 105.34–105.35.
31 Ibid. s 105.38(1).
32 Ibid. s 105.15.
33 Ibid. s 105.14A.
34 Ibid. s 105.35(1)(f).
35 Ibid. s 105.35(2).
36 Ibid. s 105.41.

returned home to Australia. These concerns led to large-scale anti-terrorism raids in Sydney and Melbourne. In the wake of these events, PDOs were issued on 18 September 2014 against three unnamed men by the Supreme Court of New South Wales. The men were released the next day.[37]

No more can be determined about these PDOs, such as why it was thought necessary to use the regime after years of inactivity, or what specific circumstances required the use of a PDO. This is because the decision to issue the PDOs was the subject of a suppression order by the Supreme Court of New South Wales that covers every aspect of the orders – including the names of the parties, the evidence relied upon by the AFP and the reasons for which the PDOs were issued. The non-publication order is so broad that even the name of the Supreme Court spokesperson who announced it could not be published. The suppression order does not have an expiry date, and as a result will remain in place indefinitely unless the Court makes a further decision to rescind it.[38]

More information was made available in relation to the fourth PDO, which was issued by the Supreme Court of Victoria on 18 April 2015[39] in relation to alleged plots to disrupt Anzac Day commemorations. The PDO was made against Harun Causevic, an 18-year-old man. This was criticised by a number of legal groups, which argued the PDO circumvented the traditional legal process.[40] Victorian Premier Daniel Andrews acknowledged these concerns, but backed the detention of the teen without charge, saying that police needed the power to be able to ensure public safety.[41]

37 Australian Federal Police, 'Clarification of Operation Appleby Numbers' (Media Release, 20 September 2014). See also Paul Farrell, 'Police Listened to Lawyer–Client Phone Call after Sydney Counter-Terrorism Raid', *The Guardian* (online), 24 November 2014, available at www.theguardian.com/australia-news/2014/nov/24/police-listened-lawyer-client-phone-call-terrorism-raid (accessed 5 September 2016).

38 Paul Farrell, 'Indefinite Ban on Reporting of Counter-Terrorism Preventive Detention Order', *The Guardian* (online), 23 September 2014, available at www.theguardian.com/world/2014/sep/23/indefinite-ban-reporting-counter-terrorism-preventative-detention-order (accessed 5 September 2016).

39 Allison Worrall, 'Police Use Controversial Anti-Terror Powers to Detain Teen Terror Suspect', *The Age* (online), 20 April 2015, available at www.theage.com.au/victoria/police-use-controversial-antiterror-powers-to-detain-teen-terror-suspect-20150419-1moe88.html (accessed 5 September 2016); 'Two held after terror raids allegedly linked to Anzac Day', *The Australian* (online), 19 April 2015, available at www.theaustralian.com.au/news/nation/two-held-after-terror-raids-allegedly-linked-to-anzac-day/story-e6frg6nf-1227310072957 (accessed 5 September 2016).

40 Worrall, above n 39: '"It's essentially throwing the Magna Carta out the window," said Greg Barns, barrister and spokesman for the Australian Lawyers Alliance. "This shows a complete contempt of the Australian Parliament for fundamental human rights which have been in existence for over 800 years." Barrister and vice president of civil liberty group Liberty Victoria, Michael Stanton, said if there was sufficient evidence, a person should be charged and face the usual court process. "Our system operates on the basis that it's for the courts and the courts alone to make the decision of whether someone's liberty should be taken away."'

41 Ibid.

On 21 April 2016, the police applied under s 130 of the *Terrorism (Community Protection) Act* 2003 to revoke the interim PDO.[42] In subsequently lifting the PDO against Causevic, Victorian Supreme Court Justice Peter Riordan said he was inclined to disclose the PDO and the reasons for Causevic's detention:

> The basis on which extreme orders are made are matters which the public is entitled to be interested in . . . The court has been asked to make extreme orders and there should be good reason why the public shouldn't be told about the basis on which the order has been made.[43]

Causevic's lawyer, Rob Stary, told the Victorian Magistrates Court it was inappropriate for his client, who had no criminal history, to be in a maximum-security prison. Causevic was subsequently released from the PDO, only to be immediately arrested and charged with planning a terrorist attack.[44]

Prior to 18 September 2014, no application had been made to issue a PDO. The Commonwealth Government stated that this reflected the policy intent of the regime, as PDOs are 'extraordinary measures which are to be used sparingly'.[45] The AFP also backed the ongoing importance of the scheme, despite its lack of use, arguing that 'continued access to preventative detention orders [is] a critical operational response of last resort, to ensure that the AFP can undertake action to quickly disrupt imminent threats'.[46] These views run counter to the findings of the COAG Review and the INSLM, which both recommended that the regime be repealed.[47]

Assessing the PDO regime

Assessing against goals and objectives

The London attacks in July 2005 provoked debate in Australia about whether new laws were needed to prevent terrorism. At a COAG meeting on 27 September 2005, leaders from all levels of government in Australia agreed that changes were required. They reached this conclusion despite the Australian Parliament having

42 IMO an Application for a Preventative Detention Order in respect of CAUSEVIC [2015] VSC 248 (3 June 2015) [4].

43 'Man Charged with Terrorism Offences Had Phone Conversation with 14yo British Suspect, Court Hears', *ABC News* (online) 23 April 2015.

44 Causevic was acquitted of the terrorism-related charges, only to be made subject to a control order. See Chapter 3 by Susan Donkin in this collection.

45 Revised Explanatory Memorandum, Counter-Terrorism Legislation Amendment (Foreign Fighters) Bill 2014 (Cth) 131 [751]: with reference to control orders under Division 104 of the *Criminal Code*.

46 AFP, Submission No 36 to Parliamentary Joint Committee on Intelligence and Security, Parliament of Australia, *Advisory Report on the Counter-Terrorism Legislation Amendment (Foreign Fighters) Bill 2014*, October 2014, 62 [2.239].

47 COAG Review, above n 5, 68; INSLM Report, above n 6, 67.

already enacted a long list of significant counter-terrorism laws in response to the September 11 and other attacks. The communiqué of the meeting stated:

> [COAG] agreed that there is a clear case for Australia's counter-terrorism laws to be strengthened. . . . COAG agreed to the Commonwealth Criminal Code being amended to enable Australia better to deter and prevent potential acts of terrorism and prosecute where these occur.[48]

Legislation to bring this about was drafted as the Anti-Terrorism Bill (No. 2) 2005 (Cth). On 2 November 2005, Prime Minister John Howard explained to the public that this new law was needed to counter a potential terrorist threat, and that it should therefore be passed immediately by Federal Parliament:

> The Government has received specific intelligence and police information this week which gives cause for serious concern about a potential terrorist threat. . . . The Government is satisfied on the advice provided to it that the immediate passage of this bill would strengthen the capacity of law enforcement agencies to effectively respond to this threat.[49]

The Bill included a range of new measures, such as PDOs and control orders, and was introduced into the House of Representatives the next day, with Attorney-General Philip Ruddock stating that 'the government would like all elements of the anti-terrorism legislation package to become law before Christmas'.[50]

The rationale for introducing PDOs was not made clear by the Government in its public statements on the Bill or in parliamentary debate. Aside from a reference to a threat based on classified information, no more specific justification was given as to why a power to detain a person for a short period of time to prevent a terrorist act or to preserve evidence was needed in addition to existing powers. Hence, no attempt was made to identify what gap in the existing law would be filled by the PDO regime, nor why it was a necessary part of Australia's legislative response to the threat of terrorism. The new regime was usually only spoken of in descriptive terms. For example, the Explanatory Memorandum to the Bill stated that it included 'a new police preventative detention regime that will allow detention of a person without charge where it is reasonably necessary to prevent a terrorist act or to preserve evidence of such an act'.[51]

Where an argument was made in favour of introducing the regime, this was done only in general, rhetorical terms by way of referring to the Bill as a whole. For example, Ruddock stated in his second reading speech that the Bill was

48 Council of Australian Governments, *Council of Australian Governments Communiqué: Special Meeting on Counter-Terrorism* (Communiqué, 27 September 2005) 3.
49 John Howard, 'Anti-Terrorism Bill' (Media Release, 2 November 2005).
50 Commonwealth, *Parliamentary Debates*, House of Representatives, 3 November 2005, 102 (Philip Ruddock, Attorney-General).
51 Explanatory Memorandum, Anti-Terrorism Bill (No. 2) 2005 (Cth) 1.

needed 'to ensure that we have the toughest laws possible to prosecute those responsible should a terrorist attack occur'.[52]

The PDO regime was thus justified as being part of the Government's 'tough' response to terrorism. Beyond the general reference to a threat based on a classified information, no specific rationale for the regime can be found on the public record, whether it be in the second reading speech to the Bill, ministerial statements or debate in Parliament. In addition, no process or inquiry had identified the need for such a scheme prior to the introduction of the Bill. Notably, there is no record indicating that any person or organisation called publicly for the introduction of PDOs. The regime apparently emerged 'out of the blue' as part of the Government's wide-ranging response to the London terrorist attacks of 2005.

The Government might have argued that PDOs were required because existing police powers and traditional criminal procedures (such as arrest) were not sufficient to meet the threat of terrorism, and that these needed to be supplemented with a special new power of detention. However, such an argument would have been highly contestable given the broad powers already available to police, and indeed this point was not put in public debate. Overall, the evidence shows that no clear role or specific purpose for the PDO regime was articulated in public. Given the many opportunities to do this, the possibility exists that the Government pressed ahead with the regime in great haste without itself having identified such a need and defined purpose. What this goes to show is that the regime cannot be justified on the basis of meeting specified goals and objectives, as such goals and objectives have never been established. This finding is not altered by recent, minor changes made to the PDO regime in response to the threat posed by 'foreign fighters'. No additional rationale emerged out of that debate to justify the need for the regime.

A comparative justification?

A possible justification for Australia's PDO regime might have been that other nations had adopted a like scheme as part of their response to the threat of terrorism, and so it was thought that the same type of measure was needed in Australia. This was certainly the case for other measures. For example, the control order regime introduced in Australia in 2005 was modelled upon legislation in the United Kingdom.[53] The fact that United Kingdom authorities

52 Commonwealth, *Parliamentary Debates*, House of Representatives, 3 November 2005, 102 (Philip Ruddock, Attorney-General).

53 John Howard, 'Counter-Terrorism Laws Strengthened' (Media Release, 8 September 2005), available online at http://pmtranscripts.dpmc.gov.au/release/transcript-21909 (accessed 5 September 2016); Bronwen Jaggers, 'Anti-Terrorism Control Orders in Australia and the United Kingdom: A Comparison' (Research Paper No 28, Parliamentary Library, Parliament of Australia, 29 April 2008); Clive Walker, *Terrorism and the Law* (Oxford University Press, 2011) 299–340. See Chapter 3 by Susan Donkin in this collection.

could impose control orders was used to explain why Australia needed a like measure.[54]

No such arguments apply with respect to Australia's PDO regime. This is because the regime appears to be *sui generis*. Detention as a method of preventing harm is not unusual in other countries, and can also be found in the Australian states and territories. For example, laws in New South Wales enable the detention of individuals with a mental illness who are a danger to themselves or others,[55] and convicted former sex offenders who still pose a risk to the community.[56] However, the use of these powers is based upon evidence as to the person's past history, an element missing in the PDO regime.

Further analogies with the PDO regime might be found in pre-trial detention in overseas jurisdictions, including in the United Kingdom and Ireland.[57] Under these schemes, pre-trial detention is used as a tool of criminal procedure to permit individuals to be held pending criminal charges and trial for terrorist acts.[58] Similar legislation authorising pre-trial detention for the purpose of investigation of terrorism was enacted in Australia in 2004.[59] However, each of these regimes is distinguishable on the basis that, unlike the PDO regime, they require an ongoing investigation into a suspected terrorist act.

The closest comparator may be the United Kingdom's system of preventive arrest without a warrant, as introduced by the *Terrorism Act 2000* (UK).[60] But even this measure is very different from the Australian PDO model – it is mostly investigative and allows the police to arrest and detain a person without a warrant if they are reasonably suspected of being a terrorist.[61] By contrast, as the COAG Review pointed out, the PDO regime does not provide for questioning of the

54 Lisa Burton and George Williams, 'What Future for Australia's Control Order Regime?' (2013) 24 *Public Law Review* 182, 186–8; Andrew Lynch, 'Control Orders in Australia: A Further Case Study in the Migration of British Counter-Terrorism Law' (2008) 8 *Oxford University Commonwealth Law Journal* 159, 174.

55 The detention of persons with mental illness dates back to more than a century ago: see e.g. *Dangerous Lunatics Act 1843* (NSW) s 3. See Chapter 4 by Bernadette McSherrry and Chapter 5 by Helen Punter in this collection.

56 See e.g. the *Crimes (High Risk Offenders) Act 2006* (NSW) which enables a 'high risk' sex or violent offender to be preventively detained or supervised in the community upon the completion of a custodial sentence.

57 Other countries include Brazil, Colombia, Denmark, France, Germany, Greece, Italy, Norway, Spain and Turkey: see Stella Burch Elias, 'Rethinking "Preventive Detention" from a Comparative Perspective: Three Frameworks for Detaining Terrorist Suspects' (2009) 41 *Columbia Human Rights Law Review* 99, 131.

58 Ibid. 133.

59 *Crimes Act 1914* (Cth) pt IC div 2 sub-div B, as amended by *Anti-Terrorism Act 2004* (Cth).

60 S 41.

61 There is a similar provision in *Crimes Act 1914* (Cth) s 3WA that gives the police a power of arrest without warrant for a terrorism offence or offence of advocating terrorism.

detainee during her or his detention and can be seen as 'purely protective', and so PDOs 'differ markedly from their counterpart in the UK legislation'.[62]

The INSLM likewise stated that '[t]here are limited analogies in similar countries of a power to detain preventively without arrest or charge'.[63] He concluded that a power to detain preventively is virtually unknown in other democracies, even looking at their past experience.[64] The closest historical analogies were identified as being the internment of Japanese Americans by the United States Government during World War II[65] and the detention of suspected Irish Republican Army members by the United Kingdom Government in the 1970s.[66] Such large-scale detention is very different to the use of PDOs, but the comparison does highlight the problematic aspect of preventative detention without arrest or charge.

In all, this demonstrates the exceptional nature of the Australian PDO regime. There are simply no other similar examples of a power of preventative detention without arrest, charge or questioning. Indeed, one academic study found that PDOs do not fit into any known framework of preventative detention.[67] It also concluded that the scheme falls under the category of the 'most rights-violative approach . . . to the detention of terrorist suspects', along with those adopted in countries such as Israel, India, Pakistan, Singapore, Malaysia, Mozambique and Kenya.[68]

Principle of preventive justice

Our analysis to this point has demonstrated how the legislation that introduced the PDO regime does not reflect clear goals or objectives and cannot be said to be based upon measures in other comparable nations. These factors make the regime difficult to assess. In these circumstances, we turn to the analytical framework developed by Ashworth and Zedner.[69]

Their work focuses on preventive measures that involve coercion or a loss of liberty, including measures enacted as part of counter-terrorism regimes.[70] They identify how such measures have become a major feature of contemporary social and other policies in many Western democracies. These policies can be seen as a response to the state's duty to protect, or to provide security. However, they can have considerable implications for liberty and other rights, and so Ashworth and

62 COAG Review, above n 5, 64.
63 INSLM Report, above 6, 47.
64 Ibid.
65 See *Korematsu v United States*, 323 US 214 (1944) in which such detention was held to be constitutional.
66 See Brice Dickson, 'The Detention of Suspected Terrorists in Northern Ireland and Great Britain' (2009) 43 *University of Richmond Law Review* 927.
67 Elias, above n 57.
68 Ibid. 180–1.
69 Andrew Ashworth and Lucia Zedner, *Preventive Justice* (Oxford University Press, 2014).
70 Ibid. 2.

Zedner seek to articulate criteria by which to establish the boundaries and limits of such preventive policies.

This case study is a distillation of the work of Ashworth and Zedner and involves two major questions of justification. The first is practical and asks if the power in question is necessary and whether a lesser or different power would be no less (or maybe even more) effective.[71] Hence, a coercive, preventive measure would be justified only where it is necessary and the least restrictive means available for achieving the identified end. The second question concerns rights protection, and requires the liberty and human rights of all persons involved to be preserved as far as is possible.[72]

The point here is not to rule out the possibility that in certain circumstances individuals may be deprived of their liberty, but to subject this to a set of conditions. These conditions are in part substantive (such as to the level of harm and degree of probability required for imposing preventive measures), in part procedural (namely, what rights and guarantees the detainee should be accorded) and in part consequential (relating to the length and conditions of detention). This produces a long list of principles of preventive justice, of which the following are the most relevant to an assessment of measures such as PDOs:[73]

1 Any restriction of, or deprivation of, liberty must be necessary for the prevention of terrorist activity, and should continue for no longer than is necessary for that purpose ('necessity' principle).
2 Any restrictions on liberty must be a last resort and the least intrusive that are consistent with the preventive purpose ('least restrictive appropriate means' principle).
3 Sufficient substantiating evidence, requiring a high standard of proof, should be present and the use of fallible secret intelligence should be avoided (principle of 'sufficient substantiating evidence').
4 The right to fair trial, including major procedural rights and guarantees such as the principle of openness, transparency and accountability (in terms of the right to know upon what grounds the measure is needed), open access to evidence, rights of appeal, legal assistance, presumption in favour of open hearings, should be protected.

We apply this framework below.

The necessity principle

The PDO regime does not comply with this principle, especially with its first element as to necessity. As Ashworth and Zedner explain, preventive measures imposing a deprivation of liberty require strong justification and should be

71 Ibid. 257.
72 Ibid.
73 Ibid. 195.

accepted only if there is concrete evidence that they are necessary for the prevention of terrorist activity. The PDO regime lacks such an evidential foundation.

The 2005 process that led to the enactment of the regime provided no specific rationale for why and how the restrictions and deprivations imposed by the PDOs are necessary to prevent future acts of terrorism or how the existing criminal law tools were inadequate for the investigation and prosecution of terrorist suspects. It is also not possible to establish the necessity of the regime based upon its operation. On the contrary, law enforcement agencies have cast significant doubt upon whether the regime is effective in preventing terrorist acts.[74] AFP officers have shown instead that they prefer to use other powers.[75]

As to the second, temporal element, the legislation that introduced the PDO regime provides that the scheme is subject to a sunset clause.[76] The legislation was originally set to expire on 15 December 2015.[77] In the lead-up to that date, the PDO regime was reviewed by the COAG Review and the INSLM, both of which recommended the abolition of the scheme. The INSLM described the regime as being 'at odds with our normal approach to even the most reprehensible crimes',[78] whereas the COAG Review remarked that such powers 'might be thought to be unacceptable in a liberal democracy'.[79]

Despite this, and without further review or response to these inquiries, the Abbott Government introduced a bill into Parliament to extend the scheme for a further ten years until December 2025. It argued for an extension, with support from the AFP,[80] on the basis that PDOs would play an 'important role' in addressing the threat of terrorism posed by Australian citizens returning home after taking part in the conflicts in Syria and Iraq.[81] The decade-long extension was subjected to criticism,[82] and a compromise position was reached whereby the *Counter-Terrorism Legislation Amendment (Foreign Fighters) Act 2014* (Cth) extended the PDO regime to 7 September 2018.[83]

The fact that the regime is subject to a now extended sunset clause is not by itself sufficient to satisfy this principle. This is because the principle suggests that the regime should continue no longer than is necessary. Given that it has not been established that it is necessary in the first place, the principle suggests that regime

74 INSLM Report, above n 6, 50.
75 Ibid. 56.
76 See generally McGarrity, Gulati and Williams, above n 3.
77 The *Criminal Code* s 105.53(2), as inserted by *Anti-Terrorism Act (No 2) 2005* (Cth), had provided: 'A preventative detention order, and a prohibited contact order, cannot be applied for, or made, after the end of 10 years after the day on which this Division commences.'
78 INSLM Report, above n 6, 47.
79 COAG Review, above n 5, 68.
80 See AFP, Submission No 36, above n 46.
81 Revised Explanatory Memorandum, Counter-Terrorism Legislation Amendment (Foreign Fighters) Bill 2014 (Cth) 144 [855]–[856].
82 See AFP, Submission No 36, above n 46, 70–9.
83 *Criminal Code* s 105.53(2) as amended by *Counter-Terrorism Legislation Amendment (Foreign Fighters) Act 2014* (Cth).

should be immediately wound up, rather than extended for any period, whether subjected to a sunset clause or not.

The least restrictive means principle

The PDO regime fails to satisfy this principle. This is because there is a less restrictive alternative to PDOs available in the form of the pre-charge detention regime provided for in the *Crimes Act 1914* (Cth). This allows the AFP to detain a suspect for questioning for up to 24 hours. This period does not include any 'dead time', which may be excluded from the 24-hour limit for a range of administrative reasons, such that the actual period of detention may extend up to more than one week.[84] Pre-trial detention is part of the ordinary criminal procedure and therefore accords all procedural rights and guarantees to the detainee. This makes it less restrictive and intrusive compared with the PDO. This alternative also has the very distinct advantage of permitting the questioning of people during the period of their detention.

It might be argued that the PDO regime should be preferred to this alternative because it is more efficient or achieves something that the pre-trial detention regime cannot. The evidence does not bear this out. For example, the INSLM stated that he had received 'no material or argument demonstrating that the traditional criminal justice response to the prevention and prosecution of serious crime through arrest, charge and remand is ill-suited or ill-equipped to deal with terrorism'.[85] Further, the INSLM referred to a discussion with AFP officers at a private hearing at which it was 'strongly suggested that "in a real, practical urgent sense" the ability to arrest a person is a more efficient and effective process for dealing with imminent terrorist threats than the complex and time consuming process of a PDO'.[86]

Principle of sufficient substantiating evidence

To apply for and issue a PDO, the AFP officer or the issuing authority, respectively, must have only 'reasonable grounds to suspect' that the person will, for example, engage in a terrorist act or possesses a thing connected with preparation for a terrorist act.[87] This involves only a single objective component.[88] As a result, neither the AFP officer nor issuing authority is required to form their own subjective suspicion about the matter. The INSLM report noted that this approach contrasts with the approach taken in all Commonwealth, state and territory arrest provisions, which require a dual objective and subjective component, meaning that a police officer must believe or suspect on reasonable grounds that a person has

84 *Crimes Act 1914* (Cth) ss 23DB, 23DD.
85 INSLM Report, above n 6, 52.
86 Ibid. 56.
87 *Criminal Code* s 105.4(4).
88 INSLM Report, above n 6, 49.

committed or is committing an offence.[89] The INSLM recommended amending the PDO regime to incorporate a dual objective and subjective formula in order to safeguard the risk of arbitrary detention.[90] As it currently stands, the PDO regime is not compatible with the principle of sufficient substantiating evidence as it permits detention in circumstances where the relevant decision maker is not themselves personally convinced that the required grounds have been made out.

A further requirement for a PDO is that a terrorist act must have occurred within the last 28 days or be imminent and expected to occur at some time within the next 14 days.[91] The imminence requirement is designed to create a high threshold for applying for and issuing a PDO.[92] On the other hand, for a PDO to be made to preserve evidence relating to a recent terrorist act, it must be 'reasonably necessary to detain the subject to preserve evidence', and the detention period must be 'reasonably necessary for the purpose'.[93] In other words, an issuing authority must be satisfied that if the person is not detained, there is a substantial risk that the evidence will not be preserved.[94]

The requirement of imminence might be described as compatible with the principle of sufficient evidence. However, the threshold is so high that it can hardly be met in practice. The INSLM argued that the imminence provision limits the efficacy of the PDO regime because '[p]ractically, it is impossible to guarantee that an event will occur. A police officer simply cannot attest that a terrorist act is expected to occur within a fortnight irrespective of any intervening event'.[95] The AFP has expressed a similar concern.[96] By contrast, the threshold for a PDO to be made to preserve evidence relating to a recent terrorist act is easier to satisfy, although it still to some degree requires the issuing authority to be convinced of a person's future actions.

Stringent secrecy measures attach to PDOs. A PDO can be issued as a result of secretive proceedings at which the person to be subjected to the PDO is not given any effective opportunity to test the material used to justify the order. Such information is not governed by any standards of evidence and will undoubtedly be largely comprised of intelligence materials. The detainee is not a party to the application process and the information the police relies upon is effectively secret. This is not consistent with the principle of sufficient substantiating evidence as it undermines the suggestion that a high standard of proof is applied. It is not

89 Ibid. 50.
90 Ibid. 50–1, Recommendation III/1.
91 *Criminal Code* ss 105.4(5)–(6).
92 INSLM Report, above n 6, 51; COAG Review, above n 5, 64.
93 *Criminal Code* ss 105.4(6)(b)–(c).
94 INSLM Report, above n 6, 52.
95 Ibid. 51.
96 Despite credible intelligence that a terrorist act is imminent, the ability to predict, in advance, the precise time frame in which the act may happen may be particularly challenging. It is not clear what a court would expect in relation to evidence given by the AFP that the terrorist act is expected to occur within 14 days. See INSLM Report, above n 6, 57 (specifically the AFP's additional submission to the INSLM, 16 August 2012).

possible to say that such a standard is met in the absence of police evidence being subjected to the possibility of effective contradiction.

Right to a fair trial

The secrecy imposed with the regime is inconsistent with the notions of open justice and transparency. The *Criminal Code* places severe limits on detainees contacting people and disclosing the fact of their being subject to a PDO. The right of the detainee to contact a person can even be removed by way of a prohibited contact order. Disclosing the existence of the PDO is also a crime punishable by up to five years' imprisonment. As a result, there is little opportunity for the public to become aware that a PDO has been issued. The law requires only that the Attorney-General prepare an annual report about the operation of the regime and lay copies of the report before each House of Parliament within 15 sitting days of the report's completion. The report must set out matters such as the number of initial and continued PDOs made, how long each person was detained for and whether any complaints were made to the Ombudsman.[97]

The regime raises a number of other related concerns. These include that: the person is not given an opportunity to present their case directly to the issuing authority; the detention under an initial PDO can be facilitated entirely by the police with no reasons given for the decision; and review of decisions made under the regime is extremely limited.[98] The making of a PDO can be reviewed by the Security Appeals Division of the Administrative Appeals Tribunal, which can declare that a decision by an issuing authority to make or extend a PDO is void.[99] However, this power cannot be exercised while the PDO is in force.[100] In addition, the legality of PDO decisions is exempted from judicial review under the *Administrative Decisions (Judicial Review) Act 1977* (Cth).[101]

The *Criminal Code* provides some safeguards to minimise the impact on individual rights and liberties of individuals detained under a PDO. An officer taking a person into detention must explain at the first practical opportunity the effect of the PDO, and the person must be supplied with a copy of the order.[102] Further, the law contains a guarantee against torture by requiring that a person who is in custody or detained under a PDO be treated with humanity and with respect for human dignity, and not be subjected to cruel, inhuman or degrading treatment. A detainee also possesses the right to make a complaint to the Commonwealth Ombudsman or similar state or territory authority,[103] and may make contact with

97 *Criminal Code* s 105.47(2).
98 Paul Fairall and Wendy Lacey, 'Preventative Detention and Control Orders Under Federal Law: The Case for a Bill of Rights' (2007) 31 *Melbourne University Law Review* 1072, 1077.
99 *Criminal Code* ss 105.51(5)–(7).
100 Ibid. s 105.51(5).
101 Ibid. s 105.51(4).
102 Ibid. s 105.32(1).
103 Ibid. s 105.36.

a lawyer to obtain advice about their legal rights in relation to the PDO and their treatment.[104]

A person detained under a PDO who is under 18 years of age is entitled to additional safeguards. These include a requirement that they not be detained with people who are 18 years or older,[105] special contact rules which allow the person to contact both parents[106] and a rule that police officers must not take identification material (other than hand prints, fingerprints, foot prints or toe prints) from the person unless this is ordered by a judge of the Federal Circuit Court of Australia.[107]

Conclusion

This chapter has set out and assessed the Australian PDO regime in light of the goals for the regime, comparative approaches and principles of preventive justice. Our analysis shows that no clear purpose or specific rationale for the PDO regime was articulated in public. Further, and more importantly, it was demonstrated there was no gap in the existing law identified as needing to be filled and no explanation has been provided as to why existing police powers and traditional criminal procedures are insufficient. As a result, the regime cannot be justified on the basis of meeting particular goals and objectives, as such goals and objectives have not been established.

A comparative justification for Australia's PDO regime cannot be accepted either. PDOs do not fit into any known framework of preventive detention, and they raise more significant human rights concerns than the detention regimes of many other nations. A power to detain preventively is virtually unknown in other democracies, even looking at their past experience.[108] The Australian PDO regime is exceptional in this respect.

The regime also cannot be justified when it is examined in light of the analytical framework developed by Ashworth and Zedner.[109] The PDO scheme is not compatible with key principles of preventive justice – in particular those of necessity, least restrictive means and right to a fair trial. As a result, the PDO regime cannot be described as necessary and proportionate.

The lack of justification for Australia's PDO regime means that it should be abolished. However, such an outcome is not likely. Rather than responding to independent reports recommending this course of action, Parliament instead extended the operation of the regime. In light of the possibility, then, that the regime will continue to operate until its official expiry, and then be extended for a further period, significant changes ought to be made to render the regime less problematic. These should include applying the regime only to people 18 years or

104 Ibid. s 105.37.
105 Ibid. s 105.33A(1).
106 Ibid. s 105.39(3).
107 Ibid. s 105.43(4).
108 INSLM Report, above n 6, 47.
109 Ashworth and Zedner, above n 69.

older, enabling review of decisions to issue PDOs on broader grounds, including while a PDO is in force, and permitting more reporting and other means of public dissemination of information about PDOs where this is in the public interest.

The reporting obligations attached to PDOs should also be enhanced. The Attorney-General's annual report about the operation of Division 105 of the *Criminal Code* should do more than include statistical data on the number of initial and continued PDOs made, length of detention and complaints made to the Ombudsman. It should, in addition, reflect on the effectiveness of the PDO regime for the purpose of preventing acts of terrorism. This would permit ongoing discussion of the necessity of the scheme.

A similar extended reporting obligation can be found elsewhere. The Director-General of the Australian Security Intelligence Organisation is obliged to provide a written report to the Attorney-General 'on the extent to which the action taken under the warrant has assisted the Organisation in carrying out its functions' in respect of each questioning or detention warrant issued under Division 3, Special powers relating to terrorism offences of the *Australian Security Intelligence Organisation Act 1979* (Cth).[110] This has the effect of 'accounting for the exercise of the questioning powers and providing an understanding ultimately by the legislators and specifically by the Attorney-General, of the usefulness of these powers'.[111] This and other changes would not only put the PDO regime on a more appropriate footing, but they might also assist in developing an understanding as to whether there is a basis for the existence the regime in the first place.

110 S 34ZH.
111 INSLM report, above n 6, 96.

Part III

Evaluating preventive justice: Assessing legitimacy and effectiveness

9 A new preventive justice framework for assessing counter-terrorism law and policy

Integrating effectiveness and legitimacy

Tim Legrand and Teneille Elliott

Introduction

> We will never sacrifice our freedoms in order to defend them – but we will not let our enemies exploit our decency either. . . . If there is a choice between latitude for suspects or more powers to police and security agencies – more often, we should choose to support our agencies.
>
> Then Prime Minister of Australia, Tony Abbott, *National Security Statement*[1]

Despite the huge economic costs of counter-terrorism (CT) policing to Australia over the past 15 years, one major debate remains divisive and unresolved: how can we develop and institute laws that are effective in diminishing violent extremism while maintaining the integrity of our democratic freedoms? As indicated by Australia's former Prime Minister, the balance between citizens' rights and policing powers has largely been tipped in favour of the latter.

Australia's legislative response to countering terrorism since September 11 has been heavily weighted towards a policy of prevention: granting policing and security agencies a wider remit to interrupt the process of terrorism at increasingly earlier junctures through new powers and the criminalisation of behaviours that manifest a predisposition towards offending, often known as 'precursor crimes'. Such laws include those granting policing and intelligence agencies enhanced surveillance, investigatory and coercive powers, laws enabling non-conviction-based schemes of preventative detention and control orders, and laws creating and punishing offences connected to (increasingly preparatory) terrorism-related activity.[2]

Publicly, politicians claim that these legislative interventions weave a security blanket intended to smother extremism before it manifests in violence – that is, to *prevent* terrorist attacks. It is important that the effects of such laws – intended and unintended – are subjected to careful evidence-based evaluation. Although the laws are ostensibly geared towards strengthening the government's CT response,

1 Former Prime Minister Tony Abbott, 'National Security Statement' (Speech delivered in Canberra, Australia, 23 February 2015).

2 See Stuart Macdonald 'Understanding Anti-Terrorism Policy: Values, Rationales and Principles' (2012) 34(2) *Sydney Law Review* 317–95.

there are concerns about the effectiveness of CT laws that 'if poorly directed, generate precisely the type of violence which [they are] intended to suppress'.[3]

In this chapter, we ask whether, and how, we can determine if CT laws are *effective* in making us safer, are *appropriate* in their alignment with our liberal freedoms, and are *necessary* in their proportionate provision of legal capabilities not otherwise available. We make the central claim that effectiveness, appropriateness and necessity should be regarded as allied and inseparable, not antagonistic and incompatible, fundaments of CT law.

In the first section, we draw attention to two trends: first, the prevailing international trend towards evidence-based policy-making and how central such approaches are to enhancing accountability and, by extension, democratic legitimacy;[4] second, the declining democratic scrutiny of CT laws across the West, the opacity of their effectiveness, their sometimes questionable necessity, and the failure to give due consideration to whether CT laws are appropriate for addressing the precepts of liberal democracy, particularly respect for fundamental human rights. These two trends show the need for preventive CT laws to ally the issue of effectiveness with appropriateness and necessity. We contend that the effectiveness of a CT law is linked to appropriateness: the more 'evidence' available that preventive measures are (or are likely to be) effective and necessary, the greater their legitimacy (both perceived and actual) among citizens required to obey these measures, which, in turn, increases the likelihood that citizens will respect and comply with those laws.[5]

The second section explores the significance of effectiveness through a study that focuses on preventive measures to deal with the threats posed by foreign fighters returning to Australia. This provides a critical analysis of CT laws and the policy justifications for these reforms, and a framework and context for exploring how new modes of evaluating effectiveness should be applied to the process of policy-making and ongoing monitoring and review of preventive measures.

Positing policy's purpose

It is fundamental to a liberal democracy that the actions of an elected government are transparent to the public who hold them accountable in free elections.[6] Since it is not in the government's interest to collect, much less make available to the

3 Jenny Hocking, 'Counter-Terrorism and the Criminalisation of Politics: Australia's New Security Powers of Detention, Proscription and Control' (2003) 49(3) *Australian Journal of Politics and History* 361.

4 For a discussion of judicial legitimacy, see Chapter 11 by Sarah Murray in this collection.

5 On procedural justice, see Tom R Tyler, 'What is Procedural Justice? Criteria Used by Citizens to Assess the Fairness of Legal Procedures' (1988) 22(1) *Law and Society Review* 103; Tom R Tyler and Robert J Bies, 'Beyond Formal Procedures: The Interpersonal Context of Procedural Justice' (1990) *Applied Social Psychology and Organizational Settings* 77, 98.

6 Adam Przeworski, Susan C Stokes and Bernard Manin, *Democracy, Accountability, and Representation* (Cambridge University Press, 1999).

public, information that reveals policy failures or ineffectiveness within government, most liberal democracies have developed sophisticated systems of 'checks and balances' in which oversight agencies independent from government (in theory at least) are empowered to audit and report on government performance impartially, providing the transparency upon which democracy relies. Yet one domain of government enterprise – in Australia and elsewhere – has not only been resistant to effectiveness audits and performance evaluation, but has in fact acquired a *de facto* blanket immunity from scrutiny: security policy.[7] Underpinned by an explicit bipartisan political consensus that security issues ought to be 'above politics', the Australian policy objectives, legal measures and effects in relation to CT have proceeded with minimal independent oversight and evaluation.

An important issue arises out of the current scholarly considerations of CT policy: in assessing whether a measure is 'fit for purpose' there is a need, first, to determine whether the policy response is necessary and adapted for its purpose and, second, to evaluate (using credible methods) the actual or likely effectiveness of that response as a means of achieving the stated policy objectives. Many scholars have expressed doubts about whether particular CT policy measures are 'fit for purpose' in the first sense, but few have taken seriously the question in its second sense – namely, whether the CT measures are, or are likely to be, effective.

We urge scholars and policy-makers to resist treating CT as a 'special' form of policy-making in which only causal questions of effectiveness matter (if at all).[8] We should not assess suitability on such a narrow basis since, if we do, we blind ourselves to the range of possibilities of why a particular policy was put in place and we are thereby insensitive to the attendant wider effects of that policy and whether it is properly aligned with core values or proportionate to its ostensible aim. Put in the context of CT laws, our central claim is relatively straightforward: it is unwise – dangerous even – to reduce debates about CT laws to questions of effectiveness, much less permit politicians to make uncontested claims about impact and measures of success. Effectiveness must be paired with an equal concern for *appropriateness* and *necessity*.

Our analysis of the scholarly literature and government reports shows that there is no consensus on how to best measure the effectiveness of CT laws. The Australian Parliament, in devising the statutory role of the Independent National Security Legislation Monitor (INSLM), developed a test that largely aligns with the framework we propose, as set out in ss 3 and 6 of the INSLM Act and as applied by the INSLMs in their reports.[9] In developing our framework, we drew from the success of this review function in providing a framework for the most holistic reviews of

7 John Mueller and Mark G Stewart, *Terror, Security, and Money: Balancing the Risks, Benefits, and Costs of Homeland Security* (Oxford University Press, 2011).

8 For an examination of the role of effectiveness in the evolution of preventive organised crime measures, see Chapter 10 by Rebecca Ananian-Welsh in this collection.

9 See e.g. Bret Walker, 'Annual Report, 16 December 2011' (Annual Report, Independent National Security Legislation Monitor, 16 December 2011) (INSLM Report) where the INSLM describes his review mandate, 1; and where the INSLM applies the review criteria in relation to CT laws, 43.

Australia's CT laws to date. This is the only similar framework applied in a public policy setting that we have been able to find, although analyses of human rights compatibility will have some overlap. Our framework remains unique for its incorporation of appropriateness, effectiveness and necessity across policy, law and practice. Our framework has a wider applicability and comprehensiveness than the more limited scope of the INSLM's statutory review mandate, or a rights-based analysis.

Exploring these questions leads to two connected contributions: the first is to draw attention to the frequent failure of policy-makers to specify the expected outcomes of CT laws, and their 'fit' with the broader principles of liberal democracy; the second is to propose a framework that invites scholars to resist taking CT policy at face value and instead consider a broader range of possible policy aims that remain unarticulated, ulterior or underdeveloped.

Evidence, effectiveness and public policy

Understanding the construction and outcomes of CT laws requires a consideration of the interaction of public policy, evidence and the notion of effectiveness. All policies including laws and resource allocations are inherently a *choice* guided by government's worldview. For Dye, public policy is merely 'anything a government chooses to do or not do',[10] whereas for Michael Howlett and M Ramesh '[p]ublic policy is, at its most simple, a choice made by a government to undertake some course of action'.[11] The sorts of policy that we are interested in here are those developed with an *action* and intended *outcome* in mind. At its purest, how policy is achieved is a matter of a causal theory, which involves constructing (a) constituency or scope – that is, what part of the world requires a change of some sort; (b) an end-point, or what government would like the constituency to resemble; and (c) the instrument(s) that needs to be employed to transform (a) to (b). While public policy decision-making can be reduced to these three basic precepts, achieving these policy aims (outcomes) is a broader matter of generating policy-relevant knowledge: what constitutes the policy context, what resources or instruments are available, what sorts of change are achievable, how it can be achieved and so on. Policy is dependent on the differing forms of evidence, and the extent to which that evidence is available and in a form accessible to decision-makers.

Florence Nightingale was one of the earliest voices calling for governments to take a firmer evidence-based approach to law-making. In a letter imploring the help of Sir Francis Galton, she wrote:

> Put down what you expect from such and such legislation; after [so many] years, see where it has given you what you expected, and where it has failed.

10 Thomas R Dye, *Understanding Public Policy* (Englewood Cliffs, NJ. Prentice-Hall, 1st edn, 1972) 2.

11 Michael Howlett and M Ramesh, *Studying Public Policy: Policy Cycles and Policy Subsystems* (Oxford University Press, 2003) 3.

> But you change your laws and your administering of them so fast, and without an inquiry after results past or present, that it is all experiment, see-saw, doctrinaire, a shuttlecock between two [rackets].[12]

For Nightingale, it was commonsensical that the intentions and outcomes of legislation should be evaluated for evidence of policy performance. The reality, as she observed, was that the chaos of Westminster politics made such sober assessments impossible. Nightingale's observation stands as valid today as it was in the nineteenth century. Today, as then, the turbulence of ideology, bartering and antagonisms within Parliament makes for an uncomfortable gauntlet for the policy development process and passage of new laws. The approach to CT law-making in Australia's federal Parliament has shown this to be equally applicable locally.

In 1997, the ascendancy of the New Labour government in the United Kingdom marked the beginning of an explicit attempt to engineer an anti-ideological, less overtly politicised approach to policy- and law-making. Led by the invocations of then Prime Minister Tony Blair, the 'what works' agenda became the mantra of government: '[T]he Government has given a clear commitment that we will be guided not by dogma but by an open-minded approach to understanding what works and why.'[13] The injunction to develop policy with an eye towards measuring achievement was echoed a decade later, in 2007, by Australia's former Labour Prime Minister Kevin Rudd who proclaimed 'evidence-based policy making is at the heart of being a reformist government'.[14]

This push to inject the rigour of evidence, and a concern for achieving the stipulated outcomes of policy, prompted Australia's Productivity Commission to host a roundtable in 2009 on 'Strengthening Evidence-Based Policy in the Australian Federation'. The then Chairman of the Productivity Commission, Gary Banks, noted that 'while there has been much talk about evidence-based policy, far less attention has been paid to how we actually go about it and how we might do it better'.[15]

Those with even a passing acquaintance with the modern policy process will not be convinced by Blair's suggestion that the evidence-based approach to policy entirely manages to shrug off dogma. Despite the intentions of the Rudd Government and modest efforts within parts of the public service, an evidence-based approach to policy-making has not occurred in Australian CT law-making at the policy design or parliamentary review stages. Instead, what we have seen is closer to the 'real world' approach described by former Australian Public Service Commissioner, Lynelle Briggs:

12 Letter from Florence Nightingale to Sir Francis Galton, 7 February 1891.

13 David Blunkett (Speech delivered at the Economic and Social Research Council, 2 February 2002).

14 Chris Aulich and Mark Evans (eds), *The Rudd Government: Australian Commonwealth Administration 2007–2010* (Australian National University E Press, 2010) 37.

15 Productivity Commission, *Strengthening Evidence-based Policy in the Australian Federation, Volume 1: Proceedings*, Roundtable Proceedings (17–8 August 2009) Productivity Commission, Canberra.

> In the real world, policy is developed in a fluid environment, is subject to competing vested and political interests, and can be driven by pressure to act quickly to solve headline-grabbing problems. Ideally, we need systems that are informed by evidence at each stage of policy development, [1] from when an issue is first identified, [2] to the development of the most appropriate response, and [3] subsequent evaluation of its effectiveness.[16]

According to advocates of this approach, evidence can, and should, be used to better inform government's knowledge of [1], [2] and [3]. Laudable and logical though this high level adoption of evidence-based policy may be, it is not one that fits comfortably with the intensely political nature of decision-making where absence of evidence can be a political advantage. As economist Lord John Maynard Keynes glibly noted, '[t]here is nothing a government hates more than to be well-informed; for it makes the process of arriving at decisions much more complicated and difficult'.[17] The political dimensions of policy-making can trump even the most rational courses of action. Where an evidence-based reversal of an entrenched policy may demonstrably reduce the overall harms to individuals and costs of policing, but attract the opprobrium of voters or other powerful stakeholders, governments are unlikely to allow such evidence to change policy.

In the course of our discussion thus far, 'evidence' has been represented as objective and uncontested when, in fact, evidence is rarely free from contestation over the methods of creation, reliability and generalisability. In the policy process, much depends on what 'counts' as evidence, whether the right evidence is collected (or, indeed, collectable), what 'right' means, how it is used and its limitations. These are well-rehearsed debates among public policy scholars,[18] who indicate that what sort of evidence is used, how, when and by whom is inherently political.[19]

Evidence and legitimacy

Far from providing a reason to diminish the public visibility of the evidence used to inform policy, the contestability of evidence should encourage open debate on the limitations of our current state of knowledge and promote critical reflection on how such evidence should (and should not) be used. Increasing transparency of these processes enhances the contestability of policy choices and how we understand the effectiveness of policy:

16 Lynelle Briggs, *Challenges of Evidence-based Policy-Making: Foreword* (19 June 2009) Australian Public Service Commission (online).

17 Robert Skidelsky, *John Maynard Keynes: A Biography. Vol. 2: The Economist as Saviour, 1920–1937* (London: Macmillan, 1992) 630.

18 Ray Pawson, 'Evidence-based Policy: In Search of a Method' (2002) 8(2) *Evaluation* 157–81; Ian Sanderson, 'Evaluation in Complex Policy Systems' (2000) 6(4) *Evaluation* 433.

19 Brian Head, 'Reconsidering Evidence-based Policy: Key Issues and Challenges' (2010) 29(2) *Policy and Society* 77.

> When dealing with questions about the effects of public policy, it is essential to take into account the influence of ideology and values on the creation of evidence, as well as the conditions under which the evidence generated (inter alia by whom, for whom and why).[20]

Enhancing the transparency of decision-making, the evidence used and how it is used can buttress the legitimacy of government:

> [W]ith increasing questioning and scrutiny of public intervention in economic and social spheres, governments are turning to evidence of performance for legitimacy since it is no longer guaranteed solely by democratic political processes.[21]

Legitimacy is seen as critical for government insofar as the public is assumed to confer its consent on government actions and undertakings that are perceived to have been made in the interests of the public and without favour to any given party or stakeholder. For Fritz W Scharpf, the benefits of legitimacy are clear, for it implies 'a socially sanctioned obligation to comply with government policies even if these violate the actor's own interests or normative preferences, and even if official sanctions could be avoided at low cost'.[22]

In relation to evidence-based policy, the development of policy ideas derived from the 'best available evidence' emerges as a crucial means to acquire the consent of the public. Even where evidence is contested – and it frequently is – the deployment of evidence to support decision-making and associated outcomes of policy can be a powerful means of injecting accountability into public administration.

What works in preventing terrorism

In the domain of CT policy, there is a manifest 'evidence problem'. Evidence-based policy-making has gained some traction in Australian policy-making circles in the areas of economic and social policy. However, those institutions concerned with national security have remained largely immune from, and unconcerned with, the requirement to demonstrate effectiveness through evidence of 'what works'. This is partly because effectiveness is an ambiguous, and contested, term in CT policy. In an attempt to demonstrate that CT practices are focused on the prevention of harm from terrorism, politicians and senior officials commonly laud the

20 Thomas Widmer, 'The Contribution of Evidence-Based Policy to the Output-Oriented Legitimacy of the State' (2009) 5(4) *Evidence and Policy: A Journal of Research, Debate and Practice* 351, 364–5.

21 Ian Sanderson, 'Evaluation, Policy Learning and Evidence-Based Policy Making' (2002) 80(1) *Public Administration* 1, 2.

22 Fritz W Scharpf, 'Problem-solving Effectiveness and Democratic Accountability in the EU' (Working Paper 03/1, Max Planck Institute for the Study of Societies, February 2003).

effectiveness of security agencies through the use of metrics, typically the number of 'attacks averted' or 'lives saved', as illustrated in the following assessments:

> Since [September 2014], there have been two attacks in Australia, and security and law enforcement agencies have disrupted a further six attacks.
>
> Prime Minister of Australia, Tony Abbott[23]

> Our review indicates that interrogations of detainees on whom [enhanced interrogation techniques] were used did produce intelligence that helped thwart attack plans, capture terrorists, and save lives.
>
> CIA Director, John Brennan[24]

Such claims often pass without comment. CT law-making has revealed the Australian Parliament's diminished capacity to scrutinise the government's CT strategies, policies, laws and narratives. The prevailing Australian party political discourse holds that '[n]ational security is a matter which goes above the day-to-day politics'.[25] The lack of serious parliamentary scrutiny of security legislation is cause for concern among Australian scholars, who observe that 'governments have few if any expectations that Parliament has a part to play in national security policy and practice'.[26] In effect, CT legislation with the potential to undermine democratic rights and freedoms can proceed almost unchallenged due to a specious claim by government and its agencies that CT laws will only operate effectively where the CT activities of agencies are cloaked in almost complete secrecy, including secrecy from Parliament. In this chapter, we contest this claim.

Measuring effectiveness in preventive CT law

If security policy-making is held to be above partisan politics, then we might expect the outcomes of those policies to be subject to even greater scrutiny, producing what Cynthia Lum, Leslie W Kennedy and Alison Sherley describe as follows: '[E]vidence-based counter-terrorism policies are those policies which not only show promise in achieving outcomes sought, but at the same time do not cause harm.'[27] It is worrisome that Australian government agencies have not provided a public account of how, or even if, they have sought to determine whether

23 Tony Abbott, 'Australia's Counter-Terrorism Strategy' (Media Release, 23 July 2015).
24 Central Intelligence Agency Director John Brennan, 'Statement from Director Brennan on the SSCI Study on the Former Detention and Interrogation Program' (Press Release, 9 December 2014).
25 Australian Broadcasting Corporation, 'Government stresses national safety as Parliament resumes', *Insiders*, 31 August 2014 (Opposition Leader Bill Shorten).
26 John Uhr, 'Terra Infirma? Parliament's Uncertain Role in the War on Terror' (2004) 27(2) *University of New South Wales Law Journal* 339, 344.
27 Cynthia Lum, Leslie W Kennedy and Alison Sherley, 'Are Counter-Terrorism Strategies Effective? The Results of the Campbell Systematic Review on Counter-Terrorism Evaluation Research' (2006) 2 *Journal of Experimental Criminology* 489, 490.

CT policies achieve their stated policy aims or whether they avoid potential unintended harms or consequences. It is unclear whether any such evaluations have taken place, and indeed what would likely be the findings of such reviews. As part of a systematic review of research in the CT field, Lum, Kennedy and Sherley concluded that there was almost no evidence base to support claims of the effectiveness of CT interventions:

> Many of these interventions (and more) have become part of our daily lives and discourse, but we have no idea whether or not they fulfill the promise of reducing terrorism, terrorism-related risk or harm as there is no research to support these interventions. Indeed, some of these interventions may also have collateral and unintended effects of reducing civil rights or our quality of life.[28]

There are a number of reasons why CT policy remains immune to sustained evaluation of effectiveness. The first is methodological: the relative scarcity of terrorist attacks means it is difficult to draw a causal link between the introduction of a specific CT measure (if, indeed, it were possible to discern the effects of any one particular initiative from others) and any attendant reduction in violence:

> Quite simply, the interplay of prevention, deterrence, prosecution, disruption, and willingness to engage in extremist violence are too complex to conclusively determine, on any one of these variables alone, which of the counter-terrorism laws is 'successful'.[29]

Yet even the determination of success, if that were possible, may not be sufficient to determine whether or not a policy – preventive or otherwise – should be instituted. As discussed below, acknowledgment of a broader set of imperatives is required.

Rethinking prevention: towards a framework of effectiveness, appropriateness and necessity

This section commences by critically examining the notion of effectiveness in the context of preventive laws. We sketch a framework that begins by considering 'effectiveness' as a coin with two distinct sides: aims and outcomes. These are ontologically distinct insofar as aims cannot be derived from outcomes, nor outcomes from aims; rather, aims logically precede outcomes, but do not, necessarily, *proceed* to intended outcomes. In this context of determining effectiveness, this is

28 Cynthia Lum, Leslie W Kennedy and Alison Sherley, 'Is Counter-Terrorism Policy Evidence-Based? What Works, What Harms, and What is Unknown' (2008) 20(1) *Psicothema* 35, 41.

29 Tim Legrand, Simon Bronitt and Mark Stewart, 'Evidence of the Impact of Counter-Terrorism Legislation' in Genevieve Lennon and Clive Walker (eds) *Routledge Handbook of Law and Terrorism* (Routledge, 2015) 305.

an important point to make: the relative success of government undertakings is gauged by comparing observed outcomes (within the targeted context) against original stipulated aims. Importantly, this almost always supposes that (a) aims are clearly stipulated and coherent, which is not always the case; and (b) the instruments used in pursuit of the stipulated aims caused the claimed outcomes: that is, that a government policy caused a series of intended and observed outcomes, rather than something entirely unrelated.

A simple example illustrates the difficulty in establishing these relationships: a town's new anti-crime website might be regarded as effective if the crime rate fell after its introduction. However, the outcome measure – the number of recorded crimes in the town – could easily be affected by a host of factors: how crimes are defined and recorded; the time period in which the data is collected; whether the 'real number' of crimes was detected (a function of the resources available to a police service) or reported (a function of whether low level crimes such as vandalism are reported). The local Crime Commissioner, tasked with reducing crime in the locality[30] and eager to claim a success, may assert that an overall reduction of crimes reported indicates their anti-crime initiative was successful. On their measure of success – number of crimes reported – they could claim success even if, for example (i) the proportion of violent crimes were to *increase*, or (ii) the falling number of crime reports was due to the fact that a local criminal gang had relocated to the adjacent locality. Thus, *what is measured* and *how it is measured* can substantially influence whether or not a policy is regarded as effective.

This is a significant issue to address. At the core of any policy is a theoretical perspective. Consider the tough preventive policing and 'zero-tolerance' policy towards minor street crime that had been vigorously promoted by New York Mayor Rudy Giuliani in the 1990s. Based on the influential article by criminologists James Q Wilson and George Kelling, the policy asserted that failure to attend to the outward signs of disorder in a community (such as 'broken windows') coupled with failure to enforce petty crime acted as an invitation for criminals to commit more serious crimes.[31] Zero-tolerance of petty crimes and cleaning up communities, according to the Broken Windows theory, would therefore act as a deterrent for criminal behaviour and reduce overall crime. This model is driven by a *causal* theory: serious crime is caused by overly tolerant policing and a neglected urban environment. This model drew considerable support at the time, but subsequent

30 Although our example is merely illustrative, it reflects a policing governance mechanism that is growing in importance. For example, in November 2012, the United Kingdom created a new layer of policing governance with the introduction of Police and Crime Commissioners (PCCs). These officials are elected by popular vote with a mandate to hold Chief Constables to account for the performance of local police forces. The PCCs have the power to set local policing budgets, determine policing priorities and targets and, crucially, appoint or dismiss Chief Constables.

31 George L Kelling and James Q Wilson, 'Broken Windows: The police and neighbourhood safety' *The Atlantic* (online), March 1982, available at www.theatlantic.com/magazine/archive/1982/03/broken-windows/304465 (accessed 5 September 2016).

systematic reviews of the literature found evidence to contest its causal claims.[32] In addition to the lack of consensus, there are also credible concerns that the United States police agencies that implemented such policies fabricated and manipulated local crime data in order to improve departmental performance and political support.[33] Further, serious unintended outcomes have been associated with the policy, including increased complaints of civil rights violations by police, the criminalisation of a wider population of petty offenders, and increased demands on frontline police officers. Zero-tolerance policing had all sorts of outcomes but few were those outwardly intended (namely, a matter of effectiveness: the difference between aims and outcomes) and had a wider suite of unintended effects.

To summarise, effectiveness as a measure of how a program has achieved its stated aims typically (i) excludes outcomes beyond the intended context; (ii) excludes unobserved, unobservable and precluded outcomes within the intended context; and (iii) includes a causal supposition that the aims have a direct and/or tangible (measurable) relationship to the intended outcomes (effects). Each of these exclusions hides information pertinent to whether a policy is normatively desirable.

Returning to our example of a Crime Commissioner tasked with reducing local crime, if the anti-crime website included information that induced criminals to commit hard-to-detect crimes, we might question its unintended, negative effects. If the website provided information about the home addresses of convicted paedophiles, ostensibly to alert parents to the potential criminal threat, but this resulted in increased attacks on those convicted individuals by members of the public, then this effect would bring into question the *appropriateness* of the website. Or if it was determined that the website was not frequented by the local public or, indeed, the cost of developing and maintaining the website exceeded the costs of crime in the area, then we would question its *necessity*. Effectiveness alone is thus an insufficient conceptual tool through which to judge a policy. Policy effectiveness should be a measure of how well a program achieves its stipulated aims and how it contributes to the government's overarching imperatives including the importance of protecting the fundamental principles of our liberal democracy.

This underlines the magnitude and importance of the challenge of acknowledging the difference between the 'effect' and 'effectiveness' of policy. According to David Marsh and Allan McConnell, 'the key problem is that these claims/assessments about policy outcomes do not establish any systematic criteria for assessing success or failure'.[34] A government may want to control the narrative of

32 Bernard E Harcourt and Jens Ludwig, 'Broken Windows: New Evidence from New York City and a Five-City Social Experiment' (2006) 73 *University of Chicago Law Review* 271–320. See also Centre for Evidence-Based Crime Policy, *Broken Windows Policing* (2013) Department of Criminology, Law, and Society, available online at http://cebcp.org/evidence-based-policing/what-works-in-policing/research-evidence-review/broken-windows-policing (accessed 5 September 2016).

33 John A Eterno and Eli B Silverman, *The Crime Numbers Game: Management by Manipulation* (CRC Press, 2012).

34 David Marsh and Allan McConnell, 'Towards a Framework for Establishing Policy Success' (2010) 88(2) *Public Administration* 564, 565.

a policy's outcomes, which is a simpler task if the intended outcomes are not easily measurable, discernible, or, perhaps, clearly articulated.

Appropriateness and necessity thus emerge as crucial but neglected considerations. Consideration of the wider range of avoidable outcomes associated with any initiative is, or rather should be, an integral component of the decision-making process. *Appropriateness* is used here as an umbrella term to capture five considerations for assessing success or failure that are typically excluded in the current approaches to effectiveness. Specifically, such considerations include attention to (i) confounding outcomes, (ii) ambiguous outcomes, (iii) unintended consequences, (iv) perverse incentives and (v) legitimacy alignment. *Necessity* operates as a corollary to appropriateness, and refers to those actions or initiatives that (i) duplicate existing powers (or are superseded), (ii) serve an unrequited purpose or (iii) are disproportionate to the aim. We expand these further in 'The Appropriateness Test' on p. 167.

In demonstrating why appropriateness and necessity are useful yardsticks to accompany effectiveness, we hold to two related premises: first, we aver that John Locke's endorsement of Cicero's injunction *salus populi suprema lex esto* ['let the welfare of the people be the supreme law'] holds as a universal value; second, we aver that the observation attributed to Benjamin Franklin has an equal value: 'Those who would give up essential Liberty, to purchase a little temporary Safety, deserve neither Liberty nor Safety.' It is, we think, therefore self-evident that all government efforts concerning terrorism should be directed towards protecting the public from violence *and* advancing simultaneously the core values on which liberal democracy is based, including the protection of human rights.

A new framework to analyse the effectiveness, appropriateness and necessity of preventive measures

The Australian government's preventive CT approach has very real consequences for the integrity of Australia's legal system and Australian society. With a strong emphasis on prevention as the default setting for CT measures, the need for a framework to understand and assess preventive measures has never been more urgent. This section proposes a new framework by which effectiveness of preventive CT measures may be assessed and applies this framework to case studies drawn from the Australian CT context. By considering the preventive measure in its broader context, and measuring policy impact and outcomes, the researcher is able to offer evidence-based (or, at least, evidence-informed) assessments of overall effectiveness, appropriateness and necessity of the measure.

Applying our framework

The first step in our framework facilitates an assessment of the policy effectiveness of preventive measures by reference to intended policy objectives. By studying their stated (express) and non-stated (implied) policy objectives, the effectiveness of preventive measures can be analysed by reference to *all* discernible policy objectives. As Kathleen Gleeson notes, 'security is a construction and the policies pursued in the name of security are based on choices and assumptions – not inevitability'.[35] Our framework therefore accounts for the security politics, seeking to combine policies of effective prevention *with* the liberal ideals of justice – in other words, to construct a new framework of 'preventive justice' that is based on evidence of effectiveness, appropriateness and necessity.

The effectiveness test (or testing effectiveness)

The effectiveness test should discern the extent to which it is anticipated that the intended aims of the particular initiative will be achieved using the laws, agencies and resources available. It should be asked:

- What are the stated policy objectives: that is, those policy objectives that members of government or government officials have publicly declared through explicit policy statements?
- Is there any evidence of non-stated policy objectives – that is, those policy objectives that are not explicitly or directly stated but can be reasonably implied from the other strategy statements or background papers, or revealed through critical discourse analysis of publicly available texts? and
- Is sufficient evidence available to support the expectation that the selected instrument of implementation will achieve the stipulated aims?

The appropriateness test (or testing appropriateness)

The appropriateness test should discern the range of wider impacts that can reasonably be anticipated by the intended initiative, and assess the extent to which these conform to, confound or otherwise align with (i) strategic government aims, (ii) existing policies and laws, and (iii) fundamental precepts of liberal democracy such as upholding human rights. In determining the appropriateness of measures, the following five questions must be examined:

- **Confounding outcomes:** Are there expected outcomes that will confound the fundamental imperatives of government, or the aims of allied initiatives?
- **Ambiguous outcomes:** Is there uncertainty of what outcomes will be generated by the preventive initiative?
- **Unintended consequences:** Are there unintended consequences that can be reasonably anticipated?
- **Perverse incentives:** Does the initiative incentivise or induce egregious behaviours?
- **Legitimacy alignment:** Does the initiative align with the values of the affected public?

35 Kathleen Gleeson, *Australia's 'War on Terror' Discourse* (Ashgate, 2014) 229.

The necessity test (or testing necessity)

The necessity test centres on the intended aim of a policy. It serves as a test of whether the intended aim is already well addressed by other instruments of government or whether it is of a magnitude that merits the required resources or effort to attain the aim. In testing the necessity, consideration may be given to:

- **Redundancy**: Is the instrument or initiative superseded by other initiatives?
- **Duplication**: Does the intended initiative replicate existing initiatives?
- **Proportionality**: Does the initiative produce outcomes that outweigh its start-up or ongoing costs?

Holistic assessment of preventive measures

To evaluate the impact of a preventive measure holistically, and policy effectiveness/appropriateness/necessity, it is necessary to assess each policy objective and outcome in context, rather than individually. Preventive measures operate within a highly complex and multifaceted CT policy context. This complex system includes 'hard' measures that rely on the exercise of state power, such as terrorism offences and administrative controls on individuals suspected of terrorism, through to 'soft' measures such as community-based programs for countering violent extremism (CVE) that rely on community goodwill and participation.[36] Preventive policy objectives and outcomes must be considered collectively because security policy problems have social and political dimensions that cannot easily be assessed in isolation. The interconnections and interactions of different policies must be exposed and their implications for policy outcomes explored.

This interconnected nature of CT policies and practices is demonstrated by the case studies in the following section. These case studies demonstrate how a preventive measure may have little to no effect, or, worse yet, completely negative unintended consequences. The case studies operate to identify gaps in effectiveness and opportunities to improve the effectiveness and appropriateness of preventive measures.

Case study 1: The use of preventative detention orders in Australian CT operations

Our framework can be applied to assess the operational effectiveness of existing preventive measures. Our framework facilitates an analysis of the effectiveness, appropriateness and necessity of preventative detention orders (PDOs) by examining how PDOs are intended to prevent terrorism, their application and the outcomes they provide. A PDO is an executive order for the limited detention of a person in order to prevent an imminent terrorist attack or preserve evidence

36 See Chapter 7 by Keiran Hardy in this collection for an analysis of CVE programs in the United Kingdom, and whether (and which) preventive justice principles might guide and limit their use.

relating to a terrorist act.[37] PDOs were used for the first time in Australia in September 2014 following raids carried out in Sydney and Brisbane as part of Operation Appleby. Three men were held for two days without charge on PDOs, and then released.[38]

We can ask: is sufficient evidence available to support the expectation that the use of a PDO will achieve stipulated aims, thus satisfying the necessity precept? As a short-term preventive measure, it is arguable that the use of the PDOs kept suspected terrorists in police detention, thereby preventing them from continuing their terrorist activity. However, PDOs have little efficacy as a long-term preventive measure given the maximum 14-day detention period.[39]

We then ask, applying our framework; what unintended consequences can be reasonably anticipated, and are there expected outcomes that will confound the fundamental imperatives of government or the aims of allied initiatives? The PDO case study highlights how preventive measures may produce negative unintended (and unforeseen) consequences as PDOs may hinder short-term preventive capabilities and long-term investigations and prosecutions. For example, an unintended negative outcome may be that the use of a PDO against a person further radicalises them and/or spurs them into further, even immediate, terrorist action upon their release (now that they are aware of police/security agency interest in them and knowledge of their plans/capabilities). That a person subject to a PDO cannot be questioned during the period of detention led the former INSLM, Bret Walker SC, to describe such powers as 'worse than useless' because 'questioning of them cannot contribute to the presumably urgent and ongoing investigation of the offending in question'.[40] The then INSLM found that 'PDOs are not enhancements of the crucial capacity of the intelligence and police agencies to detect and investigate terrorist offences . . . PDOs would rather impede investigation by way of questioning.'[41] The Australian Federal Police (AFP) submitted that 'if questioning during detention was permitted, it could elicit important

37 For a detailed discussion of the operation of the PDO regime, see Chapter 8 by Svetlana Tyulkina and George Williams in this collection.

38 The AFP confirmed that the three PDOs were made under New South Wales legislation. See e.g. Paul Farrell, 'Detention orders obtained before anti-terrorism raids were carried out', *The Guardian* (online) 19 September 2014, available at www.theguardian.com/world/2014/sep/19/detention-orders-obtained-before-anti-terrorism-raids-were-carried-out (accessed 5 September 2016); Dan Box and Paul Maley, 'Three held under preventive detention orders', *The Australian* (online) 20 September 2014, available at www.theaustralian.com.au/in-depth/terror/three-held-under-preventive-detention-orders/story-fnpdbcmu-1227064748235 (accessed 5 September 2016).

39 The maximum detention period is 14 days under the state and territory PDO provisions, with a maximum period of 48 hours under the Commonwealth PDO scheme. This longer detention period would appear to explain the preference for the use of state PDOs.

40 Steve Cannane, 'Emphasis in legislation should be on safety', *ABC Lateline*, 23 September 2014, available online at www.abc.net.au/lateline/content/2014/s4093437.htm (accessed 5 September 2016).

41 Bret Walker, 'Declassified Annual Report' (Annual Report, Independent National Security Legislation Monitor, 20 December 2012) Commonwealth of Australia.

information which could better direct police resources in preventing a terrorist attack'.[42] These are examples of ambiguous outcomes – where there is uncertainty over what outcomes will be generated by the preventive initiative (such as hindering an investigation). They are also examples of perverse incentives (such as encouraging a person to accelerate plans to commit a terrorist attack) and confounding outcomes (such as confounding the aims of the allied CVE programs by contributing to a person's radicalisation).

Unintended consequences (with negative effects) may even arise as a result of genuine efforts in the policy-making stage to incorporate provisions that safeguard individual rights, leading to a conflict between appropriateness and effectiveness. For PDOs, the desire for the policy to have a legitimacy alignment – that is, that the safeguards accord with the values of the affected public – negatively impacted the effectiveness of the policy. The provisions governing when PDOs may be sought and issued are so complex that the transaction costs (in terms of police resources and time) are too high compared with those associated with the use of general police powers. As a result, PDOs have been rarely used and therefore we may express concerns pertaining to their necessity stemming from their *proportionality* and possible *redundancy*. Through choosing to apply the PDO power over a general arrest power, the police may be delayed in their ability to detain the person. The choice to use the PDO – lauded by the government as a preventive measure – may paradoxically stop police from preventing a terrorist act.

This shows the need for those working on CT investigations to consider all available preventive measures. For example, an analysis could be undertaken as to whether the Australian Security Intelligence Organisation's (ASIO) questioning and detention powers[43] would better achieve the policy aim of detaining a person while also eliciting important information that could assist in urgent CT investigations.

Case study 2: Passport cancellation

Passport cancellation as a preventive measure is being increasingly used in the Australian CT context. In response to the escalation of Australians travelling to conflict zones abroad, and those planning and attempting to do so, there has been a substantial increase in the number of passports cancelled by the Foreign Minister on security grounds.[44] There are a number of matters to consider when measuring the effectiveness, appropriateness and necessity of passport cancellations as a

42 Ibid. 58.

43 See *Australian Security Intelligence Organisation Act 1979* (Cth) pt III, div 3.

44 ASIO issued 93 adverse security assessments in relation to passports in the 2014–15 financial year, meaning ASIO made twice as many recommendations for passports to be refused or cancelled on security grounds in 2014–15 than the previous year: Australian Security Intelligence Organisation, *ASIO Report to Parliament 2014–15* (19 October 2015) xiii. Over 30 Australian passports were cancelled on security grounds in the 2013–14 financial year, compared with just seven in 2011–12: INSLM Report, above n 9, 58.

preventive measure by preventing a person from travelling to a conflict zone. The government has described the purpose of passport cancellations as being 'to enhance the Australian government's capacity to take proactive, swift and proportionate action to mitigate security risks relating to Australians travelling overseas'.[45] However, given the flow-on consequences from cancelling a passport, such action does not necessarily, on its own, achieve the preventive policy objective.

The policy objective of preventing a person from journeying overseas and acquiring increased terrorist capabilities and intent is certainly a legitimate CT policy aim. The challenge for security and police agencies remains how to deal effectively with the threat posed by would-be foreign fighters who are prevented from travelling abroad. For example, they may turn their terrorist intentions towards a domestic plot if prevented from travelling overseas. If unable to travel abroad personally, they may support terrorism through other means such as terrorist financing or facilitating the recruitment and travel of others. Peter Dutton, Minister for Immigration and Border Protection, acknowledged the unintended consequence of passport cancellation that 'people . . . may well decide to manifest their terrorist activity domestically'.[46] Or, as former senior Australian CT officer Peter Moroney put it, cancelling the passports of extremists without any community measures to back up this move is like 'pulling the pin on a hand grenade and leaving it in a confined space'.[47]

The success of passport cancellation as a preventive measure will, in most cases, depend on the impact of other preventive measures, such as the effectiveness of CVE programs in de-radicalising persons at risk. Passport cancellation would also need to be supported by police and intelligence agency inquiries to determine whether the individual remains involved in terrorism, so that action can be taken to prevent such activity through timely arrest and prosecution. This demonstrates the need to assess how a preventive policy measure operates in relation to the government's CT preventive policy response *as a whole*. A measure cannot be singled out for evaluation, divorced from the reality of how it interacts with, supports or hinders other measures.

The consequences of 'hard' preventive measures such as prosecution on 'soft' preventive measures such as CVE efforts must be considered when assessing the effectiveness of preventive measures. Australia's legislative response may have repercussions for the effectiveness of other aspects of the Australian government's

45 Explanatory Memorandum, Counter-Terrorism Legislation Amendment (Foreign Fighters) Bill 2014 [43].

46 Peter Dutton, 'Counter-Terrorism Unit interventions; Grand Mufti comments; Indonesian death penalty; transfer of detainees; Christmas Island Detention Centre disturbance; Indonesia Australia Business Week 2015' (Speech delivered at the Doorstop Interview, Brisbane International Airport, 20 November 2015).

47 Rachel Olding, 'Cancelling passports of suspected jihadists won't deter the next Khaled Sharrouf', *Sydney Morning Herald* (online) 19 August 2014, available at www.smh.com.au/federal-politics/political-news/cancelling-passports-of-suspected-jihadists-wont-deter-the-next-khaled-sharrouf-20140818-104gwc.html (accessed 5 September 2016).

response to terrorism, such as CVE programs. Daniel Byman and Jeremy Shapiro note how '[i]ndiscriminate prosecution would also turn Muslim communities against the government, making them less likely to identify violent radicals in their midst'.[48]

From a preventive justice perspective, prevention of travel overseas and prosecution within Australia could be viewed as the most appropriate and legitimate policy objective and outcome, when compared against the alternative of citizenship revocation (discussed below).

This approach applies the rule of law and due process (assuming that the decision is amenable to challenge before the courts by way of review), and accords with Australia's international obligations to counter terrorism at home and abroad.

Case study 3: The Australian Government's CT amendments to citizenship law

Our framework can be applied as a predictive tool to anticipate the likely outcomes of CT laws. The *Australian Citizenship Amendment (Allegiance to Australia) Act 2015* (Cth) (Allegiance to Australia Act) empowers the government to terminate the Australian citizenship of dual citizens suspected of involvement in terrorism. The government described how the 'desired outcome of this Bill is to ensure the safety and security of Australia and its people'.[49] Another stated objective of the policy is 'preventing return to Australia'[50] of a person whose citizenship has been revoked. An assessment of the effectiveness of these policy objectives requires more than an analysis of how many people the government has banned from Australia using the Allegiance to Australia Act. If the policy objective were to simply keep these people out of Australia, then a headcount of how many people had been prevented from residing in Australia would be sufficient. However, the terrorist threat posed by such individuals to Australians at home or abroad is not neutralised by their removal from Australian soil.

Australian CT operations in 2014 and 2015 reveal the key role played by individuals from outside of Australia in terrorist plots against Australia. Individuals abroad have plotted terrorist attacks against Australia, encouraged others to commit a terrorist attack in Australia and facilitated travel of Australians abroad to engage in terrorism. Revoking citizenship and deporting or leaving a person offshore decreases the likelihood of the person being held legally accountable for their terrorist conduct. The countries where the majority of these dual nationals are located (for example, Syria, Iraq, Somalia) are likely incapable of prosecuting these individuals or even keeping them under state surveillance – the two key means by which the state can prevent individuals from committing terrorist atrocities. These countries generally will be unable to effectively investigate, prosecute and

48 Daniel Byman and Jeremy Shapiro, 'Homeward Bound? Don't Hype the Threat of Returning Jihadists' (2014) Nov/Dec 2014 *Foreign Affairs* 37, 45.

49 Explanatory Memorandum, Australian Citizenship Amendment (Allegiance to Australia) Bill 2015 (Cth) 1.

50 Ibid. 29.

punish these individuals for their terrorist activities. Given the state of governance and law and order in these countries, the likelihood of Australian authorities securing mutual legal assistance for the collection of evidence, or extraditing individuals back to Australia to face a criminal trial, is low. Australian authorities will not be able to monitor these individuals and collect intelligence on their terrorist activities to the extent they could if the individuals remained in Australia where measures such as control orders, telecommunications interception and surveillance device warrants could be used.

Police alleged that those detained in Sydney as part of Operation Appleby were intending to commit terrorist attacks against random members of the Australian public on behalf of Daesh and had received direct encouragement from an Australian within Daesh. Police also alleged links between the Melbourne group involved in the 2015 Anzac Day plot and Neil Prakash.[51] Prakash is believed by police and security agencies to be the highest-ranking Australian in Daesh in Syria, and the chief recruiter of Australian foreign fighters.

A series of conflicting policy objectives raise further questions about the appropriateness of the approach. For example, the preventive policy objective of keeping people out of Australia is in direct conflict with then Prime Minister Abbott's stated policy objective 'to keep people who would do us harm under the closest possible supervision'.[52] This is because the government cannot keep individuals in places such as Syria and Iraq under the 'closest possible supervision'.

Extensive research on 'suspect communities' in the United Kingdom suggests this policy is likely to be counter-productive in the longer term, as it will alienate Muslim communities in Australia and foster a feeling of distrust and fear among these communities.[53] This would make people less likely to come forward to authorities with information about suspected radicalisation or terrorist activities. Another unintended policy outcome is the creation of a tiered citizenship system with different classes of citizenship where naturalised citizens have lesser rights than other citizens.[54]

51 Twenty-four-year-old Prakash is an Islamic convert of Fijian-Indian and Cambodian background who travelled to Syria in early 2013 where he is known as Abu Khalid al Cambodi.

52 Daniel Hurst, 'Coalition to tighten laws to crackdown on alleged jihadists', *The Guardian* (online) 4 July 2014, available at www.theguardian.com/world/2014/jul/04/coalition-crackdown-alleged-jihadists (accessed 5 September 2016).

53 Pantazis and Pemberton have developed Hillyard's notion of 'suspect communities' to put forward evidence from the United Kingdom that CT measures and the political discourse around such measures have created 'suspect communities'. They argue that Muslim communities have been constructed as 'suspect communities' and specifically targeted for state surveillance, with a negative impact on social cohesion and national security. See Christina Pantazis and Simon Pemberton, 'From the "Old" to the "New" Suspect Community' (2009) 49(5) *British Journal of Criminology* 646; Paddy Hillyard, *Suspect Community: People's Experiences of the Prevention of Terrorism Acts in Britain* (Pluto Press, 1993).

54 For an excellent discussion of issues of allegiance and identity, including policy implications, see Kim Rubenstein and Niamh Lenagh-Maguire, 'Citizenship and the Boundaries of the Constitution' in Rosalind Dixon and Tom Ginsburg (eds), *The*

These examples are relevant to an effectiveness analysis (for example, the preventive measure can only be applied to dual citizens and not to suspected terrorists who hold no other nationality). They are also relevant to an appropriateness analysis (for example, is it appropriate to create 'suspect communities' or a tiered system of citizenship).

Our framework can be applied to assess if the Allegiance to Australia Act is normatively appropriate and test the government's claim that the policy is 'in the Government's view, proportionate to the legitimate goal of ensuring the security of the Australian community'.[55] The Act enables the cessation of an individual's Australian citizenship on the basis of their past criminal conviction for a terrorism offence. It also allows for an Australian citizen aged 14 years or older who is a national or citizen of a country other than Australia to have his or her Australian citizenship revoked if they act inconsistently with their allegiance to Australia by engaging in any of the activities listed in s 33AA(2) of the Allegiance to Australia Act (being conduct that would constitute a terrorism offence under the *Criminal Code Act 1995* (Cth)).[56] Australian citizenship ceases immediately on the person engaging in that conduct.[57] This provision only applies where the person was overseas when they engaged in the conduct or the person left Australia after engaging in the conduct and, at the time they left Australia, the person had not been tried for an offence related to the conduct.[58] Section 33AA of the Allegiance to Australia Act therefore enables cessation of citizenship not on the basis of a criminal conviction for a terrorism offence, but on the basis of highly classified intelligence,[59] not necessarily of an evidential standard sufficient to convict the person, and which the person will never see.

The Allegiance to Australia Act is hard to reconcile with the traditional rule of law ideal that interference with liberty and property must follow due process, which in relation to the adjudication of terrorism offences should be established in the courtroom on the criminal standard of beyond reasonable doubt, rather than through a secretive administrative process. When asked why citizenship should

Research Handbook in Comparative Constitutional Law (Edward Elgar, 2011) 143; Fiona Jenkins, Mark Nolan and Kim Rubenstein (eds), *Allegiance and Identity in a Globalised World* (Cambridge University Press, 2014), especially Part IV 'National Security Concerns and Counter-Terrorism Law'.

55 Explanatory Memorandum, Australian Citizenship Amendment (Allegiance to Australia) Bill 2015 (Cth) 29.

56 Allegiance to Australia Act s 33AA(1).

57 Ibid. s 33AA(9).

58 Ibid. s 33AA(7).

59 In explaining how the process for briefing the Minister for Immigration and Border Protect in citizenship cessation cases would work, the Secretary of the Department of Immigration and Border Protection, Michael Pezzullo, commented on the nature of the information that would be provided to the Minister and which would form the basis of the Minister's decision. Pezzullo confirmed that it is a 'fair supposition' that the brief would include largely classified information from agencies such as ASIO, and would include limited open source (public) material. See Commonwealth, *Committee Hansard*, Parliamentary Joint Committee on Intelligence and Security, 10 August 2015, 10.

cease on the basis of something other than criminal conviction by a court, Dutton stated:

> [I]f somebody had been involved in … a terrorist act within Syria: to come back to Australia, it's very hard for us to gather the evidence and prosecute beyond a reasonable doubt in our courts here. So necessarily we rely on the advice from the intelligence agencies and the information available through gathering of all of that information.[60]

The obstacles to collecting evidence adequate for prosecution before a criminal court appear to be the motivation behind s 33AA of the Allegiance to Australia Act, and indicate that another policy aim is to apply revocation of citizenship in lieu of criminal prosecution. The effect, however, is to create a process that both erodes and circumvents the fundamental human rights of citizens suspected of terrorism – foremost the right to a fair trial – but who cannot be prosecuted or have their guilt determined in the ordinary way.

A negative, unintended consequence of the citizenship revocation policy is that finite agency resources are used on applying this policy. These resources may well yield better policy outcomes if put towards a different preventive measure such as CVE efforts or in providing Turkey with capacity-building assistance to identify foreign fighters before they enter Syria and to deport them back to Australia. Likewise, it may be a better use of resources to work with the Turkish police to collect evidence of terrorist activities to facilitate prosecution on their return to Australia. By reassessing what preventive measure will provide the best overall policy outcome, government and agencies can better use their resources to support the achievement of policy objectives.

Conclusion

Security policy-making has long resisted the wider public sector trends demanding more rigorous evaluation of policy outcomes. It is clear that CT is an area in which assessing the effects of government initiatives should be considered not merely useful but in fact crucial for developing more evidence-based policy. Yet considerations of 'effectiveness', as we have argued here, offer only a dangerous, one-eyed view of the full implications of government action in this fraught space. The dominant rationale of CT practice has been to build a 'better' mousetrap, geared to meet one simple aim: to steadily break the back of violent extremism. Yet this effort towards making better policy has occurred with little regard to the accompanying financial, moral or political cost. As suggested here, we think that applying the twin tests – of effectiveness and appropriateness – to preventive CT legislation offers a series of important analytical and normative pay-offs. For those

60 Australian Broadcasting Corporation, 'Government divided about removing citizenship of foreign fighters without dual nationality', *7.30 Report,* 26 May 2015 (Peter Dutton).

concerned with understanding the circumstances under which policy should, or should not, be instituted, the effectiveness/appropriateness framework operates as a means to divine the likely risks and benefits. As McConnell claims, '[policy] success and failure are not mutually exclusive'.[61] We suggest it is normatively desirable that government move beyond questioning effectiveness – although even this is not a well-worn topic in the CT policy domain – to capture broader questions concerned with appropriateness. Appropriateness requires consideration of whether the measure is producing confounding or ambiguous outcomes; unintended consequences; perverse incentives; and legitimacy alignment. By applying this structured approach to CT policy measures, we hope that our framework can alert analysts to those possibilities of achieving both effective *and* appropriate outcomes, and, in so doing, strengthen the arm of those charged with pursuing the ultimate safety of the public.

61 Allan McConnell, 'Policy Success, Policy Failure and Grey Areas In-Between' (2010) 30(3) *Journal of Public Policy* 345, 359.

10 'If at first you don't succeed . . .'

Effectiveness and the evolution of preventive organised crime measures

Rebecca Ananian-Welsh

Introduction

The impact of a preventive measure is generally experienced before a wrong has occurred. However, as chapters in this volume have identified, such measures often involve serious impositions on liberty.[1] It is these kinds of measures that Ashworth and Zedner describe as 'coercive preventive measures'.[2] The primary justification[3] for a preventive measure therefore tends to focus on its effectiveness: an intrusion on liberty may be acceptable because it avoids a much greater wrong. But what if the effectiveness of a preventive measure is never demonstrated? One might expect that measure to be repealed, thereby avoiding an unnecessary intrusion on liberty.

This chapter considers the role that proven effectiveness may play in guiding the evolution of a preventive measure. I focus on the migration of control orders in Australia – from the anti-terrorism context to that of organised crime, and across domestic jurisdictions. I then trace the role of proven effectiveness in the extension of the control order paradigm to a new extreme. I do not attempt a realistic assessment of whether control orders are, in fact, effective at preventing crime.[4] Rather, I focus on the rhetoric of effectiveness and query whether proof of the (in) effective functioning of these laws facilitated or stalled their adoption, their migration or their escalation to new levels of severity.

Control orders: from terrorists to bikies

Federal anti-terrorism control orders

It is widely accepted that the prevention of criminal acts is preferable to simply reacting to crimes that have already occurred. This paradigm of preventive justice

1 See e.g. the preventive detention of the mentally ill discussed by Bernadette McSherry in Chapter 4 and Helen Punter in Chapter 5.
2 Andrew Ashworth and Lucia Zedner, *Preventive Justice* (Oxford University Press, 2014) 20–1.
3 For a discussion of the justifications and rationales for coercive preventive measures, see ibid. 20–5.
4 For discussion on measuring the effectiveness of preventive measures, see Chapter 9 by Tim Legrand and Teneille Elliot in this collection.

was rekindled in the wake of September 11, when the threat of terrorism entered the global consciousness and we witnessed the potential devastation that may be wrought by a single act of terror. Australia, like most nations, responded to the threat of global terrorism by enacting new anti-terrorism laws.[5] Many of these laws were aimed squarely at the prevention, rather than the prosecution, of terrorist acts.

Control orders were one of the preventive anti-terrorism measures introduced by the Australian government in 2005.[6] Adapted from the United Kingdom's anti-terrorism control order scheme,[7] Australia's control orders are civil orders, issued by a court and capable of imposing a wide array of restrictions and obligations on an individual in the absence of a criminal charge. For example, a control order may impose curfews or restrictions on a person's location, use of technology or contact with certain people, or it may require a person to report to police or wear an electronic tag.[8]

Federal anti-terrorism control orders may be issued in respect of adults not suspected of involvement in criminal wrongdoing. In this sense, control orders are an alternative, rather than an adjunct, to the criminal justice system. A child aged 16 or 17 years may also be subject to a control order of up to three months duration.[9] The maximum duration of a regular control order is 12 months from the date that the initial 'interim' order is served on the person,[10] and there are no limits on seeking successive control orders over an individual.[11]

The control order provisions enable the Australian Federal Police (AFP) to seek two kinds of orders from an issuing court.[12] With the consent of the Attorney-General, the AFP may first seek an interim control order. Interim orders are issued

5 See generally Andrea Bianchi, 'Security Council's Anti-terror Resolutions and Their Implementation by Member States: An Overview' (2006) 4(5)*Journal of International Criminal Justice* 1044. Cf. e.g. Argentina and Brazil discussed in Rebecca Welsh, 'Understood But Undefined: Why Do Argentina and Brazil Resist Criminalising Terrorism?' (2013) 7 *Vienna Journal on International Constitutional Law* 327.

6 *Criminal Code Act 1995* (Cth) (Criminal Code) ch 5 pt 5.3 div 104. For detailed examination of control orders in Australia and the United Kingdom, see Chapter 3 by Susan Donkin in this collection.

7 Andrew Lynch, Tamara Tulich and Rebecca Welsh, 'Secrecy and Control Orders: The Role and Vulnerability of Constitutional Values in the United Kingdom and Australia' in David Cole, Federico Fabbrini and Arianna Vedaschi (eds) *Secrecy, National Security and the Vindication of Constitutional Law* (Edward Elgar, 2013) 154. Control orders in the United Kingdom have since been repealed and replaced with the similar, but less onerous, Terrorism Prevention and Investigation Measure (TPIM) scheme prescribed by the *Terrorism Prevention and Investigation Measures Act 2011* (UK).

8 Criminal Code s 104(5)(3).

9 Ibid. s 104.28.

10 Ibid. s 104.16(1)(d).

11 Ibid. s 104.5(2).

12 Ibid s 100.1 defines issuing courts as the Federal Court of Australia, the Family Court of Australia and the Federal Circuit Court of Australia. The court receives the application in the same form it was presented to the Attorney-General, subject to any changes required by the Attorney-General, as well as information sworn by the applicant and the written consent of the Attorney-General: s 104.3.

By making findings of constitutional invalidity in *Totani* and *Wainohu*, the High Court indicated that control order schemes would need to be carefully drafted so as to protect the institutional integrity and independence of state courts. However, by grounding invalidity in very narrow bases that seemed to overlook some of the more troubling features of control order schemes (such as their imposition of preventive restraints on liberty on the basis of untested evidence and predictive, even vague, criteria), the High Court also indicated that the control order framework was not necessarily at odds with constitutional values.

The states harnessed this latter suggestion and continued to implement bikie control order schemes. This was reflected, for example, in a statement by Western Australian Attorney-General Michael Mischin when that State's control order scheme was introduced to parliament in 2012. For Mischin, the High Court in *Wainohu* 'found that there is nothing constitutionally or legally objectionable about the principal underlying objectives of these laws'.[50]

The constitutional legitimacy of control orders was cemented in 2013 when the High Court upheld Queensland's *Criminal Organisation Act 2009* (Qld) in *Assistant Commissioner Michael James Condon v Pompano Pty Ltd*.[51] Following this case, the processes of migration and normalisation for bikie control orders seemed to be complete. Bikie control orders had been enacted in most Australian jurisdictions, and the prospect of a successful constitutional challenge no longer posed a significant threat. But, despite the spread and normalisation of control orders, stories pointing to their effectiveness as a preventive justice tool were nowhere to be seen.

From control to criminalisation: the new offence provisions

In 2013, not long after the High Court upheld Queensland's bikie control order scheme, the government of that State abandoned its only control order application. The government, then led by Premier Campbell Newman, declared control orders to be 'a failure',[52] thereby acknowledging their lack of proven effectiveness. Instead of repealing the control order provisions, the Newman government harnessed the ineffectiveness of control orders to justify the introduction of more severe preventive measures.

In October 2013, the Newman government introduced a new suite of preventive justice measures that harnessed the *criminal* law to fight the continuing 'war on bikies'.[53] These laws included a set of new offences, criminalising certain acts performed by 'participants in a criminal organisation' (the new offence

50 Western Australia, *Parliamentary Debates*, Legislative Council, 22 March 2012, 1148 (Michael Mischin).
51 (2013) 252 CLR 38.
52 Queensland, *Parliamentary Debates*, Legislative Assembly, 15 October 2013, 3114 (Campbell Newman) 3248 (Jarrod Bleijie).
53 See e.g. *Criminal Law (Criminal Organisations Disruption) and Other Legislation Amendment Act 2013* (Qld); *Vicious Lawless Association Disestablishment Act 2013* (Qld); *Tattoo Parlours Act 2013* (Qld).

provisions).[54] As in the bikie control order schemes, the first stage of the new offence provisions involves the declaration of a criminal organisation. This declaration may be made by either the courts or the Attorney-General.[55] The courts may declare an organisation if its purposes relate to engagement in serious criminal activity, or if it represents an unacceptable risk to the community.[56] The Attorney-General may simply declare organisations at his or her (unreviewable) discretion.[57] Former Queensland Attorney-General Jarrod Bleijie declared 26 organisations, and said that the reasons behind these declarations may never be made public.[58]

Participants in a declared organisation then face prosecution if they meet in a group of three or more in public,[59] go to a prescribed place or event (which non-participants are free to attend)[60] or recruit to the organisation.[61] It is also an offence for anyone to wear logos, clothing or other icons associated with a declared criminal organisation on licensed premises.[62] These offences attract a minimum sentence of six months' (and a maximum of three years') imprisonment.[63] 'Participants' include not only directors or officers of declared organisations but those who in any way assert, declare, seek or advertise an association with a declared organisation, or who have attended more than one gathering of such an organisation, or who participate or take part in the affairs of a criminal organisation in any way.[64] The one stated exception from this broad definition is for lawyers acting in a professional capacity.[65]

It is clear that the new offence provisions aim to prevent future crimes rather than respond to past criminal actions. It is not suggested that there is something inherently criminal or deserving of incarceration in, for example, three people meeting in public or wearing insignia in a bar. By targeting 'participants in criminal organisations', these laws aim to dismantle organised crime groups and prevent serious criminal activity, rather than merely deterring or punishing reprehensible conduct. Like control orders, the new offence provisions harness the basic idea of guilt by association to restrict the freedoms and liberties of those associated with declared 'criminal' groups. But, unlike control orders, these new measures are

54 *Criminal Code Act 1899* (Qld) (Criminal Code Qld) ss 60A–60C.
55 Although, since *Totani*, all state and territory control order schemes have placed this declaration process within the judicial branch. See e.g. legislative references, above n 28.
56 Criminal Code (Qld) s 1 (definition of 'criminal organisation').
57 Ibid.
58 Marty Silk, 'Bikie evidence to be secret forever' (15 January 2014) *Brisbane Times* (online), 15 January 2014, available at www.brisbanetimes.com.au/queensland/bikie-evidence-to-be-secret-forever-20140115-30vg3.html (accessed 5 September 2016).
59 Criminal Code (Qld) s 60A.
60 Ibid. s 60B.
61 Ibid. s 60C.
62 *Liquor Act 1992* (Qld) ss 173EB, 173EC, 173ED.
63 Criminal Code (Qld) ss 60A–60C.
64 Ibid. s 60A(3).
65 Ibid.

within the criminal sphere and impose harsh terms of imprisonment rather than civil obligations and restrictions (which only attract criminal sanctions if a breach of a control order can be established).

The migration of the new offence provisions

The new offence provisions were introduced, debated and enacted in a single sitting of the Queensland parliament in October 2013. The apparent failure of control orders to effectively prevent crime helped to justify the introduction of these harsh new laws. Beyond this, the same factors underpinned the enactment of the new offence provisions and bikie control orders. A brawl between rival bikie gangs on Queensland's Gold Coast had brought gang violence to the forefront of political debate. The Newman government had adopted a 'tough on crime' policy platform, and was actively seeking to introduce the toughest anti-bikie laws in the world.[66] Bikies were again painted as 'urban terrorists' and the rhetoric of 'war' was invoked.[67]

By the end of 2014, the new offence provisions had withstood constitutional challenge, and had thereby gained constitutional legitimacy.[68] The Commonwealth, as well as those states and territories that had already enacted bikie control order laws, intervened in this case to argue for the validity of the impugned provisions. Following the High Court's ruling, Attorneys-General from Western Australia, South Australia and the Northern Territory said they would be considering the decision very carefully, with an eye to introducing similar schemes in their own jurisdictions.[69]

It seemed, therefore, that the spread and perhaps even the normalisation of the new offence provisions were inevitable. However, unlike control orders, the new offence provisions have been slow to migrate to other states or territories.

Within weeks of the enactment of Queensland's new bikie laws, the Western Australian government had introduced legislation criminalising participation in, and recruitment to, criminal organisations.[70] Each of these offences is punishable by five years' imprisonment. Then, in July 2015, the South Australian parliament enacted the *Statutes Amendment (Serious and Organised Crime) 2015* (SA). This

66 See e.g. ABC Television, 'Queensland to introduce the world's toughest bikie laws', *Lateline*, 30 September 2013 (Jarrod Bleijie), available online at www.abc.net.au/lateline/content/2013/s3859470.htm (accessed 5 September 2016); Jarrod Bleijie, 'How to win war with bikie gangs', *The Australian* (online), 20 December 2013, 10; Queensland, *Parliamentary Debates*, Legislative Assembly, 15 October 2013, 3114 (Campbell Newman), 3120 (Jarrod Bleijie).

67 See Ananian-Welsh and Williams, above n 38, 390.

68 *Kuczborski v Queensland* (2014) 254 CLR 51.

69 Cleo Fraser, 'States, NT May Adopt Qld Anti-Bikie Laws', *news.com.au* (online), 14 November 2014, available at www.theaustralian.com.au/news/latest-news/court-rejects-challenge-to-qld-bikie-laws/news-story/88be798f38e0ca723f734938b04b6551 (accessed 5 September 2016).

70 *Criminal Organisation Control Act 2012* (WA). See also Michael Mischin, 'Crackdown Set to Begin on WA's Criminal Gangs' (Media Statement, 29 October 2013).

Act contained a suite of measures aimed at dismantling organised crime gangs, including provisions that mirrored Queensland's new offence provisions.[71]

The effectiveness of the new offence provisions is debatable. On the one hand, police claim that the laws have had an impact on organised crime gangs, beyond merely decreasing their visibility and causing them to vacate clubhouses.[72] On the other hand, some have argued that any decreases in crime are attributable to other factors such as increased levels of funding for the Queensland Police Service.[73]

In April 2016, the Queensland Department of Justice and Attorney-General's 'Taskforce on Organised Crime Legislation' (Taskforce) issued its 416-page report on the State's anti-bikie laws. This Taskforce was chaired by retired judge Alan Wilson and its members included representatives from the Queensland Bar Association, Law Society, Police Service and Union, and Departments of Justice and of Premier and Cabinet. The Taskforce's Report was damning of the new offence provisions, concluding that they 'represent a significant breach of Queensland's fundamental legislative principles, and compromise civil liberties and democratic rights',[74] and that this was apparently for no tangible crime prevention outcome: 'In their current form the offences will be difficult to prosecute successfully, and may be constitutionally invalid.'[75]

The Taskforce reported that, despite 42 persons being charged with the offence of participants in a criminal organisation meeting in public, five people being charged with going to a prescribed place, and five people being charged with the recruitment offence, *no one* had been successfully prosecuted under the laws.[76]

This lack of convictions has not saved the provisions from public controversy. In one highly publicised case, Sally Kuether, a librarian and community service award holder with no criminal history, was arrested for meeting her partner and a friend at a hotel for a drink. Kuether was wearing the insignia of a declared organisation, the Life and Death Motorcycle Club, to which her partner and his friend allegedly belonged. The police arrested all three for committing the offence of 'participants in a criminal organisation being knowingly present in public places' and for

71 There are some minor differences between the Queensland and South Australian new offence provisions. For example, the South Australian provisions do not proscribe mandatory minimum sentences.

72 Chris O'Brien, 'Queensland police fight to keep anti-bikie laws, Premier says' *ABC News* (online), 17 August 2015, available at www.abc.net.au/news/2015-08-17/qld-police-can-fight-for-anti-bikie-laws/6702540(accessed 5 September 2016); Queensland Police, *Anti-criminal gang laws – FAQs* (25 August 2014), available online at www.police.qld.gov.au/programs/acglfaq.htm (accessed 5 September 2016).

73 Terry Goldsworthy, 'Crime stats provide reality check in Queensland's bikie crackdown' (1 September 2014) *The Conversation*, available online at https://theconversation.com/crime-stats-provide-reality-check-in-queenslands-bikie-crackdown-30908 (accessed 5 September 2016)..

74 Queensland Department of Justice and Attorney-General, Taskforce on Organised Crime Legislation, *Report of Taskforce on Organised Crime Legislation* (31 March 2016) Queensland Government 169.

75 Ibid.

76 Ibid. 172, 174–5.

entering and remaining in a licensed premises wearing prohibited items, being Life and Death Club vests. The police opposed bail and raided Kuether's home.[77] Following her release on bail, Kuether said to the media: 'I can't see what I've done wrong, all I did was have a beer with my partner and my mate.'[78] The more serious charges were eventually dropped against Kuether before the Brisbane Magistrates Court, although she was fined $150 for wearing the insignia of a declared organisation on licensed premises.[79]

In another instance, Daniel Lovett, Bane Ajajbegovic, Dario Halolovic, Kresmir Basic and Darren Hayley – a group of childhood friends from Victoria on holiday on the Gold Coast – were on their way to Cold Rock ice creamery when they were charged with the offence of 'participants in a criminal organisation' meeting in public. Their solicitor would report that the men had spent some of their three weeks in prison in prolonged solitary confinement, 'and that Queensland taxpayers had paid $500,000 for the case to be pursued'.[80] The prosecution eventually dropped all charges against the 'Ice Cream Bikies' for lack of evidence.[81]

At the time of writing, parliamentary inquiries have been convened in Queensland and South Australia to review organised crime legislation. The impact of these inquiries remains to be seen – although the Taskforce Report indicates that support for the new offence provisions is highly unlikely.

There are a variety of reasons why the new offence provisions have not been adopted outside of Queensland and South Australia. First, these laws played a role in the Newman government's defeat in the January 2015 State election. The tough bikie laws introduced by that government arguably went too far in encroaching on civil liberties to prevent crime, and became politically unpalatable. By the 2015 election, not only had the laws attracted critique from leading lawyers, but widespread protests had been staged across Queensland and even outside Australia.[82] Critics and supporters of the laws argued about the effectiveness of the laws at preventing crime,[83] but this issue was not given prime attention. Instead,

77 Frank Robson, 'Crack down: Queensland's anti-bikie laws are resulting in some unusual arrests – and not just of bikies. Is the war on outlaw gangs backfiring?', *Sydney Morning Herald* (online), 14 June 2014, available at www.smh.com.au/lifestyle/crack-down-20140613-39rul.html (accessed 5 September 2016)..

78 Brooke Baskin, 'Librarian and accused bikie Sally Louise Kuether freed on bail', *The Courier-Mail* (Brisbane), 31 January 2014, 3.

79 'Anti-association charges dropped against first woman charged under Queensland's anti-bikie laws', *ABC News* (online), 8 April 2015, available at www.abc.net.au/news/2015-04-08/a-librarian-who-was-charged-under-queenslands-antibikie-laws-ha/6377062 (accessed 5 September 2016)..

80 Queensland Department of Justice and Attorney-General, above n 74, 172.

81 Ibid.

82 Amy Remeikis, 'Bikie protests go international', *Brisbane Times*, 14 January 2014, available online at www.brisbanetimes.com.au/queensland/bikie-protests-go-international-20140114-30t4z.html (accessed 5 September 2016).

83 See e.g. 'Qld's bikie laws aren't working: academic', *news.com.au* (online) 20 January 2014, available at www.news.com.au/national/breaking-news/qlds-bikie-laws-arent-working-academic/story-e6frfku9-1226806008628 (accessed 5 September 2016); Terry Goldsworthy, 'The revealing facts on bikie laws and crime in Queensland', *The*

criticism tended to focus on the impact of the laws on basic rights and civil liberties, and the laws' potential for overreach.[84]

In the lead-up to the 2015 election, the Queensland Labor Party, led by Anastacia Palaszczuk, promised to review and even repeal the bikie laws, including the new offence provisions. No longer was an uncompromising 'tough on crime' policy platform a ticket to political success. Once elected, Premier Palaszczuk convened the parliamentary inquiry and Taskforce mentioned above with a view to replacing the new offence provisions and other anti-bikie laws enacted by the Newman government.

In South Australia, the enactment of new offence provisions attracted heated parliamentary debate before they were passed into law in July 2015. Just as in Queensland when Newman introduced his government's anti-bikie legislation, in the course of the South Australian debate control orders were recognised as a 'demonstrable failure'.[85] Although the Queensland Taskforce was yet to report when the South Australian bill was before parliament, some attention was directed at whether the new offence provisions had been shown to be an effective crime prevention measure in Queensland. As Vickie Chapman, Deputy Leader of the Liberal Party (in opposition) noted, the effectiveness of the new offence provisions was not only unproven, but was at that time under review with a view to possible repeal by the Queensland government. Against this background, Chapman said:

> It just seems bizarre to me that the government are coming in here to ask us to approve a Queensland model . . . and adhere to that formula when they themselves are reviewing this and we have really only been able to have anecdotal material . . . and information they have been able to glean about what is happening in Queensland. I think this is very concerning.[86]

While these kinds of concerns over the uncertain effectiveness of the new offence provisions were being raised, more attention was being paid to other factors. First, the failure of bikie control orders was again being harnessed to justify the introduction of new measures.[87] Second, constitutional concerns were raised and given

Conversation (online), 20 January 2015, available at https://theconversation.com/the-revealing-facts-on-bikie-laws-and-crime-in-queensland-35892 (accessed 5 September 2016); Jonathan Green, 'Background Briefing: VLAD the bikie jailer', *Radio National ABC*, 2 February 2014, available online at www.abc.net.au/radionational/programs/backgroundbriefing/2014-02-02/5225444 (accessed 5 September 2016).

84 See e.g. Andrew Trotter and Harry Hobbs, 'The Great Leap Backward: Criminal Law Reform with the Hon Jarrod Bleijie' (2014) 36 *Sydney Law Review* 1; 'Anti-bikie laws: Rallies held around country to protest anti-association laws in Queensland, NSW, Victoria and South Australia', *ABC News* (online), 4 July 2015, available at www.abc.net.au/news/2015-07-04/anti-bikie-law-rallys-held-around-australia/6595206 (accessed 5 September 2016).

85 See e.g. South Australia, *Parliamentary Debates*, House of Assembly, 16 June 2015, 1593 (Vickie Chapman).

86 Ibid. 1603.

87 See e.g. ibid. 1593.

priority – it was clear that the South Australian government was keen to avoid another defeat in the High Court, as it had suffered in *Totani*.[88] Ultimately, the new offence provisions were enacted in South Australia after only slight amendment.[89] Concerns over their potential ineffectiveness as a crime prevention measure were, again, overshadowed and sidelined – even though in Queensland the government was actively reviewing the provisions, and effectiveness was at the forefront of this review.

At the time of writing, there have been no further indications that other states will be enacting similar provisions, although it remains to be seen whether outbreaks in gang violence or a resurgence in 'tough on crime' politics may drive other states or territories to adopt similar laws.

The role of effectiveness

The rapid migration of control orders across contexts, their normalisation and the introduction of the new offence provisions were supported by factors that include the widespread adoption of 'tough on crime' policy platforms, outbreaks of gang violence and High Court cases in which these laws gained constitutional legitimacy. The failure of the new offence provisions to undergo a similar process of migration and normalisation may reflect a shift in political ethos – perhaps the controversy over the Newman government's anti-bikie laws demonstrated that 'tougher' is not always the most politically popular approach. But what role has 'effectiveness' played in the evolution of control orders and the new offence provisions?

When control orders migrated to the organised crime sphere, there was no evidence that they had been in any way effective as a federal anti-terrorism measure. Inquiries had been convened to investigate the measure's effectiveness, and the INSLM had concluded that control orders were both unnecessary and ineffective. As an anti-organised crime measure, again the effectiveness of control orders was undemonstrated. However, this presented no real obstacle to the adoption of bikie control order laws in South Australia, New South Wales, Western Australia, the Northern Territory, Victoria or Queensland.

This demonstrates that effectiveness can be a side issue in the migration of preventive justice measures. Strong arguments of ineffectiveness will not necessarily stall the spread of a preventive measure or prompt its repeal – even when that measure has the capacity to severely impact civil liberties or those arguments are made by reputable sources such as the INSLM. Arguments pointing to a lack of demonstrated effectiveness have been met by emphasis on the urgent need to crack down on an imminent threat, or pressure to align with surrounding jurisdictions so as to avoid any chance of becoming a safe haven. Such rhetoric plays to public fears on the subject and a perceived need to do *something*.

88 See e.g. Tom Fedorowytsch, 'Anti-bikie legislation passes South Australian parliament', *ABC News* (online), 30 July 2015, available at www.abc.net.au/news/2015-07-30/anti-bikie-legislation-passes-sa-upper-house/6660280 (accessed 5 September 2016).

89 The list of criminal organisations was reduced from 27 to ten.

The new offence provisions have presumably succeeded in deterring certain actions – for instance, the wearing of gang insignia on licensed premises and the use of prescribed premises as bikie clubhouses.[90] The Taskforce Report also annexed a Queensland Police Service survey of Gold Coast business owners, which demonstrated that 66 per cent of those surveyed felt safer since the 'crack-down' on bikie gangs. This may have been the way in which these laws have been effective – even though actual (not perceived) community safety was their stated objective. This highlights the importance of distinguishing between aims and outcomes when considering the effectiveness of preventive measures, as discussed by Tim Legrand and Teneille Elliot in Chapter 9 of this collection.

Whether the new offence provisions – or control orders for that matter – have impacted levels of organised crime or dismantled criminal gangs remains open for debate and has, appropriately, been the subject of inquiries. Suffice to say, the effectiveness of the new offence provisions was far from clear when the South Australian provisions were enacted, just as the effectiveness of control orders was undemonstrated during their spread and normalisation.

Had Queensland's Taskforce reported that the new offence provisions were highly effective at preventing gang crime, there would have been every chance that other states and territories would have enacted similar laws. But what is likely to follow the finding that the laws are ineffective at achieving this aim? The control order case study suggests that this finding alone would provide little obstacle to the retention of the new offence provisions by Queensland and South Australia, or even to their adoption by other states and territories – as long as governments consider the laws to be politically expedient. Importantly, the Taskforce Report makes positive suggestions for alternative schemes to replace the new offence provisions (such as consorting laws). This may satisfy the political need for tough criminal justice measures while also bringing about the repeal of the highly problematic new offences.

The ineffectiveness of control orders at preventing criminal activities eventually justified the introduction of the new offence provisions in both Queensland and South Australia, which harness the same rights-offensive frameworks in a *more* onerous way. This suggests that if the new offence provisions are proven to be ineffective at preventing crime, they may nonetheless lead to even harsher preventive laws. For example, the consorting laws proposed by the Taskforce may not be more severe, but they are nonetheless highly controversial.[91] In sum, far from prompting the winding back of these preventive measures, proven ineffectiveness was largely irrelevant to the initial introduction, migration and normalisation of

90 See e.g. Queensland Police, *Anti-criminal gang laws – FAQs* (25 August 2014), available online at www.police.qld.gov.au/programs/acglfaq.htm (accessed 5 September 2016).

91 These laws were subject to an unsuccessful constitutional challenge in *Tajjour v New South Wales; Hawthorne v New South Wales; Forster v New South Wales* (2014) 254 CLR 508. For critique of consorting provisions, see e.g. Anthony Gray, 'Freedom of Association in the Australian "Constitution" and the Crime of Consorting' (2013) 32 (2) *University of Tasmania Law Review* 149.

bikie control orders, and assisted in the escalation of the control order paradigm to a new level of severity in the new offence provisions.

Conclusion

Preventive measures such as control orders and the new offence provisions impact the rights and liberties of citizens before a wrong has necessarily occurred. This imposition is often justified on the basis that a much greater wrong – such as an act of terrorism or gang violence – is being avoided. Logically, one would expect an effective preventive measure to thrive and be adapted to new contexts, and an ineffective measure to be repealed. This chapter has demonstrated that this is not necessarily the case.

Despite their potentially onerous impact on civil liberties, the ineffectiveness of control orders as a crime prevention measure provided no obstacle to their migration from the anti-terrorism sphere to that of organised crime, or the enactment of bikie control orders in almost every Australian state and territory. Disturbingly, the ineffectiveness of bikie control orders then supported the escalation of the control order paradigm to a new level of severity, with the introduction of new offence provisions in Queensland and South Australia. Thus, an ineffective and liberty-intrusive preventive measure spread across jurisdictions and contexts, normalised and escalated to a new extreme.

This is a troubling trend. Testing the effectiveness of a measure in reaching its preventive justice goal is a notoriously difficult task,[92] but some attempt to realistically grapple with and reflect on a measure's effectiveness is crucial in justifying and maintaining its legitimacy. If effectiveness becomes a substantively irrelevant consideration in parliaments' decisions to enact a particular preventive justice measure, then the law and its consequent intrusions on liberty are unjustified and arguably illegitimate. The enactment of control orders and the new offence provisions may have been effective in reassuring the community and improving perceptions of public safety, and of conveying an image of a responsive government, protecting security and looking out for the interests of citizens, but there remains clear evidence that these measures were ineffective in achieving their stated aims of preventing gang crime, despite severely undermining civil liberties.

The trends described in this chapter are by no means limited to the control order or organised crime contexts. When a 'tough on crime' policy platform is adopted that targets a minority and plays to majority fears, there is a real potential for an ineffective preventive measure to thrive. There is little public sympathy for bikies, drug traffickers, people smugglers, sex offenders, terrorists or even asylum seekers, making these groups vulnerable to ineffective but liberty-intrusive laws enacted for short-term political gain. As most Australian jurisdictions lack a Charter of Human Rights, the risk of such measures being adopted, migrating and normalising is heightened, as there is little scope for legal challenge that might constrain the impact of the laws or embarrass the government in court. Recent

92 See generally Chapter 9 by Tim Legrand and Teneille Elliot in this collection.

events in Queensland, however, demonstrate that enacting severe preventive measures may not always be politically popular. The new offence provisions may signal a tipping point wherein the incursion on civil liberties no longer seems necessary or appropriate. Indeed, the Newman Government's anti-bikie laws smoothed the way towards an inquiry into the adoption of a human rights Act in Queensland. It remains to be seen whether the new offence provisions will spread and be adopted outside of Queensland and South Australia, or if they will be repealed in Queensland following the outcomes of current inquiries. It is clear enough, however, that the future of the new offence provisions is unlikely to depend on whether or not they are actually effective at preventing crime.

11 Preventive justice, the courts and the pursuit of legitimacy

Sarah Murray

Introduction

The role of the courts in the preventive justice enterprise is particularly important from a rule of law perspective. They can provide an institutional check on the exercise of actions that are potentially highly disruptive or invasive. However, their involvement can cut both ways. It is clear that although the judiciary can lend independent oversight and impartial review to preventive measures, there is a risk that the role of the courts may be compromised in the process. This chapter explores this tension and, particularly, what preventive justice might mean for the legitimacy of the courts as an institution. Rather than exploring the operation or constitutionality of such measures, this chapter unpacks the delicacy of the courts' role and the legitimacy crisis that preventive justice potentially poses.

Preventive justice and the courts

As detailed in Part I of this collection, preventive justice is a theoretical perspective that concentrates upon the role of the state in preventing the infliction of future harm.[1] Inevitably, to the extent that it operates forcibly, preventive measures can meddle with individual liberty so as to serve the ultimate goal of protecting society, while at the same time 'give the state much greater power over and much greater knowledge about its citizenry'.[2]

For Andrew Ashworth and Lucia Zedner, it is frequently the case that the risk of harm means that preventing it becomes the favoured solution.[3] They have therefore sought to argue for preventive regulation that draws an appropriate

1 Carol Steiker, 'The Limits of the Preventive State' (1998) 88(3) *Journal of Criminal Law and Criminology* 771, 774; Andrew Ashworth and Lucia Zedner, *Preventive Justice* (Oxford University Press, 2014); Andrew Ashworth, Lucia Zedner and Patrick Tomlin (eds), *Prevention and the Limits of the Criminal Law* (Oxford University Press, 2013).
2 Steiker, above n 1, 806.
3 Ashworth and Zedner, *Preventive Justice*, above n 1, 252. See also Andrew Lynch and Alexander Reilly, 'The Constitutional Validity of Terrorism Orders of Control and Preventive Detention' (2007) 10(1) *Flinders Journal of Law Reform* 105, 105.

balance between coerciveness and harm prevention, drawing out 'the proper limits of the preventive state'.[4] This is based on identifying:

> the state's duty to protect . . . but also the state's duty to respect individuals and autonomous beings – which means, among other things, respect for rights, the maintenance of rule of law values, the avoidance of arbitrariness, and kindred principles.[5]

Similarly, Steiker has queried: 'What constitutional and/or policy limits are there on the non-punitive "preventive" state?'[6] These questions are particularly important in the curial context as courts are frequently called on to review preventive measures, often outside the standard 'punishment' context.[7]

Control orders as a preventive measure have been the subject of extensive discussion in the literature.[8] They represent an example of preventive regulation

4 Ashworth and Zedner, *Preventive Justice*, above n 1, 253. See also Andrew Ashworth and Lucia Zedner, 'Prevention and Criminalization: Justification and Limits' (2012) 15 *New Criminal Law Review* 542.

5 Ashworth and Zedner, *Preventive Justice*, above n 1, 6, 251 ('duty to protect' versus 'duty of justice'). See also Andrew Ashworth and Lucia Zedner, 'Defending the Criminal Law: Reflections on the Changing Character of Crime, Procedure and Sanctions' (2008) 2 *Criminal Law and Philosophy* 21.

6 Steiker, above n 1, 777.

7 Ashworth and Zedner, *Preventive Justice*, above n 1, 20–1. Cf. Douglas Husak, 'Preventive Detention as Punishment? Some Possible Obstacles' in Ashworth, Zedner and Tomlin, above n 1, ch 9; Bernard E Harcourt, 'Punitive Preventive Justice: A Critique' in Ashworth, Zedner and Tomlin, above n 1, ch 13. See also Kimberly Kessler Ferzan, 'Beyond Crime and Commitment: Justifying Liberty Deprivations of the Dangerous and Responsible' (2011) 96 *Minnesota Law Review* 141; Jennifer C Daskal, 'Pre-Crime Restraints: The Explosion of Targeted, Non-Custodial Prevention' (2014) 99 *Cornell Law Review* 327, 340, 371–2.

8 Denise Meyerson, 'Using Judges to Manage Risk: The Case of Thomas v Mowbray' (2008) 36 *Federal Law Review* 209; Jude McCulloch, 'Australia's Anti-Terrorism Legislation and the Jack Thomas Case' (2006) 18(2) *Current Issues in Criminal Justice* 357; Lynch and Reilly, above n 3; Paul Fairall and Wendy Lacey, 'Preventative Detention and Control Orders Under Federal Law: The Case for a Bill of Rights' (2007) 31 *Melbourne University Law Review* 1072; Lucia Zedner, 'Preventive Justice or Pre-Punishment? The Case of Control Orders' (2007) 60(1) *Current Legal Problems* 174; Andrew Lynch, 'Thomas v Mowbray – Australia's "War on Terror" Reaches the High Court' (2008) 32 (3) *Melbourne University Law Review* 1182; Sascha-Dominik Bachmann and Matthew Burt, 'Control Orders Post 9-11 and Human Rights in the United Kingdom, Australia and Canada: A Kafkaesque Dilemma?' (2010) 15(2) *Deakin Law Review* 131; Tamara Tulich, 'Adversarial Intelligence? Control Orders, TPIMs and Secret Evidence in Australia and the United Kingdom' (2012) 12(2) *Oxford University Commonwealth Law Journal* 341; Clive Walker and Alexander Horne, 'The Terrorism Prevention and Investigations Measures Act 2011: One Thing But Not Much the Other' [2012] *Criminal Law Review* 421; Clive Walker, 'The Reshaping of Control Orders in the United Kingdom: Time for a Fairer Go, Australia!' (2013) 37 *Melbourne University Law Review* 143; Ben Middleton, 'Terrorism Prevention and Investigation Measures: Constitutional Evolution, Not Revolution?' (2013) 77(6) *Journal of Criminal Law* 562; Alexander Horne and Clive Walker, 'Lessons Learned for Political Constitutionalism? Comparing the

having potentially deleterious consequences for an individual's freedoms in the name of averting a possible harm to the state.[9] The degree to which they do so varies depending on the legislative regime and the nature of the restrictions which are imposed on a particular individual. However, they are typically applied without a conviction and often in the absence of the standard rights and processes associated with criminal trials.[10] Control orders, therefore, provide a good example of a preventive measure placing the judiciary in a problematical position and provide a good case study to illustrate the legitimacy issues that can potentially arise.

Thomas v Mowbray[11] was an Australian High Court decision concerning the constitutionality of the control order powers conferred by Division 104 of the *Criminal Code Act 1995* (Cth).[12] In forming part of the majority finding that the powers were ultimately valid, Gleeson CJ said:

> the argument for the plaintiff is that the power involved in making anti-terrorist control orders is exclusively non-judicial and, in its nature, antithetical to the judicial function. Put another way, the argument is that, even assuming it is within the power of the federal Parliament to legislate for such restraints upon the liberty of individuals, the power to make control orders cannot be given to judges. The corollary appears to be that it can only be exercised by the executive branch of government. The advantages, in terms of protecting human rights, of such a conclusion are not self-evident. In *Fardon*, I indicated that the exercise of powers, independently, impartially and judicially, especially when such powers affect the liberty of the individual, would ordinarily be regarded as a good thing, not something to be avoided. An argument, as a matter of policy, that legislation for anti-terrorist control orders ought to be

Enactment of Control Orders and Terrorism Prevention and Investigation Measures by the UK Parliament' [2014] *Public Law* 267; Lisa Burton and George Williams, 'What Future for Australia's Control Order Regime?' (2013) 24 *Public Law Review* 182; Rebecca Ananian-Welsh and George Williams, 'The New Terrorists: The Normalisation and Spread of Anti-Terror Laws in Australia' (2014) 38(2) *Melbourne University Law Review* 362; See also the Department of the Prime Minister and Cabinet, *Independent National Security Legislation Monitor* (18 March 2015), Australian Government. Note also the Independent National Security Legislation Monitor, available online at www.inslm.gov.au (accessed 18 March 2015). See also Chapter 3 by Susan Donkin and Chapter 10 by Rebecca Ananian-Welsh in this collection.

9 See e.g. Andrew Ashworth and Lucia Zedner, 'Prevention and Criminalization: Justifications and Limits' (2012) 15 *New Criminal Law Review* 542.

10 Ashworth and Zedner, *Preventive Justice*, above n 1, 184–90. In the Australian context of terrorism legislation, see also Justice Anthony Whealy, 'Terrorism and the Right to a Fair Trial: Can the Law Stop Terrorism?' (Paper presented to the British Institute of International and Comparative Law, April 2010) 23; Justice Anthony Whealy, 'The Impact of Terrorism Related Laws on Judges Conducting Criminal Trials' (Paper presented at the Supreme and Federal Court Conference, November 2007) 12.

11 (2007) 233 CLR 307.

12 Ibid. 356 [116]. Gummow and Crennan JJ explicitly alluded to 'preventative justice' in this context.

> subject to some qualification in aid of the human rights of people potentially subject to such orders is one thing. An argument that the making of such orders should be regarded as totally excluded from the judicial function is another. . . To decide that such powers are exclusively within the province of the executive branch of government would be contrary to our legal history, and would not constitute an advance in the protection of human rights.[13]

In contrast, Kirby J, in a strong dissent, stated that Division 104:

> provides for the deprivation of liberty because of an estimate of some future act, not necessarily one to be committed by the person subject to the proposed order. To uphold the validity of that type of control order for which Div 104 of the Code provides would be to erode the well-founded assumption that the judiciary in Australia under federal law may only deprive individuals of their liberty on the basis of evidence of their past conduct. It would seriously undermine public confidence in federal courts for judges to subject individuals to any number of 'obligations, prohibitions and restrictions' for an indeterminate period on the basis of an estimate that some act, potentially committed by somebody else, may occur in the future. To do this is to deny persons their basic legal rights not for what they have been proved to have done (as established in a criminal trial) but for what an official suggests that they might do or that someone else might do. To allow judges to be involved in making such orders, and particularly in the one-sided procedure contemplated by Div 104, involves a serious and wholly exceptional departure from basic constitutional doctrine unchallenged during the entire history of the Commonwealth . . . Unless this Court calls a halt, as it did in that case, the damage to our constitutional arrangements could be profound.[14]

In the United Kingdom, as compared with Australia, the courts' role in the control order context is arguably strengthened, at least to some extent, by the role of special advocates as well as the greater place for considerations of the human rights implications of the measures.[15] However, even in the United Kingdom, a greater parliamentary oversight of control order legislation is often advocated.[16] In the House of Lords decision of *A v Secretary of State for the Home Department*,[17] the Court considered the legality of the *Anti-terrorism, Crime and Security Act 2001* (UK). The plurality found that the detention of non-British citizens by that Act was, in the circumstances, disproportionate. Lord Bingham of Cornhill contended that the 'Parliament, the executive and the courts have different functions':

13 Ibid. 329 [17] (citations omitted).
14 Ibid. 432 [357] (citations omitted).
15 Walker, above n 8, 180–1; Fairall and Lacey, above n 8, 1087, 1092; Bachmann and Burt, above n 8, 153.
16 Middleton, above n 8, 582; Horne and Walker, 'Lessons Learned for Political Constitutionalism?', above n 8.
17 [2005] 2 AC 68.

> But the function of independent judges charged to interpret and apply the law is universally recognised as a cardinal feature of the modern democratic state, a cornerstone of the rule of law itself. The Attorney General is fully entitled to insist on the proper limits of judicial authority, but he is wrong to stigmatise judicial decision-making as in some way undemocratic.[18]

Similarly, Lord Nicholls of Birkenhead stated that:

> All courts are very much aware of the heavy burden, resting on the elected government and not the judiciary, to protect the security of this country and all who live here. All courts are acutely conscious that the Government alone is able to evaluate and decide what counter-terrorism steps are needed and what steps will suffice. Courts are not equipped to make such decisions, nor are they charged with that responsibility. But Parliament has charged the courts with a particular responsibility . . . The duty of the courts is to check that legislation and ministerial decisions do not overlook the human rights of persons adversely affected.[19]

Preventive control orders arguably place courts in an unenviable catch-22 situation.[20] The involvement of the judiciary in reviewing preventive justice measures, such as control orders, is clearly important. The courts can provide an independent and impartial check on the exercise of powers which have the potential to undermine individual liberty in a raw sense.[21] The rule of law, even in its thinnest conception, looks to judicial review as vital to ensure that arbitrary power is not exercised in the name of political expediency.[22] As noted above, this perspective is evident in Gleeson CJ's contention in *Thomas* that '[t]o decide that such powers are exclusively within the province of the executive branch of government would be contrary to our legal history, and would not constitute an advance in the protection of human rights'.[23]

18 Ibid. [42].
19 Ibid. [79]–[80]. See also Lord Walker of Gestingthorpe at [192]. For a comparison of this case with *Secretary of State for the Home Department v Rehman* [2003] 1 AC 153, see David Dyzenhaus, *The Constitution of Law: Legality in a Time of Emergency* (Cambridge University Press, 2006) 174–8.
20 See also Kent Roach, *The 9/11 Effect: Comparative Counter-Terrorism* (Cambridge University Press, 2011) 452.
21 Dyzenhaus, *The Constitution of Law*, above n 19; Helen Fenwick and Gavin Phillipson, 'Covert Derogations and Judicial Deference: Redefining Liberty and Due Process Rights in Counterterrorism Law and Beyond' (2011) 56 *McGill Law Journal* 863; Daskal, above n 7; Tom R Hickman, 'Between Human Rights and the Rule of Law: Indefinite Detention and the Derogation Model of Constitutionalism' (2005) 68(4) *Modern Law Review* 655.
22 See e.g. discussion in Lynch, above n 8, 1209. See also David Bonner, *Executive Measures, Terrorism and National Security* (Ashgate, 2007) 352.
23 (2007) 233 CLR 307, 329 [17] (citations omitted).

The judicial dilemma, however, is the point at which this supervisory involvement comes at too high a price. Even if measures are strictly constitutional, they can begin to sap the judiciary of legitimacy if they compromise, or are seen to compromise, the traditional elements of the criminal or civil process, or if they entangle judges in highly political or partisan issues.[24] As Andrew Lynch and Alex Reilly have noted, 'the more often the executive uses judicial independence to bolster the legitimacy of its actions, and the more often the judiciary participate in processes that are not judicial in nature, the more eroded judicial independence becomes'.[25] Further, Lynch has separately noted that even if rule of law considerations are weighed in, that it can still impair the courts as an institution.[26] Hayne J, in dissent in *Thomas*, echoed these sentiments in declaring that 'to the extent that federal courts are left with no practical choice except to act upon a view proffered by the Executive, the appearance of institutional impartiality and the maintenance of public confidence in the courts are both damaged'.[27]

This is a particular concern in instances where preventive regimes come into play in situations when the evidence for criminal prosecution is lacking,[28] or when due process guarantees are not preserved.[29] It can then become an issue of whether the preventive measures contain the appropriate legal protections to ensure that the judicial role is not rendered unbecoming.[30]

There are also serious questions as to whether the courts are the appropriate governmental arm to be vested with monitoring preventive functions when national security concerns are at stake, and certain issues, including those relating to intelligence information, may not be justiciable.[31] Lord Hoffmann's comments in *Secretary of State for the Home Department v Rehman*[32] (*Rehman*) are often cited in this context as his Lord Justice referred to:

24 See, further, Lynch and Reilly, above n 3, 138.
25 Ibid. 109, 138.
26 Lynch, above n 8, 1209.
27 233 CLR 307, 477–8 [512].
28 Middleton, above n 8, 563; Burton and Williams, above n 8, 194–5; Ananian-Welsh and Williams, above n 8, 400.
29 See e.g. Zedner, above n 8; Jonathan M Coady, 'Conditional Release of Terror Suspects in Canada: Lessons from the United Kingdom' (2010) 36 *Queens Law Journal* 251; Walker and Horne, above n 8; Walker, above n 8; Bonner, above n 22, 286–7, ch 9.
30 Meyerson, above n 8, 222.
31 See e.g. *Secretary of State for the Home Department v Rehman* [2003] 1 AC 153 [62] (Lord Hoffmann); *A v Secretary of State for the Home Department* [2005] 2 AC 68 [29] (Lord Bingham of Cornhill); *Thomas v Mowbray* (2007) 233 CLR 307, 477 [510] (Hayne J). Cf. Aileen Kavanagh, 'Judging the Judges under the Human Rights Act: Deference, Disillusionment and the "War on Terror"' [2009] *Public Law* 287, 299–301 although acknowledging the 'expertise and legitimacy' of the 'legislature and executive . . . in the national security context'; Dyzenhaus, *The Constitution of Law*, above n 19, 219.
32 [2003] 1 AC 153.

> the need for the judicial arm of government to respect the decisions of ministers of the Crown on the question of whether support for terrorist activities in a foreign country constitutes a threat to national security. It is not only that the executive has access to special information and expertise in these matters. It is also that such decisions, with serious potential results for the community, require a legitimacy which can be conferred only by entrusting them to persons responsible to the community through the democratic process. If the people are to accept the consequences of such decisions, they must be made by persons whom the people have elected and whom they can remove.[33]

This question of expertise and the evident risks involved can mean that deference to executive and legislative judgment becomes the safest course.[34] However, scholars argue that courts have a crucial role in safeguarding individual rights in the climate of declared 'emergencies'[35] and that this reinforces the legitimacy of other governmental branches.[36] As Jonathan Coady has argued, '[a]ny tension between the government and the court in matters of security is not an unwelcome consequence of democracy, but a sign that it is functioning properly'.[37]

Ultimately, the question becomes how courts can walk the appropriate line, by supervising the other governmental branches while not marring the legitimacy of the courts as an institution.

Judicial legitimacy in the preventive justice space

> The quality which sustains judicial legitimacy is not bravery, or creativity, but fidelity . . . Like fairness, legitimacy should be constantly on display in courts.[38]

Unravelling the implications for judicial legitimacy is key as the judiciary are increasingly playing central roles in preventive justice regimes. But what is even meant by judicial legitimacy? In the literature, legitimacy is connected with what makes decisions of courts listened to, accepted and observed.[39] But this is an

33 Ibid. [62]. See, further, the discussion in Dyzenhaus, *The Constitution of Law*, above n 19, 174.

34 Kavanagh, above n 31, 301; Fiona de Londras and Fergal F Davis, 'Controlling the Executive in Times of Terrorism: Competing Perspectives on Effective Oversight Mechanisms' (2010) 30(1) *Oxford Journal of Legal Studies* 19, 27. For a discussion of Lord Hoffmann's dissatisfaction with the word 'deference' in the context of judicial-legislative relations, see Jeffrey Jowell, 'Judicial Deference: Servility, Civility or Institutional Capacity?' (2003) *Public Law* 592.

35 For an excellent discussion of this context, see Bruce Ackerman, 'The Emergency Constitution' (2004) 113 *Yale Law Journal* 1028.

36 Coady, above n 29, 294–5; Fenwick and Phillipson, above n 21, 894, 906.

37 Coady, above n 29, 284.

38 Chief Justice Murray Gleeson, 'Judicial Legitimacy' (Paper presented at the Australian Bar Association Conference, New York, 2 July 2000).

39 Nick Huls, 'Introduction: From Legitimacy to Leadership' in Nick Huls, Maurice Adams and Jacco Bomhoff (eds), *The Legitimacy of Highest Courts' Rulings: Judicial Deliberations and Beyond* (2009, TMC Asser Press) ch 1.

over-simplification. Might a decision be seen as legally acceptable but morally doubtful? Does this disjunction matter or is the legitimacy of a court's decisions removed from the legitimacy of the courts as an institution? The complexity of the concept means that, ultimately, judicial legitimacy becomes the end game: it becomes the bundle of 'factors justifying . . . public trust'.[40]

Judicial legitimacy cannot be entirely separated from concepts such as judicial independence, judicial impartiality and judicial transparency.[41] These concepts serve the wider goal of respect and legitimacy in the curial arm, for without the perception and reality of a neutral and self-functioning bench, judicial legitimacy will inevitably wane. It is not, however, a binary or zero sum game. Instead, the degree of judicial legitimacy within a system is best placed along a continuum.

Richard Fallon has exposed some of the difficulties latent in the legitimacy concept and the way it is often used, often without probing its meaning.[42] For Fallon, legitimacy is better understood as resting on 'shifting sands' than a 'single rock of legitimacy' and understanding how these various bases interweave is crucial.[43] He concludes that it is tricky to try to speak of an 'overall' overarching legitimacy which takes these different brands of legitimacy into account when each type is not necessarily of the same 'normative' or 'empirical' character.[44] Fallon sees benefit in 'pay[ing] closer heed to what we and others mean when we talk about legitimacy'.[45]

What is clear is that judicial legitimacy should not be equated with public confidence. The confidence in which courts are held is a contributing factor but is narrower than judicial legitimacy as it is understood here. Public confidence as a useful tool has fallen out of favour somewhat in recent years. Following *Kable v Director of Public Prosecutions (NSW)*,[46] public confidence was used as the barometer for whether laws of the Australian States affected or tainted the ability of federal jurisdiction to be conferred on such courts and hence rendered them unconstitutional. In *Fardon v Attorney-General (Qld)*,[47] this approach was criticised. Gummow J concluded that public confidence was more useful as an 'indicator, but not the touchstone, of invalidity'.[48] Heydon J in *Wainohu v New South*

40 Marc A. Loth, 'Courts in a Quest for Legitimacy: A Comparative Approach' in Nick Huls, Maurice Adams and Jacco Bomhoff (eds), *The Legitimacy of Highest Courts' Rulings: Judicial Deliberations and Beyond* (2009, TMC Asser Press) 267, 268.
41 See e.g. Mitchel Lasser, *Judicial Deliberations: A Comparative Analysis of Judicial Transparency and Legitimacy* (Oxford University Press, 2009) 3. See also the discussion of core concepts in Enid Campbell and H P Lee, *The Australian Judiciary* (Cambridge University Press, 2nd edn, 2012), ch 1.
42 Richard H Fallon Jr, 'Legitimacy and the Constitution' (2005) 118 *Harvard Law Review* 1787, 1789–90.
43 Ibid. 1793.
44 Ibid. 1851.
45 Ibid. 1852.
46 (1996) 189 CLR 51.
47 (2004) 223 CLR 575.
48 Ibid. 617–18 [102].

Wales[49] was censorious of 'public confidence' as a decision-making tool. His Honour queried whether 'public confidence' had 'any more meaning than expressions like "social justice" or "value to society"'.[50] His Honour also indicated that 'it is often the duty of courts to resist conduct which would increase the confidence in them of some sections of the public'.[51]

Fallon and Nick Huls argue that there are different kinds of legitimacy, such as legal, political, sociological and moral legitimacy, and that these feed off and intersect with each other.[52] Legal legitimacy refers to the legal logic on which a decision is made and the sense that a decision is legally determinative.[53] As Fallon points out, legal illegitimacy does not automatically translate to decisional disobedience.[54] Political legitimacy suggests that a governmental institution or branch is accepted within that framework as having a particular capacity or function.[55] This is particularly relevant in the preventive justice space. For example, the institutional appropriateness of a particular preventive function and its assignment to the courts, which is arguably a political conception of legitimacy, is also bound up in the legality of the conferral of that function and the statutory or constitutional mechanism by which this occurs. Sociological legitimacy is most often seen in Weberian terms as bound up in a community or section of community's *belief* and internalisation of something.[56] Fallon traces how the sociological legitimacy literature allows a further compartmentalisation into institutional legitimacy (public confidence in a governmental body), substantive legitimacy (the 'rightness' of a decision) and authoritative legitimacy (whether a decision should be followed). To say that a decision or institution is morally legitimate is to comment on the degree to which its actions demonstrate a moral truth or principled basis.[57]

On the other hand, Marc Loth compartmentalises judicial legitimacy into 'input' and 'output' factors.[58] The former are more institutionally framed: the aspects that guarantee judicial independence, how judges are selected and how courts are administered and funded. The output factors concentrate on the social, legal and political dimensions: how courts interact with litigants, the community and the other governmental arms, and, vitally, the matters the courts hear and the judgments they hand down. These ideas of legitimacy also intersect with theories of procedural justice. It is Tom Tyler's work in this area that is most frequently

49 (2011) 243 CLR 181, 248–9 [173]–[177].
50 Ibid.
51 Ibid.
52 Huls, above n 39, 14–17; Fallon, above n 42.
53 Huls above n 39, 15.
54 Fallon, above n 42, 1794.
55 For examples, see Huls above n 39, 14.
56 Fallon, above n 42, 1795 (noting that in its 'weak' sense it alludes to 'acquiescence' rather than acceptance of legitimacy); Huls, above n 39, 16; Tom Tyler, 'Procedural Justice, Legitimacy and the Effectiveness of the Rule of Law' (2003) 30 *Crime and Justice* 283, 307.
57 Huls, above n 39, 17; Fallon, above n 42, 1796.
58 Loth, above n 40, 269. See also Marc A Loth, 'Courts in Search of Legitimacy: The Case of Wrongful Life' (2007) 13 *IUS Gentium* 73.

cited.[59] Procedural justice research demonstrates that the fairness of, and the way a person experiences, the legal process can influence the person's impression of the courts and the degree to which they perceive it as legitimate.

For David Dyzenhaus, legitimacy in the preventive justice space is knotted up with the concept of legality and particularly 'rule-by-law legitimacy' and 'rule-of-law legitimacy'.[60] Dyzenhaus uses these concepts to distinguish between the legal backing for preventive measures as opposed to the application of rule of law standards to those measures. The risk for Dyzenhaus with preventive measures is the presence of a rough shadow of legality, which he describes as 'grey holes' which have 'just enough legality to provide [the] government with a basis to claim that it is still governing in accordance with the rule of law, and thus to garner some legitimacy'.[61] However, these sheer measures threaten the judicial role to the extent that they cast it with 'legality' and make them 'complicit not only in maintaining the grey hole, but also in creating it'.[62] For this reason, they are potentially more destructive than 'black holes'.[63]

For example, Lisa Burton and George Williams note that one Special Advocate in the United Kingdom departed from the role on the basis that they were bestowing '"legitimacy" to an "odious process"'.[64] Similarly, Helen Fenwick and Gavin Phillipson have identified the tendency for judicial deference to render United Kingdom courts parties to a narrowing, in the security context, of the interpretation of the 'deprivation of liberty' requirement in the *European Convention of Human Rights*.[65] The courts must therefore reconcile the competing forces playing upon them to ensure that judicial legitimacy does not become a victim in the process. Dyzenhaus is emphatic that the courts have an important role to play. For Dyzenhaus, the risk lies in judges giving their legal blessing to

59 See e.g. Tom Tyler, 'What is Procedural Justice? Criteria Used by Citizens to Assess the Fairness of Legal Procedures' (1988) 22 *Law and Society Review* 103; Tom Tyler and Kenneth Rasinski, 'Procedural Justice, Institutional Legitimacy and the Acceptance of Unpopular U.S. Supreme Court Decisions: A Reply to Gibson' (1991) 26 *Law and Society Review* 621; Tom Tyler, 'Citizen Discontent with Legal Procedures: A Social Science Perspective on Civil Procedure Reform' (1997) 45 *American Journal of Comparative Law* 871; Tom Tyler, 'Procedural Justice, Legitimacy and the Effective Rule of Law' (2003) 30 *Crime and Justice* 283.

60 David Dyzenhaus, 'Preventive Justice and the Rule-of-Law Project' in Ashworth, Zedner and Tomlin, above n 1, 91. See also Chapter 2 by Jocelyn Stacey in this collection.

61 Ibid. 99. See also Dyzenhaus, *The Constitution of Law*, above n 19, 42.

62 Dyzenhaus, 'Preventive Justice and the Rule-of-Law Project', above n 60, 99, 114. See also David Dyzenhaus and Rayner Thwaites, 'Legality and Emergency: The Judiciary in a Time of Terror' in Andrew Lynch, Edwina MacDonald and George Williams (eds), *Law and Liberty in the War on Terror* (Federation Press, 2007) 9, 11. Dyzenhaus is also critical of the fact that judges can sometimes 'rewrite history' and hence 'support a continuation of the dismal judicial record': Dyzenhaus, *The Constitution of Law*, above n 19, 63.

63 Dyzenhaus, *The Constitution of Law*, above n 19, 50.

64 Burton and Williams, above n 8, 198.

65 Fenwick and Phillipson, above n 21, 886.

legislation which thwarts the rule of law without at the same time acknowledging this reality. Dyzenhaus explains that even if the courts cannot intervene:

> they should certainly not give in to the temptation to assert that all is well in order to maintain that they still have their role . . . it [is] their duty to point out publicly [in their judgments] that a matter that is susceptible to the control of the rule of law . . . has been deliberately removed from such control.[66]

Ron Kahn and Ken Kersch have, for example, described the importance of the dynamic position in which courts are placed in which, 'temporally', they are subject to 'internal' but also 'external influences'.[67] Indeed, these influences are not mutually exclusive but interact in 'complex, bidirectional and mutually constitutive way[s]'.[68] This means that not only are courts, and the way they interpret and reinterpret their role, central to their own legitimacy, but so are the outward forces, political, constitutional, social and financial, which impinge upon them as part of a 'continual process'.[69] As Aileen Kavanagh wisely notes, a proper critique of the role of the courts can only be undertaken mindful of the 'nature, limits and functions of that institution'.[70] It is for this reason that an institutionalist conception of legitimacy is of particular utility.

This chapter argues that, to understand judicial legitimacy, it is most helpful to conceive of the judicial role in a broader neo-institutional sense.[71] Although this overlaps with Loth's input and output model, it also allows the complexity of the role played by the courts and the factors that play on them to be understood – something particularly evident in the preventive justice context. What stands out from this analysis is that the judiciary are not passive actors in the legitimacy game. Instead, as institutions, and alongside other institutional actors, the courts contribute (and re-contribute) to their own legitimacy.

66 Dyzenhaus, *The Constitution of Law*, above n 19, 218.
67 Ronald Kahn and Ken I Kersch, 'Introduction', in Ronald Kahn and Ken I Kersch (eds), *The Supreme Court and American Political Development* (University Press of Kansas, 2006) 17–19.
68 Ronald Kahn and Ken I Kersch, 'Conclusion: Supreme Court Decision Making and American Political Development' in Ronald Kahn and Ken I Kersch (eds), *The Supreme Court and American Political Development* (University Press of Kansas, 2006) 443, 453.
69 Kahn and Kersch, 'Introduction', above n 67, 20.
70 Kavanagh, above n 31, 303.
71 For general neo-institutionalist literature, see James G March and Johan P Olsen, 'Elaborating the "New Institutionalism"' in R A W. Rhodes, Sarah A Binder and Bert A Rockman (eds), *The Oxford Handbook of Political Institutions* (Oxford University Press, 2006) 4–20; André Lecours, *New Institutionalism: Theory and Analysis* (University of Toronto Press, 2005); Sarah Murray, *The Remaking of the Court: Less-Adversarial Practice and the Constitutional Role of the Judiciary in Australia* (Federation Press, 2014) ch 2.

Judicial legitimacy at the preventive justice coalface

In the preventive justice context, how does the legitimacy minefield present itself? In cases such as *Thomas*, a court is placed in a push-me-pull-you situation. In scrutinising preventive measures, they are to some extent 'damned if they do, and damned if they don't'. Courts, whether or not they are dealing with preventive action, have some core legitimacy touchstones that have already been identified. These include the respect that comes from the institutional attributes of independence and impartiality, including methods of appointment, security of tenure and salary, and separation from the more political arms. They also rely on their legal reasoning traditions, including the use of doctrine, case law and precedent, but also the wider legal culture in which they operate. These regulate the hearing process, the expectations of judgments as well as the role of judges within the wider community. Further, judicial attributes are often reinforced by judicial action and by the legal community in which they operate.[72] For instance, when judges speak publicly, their chosen or assigned topics often concern issues such as judicial independence, separation of powers or the importance of the rule of law.[73] These topics themselves become legitimacy-buttressing and continually reinforce the judicial attributes which the courts and legal community expect the courts to bear.

All cases present their own challenges; however, preventive measures, such as control orders, place courts in a unique style of realpolitik. For example, public opinion may support heavy-handed legislative responses against suspected terrorists, particularly in the aftermath of acts of terrorism, and oppose any mildness in the treatment of people posing a threat to 'good society'.[74] This external pressure feeds into a perception, actively encouraged by the elected government, that the executive is peculiarly well placed to defend the legitimacy of national security measures and therefore an anticipation of deferential judicial responses. These pressures rub against an expectation within the legal community (to an extent both an internal and external operating force)[75] that constitutional, human rights and rule of law considerations must be accorded appropriate weight and the government's response adequately assessed by an impartial judicature.

How do courts respond to this challenge? Often, wittingly or unwittingly, they seek to strengthen their own legitimacy and, in so doing, become co-creators of it. This can occur in a variety of ways. Reliance on reasoning and legal doctrine is often supplemented by an explanation of the institutional position in which the court is placed. For example, judgments often recount the threat that has justified the measure and what this means for the judiciary in terms of scrutinising the actions of the executive in the national security context. This can either justify judicial deference or be used as a precursor to explain the necessity of judicial

72 Campbell and Lee, above n 41, 289–90, 314–15.

73 The Australasian Institute of Judicial Administration Incorporated, *Guide to Judicial Conduct* (AIJA, 2nd edn, 2007) 25.

74 Stuart Macdonald, 'Understanding Anti-Terrorism Policy: Values, Rationales and Principles' (2012) 34 *Sydney Law Review* 317, 344.

75 Kahn and Kersch, 'Conclusion', above n 68, 455.

intervention as the following cases illustrate (even if contemporaneously recognising the limited institutional role of the courts in this context).[76]

Gleeson CJ in *Thomas* emphasised the important institutional function played by the court, while at the same time finding Division 104 a valid constitutional preventive measure.[77] Gummow and Crennan JJ, in forming part of the majority, sought to make clear that courts are not to second-guess governmental conclusions as to a 'terrorist threat',[78] but did not dispute that risk assessment could still be 'a distinctively judicial activity'.[79] Gummow and Crennan JJ also recognised that the case had implications for the rule of law and the constitutional role for the courts (via Chapter III of the *Commonwealth Constitution*), posing rhetorically, 'But what does the rule of law require?'[80] Callinan J affirmed the role for the courts, even if it was subject to inevitable limitations. His Honour explained:

> Risks to democracy and to the freedoms of citizens are matters of which courts are likely to have a higher consciousness. That the material upon which the courts may be forced by the exigencies to rely, may be incomplete, fragmentary and conflicting does not deprive the process which the Code requires them to undertake of its judicial character, or mean that the issues are not justiciable. If courts could only decide cases in which the materials were complete and the facts not in conflict, there would be little work for them to do and many controversies left unquelled.[81]

Joining Kirby J in dissent, Hayne J found that the law was within the defence power,[82] but that the review function was non-judicial in nature and therefore had been unconstitutionally conferred on the judiciary. While His Honour did not conclude that the function could be seamlessly conferred on the executive,[83] in the legislation's current form, he was concerned about 'the nature of the material . . . present[ing] issues of a kind not suited to judicial determination',[84] the fact that the courts may be compromised by having to rely on executive intelligence,[85] and that it conferred on 'courts the decision of what is necessary to protect the public and . . . offers the courts no standard by which to decide that question'.[86] His Honour therefore struck down the legislation, in an effort to not taint the exercise of judicial power by the courts, and in so doing their integrity and legitimacy as an institution.

76 For Dyzenhaus, it is vital that judges are fulsome in their reasons and 'make their commitments explicit': *The Constitution of Law* above n 19, 66–7, 179–80, 212.
77 (2007) 233 CLR 307, 327–35 [15], [17]–[19], [30].
78 Ibid. 354 [107].
79 Ibid. 354–5 [108], [110].
80 Ibid. 342 [61].
81 Ibid. 508 [599].
82 *Commonwealth Constitution* s 51(vi).
83 Ibid. 476 [506].
84 Ibid. 477 [510].
85 Ibid. 477 [512].
86 Ibid. 478–9 [513], [516].

In *A v Secretary of State for the Home Department*,[87] Lord Bingham of Cornhill recognised the superior terrorism expertise of the executive, while highlighting (the expectation and) the judiciary's capacity to conduct an assessment of the proportionality of the government's response.[88] Lord Hope of Craighead,[89] Lord Rodger of Earlsferry[90] and Baroness Hale of Richmond[91] agreed in emphasising the crucial scrutinising role to be played in such cases by the courts. Lord Hoffmann, dissenting, stressed the importance of the case (and hence the consideration that the House of Lords had given to it) due to its implications for the allowance of arbitrary detention.[92] Removed from his more deferential position in *Rehman*, Lord Hoffmann found the requisite state of emergency was lacking in not sufficiently 'threatening the life of the nation',[93] even in accepting the likelihood of terrorists strategising in the United Kingdom, and identified the danger as 'not from terrorism, but from laws such as these'.[94] For Lord Hoffmann, the House of Lords had a duty to intervene in the assessment of whether derogation from fundamental human rights obligations was justified and that monitoring Parliament's position in such cases was vital in ensuring that terrorism did not see fundamental obligations unnecessarily cast aside.

This legitimacy-reinforcing pattern is also evident in the United States decision of *Hamdi v Rumsfeld*.[95] In that case, the majority acknowledged the 'weighty and sensitive governmental interests' at stake and that the 'core strategic matters of warmaking belong in the hands of those who are best positioned and most politically accountable for making them',[96] before finding that due process protections still had to be made available to 'enemy combatants'. The majority concluded that:

> Striking the proper constitutional balance here is of great importance to the Nation during this period of ongoing combat. But it is equally vital that our calculus not give short shrift to the values that this country holds dear or to the privilege that is American citizenship. It is during our most challenging and uncertain moments that our Nation's commitment to due process is most severely tested; and it is in those times that we must preserve our commitment at home to the principles for which we fight abroad. . . we necessarily reject the Government's assertion that separation of powers principles mandate a heavily circumscribed role for the courts in such circumstances. Indeed, the position that the courts must forgo any examination of the individual case and

87 [2005] 2 AC 68.
88 Ibid. [29], [41], [42]. As to the complexity of Human Rights Charters in this context, see Dyzenhaus, *The Constitution of Law*, above n 19, 184–5.
89 [2005] 2 AC 68 [108], [116].
90 Ibid. [178].
91 Ibid. [226].
92 Ibid. [86].
93 Ibid [95]–[96].
94 Ibid. [97].
95 542 US 507 (2004).
96 Ibid. 531 (O'Connor J, joined by Rehnquist CJ, Kennedy and Breyer JJ).

> focus exclusively on the legality of the broader detention scheme cannot be mandated by any reasonable view of separation of powers, as this approach serves only to *condense* power into a single branch of government.[97]

What is particularly evident in the judgment of Connor J is a focus on the 'legal' aspects of the curial role. This emphasis on legality as opposed to the policy or security aspects serves to reinforce 'legal legitimacy' of the role to be played by courts.[98]

Agreeing with Connor J in part, Souter J (joined by Ginsburg J) noted that the separation of powers meant:

> deciding finally on what is a reasonable degree of guaranteed liberty whether in peace or war (or some condition in between) is not well entrusted to the Executive Branch of Government, whose particular responsibility is to maintain security.[99]

In dissent, Scalia J (Stevens J concurring) doubted the suitably of courts usurping executive and legislative judgment.[100] His Honour asserted that:

> The plurality seems to view it as its mission to Make Everything Come Out Right . . . The problem with this approach is not only that it steps out of the courts' modest and limited role in a democratic society; but that by repeatedly doing what it thinks the political branches ought to do it encourages their lassitude and saps the vitality of government by the people.[101]

Similarly, Thomas J disapproved the majority's understanding of how security matters were to be institutionally dealt with and that the court was acting out of its depth in scrutinising this exercise of war powers.[102] Like Scalia J, Thomas J justified the importance of judicial deference in such cases, marking out the politically legitimate line that courts must pay heed to.

Interfering with security measures, particularly in the terrorism context, can face an unwelcome reception.[103] One of the difficult issues for the judiciary is that it may not be seen as appropriate for the courts to directly and publicly respond to criticism of their decisions.[104] For this reason, much of this must be done

97 Ibid. 532, 535–6.

98 See e.g. *Fardon v Attorney-General (Qld)* (2004) 223 CLR 575, 593 [23] (Gleeson CJ). As to the difficulty of this distinction, see *Thomas v Mowbray* (2007) 233 CLR 307, 348–9 [81], [88] (Gummow and Crennan JJ).

99 *Hamdi v Rumsfeld* 542 US 507, 545 (2004).

100 Ibid. 577–8.

101 Ibid. 576–7.

102 Ibid. 579–82.

103 Roach, above n 20, 454.

104 Australasian Institute of Judicial Administration, above n 73, 23–4; Campbell and Lee, above n 41, 13–14, 287–8.

pre-emptively in the judgment itself. The response of the legal community also feeds into the ultimate way the judgment is received, and this in turn shapes and responds to the government's and media's reaction to the court's finding. This complex dialectic all contributes to the legitimacy barometer of the judiciary. Although this is not to suggest that one decision can itself permanently recalibrate the regard had for the courts, each decision feeds into the legitimacy continuum with which the curial arm must grapple. As French CJ explained in *International Finance Trust Company Ltd v New South Wales*[105] when deciding a state restraining order case:

> Nor is it to the point to say that the particular intrusion upon the judicial function . . . is confined in scope and limited in effect both in time and by the facility to seek ancillary or exclusion orders. Such a calculus will not accord sufficient significance to the quality of the intrusion upon the judicial function. An accumulation of such intrusions, each 'minor' in practical terms, could amount over time to death of the judicial function by a thousand cuts.[106]

Conclusion

Judicial legitimacy is best conceived as a form of institutional ecosystem, with a delicate balance of factors and players to keep it in a healthy state. As Huls has contended, the various 'senses' in which legitimacy can be used, whether in a legal, political, moral or socio-cultural sense, all contribute to judicial legitimacy in an aggregate sense.[107] It is difficult to consider aspects of this legitimacy in isolation.

In the preventive justice context of control orders, there is a particular risk of judicial legitimacy being sapped by the courts either interfering or shying away from interfering in such a politically and rights-charged issue. Institutionally, there are several aspects of the courts' architecture which prepare it for such challenges, and judges themselves play a key part, along with the legal and wider community.

Fundamentally, it is contended that the ecosystem that nourishes judicial legitimacy, though robust, is not impenetrable. Preventive measures can place courts in a particularly vulnerable position, and although they are not passive actors in this context, it cannot be assumed that the courts will continue to be respected as institutions simply because they have been in the past.

105 (2009) 240 CLR 319.
106 Ibid. 355 [57].
107 Huls, above n 39, 13–17.

12 Regulatory bargaining in the shadows of preventive justice

Deferred prosecution agreements

Simon Bronitt[*]

Introduction

Regulatory crime is ubiquitous. Odds are that some readers of this chapter have recently paid a prescribed penalty in response to an infringement or enforcement notice to avoid some type of regulatory action. These legal processes are commonplace, though largely forensically invisible; matters are only rarely disputed and, even then, contested cases rarely escape the lower levels of the court system. Described by Pat O'Malley as a form of 'technocratic justice' that has 'de-moralised' the criminal law,[1] infringement or enforcement notice schemes nevertheless generate significant state revenues and cost savings in the administration of justice. However, it would be wrong to conclude that such diversionary tools have been confined to the policing of less serious violations of the criminal law such as road traffic offences or minor 'regulatory' offences. Over the past two decades, these tools have been used to police an increasingly wide range of crime, with the effect that in the field of corporate and securities law the use of civil penalties and settlements, rather than criminal prosecution, is now the dominant regulatory norm.[2]

In relation to policing corporate wrongdoing, the pecuniary stakes for enforcement agencies are much higher since the penalties, which are typically aggravated for corporate offenders, potentially generate significant million-dollar revenue streams for the state. The most prominent example is the enforcement action taken by the United States Department of Justice in 2012 against the global banking conglomerate HSBC for its knowing and reckless facilitation of money laundering for Mexican drug cartels and international sanctions violation. In exchange for terminating prosecution, HSBC paid $1.92 billion (USD) to United States regulators.[3]

* I would like to thank Professors John Braithwaite (ANU) and Nicola Padfield (University of Cambridge) for providing feedback on earlier drafts, and also Michael Potts, UQ, for his excellent research assistance. I would also like to acknowledge the generous funding received from the Herbert Smith Freehills Visitor Scheme at the University of Cambridge, which supported my visitor position at the Faculty of Law, June–July 2016.

1 Pat O'Malley, 'Technocratic Justice in Australia' (1984) 2 *Law in Context* 31.

2 Vicky Comino, *Australia's 'Company Law Watchdog': ASIC and Corporate Regulation* (Thomson Reuters 2015).

3 Ben Protess and Jessica Silver-Greenberg, 'HSBC to Pay $1.92 Billion to Settle Charges of Money Laundering', DealBook, *The New York Times* online, 10 December

This chapter examines the issues of legal principle and policy arising from agreements to terminate or defer prosecution, critically reviewing the 'payoffs' and 'pitfalls' of using such agreements to deal with serious corporate crime. In the United States and United Kingdom, the advent of deferred prosecution agreements, or DPAs, has been heralded as another valuable tool for regulators, and the adoption of a DPA scheme is currently under consideration in Australia.[4] However, as revealed below, the purposes and principles governing DPA schemes remain nascent and ill-defined. This chapter calls for the adoption of a more principled approach to deferred prosecution, one that prioritises preventive justice over regulatory pragmatism and expediency.

What is a deferred prosecution agreement?

Agreements to defer prosecution are collectively and commonly known as DPAs, although this label belies the diversity in how DPAs are legally conceived and applied in practice. In the United States, for example, the legal basis for negotiating a DPA derives from the *Speedy Trial Act of 1974* 18 USC § 3161 (1974) and the statutory provisions that define the general powers and duties of federal prosecutors.[5] However, the Act itself does not create or define DPAs, with the result that the purpose, principles and restrictions on their use are not to be found in positive law, but rather are governed by prosecution discretion, policy and administrative practice.

The United States' position may be contrasted with the legislative DPA scheme recently enacted in the United Kingdom. The *Crime and Courts Act 2013* (UK) defines the DPA as 'an agreement between a designated prosecutor and a person . . . whom the prosecutor is considering prosecuting for an offence specified in Part 2'.[6] These agreements have a more restricted operation than their United States counterparts. For example, the United Kingdom DPA applies only to 'legal persons' (that is, corporations, not natural persons), and prescribed economic crimes; moreover, the processes of negotiating, executing and enforcing breaches of the

2012, available at http://dealbook.nytimes.com/2012/12/10/hsbc-said-to-near-1-9-billion-settlement-over-money-laundering/?_r=0 (accessed 5 September 2016).

4 For an excellent essay on this topic, see Justin O'Brien, 'The Sword of Damocles: Deferred Prosecutions and the Search for Accountability' in Justin O'Brien and George Gilligan (eds), *Integrity, Risk and Accountability in Capital Markets: Regulating Culture* (Oxford: Hart Publishing, 2013) 161.

5 To address the issue of undue delay in the administration of justice, the *Speedy Trial Act of 1974*, 18 USC (1974) prescribed specific time limits, which would be suspended during '[a]ny period of delay during which prosecution is deferred by the attorney for the Government pursuant to written agreement with the defendant, with the approval of the court, for the purpose of allowing the defendant to demonstrate his good conduct': § 3161(h)(2). This provision recognised, albeit indirectly, legal space for prosecutors to enter into written agreement to defer prosecution, which became known as DPAs.

6 See *Crime and Courts Act 2013* (UK) c 22, sch 17, part 1, s 1(1).

DPA require judicial involvement.[7] This scheme has only been available in the United Kingdom since 2014, although the Serious Fraud Office has moved quickly to test these new provisions, entering into the first DPA in late 2015.[8]

At its core, the DPA is an agreement to discontinue prosecution in relation to specific crimes, conditional upon the party (putative defendant) complying with a set of 'terms and conditions' that have been negotiated with and agreed to by prosecutors. Once the DPA has been negotiated, agreed and judicially approved, a stay of prosecution continues until its expiry or breach. In cases where the DPA is 'breached',[9] the stay of prosecution is discharged with the effect that prosecution of the original charges will resume. Prosecutors must then establish these offences, applying the usual criminal standard of proof 'beyond reasonable doubt'.

There is significant diversity in the types of terms and conditions that may be included in a DPA. After reviewing the diversity of DPAs negotiated in United States, it is clear that their scope is only limited by prosecutorial imagination. According to Eugene Illovsky, DPA terms and conditions are often borrowed or inspired from the United States Sentencing Guidelines for the relevant offences, and typically include some admission of wrongdoing, payment of fines, cooperation with the government, adoption of compliance programs and waiving of speedy trial rights and statute of limitations defences that would otherwise apply in respect of the identified offences.[10] DPA terms have also included public apology, restitution for those harmed by the corporate misconduct, forfeiture of illicit assets and profits as well as undertaking to make ongoing disclosures to the authorities and regulators.

The United Kingdom's DPA scheme provides statutory guidance concerning the types of terms and conditions that may be included. The *Crime and Courts Act 2013* (UK) includes the following list of approved DPA terms to:

- pay to the prosecutor a financial penalty;
- compensate victims of the alleged offence;
- donate money to a charity or other third party;
- disgorge any profits made from the alleged offence;
- implement a compliance programme or make changes to an existing compliance programme relating to policies or to the training of employees or both;

7 As the United Kingdom Serious Fraud Office notes: 'A DPA is an agreement reached under judicial supervision between the prosecutor and an organisation. The agreement allows a prosecution to be suspended for a defined period provided the organisation meets certain specified conditions. DPAs will only apply to organisations in cases of economic crime': Serious Fraud Office (UK), 'Deferred Prosecution Agreements: New Guidance for Prosecutors' (News Release, 14 February 2014).

8 Serious Fraud Office (UK), 'SFO agrees first UK DPA with Standard Bank' (News Release, 30 November 2015).

9 Unlike the situation in the United States, the breach of a DPA is judicially determined following a hearing. The court must publish reasons for its determination and, if a breach is found, order its termination: *Crime and Courts Act 2013* (UK) c 22, sch 17, part 1, s 9(4).

10 Eugene Illovsky, 'Corporate Deferred Prosecution Agreements: The Brewing Debate' (2006) 21(2) *Criminal Justice* 36, 36.

- co-operate in any investigation related to the alleged offence; [or]
- pay any reasonable costs of the prosecutor in relation to the alleged offence or the DPA.[11]

The list is non-exhaustive. The Act requires simply that the terms included in the DPA be 'fair, reasonable and proportionate'.[12] This approach ensures a high degree of flexibility, as the DPA Code of Practice notes '[w]hat terms are fair, reasonable and proportionate, including the length of the DPA, will be determined on a case by case basis'.[13] That said, the Code of Practice identifies three terms that 'normally' should be included in the agreement: a financial order (also described as a 'financial penalty'), recovery of the 'reasonable costs' incurred by the prosecution, and party cooperation with the investigation related to the alleged offence.[14] The inclusion of terms that offer redress for victims is also viewed as 'particularly desirable'.[15]

The limitless range and diversity of terms and conditions available for inclusion in a DPA stem, in part, from the lack of consensus about its underlying regulatory rationale or purpose. Strictly speaking, the DPA is *not* a form of 'punishment'; nor is financial payment or asset forfeiture a 'penalty' in the formal legal sense.[16] Nonetheless, the agreements themselves and supporting DPA Codes of Practice often use the language of 'penalties' and 'fines'.[17] Unhelpfully, neither the United Kingdom DPA scheme nor its United States counterpart includes a statutory

11 *Crime and Courts Act 2013* (UK) c 22, sch 17, part 1, s 5(3)(a)–(g).
12 *Crime and Courts Act 2013* (UK) c 22, sch 17, part 1, ss 7(1), 8(1).
13 Serious Fraud Office and Crown Prosecution Service (UK), *Deferred Prosecution Agreements Code of Practice: Crime and Courts Act 2013* (14 February 2014) ('*United Kingdom DPA Code of Practice*') 12, available online at www.sfo.gov.uk/?wpdmdl=1447 (accessed 5 September 2016).
14 Ibid.
15 Ibid. Although desirable, recent research commissioned by the World Bank and United Nations Office of Drugs and Crime (UNODC) suggest that settlements in foreign bribery cases have not achieved substantial repatriation of illicit assets or funds to those developing countries whose economies and public sectors are most severely affected: Jacinta Odour, Jeanne Hauch, Marianne Mathias, Ji Won Park, Oliver Stolpe, Agustin Flah, Dorothee Gottwald, Francisca M U Fernando, 'Left out of the Bargain: Settlements in Foreign Bribery Cases and Implications for Asset Recovery' (27 November 2013) Stolen Asset Recovery Initiative – The World Bank and UNDOC.
16 In the United Kingdom, civil forfeiture generally is seen to not carry a criminal character: see e.g. *Director of the Assets Recovery Agency v Walsh* [2004] NIQB 21 (1 January 2005), upheld on appeal in *Walsh v Director of the Assets Recovery Agency* [2005] NICA 6 (26 January 2005).
17 In the United States, these DPA terms are expressed variously as a 'monetary penalty' or 'fine', applying the terminology from the United States Sentencing Guidelines, see e.g. the DPA in *United States of America v Commerzbank AG* (10 March 2015), available online at www.justice.gov/sites/default/files/opa/press-releases/attachments/2015/03/12/commerzbank_deferred_prosecution_agreement_1.pdf (accessed 5 September 2016). Cf. the *United Kingdom DPA Code of Practice* which describes this type of term as a 'financial order', above n 13, 12.

objects or purpose clause.[18] This lack of clear underlying 'philosophy of justice' is a significant weakness in the current regulatory framework governing DPAs in both the United States and the United Kingdom. As argued below, DPAs are likely to have greater legitimacy and regulatory impact if reconceived as tools of preventive, rather than punitive, justice.

My proposals for reform, elaborated in Part II below, are not inconsistent with the underlying philosophy that motivated the initial development of DPAs in the United States in the 1980s as new diversionary tools for prosecutors dealing with high levels of juvenile delinquency.[19] The extension of DPAs beyond 'juvenile crime on the streets' to 'white collar crime in the suites', has tended to suppress the DPA's restorative rationale and preventive potential in favour of expediency and other pragmatic public interest considerations. Before considering how DPAs can be reconfigured as tools of preventive justice, Part I examines how current schemes in the United States and the United Kingdom balance the payoffs and pitfalls of using DPAs as tools for regulating corporate criminality.[20]

Part I

Deferred prosecution and the public interest: balancing payoffs and pitfalls

DPAs have gained wide support from both the regulatory and corporate sectors in the United States over the past decade, and have been applied to an expanding range of offences, including corporate bribery under the *Foreign Corrupt Practices Act of 1977* 15 USC § 78dd-1 (1977). The major 'payoff' for the public interest is that the DPA avoids the risk that enforcement action may precipitate major corporate failures, cause harm to innocent third parties (investors and employees) and undermine public confidence in local markets and even, in some cases, the global economy.[21] The claim that some major corporations are now 'too big to

18 The United Kingdom Government in its consultation paper canvassing DPAs skirted this issue, noting only that such agreements 'provide prosecutors with an extra tool to tackle economic crime in England and Wales which currently too often goes without redress', cited in Michael Bisgrove and Mark Weekes, 'Deferred Prosecution Agreements: A Practical Consideration' (2014) (6) *Criminal Law Review* 416, 416.

19 Peter Spivack and Sujit Raman, 'Regulating the "New Regulators": Current Trends in Deferred Prosecution Agreements' (2008) 45(2) *American Criminal Law Review* 159, 163.

20 Corporate criminality is not limited to economic or financial crime. The potential application of DPAs to combat institutional child sexual abuse is explored in Simon Bronitt, 'New Regulatory Paradigms for Preventing Institutional Child Sexual Abuse' in Yorick Smaal, Andy Kaladelfos and Mark Finnane (eds), *The Sexual Abuse of Children: Recognition and Redress* (Monash University Publishing, 2016) ch 13.

21 The risk has been termed as the 'Arthur Anderson effect' after the notorious collapse of a United States-based global accounting firm following the investigation into its complicity in the Enron scandal: Federico Mazzacuva, 'Justifications and Purposes of Negotiated Justice for Corporate Offenders: Deferred and Non-Prosecution Agreements in the UK and US Systems of Criminal Justice' (2014) 78(3) *Journal of Criminal Law* 249, 250. Underscoring the potential value of submitting to the terms of a

fail' has been challenged, although the regulatory preference for DPAs over the past decade is often justified in terms of the public interest in avoiding or mitigating the risk of economic harm. As the then United States Attorney-General Eric Holder told a Senate Hearing in 2012:

> I am concerned that the size of some of these institutions has become so large that it does become difficult for us to prosecute them when we are hit with indications that if you do prosecute, if you do bring a criminal charge, it will have a negative impact on the national economy, perhaps even the world economy. And I think that is a function of the fact that some of these institutions have become too large. I think it has an inhibiting influence and impact on our ability to bring resolutions that I think would be more appropriate.[22]

The United States Attorneys' Manual permits prosecutors to consider such 'collateral consequences', and there is no doubt that these interests are given weight, although the United States Department of Justice is at pains to point out that potential economic consequences are only one of the factors (among nine others) to be weighed in the balance in determining whether deferral of prosecution is in the public interest.[23] Even if economic considerations are accepted as relevant to the public interest determination, the weight attached to potential collateral economic harm has attracted criticism, not least in relation to the methodology applied, level of transparency and role of 'experts' in such risk assessments.[24]

In relation to the relevance of such economic considerations, the United Kingdom DPA scheme has adopted a different position to its United States

DPA offered by prosecutors, three months prior to the conviction of Arthur Anderson, DPA negotiations stalled because the company's senior executives believed the demands of the prosecutors were excessive: Spivack and Raman, above n 19, 165. Not all commentators have accepted that enforcement action was the cause of the collapse: Brandon Garrett, *Too Big to Jail: How Prosecutors Compromise with Corporations* (Harvard University Press, 2014) 42.

22 *Oversight of the US Department of Justice* (Hearing Before the Subcommittee on the Judiciary, 113th Congress, 6 March 2013) quoted in the submission of Mythili Raman, Acting Assistant Attorney-General, Criminal Division, United States Department of Justice, 'Who Is Too Big to Fail: Are Large Financial Institutions Immune from Federal Prosecution?' (Hearing Before the Subcommittee on Oversight and Investigations of the House Committee on Financial Services, United States House of Representatives, 22 May 2013) 2.

23 Garrett, above n 21, 63, noted that economic 'collateral consequences' may support the case for prosecution deferral. The concept is explained in the United States Department of Justice, *U.S. Attorneys' Manual* (December 2014) Offices of the United States Attorneys ('*United States Attorneys' Manual*') Title 9–27.240, available online at www.justice.gov/usam/united-states-attorneys-manual (accessed 5 September 2016).

24 Members of the United States Congressional Committee have raised concerns relating to the lack of transparency in how risks of corporate collapse were assessed: Raman, above n 22.

counterpart. The United Kingdom Code of Practice, citing international legal obligations under the Organisation for Economic Co-operation and Development (OECD) Convention on Combating Bribery of Foreign Public Officials in International Business Transactions, proclaims that the decision to prosecute foreign bribery offences should 'not be influenced by considerations of national economic interest, the potential effect upon relations with another State or the identity of the natural or legal persons involved'.[25] That said, the Code of Practice subsequently states that prosecutors may consider (presumably in cases not involving foreign bribery) as an 'additional public interest' that the 'conviction is likely to have collateral effects on the public, the corporation's employees, shareholders and/or institutional pension holders.[26] This inconsistent approach to collateral economic impacts in the United Kingdom's Code of Practice is regrettable, leaving scope for submissions by corporate lawyers that their clients, in relation to allegations not involving foreign bribery, are indeed 'too big to fail'.

Another public interest 'payoff' is that entering into a DPA offers substantial savings for all parties involved, avoiding the potential for uncertainties, delays and high costs of criminal litigation. It is estimated in the United Kingdom that the investigation and prosecution of a case involving a late guilty plea takes on average eight years to finalise and costs the Serious Fraud Office £1.6 million.[27] The problem of delay appears to be even more acute in Australia: the OECD's most recent review of Australia's enforcement record noted that 17 foreign bribery investigations were ongoing, with only one prosecution reaching the courts since the legislation was introduced in 1999.[28] Another 'payoff' of entering into a DPA is that the corporation avoids the negative media publicity caused by protracted investigations and delayed trials.

From a crime prevention perspective, the DPA provides an enforceable (not merely voluntary) mandate for the corporation to introduce organisational reform, and enhanced governance and compliance programs. It also offers regulatory authorities a pathway to recoup, fully or in part, the costs of investigation and enforcement action.[29] From the standpoint of persons adversely affected by corporate crime, DPAs instituted by state authorities may offer access to compensation without the costs or delays of instituting litigation individually. As the above discussion reveals, the perceived public benefits favour the increased use of DPAs and following the trends in the United States and United Kingdom, Australian policy-makers and legislators are actively considering introducing DPA

25 *United Kingdom DPA Code of Practice*, above n 13, 5, citing Article 5 of the *OECD Convention on Combating Bribery of Foreign Public Officials in International Business Transactions*, opened for signature 17 December 1997 [1999] ATS 21 (entered into force 15 February 1999).

26 Ibid. 6.

27 Bisgrove and Weekes, above n 18, 418; Mazzacuva, above n 21, 251.

28 OECD, *Australia: Follow-Up to the Phase 3 Report and Recommendations* (April 2015) 4, available online at www.oecd.org/daf/anti-bribery/Australia-Phase-3-Follow-up-Report-ENG.pdf (accessed 5 September 2016).

29 Bisgrove and Weekes, above n 18, 418.

schemes to deal with foreign bribery offences,[30] as well as serious corporate crime generally.[31]

In terms of 'pitfalls', however, the use of a DPA poses a number of threats to the legitimacy of state action. A key concern relates to the potential threat that such bargaining practices and settlements pose to constitutional values such as the rule of law.[32] Applying prosecutorial leniency in exchange for payments from wealthy defendants (either corporations or individuals) is hard to reconcile with the principle of equality before the law.[33] Also, from an ethical standpoint, commentators have expressed concern about the corrosive effect of legitimating state-sanctioned 'legal bribes' to cease enforcement action,[34] with undue pressure placed on public officials to settle matters rather than proceed to trial. This pressure may be particularly acute during times of public sector austerity, and growing agency and governmental dependence upon billion-dollar DPA-generated revenue streams.[35] With diminishing moral force associated with this bargaining process, there is a risk that corporations may come to view settlements in transactional terms as simply a 'cost of doing business', rather than as acts of genuine redress or commitment to prevention and governance reform.[36]

Another 'pitfall' relating to legitimacy is the lack of transparency in the administration of DPAs. The United States Attorneys' Manual sets out the general principles of federal prosecution; however, it contains limited guidance on the precise processes governing deferral of prosecutions. The United States Attorneys' Manual contains some guidance on negotiating non-prosecution agreements (NPAs), which has been presumed to apply equally to agreements to defer prosecution 'under certain conditions'. However, it contains scant guidance on how the

30 The inquiry of the Australian Senate Standing Committee on Economics into foreign bribery has invited public submissions on the introduction of DPA schemes: Senate Standing Committee on Economics, Parliament of Australia, *An Inquiry into The Measures Governing the Activities of Australian Corporations, Entities, Organisations, Individuals, Government and Related Parties with Respect to Foreign Bribery* (2015).

31 The Attorney-General recently released a public consultation paper: Attorney-General's Department, *Improving Enforcement Options for Serious Corporate Crime: Consideration of a Deferred Prosecution Agreements Scheme in Australia – Public Consultation Paper* (March 2016) Australian Government, available online at www.ag.gov.au/Consultations/Pages/Deferred-prosecution-agreements-public-consultation.aspx (accessed 5 September 2016).

32 See generally Karen Yeung, *Securing Compliance: A Principled Approach* (Hart Publishing, 2004) ch 6.

33 Ibid. 168ff.: the threat to the right to fair and equal treatment in the context of administrative settlements is discussed. On the significance of these liberal constitutional values in the context of A V Dicey's writings, see Stephen Bottomley and Simon Bronitt, *Law in Context* (Federation Press, 4th edn, 2011) ch 2.

34 Simon Bronitt, 'Policing Corruption and Corporations in Australia: Towards a New National Agenda' (2013) 37(5) *Criminal Law Journal* 283, 288.

35 Bisgrove and Weekes, above n 18, 418.

36 N Richard Janis, 'Deputizing Company Counsel as Agents of the Federal Government' (White Paper, Cato Institute, 2008) 4; Kurt Eichenwald, *Serpent on the Rock* (Harper Business, 1995) xiii–ix.

negotiation should be conducted, simply suggesting that prosecutors should enter into such agreements in return for cooperation only where: (i) other means of obtaining cooperation are unavailable or ineffective; (ii) cooperation serves the public interest; and (iii) the course of action is approved by an appropriate supervisory official.[37]

United States Attorneys are empowered and accustomed to 'striking bargains' with defendants through the application of prosecutorial discretion, balancing a range of interests pursuant to the general duty of prosecutors to proceed in cases where there is sufficient evidence to obtain a conviction and that prosecution serves the 'public interest'.[38] The United States Attorneys' Manual requires that a written record of the final agreement be made publicly available,[39] although judges are not involved in the negotiation process or in the approval of the final agreement. This may be contrasted with the judicial oversight of DPAs in the United Kingdom, which extends to both the negotiation phase and the final agreement.[40] The United Kingdom legislation has attempted to address these legitimacy deficits by requiring that the prosecutor's decision to commence negotiations must likely be in the 'interests of justice' and that the proposed terms and final agreement are 'fair, reasonable and proportionate'.[41] Judicial involvement in this process seeks to address the legitimacy deficit and mitigates the risk that a party may be unduly pressured by the prosecution to submit to the terms of an agreement that is not in the public interest, or is unfair, unreasonable or disproportionate.[42]

Another source of potential unfairness at the systemic level arises from the interaction between the DPA and other concurrent legal processes that may lead to the imposition of civil penalties, civil forfeiture orders and/or, ultimately, criminal conviction by a court. An unresolved question relates to the relationship between civil and criminal enforcement actions that arise 'on the same facts', and the extent to which 'concurrence' of a parallel proceeding has the potential to prejudice or undermine the fairness of the other proceeding. As noted above, there are some significant and obvious differences between civil and criminal proceedings. For example, many of these civil proceedings diverge from the usual criminal burden and standard of proof, liberally reversing the onus of proof and

37 *United States Attorneys' Manual*, above n 23, 9–27.650

38 *United States Attorneys' Manual*, above n 23. The twin threshold of sufficiency and public interest are discussed at 9–27.600. The manual identifies a non-exhaustive list of considerations relevant to the decision to desist or defer prosecution, including '(1) the importance of the investigation or prosecution to an effective program of law enforcement; (2) the value of the person's cooperation to the investigation or prosecution; and (3) the person's relative culpability in connection with the offense or offenses being investigated or prosecuted and his/her history with respect to criminal activity': 9–27.620.

39 Ibid. 9–27.650.

40 See *Crime and Courts Act 2013* (UK), c 22, sch 17, ss 7–8.

41 Ibid. s 8(1): these thresholds apply to the entry into negotiation, proposed terms and final agreement.

42 For a discussion of judicial legitimacy in the context of preventive justice, see Chapter 11 by Sarah Murray in this collection.

lowering the evidence threshold to a preponderance of probability, rather than proof beyond reasonable doubt.[43] Questions have also arisen about the status of evidence obtained through these civil proceedings, and the extent to which its admission in parallel or subsequent criminal proceedings may prejudice the defendant's right to a fair trial.[44]

In the United Kingdom, some of these uncertainties have been addressed by legislation, clarifying that the 'statement of facts' included in a DPA is to be treated as an admission in any subsequent criminal proceeding vis-à-vis the relevant offence.[45] United States Attorneys have sought to achieve the same outcome administratively by requiring the DPA to include comprehensive 'agreed' statements of facts, which purport to bind the defence in any subsequent prosecution triggered by a breach of the DPA. Further minimising the scope for future challenges,[46] DPAs also include 'non-contradiction provisions' (that is, clauses that bind the corporation not to make statements or claims contradicting these 'agreed' facts).[47] The 'conclusiveness' of such provisions has not been challenged, and it may be argued that the party should be able to resile from earlier admissions of fact due to the subsequent discovery of new material that changes the relevance, weight or indeed admissibility of the earlier evidence. For example, further enquiries by the defendant may reveal that the prosecution case was based on evidence of incriminating 'facts' obtained by entrapment (which is a substantive defence in the United States), or otherwise illegally or improperly obtained, which would be likely be excluded if the case proceeded to trial.

To avoid such legitimacy deficits, it is vital that DPAs are comprehensively regulated by statute not merely by administrative guidelines (as in the United

43 Confiscations and civil forfeiture in Australia and the United Kingdom are based upon a determination of criminal or unlawful conduct on the balance of probabilities: see *Proceeds of Crime Act 2002* (UK) c 29, pt 5, ch 1, s 240; *Proceeds of Crime Act 2002* (Cth) s 317(2). For an excellent article examining the evolution and human rights challenges to these powers, see Colin King, 'Using Civil Processes in Pursuit of Criminal Law Objectives: A Case Study of Non-Conviction Based Asset Forfeiture' (2012) 16 *International Journal of Evidence and Proof* 337.

44 See *Commissioner of the Australian Federal Police v Zhao* (2015) 255 CLR 46, where the High Court recognised that judges may stay civil proceedings relating to the forfeiture of tainted property under s 49 of the *Proceeds of Crime Act 2002* (Cth) pending the outcome of concurrent criminal proceedings. The High Court noted that the coercive civil measures (requiring respondents to make incriminating disclosures) gave the prosecution an undue advantage, prejudicing the right to a fair trial in the concurrent criminal proceedings.

45 *Crime and Courts Act 2013* (UK) c 22, sch 17, s 13(2).

46 A recent analysis of DPAs in the United Stated revealed that 91 per cent of DPAs (and 79 per cent of NPAs) require agreement to the admissibility of a statement of facts: Cindy R Alexander and Mark A Cohen, 'The Evolution of Corporate Criminal Settlements: An Empirical Perspective on Non-Prosecution, Deferred Prosecution, and Plea Agreements' (2015) 52 *American Criminal Law Review* 537, 588.

47 Illovsky, above n 10, 38; Julie R O'Sullivan, 'How Prosecutors Apply the "Federal Prosecutions of Corporations" Charging Policy in the Era of Deferred Prosecutions, and What That Means for the Purposes of Federal Criminal Sanction' (2014) 51 *American Criminal Law Review* 29, 56.

States), and that the settlement terms are publicly accessible and judicially approved (as in the United Kingdom). Also, it is desirable that, as a matter of procedural fairness, all parties (including proxies representing those adversely affected by the corporate wrongdoing such as shareholder groups) have standing to make submissions before any agreement is judicially approved.

In both the United States and United Kingdom, the process of regulatory bargaining under these DPA schemes rests firmly on the shoulders of state officials and their general discretion not to prosecute in the 'public interest'. Yet the tests for balancing competing public interests are notoriously amorphous, as revealed in controversial cases where investigations and prosecutions have been halted, citing potential negative impacts upon global and local markets, diplomatic relations and even national security.[48] On the other side of the balance, the public interest encapsulated in the Latin maxim *fiat justitia et ruant coeli* ('let justice be done though the heavens fall') weighs equally heavily: namely, the fundamental importance of upholding the core rule of law values that no one is above the law, and that breaches of the law must be prosecuted in a fair and consistent manner. From the perspective of corporate governance in the aftermath of the global financial crisis, there is also a compelling public interest in promoting a more assertive prosecution policy that signals the end of cultures of corporate impunity.

To avoid the risk that decision-making based on discretion descends into a 'tyranny of arbitrariness',[49] legislatures have required or empowered administrative agencies to develop codes and guidelines. Typically, these administrative norms require the relevant decision-makers (prosecutors and judges) to consider a range of interests in reaching their decision, and also ensure compliance with the requisite standards of 'fairness, reasonableness and proportionality' (as discussed above). Although in the United Kingdom these 'constitutional' standards have become more prominent since the adoption of the *Human Rights Act 1998* (UK), they do not address one of the key concerns raised above – namely, the importance of identifying, more precisely, the *purpose* of this new regulatory tool. Part II of this chapter explores the preventive potential of DPA schemes, and how current law and practice may be realigned to prioritise prevention or minimisation of harms by corporations, and, where that proves impossible, to ensure adequate redress and compensation.

Part II

Towards principled prosecution: rethinking expediency and the public interest

As noted in Part I, DPA schemes in the United States and United Kingdom emerged as expedient measures without clearly articulated or coherent purposes.

48 For a review of cases in which these issues have arisen, see Philip Stenning, 'Discretion, Politics, and the Public Interest in "High-Profile" Criminal Investigations and Prosecutions' (2009) 24(3) *Canadian Journal of Law and Society* 337.

49 See generally Denis Galligan, 'Regulating Pre-Trial Decisions' in Nicola Lacey (ed.), *A Reader on Criminal Justice* (Oxford University Press, 1994).

Although *not* an instrument of punishment (since this requires a formal determination of guilt following due process of law), DPAs nevertheless manifest quasi-punitive elements. In the United Kingdom, for example, a DPA can only be approved if the judicial officer considers the terms and conditions proportionate to the degree of culpability and harm caused by the corporation – conditions shadowing the twin core ideas central to the retributive philosophy of 'just deserts'. The alternative approach is to view the DPA as an administrative tool for regulating executive leniency, mitigating potential 'penalties' in proportion to the extent to which the corporation promptly notified authorities of suspected criminality, cooperated fully with investigators, and assisted to identify other parties responsible. However, in the absence of judicial involvement in guilt determination, the legitimacy of these 'quasi-punitive' or leniency processes is open to serious challenge. As Karen Yeung perceptively observed in her excellent study of regulatory bargaining:

> Whilst the line between 'administrative' and 'judicial' functions may be notoriously difficult to draw, at least at the margins, it is well-established that the imposition of punishment is a quintessentially judicial function. On this basis, it is suggested that administrative settlements are unsuited to securing penal purposes, at least in the absence of judicial oversight to oversee the fair and accurate application of legal standards so as to ensure the innocent are not punished.[50]

DPA schemes, it is submitted, are better viewed not as civil or pecuniary penalty schemes,[51] but as diversionary tools of preventive justice. In this way, a DPA has the potential to both prevent and repair harms caused by corporate wrongdoing:

50 Yeung, above n 32, 166.

51 Australia has an extensive system of civil or pecuniary penalties operating alongside, or as an alternative to, criminal prosecution across a range of regulatory spheres including trade practices, corporations and industrial relations law. Such penalties, while not contingent upon criminal conviction, nevertheless have significant financial and regulatory consequences. In a recent decision, the High Court reviewed where certain restrictions in sentencing law should be applied to the administration of civil penalties: see *Commonwealth of Australia v Director, Fair Work Building Industry Inspectorate* [2015] HCA 46. Noting that the imposition of civil penalties lacked the moral stigma of criminal conviction and punishment (see [17] and [54]–[55]), the Court held that legal protections applied to criminal trials did not apply to civil penalty proceedings. Moreover, the Court held that regulators in civil penalty proceedings, though statutory office holders, were acting as civil litigants and not prosecutors. Regulators were not bound by the same duties as prosecutors, thus leaving scope for the parties to settle disputes by agreement as to appropriate penalties. In these cases, the role of the court is only to be persuaded that the agreement reached is appropriate, within the permissible range in all the circumstances. For further discussion of the legal issues prior to the High Court ruling, see Rebecca Ananian-Welsh and Katie Glover, 'Before the High Court: Commonwealth v Director, Fair Work Building Industry Inspectorate: The End of Penalty Agreements in Civil Pecuniary Penalty Schemes?'(2015) 37 *Sydney Law Review* 417.

reparation may involve asset forfeiture and restitution, as well as prevention of ongoing and future harm through education and monitoring programs. Framed around this preventive justice paradigm, DPAs have much greater potential for transforming organisational cultures that perpetrate, facilitate or condone corporate crime.

The need for more strategy behind DPAs has been identified by John Braithwaite, who notes the lack of any coherent philosophy in relation to the policies and practices governing deferral of prosecution:

> What formal western law lacks when it applies techniques such as deferred prosecution is a philosophy of why allowing justice as repair and redemption should be the mainline response even when doing so involves a breach of the principle of proportional punishment. A restorative justice philosophy allows us to accept that if a victim wishes to forgive in return for some other dimension of justice beyond proportional sanctioning, after discussing the option with other stakeholders, this can be just.[52]

In the next section, I explore how this 'alternate' philosophy may be applied to DPAs in the context of corporate crime.

Rethinking corporate responsibility and reactive fault

In this section, I return to the model of corporate blameworthiness, known as 'reactive fault', devised by Brent Fisse in the 1980s and further developed in his writings with John Braithwaite.[53] Reactive fault has the potential to reframe how DPAs are both conceptualised and administered. The effect of reactive fault is to reframe the legal window for assessing corporate fault, focusing attention upon how those agents responsible for the harm reacted and responded 'restoratively'. Reactive fault disputes the criminal law's traditional obsession with assessing fault by the identification of a guilty mind (such as intention or knowledge) either before or concurrently with the harmful conduct (such as injury or death).[54] Since restorative justice focuses primarily on physical manifestations of offending behaviour (actions and consequences), the reactive fault model shifts attention from 'fault which is causally prior to the crime, of which intention is the most important

52 John Braithwaite, 'Cultures of Redemptive Finance' in Justin O'Brien and George Gilligan (eds), *Integrity, Risk and Accountability in Capital Markets: Regulating Culture* (Hart Publishing, 2013) 282.

53 Brent Fisse, 'Reconstructing Corporate Criminal Law: Deterrence, Retribution, Fault, and Sanctions' (1983) 56(6) *Southern California Law Review* 1141. This idea was further developed and elaborated upon in Brent Fisse and John Braithwaite, *Corporations, Crime and Accountability* (Cambridge University Press, 1993).

54 Braithwaite has extended his model of reactive fault beyond the corporate crime realm, contending that the general focus on 'intention' in the criminal law, from both normative and sociological perspectives, is mistaken: John Braithwaite, 'Intention Versus Reactive Fault' in Ngaire Naffine, Rosemary Owens and John Williams (eds), *Intention in Law and Philosophy* (Ashgate, 2001) ch 16.

variant, to fault based on how restoratively the offender acts after the crime'.[55] Once aware of the harm caused, the corporation has a duty to take reasonable steps to engage in restorative action, but also to prevent future harms. If the corporation's reaction is adequately restorative, then only civil liability applies to rectify the harms caused. Fisse and Braithwaite are not, however, proposing a strict 'no-fault' model of civil liability to substitute for corporate criminal responsibility. As noted above, where the reaction to harm caused is insufficiently restorative, then the use of criminal prosecution should be used, but only then as a matter of last resort.[56]

How, then, does this model of reactive fault transpose on to DPA schemes? Federico Mazzacuva in a recent article noted how some rehabilitative aspects of DPA schemes in the United Kingdom and United States conformed to the theory of reactive fault.[57] Elaborating upon Mazzacuva's insight, the reactive fault model would prioritise the preventive purpose of DPA schemes. The model of reactive fault has profound implications for responses to alleged corporate wrongdoing. There is no need to establish that the corporate conduct was accompanied by any fault element – the corporation only need acknowledge its 'responsibility' for the prohibited acts or omissions.[58] Consistent with the reorientation towards prevention, prosecutors need not believe there is a reasonable prospect of conviction, or, further, that the corporation must admit its guilt as a precondition of being eligible to engage in a DPA. Since this process is entirely administrative, the usual civil standard of proof on the 'balance of probabilities' would apply. Under this model, once aware of the harm caused, the corporation has a duty to take reasonable steps to engage in restorative action, but also to prevent future harms. If the corporation breaches either duty, then prosecution may be instituted in the ordinary way. At that stage, guilt is determined by assessing corporate blameworthiness before and

55 Ibid. 345.

56 These ideas form part of a broader theory of responsive regulation, and the enforcement pyramid developed by Ian Ayres and John Braithwaite, over many years. The literature is voluminous, and has been influential in a range of fields, from occupational health and safety to domestic violence, and even terrorism law. See generally Arie Freiberg, *The Tools of Regulation* (Federation Press, 2010). Yeung, above n 32, 167–70, offers a critique of the enforcement pyramid for its failure to give sufficient attention to legitimacy issues, specifically the rights of persons and entities subjected to regulatory actions, and overlooking the 'constitutional values of proportionality and consistency, which are themselves rooted in the right to fair and equal treatment'.

57 Federico Mazzacuva, 'Justifications and Purposes of Negotiated Justice for Corporate Offenders: Deferred and Non-Prosecution Agreements in the UK and US Systems of Criminal Justice' (2014) 78(3) *Journal of Criminal Law* 249, 262.

58 This approach is adopted in the Australian Capital Territory with respect to restorative justice conferencing for minor offences under the *Crimes (Restorative Justice) Act 2004* (ACT). Under s 19, the major eligibility requirement for offenders to engage in restorative justice processes is that he or she 'accepts responsibility for the commission of the offence'. This act of accepting responsibility does not constitute a formal admission of guilt that would restrict a plea of not guilty in criminal proceedings, nor is it a mandatory mitigating factor in sentencing (s 20). Processes for restorative justice agreements, which include reparative action, are contained in pt 8, div 8.4.

during the alleged offences. The extent to which a corporate defendant manifested reactive fault *after* the alleged offence occurred would be relevant only to sentencing; for example, proof that it took steps to prevent future harm, compensate victims and cooperate with authorities may mitigate the sentence imposed in accordance with the ordinary principles of sentencing law.[59]

Reactive fault applied to DPA schemes requires a radical rethink of our existing model of corporate responsibility based on the binary of criminal *versus* civil liability,[60] and may be viewed, at the systemic level, as further evidence of the trend towards hybrid models of legal responsibility.[61] As previously observed in the context of counter-terrorism measures, the question is not the extent to which these hybrid models deviate from the conventional civil/criminal binary, but whether the responses are both effective and legitimate (particularly in respect of upholding human rights).[62] Law reform in relation to DPA schemes, as well as future policy and practice, should be guided in equal measure by the principles of preventive justice, rather than 'shadow' forms of retributive justice or pragmatic expediency.

Conclusion

A number of chapters in this collection explore how the fight against serious and organised crime and terrorism has spawned a wide range of preventive justice measures. In Australia, and elsewhere, legal measures have extended beyond the traditional reactive criminal law paradigm based on prosecution, conviction and punishment. There is now an increasing array of legal hybrids traversing civil and criminal law, which apply both pre-trial and post-conviction. These include anti-association and control orders, as well as confiscation of assets through freezing, restraining and forfeiture orders. The significant change in recent years, as illustrated in the example of the DPA scheme, is that conviction following 'due process of law' is no longer the critical pivot point for legal intervention. As this

59 The *Criminal Justice Act 2003* (UK) c 44, pt 12, ch 1, s 166(1) leaves it open to the sentencing judge to take any factor they considers relevant to mitigate sentence: see, further, Sentencing Guidelines Council (UK), *Overarching Principles: Seriousness* (December 2004) 1.26.

60 The civil/criminal binary has been rejected in analyses of civil penalty schemes under Corporations Law: see e.g. Peta Spender, 'Negotiating the Third Way: Developing Effective Process in Civil Penalty Litigation' (2008) 26(4) *Company and Securities Law Journal* 249; Vicky Comino, 'Effective Regulation by the Australian Securities and Investments Commission: The Civil Penalty Problem' (2009) 33(3) *Melbourne University Law Review* 802.

61 The trend towards hybridity in the field of terrorism law, revealed through adoption of control orders, preventive detention and other preventive measures, are explored in Simon Bronitt and Susan Donkin, 'Australian Responses to 9/11: New World Legal Hybrids?' in Aniceto Masferrer (ed.), *Post 9/11 and the State of Permanent Legal Emergency* (Springer, 2012) 223. See also Chapter 3 by Susan Donkin, Chapter 8 by Svetlana Tyulkina and George Williams, and Chapter 10 by Rebecca Ananian-Welsh in this collection.

62 Ibid. 237.

chapter has revealed, it is the decision to prosecute – *not* conviction and/or punishment – that is the 'Sword of Damocles' hanging over corporate defendants.[63]

An agreement to defer prosecution with 'strings attached' can be viewed in a range of ways. It may be viewed as serving a retributive function, shadowing just deserts (imposing civil penalties proportionate to putative corporate wrongdoing or harm caused) or as an expedient policy of expiation (imposing discounted civil penalties in exchange for early and ongoing cooperation with state authorities and regulators). Alternatively, DPAs may be reconfigured to prioritise the objectives, principles and practices of restorative justice (what Braithwaite termed 'justice as repair and redemption').[64] Applying this approach, DPAs would be a means of repairing the significant and ongoing harms caused by corporate wrongdoing and preventing future harms. This may involve forfeiture and restitution, as well as education and monitoring programs aimed at prevention.

In my view, it has been a serious mistake, conceptually, to link the rationale for DPAs to retributive philosophy of 'just deserts', albeit one which is prospectively stayed on the grounds of leniency, expediency or some other 'public interest'. The danger of this model is that the process itself has become a form of punishment, offending the ideal that matters of legal liability (whether civil or criminal) should be determined by a court of law. This chapter argues that DPAs should be reconfigured, linked explicitly to the principles of preventive justice. With growing interest in the regulatory trends in the United States and United Kingdom, the introduction of a DPA scheme to deal with specified categories of corporate crime in Australia appears increasingly likely.[65] However, before such reform is introduced, it is vital that the policy and legislative community take further steps to clarify the purposes, principles and philosophy of preventive justice, which should guide the use of DPAs.

63 As Braithwaite perceptively observed, '[m]ost punishments are more feared in anticipation than they are once experienced. A criminal justice system that privileges restorative justice ahead of punitive justice thereby increases the deterrent power of punitive justice through a Sword of Damocles effect': John Braithwaite, *Restorative Justice and Responsive Regulation* (Oxford University Press, 2002), 241. See generally Justin O'Brien, 'The Sword of Damocles: Deferred Prosecutions and the Search for Accountability' in Justin O'Brien and George Gilligan (eds), *Integrity, Risk and Accountability in Capital Markets* (Hart Publishing, 2013) 161.

64 Braithwaite, 'Cultures of Redemptive Finance', above n 52, 282.

65 Australian Senate Standing Committee, above n 30, and Attorney-General's Department, above n 31.

Index

For Product Safety Concerns and Information please contact our EU
representative GPSR@taylorandfrancis.com
Taylor & Francis Verlag GmbH, Kaufingerstraße 24, 80331 München, Germany

www.ingramcontent.com/pod-product-compliance
Ingram Content Group UK Ltd.
Pitfield, Milton Keynes, MK11 3LW, UK
UKHW022134190926
475702UK00013B/1800
9780367025199